Rape-Revenge Films
Second Edition

ALSO BY ALEXANDRA HELLER-NICHOLAS

The Giallo *Canvas: Art, Excess and Horror Cinema* (McFarland, 2021)

Found Footage Horror Films: Fear and the Appearance of Reality (McFarland, 2014)

Rape-Revenge Films
A Critical Study
Second Edition

Alexandra Heller-Nicholas

McFarland & Company, Inc., Publishers
Jefferson, North Carolina

Permission has been granted to reprint portions
of this book derived from these earlier published essays by the author:

"Silence and Fury: Rape and *The Virgin Spring*," *Screening the Past* 28 (2010)
<http://www.latrobe.edu.au/screeningthepast/28/rape-and-the-virgin-spring.html>.

"Last Trope on the Left: Rape, Film and the Melodramatic Imagination,"
Limina: A Journal of Cultural and Historical Studies 15 (June 2009)
<http://www.limina.arts.uwa.edu.au/previous/vol11to15/vol15/hellernicholas>.

"Comedy and the Castratrice: Věra Chytilová's *Traps* (1998),"
Senses of Cinema 87 (June 2018) <https://www.sensesofcinema.com/2018/
cteq/comedy-castratrice-vera-chytilovas-traps-1998/>.

ISBN (print) 978-1-4766-8649-3
ISBN (ebook) 978-1-4766-4490-5

LIBRARY OF CONGRESS AND BRITISH LIBRARY
CATALOGUING DATA ARE AVAILABLE

Library of Congress Control Number 2021935621

© 2021 Alexandra Heller-Nicholas. All rights reserved

*No part of this book may be reproduced or transmitted in any form
or by any means, electronic or mechanical, including photocopying
or recording, or by any information storage and retrieval system,
without permission in writing from the publisher.*

Front cover design © 2021 Darren Cotzabuyucas/DC Design

Printed in the United States of America

*McFarland & Company, Inc., Publishers
Box 611, Jefferson, North Carolina 28640
www.mcfarlandpub.com*

For Jan Napiorkowski, 1975–2020

"Anger is destructive, but very active."
—Virginie Despentes

Table of Contents

PREFACE TO THE SECOND EDITION	1
INTRODUCTION	9
Chapter One: The Rape-Revenge Film Canon	25
Chapter Two: The Rape-Revenge Film Across Genres	55
Chapter Three: The Rape-Revenge Film Around the World	97
Chapter Four: Women-Directed Rape-Revenge Films	152
AFTERWORD	175
CHAPTER NOTES	179
BIBLIOGRAPHY	191
INDEX	197

Preface to the Second Edition

This revised edition marks ten years since this book's original release, and, to put it mildly, a lot has happened in that time regarding this subject, both for myself personally and in relation to the mass public discourse sparked by the publication of the allegations of a decades-long reign of terror by once-revered Hollywood producer Harvey Weinstein. Under the umbrella of #MeToo—a term coined by activist Tarana Burke in 2006 and appropriated by Hollywood 11 years later—that someone of now-convicted Weinstein's caliber could be held accountable felt for many that a pressure relief valve firmly welded shut was loosened, granting sexual assault survivors a discursive context to share their stories. It happened to you? Yeah, me too.

The publication of the Weinstein allegations in the *New York Times* and *The New Yorker* in October 2017 has retrospectively largely been configured as a concrete turning point where, almost overnight, the meaning and value of rape-revenge films—for better or for worse—could be conceived in an entirely new way. There was a sudden critical awareness, for instance, of women-directed rape and rape-revenge films which, despite having existed long before 2017, allowed their reassessment. This is where the bulk of the new work in this second edition is most apparent, Chapter Four focusing on women-directed rape-revenge films. Importantly, however, it's worth stating that while the Weinstein allegations were for many the straw that broke the camel's back, widespread anger, fury and frustration had already been increasing in intensity concerning the growing global epidemic of sexual violence (particularly against women). Think of phenomena such as SlutWalk, public rallies held internationally from 2011 to protest victim blaming and raise awareness of the toxic impact of rape culture more broadly. Global in nature, SlutWalk marches were held in countries including Australia, Brazil, Iceland, Israel, North America, Singapore, South Korea, and the United Kingdom, propelled partially by public fury over many high-profile rape cases, such as that of now-convicted U.S. comic Bill Cosby, the Shakti Mills case in India, and the Saxon Mullins case in Australia.

So while women-directed rape-revenge films like Natalia Leite's *M.F.A.* and Coralie Fargeat's *Revenge* were broadly framed as groundbreaking films that heralded a #MeToo next wave, these two movies premiered in 2017 well before the Weinstein allegations surfaced. *Revenge* premiered at the Toronto International Film Festival almost exactly a month before the *New York Times* and *New Yorker* stories broke the Weinstein case open, while *M.F.A.* premiered at Austin's SXSW in March earlier that same year. In extraordinary timing, *M.F.A.* was released in U.S. cinemas on 13 October 2017, three days *after* Ronan Farrow's "From Aggressive Overtures to Sexual Assault: Harvey Weinstein's Accusers Tell their Stories" was published in *The New Yorker*[1] and eight days after Jodi Kantor and Megan Twohey's "Harvey Weinstein Paid Off Sexual Harrassment Accusers for Decades"[2] went to print in the *New York Times*, winning Pulitzer Prizes for all three journalists.

While #MeToo provided a useful lens for both critics and audiences to re-think and re-approach the broader context of rape-revenge, the social and political concerns of the movement had been around for a long time. Though #MeToo had sparked a potential newfound sensitivity to rape-revenge—and questions about the on-screen representation of gendered violence more broadly—in the context of my earlier book, intrinsically my central argument remained the same. If there is one rhetorical drumbeat that marks my approach to rape-revenge, it is that borrowed from art historian Diane Wolfthal's book *Images of Rape: The "Heroic" Tradition and Its Alternatives* (1999). Although much attention has been paid to so-called "heroic" rape imagery of the Italian Renaissance, Wolfthal argued that when looking at other representations of rape produced elsewhere in Europe during this period, it becomes apparent that "diverse notions coexisted contemporaneously."[3] Working my way through hundreds of rape-revenge films for the first book, I was struck that there was no singular or unified treatment of rape—even within the specific configuration of man-against-women rape—when the category was surveyed as a whole. In the rape-revenge film, too, "diverse notions coexisted contemporaneously." If there exists a broad cultural confusion about what sexual violence "means," these films offer a notable contemporary example of why and how contradictory and often hypocritical attitudes can co-exist more generally.

The prevailing diversity of attitudes and values regarding sexual violence is evident in the fact that #MeToo has not seen a consolidation of opinion towards the rape-revenge film, nor has it resulted in homogenizing how rape is represented across the films themselves. Again, to reiterate Wolfthal's point, we continue to find, more so now than ever, that "diverse notions coexist … contemporaneously." These variances are immediately apparent in the often eye-openingly contradictory responses they provoke from critics. For example, Richard Shepard's *The Perfection* (2018) was on one hand was lambasted by reviews titled "*The Perfection* Turns the Rape Revenge Fantasy Into Spectacle,"[4] "Netflix's *The Perfection* learned all the Wrong Lessons from #MeToo,"[5] and "*The Perfection* Is a Problematic Body Horror Drama You'll Likely Want to Avoid."[6] Yet the very same film was celebrated by the highly regarded Ashlee Blackwell—founder of the blog *Graveyard Shift Sisters* and co-writer and producer of Xavier Neal-Burgin's 2018 documentary *Horror Noire: A History of Black Horror*—whose review sought to "boost … *The Perfection*'s savory brilliance on every emotional and intellectual level imagined. Possibly hyperbole, yet I want to promise this will be one of the best film viewing experiences you'll ever have."[7]

As this book explores, there is a long history of the divisive nature of this material. This is not a product of #MeToo, but rather what has shifted now is the critical framing of rape-revenge, now unavoidably tethered to this contemporary phenomenon. Anne Billson mapped out the "problem" of the rape-revenge film in both its pleasures and challenges: "On the one hand, what could be more empowering than watching a woman wreaking violent vengeance on her abusers? I'm not aware of this being something that happens in real life, but what's wrong with a little fantasy wish fulfilment? Unlike #MeToo accusers, who have to go through the courts (yet another ordeal) or make do with naming and shaming, the rape-revenge protagonist can let rip with Old Testament vengeance."[8] Others reject this position wholesale, emphatically denying any feminist potential in the category whatsoever. For Phillipa Snow, "to take the rape-revenge film and to make it fully, functionally feminist would seem to be impossible, despite the fact that many feminists … might say that women taking out male rapist trash, either by death or by dismemberment, is the most satisfying story arc of all." Snow continues, "The subgenre's exploitation roots are too strong, and there cannot help but be a minor note of trash in more than just its men: its heroines' eventual leveling up to empowerment is necessarily borne of debasement."[9]

Although anchored to the context of #MeToo, Snow's position is hardly a new one, and in large part addressing these tendencies such as this—reducing rape-revenge to one cohesive, singular, unified whole—was the goal when this book was first published. But one element of her phrasing is vital to address: the question of feminism itself. Statements such as this actively deny the depth and breadth of debates regarding definitions of feminism, which erupted during the Second Wave and shows no signs of slowing down. There are, to be blunt, different kinds of feminism, and self-identifying feminists are often in open, even hostile, opposition to each other on many key issues. If we accept Woflthal's position that when it comes to the representation of rape, "diverse notions coexisted contemporaneously," we could do well to conceive of feminism itself in the same way when approaching rape-revenge films. As Peggy Phelan noted, while a definition is hard to lock down, at its most general level the best we may agree on is the idea that "feminism is the conviction that gender has been, and continues to be, a fundamental category for the organization of culture. Moreover, the pattern of that organization usually favors men over women."[10]

To lock rape-revenge in its entirety down to a reductive and commonly ideologically weaponized binary between "feminist" or "not feminist" fundamentally disrespects the *diversity* of responses these films provoke in people, *including women*. These responses are all valid in the sense that as contradictory as they are, every person who watches a rape-revenge film (whether they identify as "feminist" or not, whether they are a sexual assault survivor, whatever their gender identity, sexuality, class, race, etc.) has a fundamental right to their own reaction. Inescapably, this ties into my own personal experience and my relationship to my work in this area in a way that is—without being self-indulgent, I hope—worth elaborating on briefly here. Most immediately, I consciously and very deliberately choose not to speak here of my own experiences of gendered violence, harassment, and discrimination, although I too have stories to tell. Largely, this is perhaps a knee-jerk but deeply held reaction that stems from the way that older male academics especially would look at me when they learned about my research in this field, with a very specific, questioning stare that unambiguously revealed their inner thinking: *what happened to you?* Implicit here was that the answer would somehow be pertinent to how they judged my abilities as a researcher and my critical thinking, which I could palpably sense stemmed from not just curiosity but, in the case of the most regressive, conservative and privileged of these self-appointed tribal elders of cinema studies, would allow them the luxury of corralling me silently into the "hysterical woman" category. It would mean that my work did not matter, that I was just some angry woman with a chip on her shoulder, using the field of which they far too often claim explicit ownership over to exorcize my own inner demons.

If I sound angry, it is because I am. I'm conscious here of not wanting this to sound like "quit lit" because I still have the enormous privilege of working in universities as a research academic, albeit on other people's (excellent) projects and not my own. But in the ten years since this book was published, I have gone on an extraordinary professional and personal journey. When I first wrote this book, I was wide-eyed and ambitious and assumed a dazzling academic career lay before me. When it came to the research I was passionate about, however, I was dead wrong. Partially this is because the university sector in Australia where I live was collapsing, but mostly because as I moved further away from academia and focused my career on film criticism and working as a programmer and consultant for film festivals, I realized that academia was not where my work on rape-revenge seemed to really matter. To be clear, genuinely excellent work on rape-revenge has since been published in an academic context, primarily Claire Henry's essential *Revisionist Rape-Revenge: Redefining a Film Genre* (2014). But for a number of reasons, I found myself drifting away from universities and what I see as my once naïve and somewhat arrogant belief that this mode of discourse was the be-all and end-all. I wanted to reach out beyond the insularity of that context, stuck as I was for many years in unsatisfying and unstable casual teaching and frustrated that the conversations I wanted to have were not about the intricacies of genre theory or continental philosophy; these things of course have a place, but for me personally, I wanted to talk about the lived experience of rape survivors and other audiences of these films beyond a speculative length. So I took a different path and found both my people and my voice. I found them in fan circles, in the conversational arena of the film festival circuit and film collectives like Melbourne's Cinemaniacs, and online, where people who had read my book would approach me to chat. I found my people on film festival programming teams where the conversations felt more urgent and important to me than any conversation I had experienced in an academic context. And through this work, I had the enormous luxury of meeting and talking to filmmakers, a number of whom are survivors of sexual assault themselves. These conversations are worth more to me than any academic citation, and realizing that felt like being born anew.

That being said, the donation of Henry's work to the area of critical engagement with rape-revenge cinema cannot be underplayed. She has urged for rape-revenge to be considered through the lens of genre theory, amplifying her perception of what she calls the emergence of "revisionist rape-revenge" which she claims demonstrates an increasing ambivalence to the justice fantasies of earlier films in the category. A rich and deeply researched book, it reveals Henry's impressive engagement with the films in question, an admirable task for films that so many entrenched in academia have historically struggled to pull closer than arm's length. But as convincingly as Henry's argument is that "contemporary rape-revenge films hold great critical value for opening up questions about various social, political, and ethical attitudes toward rape, representation and response,"[11] her privileging of genre studies at the core of her argument reveals the academic specificity of such work. In my experience, for rape-revenge film fans and people in industry (film festival programmers, filmmakers, etc.) this is not the most urgent, probing question that comes up when rape-revenge film is discussed. People outside of academia simply want to talk about other things, and so Henry's claim that "Heller-Nicholas … shies away from terming rape-revenge a genre and avoids theorizing what rape-revenge is (whether it is a cycle, narrative pattern, or genre)"[12] and her articulation of a counter-position that "denying that rape-revenge is a film genre risks closing off the rich insights afforded by the field of genre studies"[13] perhaps reveals where our perceived audiences diverge. For Henry, "genre is a preferable term for rape-revenge because genre studies help us to understand its processes of flux and inter-genre mutation."[14] Maybe my "us" and Henry's "us" are different, however; I would argue in response that rather than shying away from calling rape-revenge a genre, I simply do not share Henry's deep and explicit investment in the field of academic genre studies on this subject because I understand that the bulk of my readership do not share that investment, either. They want to talk about their *own experiences* of rape, trauma, and survival. To be fair to Henry, this clearly reflects my own shift towards public-facing criticism and industry away from academia that retrospectively began with the first edition of this project itself as I have actively sought to speak beyond what I felt was the restrictive echo chamber of academic discourse. This is not to be anti-intellectual; rather, I found for my work a space *between* my academic background and a passionate, engaged public audience that could be bridged, which has been my primary focus between the first and second editions of this book.

In the last ten years, I haven't talked to many people about the academic nuances of genre theory, but I have talked to a *hell* of a lot of people about their experiences of rape. Without any question, talking to survivors about rape-revenge film especially was the most important thing that came from writing this book; it opened my eyes to the diversity of experience more than anything I'd ever read. Every time I speak publicly on this topic—while certainly not indicative of every rape survivor, of course—I have at least one person approach me as if to ask for my permission to find these films cathartic; "I am a rape survivor and these films have helped me so much—does that make me a freak?" is a question I have heard more than once, from both women *and* men. To hear filmmakers who are rape survivors themselves go on the record about their own experiences feels like an extension of this, a public acknowledgment of why their work matters to them and why they have the unquestionable right to represent rape on their own terms and in their own way based on their *own* experiences. All of these people frankly make me wish I was braver in being able to talk about my own stories, but I sit comfortably with the fact that as of yet at least I cannot. As hypocritical as this may appear, it's something I allow myself the right to decide on my own terms.

There is, I believe, a broad assumption that rape-revenge films somehow intrinsically act in opposition to the lived experience of rape survivors, of whom the numbers are unambiguously devastating. According to the World Population Review, in 2020 "it is estimated that approximately 35% of women worldwide have experienced sexual harassment" and that "in most countries with data available on rape, less than 40% of women who experience sexual violence seek help," with under 10 percent of those turning to law enforcement.[15] For many survivors, rape-revenge films must be unimaginably painful, triggering trauma so deep and personal that to find a descriptive catch-all is an insult to the individuality of those experiences. And yet for some—who may be a minority but are still important to acknowledge—these films can be hugely cathartic, despite how widely ignored this position is. My own experience of being approached by rape survivors is mirrored by that of a number of filmmakers who have worked in the rape-revenge space; director Karen Lam told me she has "had incredible feedback from women's shelters and rape centres who showed *Doll Parts* (2011) and *Evangeline* (2013) to some of their members. I think it's clear to those women that my intent was not about exploitation but about exploration, and taking on the story from the perspective of the victim."[16] Filmmaker Jim Hemphill likewise has said that "one of the biggest—and most pleasant—surprises for me about the response to *Bad Reputation* (2005) was that its biggest fans tended to be rape survivors." Hemphill continued, "right from the first public screening, I had girls and women come up to me—or, in most cases, email me or contact me on social media—and tell me that they were survivors and that they loved the movie and that it made them feel safe."[17] In one best pieces ever written on rape-revenge cinema, critic and filmmaker BJ Colangelo speaks of her own experience as a rape survivor and her relationship to rape-revenge, telling her story with extraordinary power, writing: "I'm never going to track down my rapist and murder him, but *I Spit on Your Grave* and rape-revenge movies like it showed me that he didn't have to destroy me when absolutely nothing else in my life told me otherwise. It showed me that I don't have to be a victim, and that being a survivor of sexual assault doesn't render me this weak, fragile, or damaged creature." She continues, "I'm still here, and I'm still strong, and no amount of therapy could ever show that to me.... So whenever people tell me how much they hate rape-revenge movies and think I'm a freak for liking them.... I just look at them and say, 'You just don't understand it, and I hope you never will.'"[18]

Similarly, often denied a place in critical discourse on rape-revenge film is the fact that rape survivors themselves have made these films. Both *Baise-Moi* (2000) directors Virginie Despentes and Coralie Trinh Thi and their two lead actors Karen Lancaume and Raffaëla Anderson are sexual assault survivors. *M.F.A.* director Natalie Leite has spoken openly of her experience, noting, "I felt like I had to make this movie because I have a personal connection to it.... I had been sexually assaulted during art school." For Leite, "this is me being able to go back and process it and speak openly about it." For Leite, the catharsis worked. "I highly recommend it! Being able to do that as therapy is very powerful."[19] Madeleine Sims-Fewer and Dusty Mancinelli have spoken at length about their own experiences and how those culminated in their powerful 2020 rape-revenge film, *Violation*. Despite noting a resistance on the part of some critics and male programmers in particular to their film, they speak with great precision about how their experience as survivors manifests in their creative work. For Mancinelli, it was #MeToo that led him to address his experience: "I came forward and confronted someone and it blew up in my face. It was all so fresh and so there was a lot of anger and resentment." *Violation* grew from this in discussion with Sims-Fewer about her own experience as a survivor, who also stars in the film as the rape-avenging protagonist Miriam. While developing the film, Sims-Fewer noted "something that we talked about a lot with our own experiences is the idea of feeling so impotent in the moment and feeling so completely helpless and then that creating the anger later. So you go away and the longer space there is between the assault and the time passing, you just start to feel more and more angry with yourself and angry with the other person and angry at the situation because you weren't able to do anything."[20]

It's stating the obvious, but not all people who watch rape-revenge films will feel the same as Colangelo, and not all filmmakers who make rape-revenge films will have the same experiences as filmmakers like Lam, Hemphill, Leite, Sims-Fewer and Mancinelli. *And nor should we expect them to*. It is enormously important to respect people's individual limits and responses to these films. But neither are right or wrong. Again, I return to the spirit of Wolfthal and emphasize again that "diverse notions coexist ... contemporaneously" when it comes to the representation of rape, and not just representation but diverse experiences and diverse responses, too. In this spirit I approach the task of revising the second edition of this book which, while providing a necessary updating of my earlier work, also seeks to further consolidate this intrinsic diversity.

There are many people to thank for a project of this size, most immediately, Dr. Josh Nelson for his support, solidarity and almost supernaturally keen eye has been essential to this edition. I thank also Dré Person and the team at McFarland. Deep gratitude to

Bill Ackerman, Mark Angeli, Sam Ashurst, David Barker, Bret Berg and AGFA, Anton Bitel, Ashlee Blackwell, Michael Blake, Anna Bogutskaya and Final Girls UK, Dean Brandum, Heather Buckley, Thomas Caldwell, Rolando Caputo, Michelle Carey, Abraham Castillo Flores, Sally Christie, Cinemaniacs (all of you!), BJ Colangelo, Martyn Conterio, Darren Cotzabuyucas, Johnboy Davidson, Samm Deighan, Wheeler Winston Dixon, Mattie Do, Heather Drain, John Edmond, Giles Edwards, Kat Ellinger, Brad Michael Elmore, Evrim Ersoy, Final Girls Berlin Film Festival (Elinor Lewy, Sara Neidorf and the team), Hannah Foreman, Gwendolyn Audrey Foster, Lee Gambin, Jack Geary, Ian Gouldstone, Jade Henshaw, Jim Hemphill, Brad Henderson and Vinegar Syndrome, Heidi Honeycutt, Chris Holden and Second Sight, Cerise Howard, Josh Hurtado, Sarah Jacek, Kier-La Janisse, Alexia Kannas, Martin Kingsley, Jacob Knight, Karen Lam, Clare Leaver, Ramon Lobato, Elf Lyons, Michael Mackenzie, Dusty Mancinelli, Anne Marsh, Kristy Matheson, Ernest Mathijs, Geoff Mayer, Donna McCrae and the Keylight ladies, Lou Mentor, Jennifer Merin, Luke Mullen, Angela Ndalianis, Anthony Nield and Indicator, Phil Nobile, Jr., Martyn Pedler, Gigi Saul Guerrero, Madeleine Sims-Fewer, James Shapiro, Francesco Simeoni and Arrow, Neil Snowdon, Matthew Sorrento, Static Vision (Conor Bateman, Felix Hubble and the team), Peter Strickland, David Surman, Marek Szold, Alison Taylor, and Emma Westwood, Cam Williams, Bret Wood and Kino Lorber. Special thanks to my family, Raibell, Richard, Max, Fiona, Rob, Rumpole, and my special magic men, Casper and Christian, and to the late Jan Napiorkowski, whose friendship was one of the greatest gifts in my life.

Introduction

Surely a definition of rape-revenge is simple: a rape-revenge film most immediately features a rape (or rapes, or attempted rapes) and an act of revenge. A rape-revenge film is one whereby a rape central to the narrative is punished by an act of vengeance, either by the victim themselves or an agent (most commonly, a partner or family member). For Sarah Projansky, the distinction between these two categories in the woman-centered rape-revenge film contains crucial ideological meaning:

> The films in the first category depend on rape to motivate and justify a particularly violent version of masculinity, relegating women to minor "props" in the narrative. The films of the second category, however, can be understood as feminist narratives in which women face rape, recognize that the law will neither protect nor avenge them, and then take the law into their own hands.[1]

If it is not the rape survivor themselves seeking vengeance, there is perhaps surprising diversity in the agents who act on their behalf. It can be fathers as in *Revenge for My Daughter* (*Salige er de som tørster*, Carl Jørgen Kiønig, 1997), *Serpent's Path* (*Hebi no michi*, Kiyoshi Kurosawa, 1998), *7 Days* (Daniel Grou, 2010), *Big Bad Wolves* (Aharon Keshales and Navot Papushado, 2013); husbands, lovers or boyfriends as in *Red White & Blue* (Simon Rumley, 2010) or *Frank & Lola* (Matthew Ross, 2016); or brothers like in *Nail Gun Massacre* (Terry Lofton and Bill Leslie, 1985) or *Sin* (Michael Stevens, 2003). Agents can also be women, acting on behalf of other women; this is particularly the case with mothers as in *A Mother's Revenge* (Armand Mastroianni, 1993), *Eye for an Eye* (John Schlesinger, 1996) and *Three Billboards Outside Ebbing, Missouri* (Martin McDonagh, 2017); sisters like in *'Gator Bait* (Beverly and Ferd Sebastian, 1974), *Savage Streets* (Danny Steinmann, 1984) and *Sweet Karma* (Andrew Thomas Hunt, 2009); and even grandmothers as in *Miss Violence* (Alexandros Avranas, 2013) and *Ajji* (Devashish Makhija, 2017).

But this distinction regarding *who* exacts vengeance is not the only important difference. In the case of Projansky's first designation—where an agent takes revenge on behalf of a raped woman—there are substantial points of distinction that separate some rape-revenge movies from others. The basic storyline of *The Virgin Spring* (*Jungfrukällan*, Ingmar Bergman, 1960) and *The Crow* (Alex Proyas, 1994) are perhaps surprisingly similar: a man systematically enacts revenge upon those who raped and murdered a woman loved one. So how can one of these films be considered one of the most significant rape-revenge movies of all time, while the other barely rates a mention? *Narrative focus* thus becomes crucial. As examined in Chapter One, Karin's (Birgitta Petterson) rape and murder is shown at painful, intimate length in *The Virgin Spring*, and spectatorial engagement with the ensuing revenge is a direct result of our emotional investment in that event. In *The Crow*, that part of the story is skipped over to provide the basic motivation for the ensuing action: we have little exposure to or interest in the raped and murdered woman outside her relationship to the film's protagonist, Eric Draven (Brandon Lee).

The power of the rape-revenge scenario is in the calculable intensity that sexual violence (or the threat of sexual violence) holds over the film as a whole. This does not necessarily mean the rape must be shown, and intensity and centrality do not automatically translate to visibility—in *The Accused* (Jonathan Kaplan, 1988) rape is only shown at the end of the film, while in *Shame* (Steve Jodrell, 1988), rape is not shown at all. The very words "rape" and "revenge" evoke associations between serious physical acts of violence with equally weighty moral and emotional responses. Regardless of how challenging the ideology or intent of a film, rape-revenge movies tend to make it explicit that rape (or the threat of rape) has triggered revenge. It is often—but not always—*how* those rapes are depicted, as well as the contexts of those depictions, that propel narratives and the spectator's experiences more generally. Rape cannot be incidental—it must be the core action that provokes revenge.

But do the films themselves fit so neatly into such a tidy definition? Many of the women-centered rape-revenge films addressed in this book are undeniably sensational attempts to profit from the ugly desire to watch sexual violence, while other examples have been critically beatified. If there's broader cultural confusion regarding how to tackle rape-revenge films, it is because the films themselves reflect a broader cultural confusion about rape more generally. That these films are both so uncomfortable and also so hard to comprehend in their sheer scale and diversity is one of the reasons they have proven so challenging for critics to fully get a handle on: when the wide range of movies this book explores is considered, many rape-revenge films are united only through their ability to demonstrate that conflicting attitudes toward rape have and continue to co-exist. Because of this diversity, the rape-revenge film allows a broad range of ideological debates to be explored. The survey of films that follows will not be a pleasant journey, and some of these examples have garnered great controversy. But at their most powerful, rape-revenge films expose and collapse simplistic assumptions about the ethics of representing rape onscreen and remind us that what we see is only a brief glance through a small, controlled window into the true horror of rape and sexual violence in terms of the very real experience of far too many men, women and children. As Claire Henry shrewdly notes, rape-revenge films are "a cultural key that can help to reveal and interrogate the meanings of rape and the political, ethical, and affective responses to it (on both individual and social levels)."[2] No matter how harrowing some of these films are, there are ethical complications to the fact that ultimately—as the famous tagline to the original *The Last House on the Left* (Wes Craven, 1972) taunted so mercilessly—what we see is "only a movie." Rape-revenge films are fluid, dynamic and elastic. Despite being broadly synonymous with horror film in the United States during the 1970s, they span genres, time and national borders. This book journeys through this surprisingly diverse, often shocking and frequently bizarre terrain, presenting a complicated history of rape-revenge films.

The Politics of Inclusion

This book explores the intersection of rape and revenge in film, surveying both mainstream and exploitation examples across time, national boundaries and genres.

It pays particular note to films situated outside traditional debates surrounding sexual violence in the cinema, but there is no intent to rescue, liberate, or defend these films. Nor are they necessarily offered to suggest broader trends; as Philip Green suggests, rape-revenge "is far from being either stylistically or ideologically monolithic, and to say that a movie 'belongs' to it is not necessarily to describe that movie's psychopolitics."[3] From this perspective, the films in this book present a contemporary continuation in cinema of art historian Diane Wolfthal's observation that, in the case of depictions of rape in medieval and early modern art, "diverse notions coexisted contemporaneously."[4] So central is this statement to the analyses that construct the bulk of this book that it can be considered its primary argument. Wolfthal's observations regarding the representation of rape in art from this period can be applied equally to the depiction of sexual violence in the rape-revenge film. She states:

> In addition to differences in style, function and patronage, rape imagery shows a broad range in tone and meaning. Some depictions represent rape symbolically, others explicitly; some clearly condemn rape, others blur the distinction between rape and seduction; some are comedic in tone, others tragic, celebratory, or horrific.[5]

Just as filmic rape is diverse, so too are debates that circulate around rape more generally. This impacts both how rape films are consumed, and also adds to how the figure of rapists and their victims and survivors are constructed in the broader popular consciousness. As Joanna Bourke observed, rapists "choose from a pool of circulating meaning. Rapists are not born; they become."[6] Much of the meaning that circulates in the public imagination about rape stems from films such as those examined here, and this alone renders an examination of their nuances, contradictions and tensions a necessary (although often distasteful) endeavor.

That is not to say that these films have nothing in common; at the very least, the eponymous features of rape and revenge rate highly on the list of defining features. These films also share a fundamental desire to represent sexual violence in a fictional context—whether shown, verbally described, or merely alluded to, actors pretend to rape or to be raped. This may provide little comfort in what is often a nasty viewing experience, but our psyches are often cushioned in more significant ways from the brutality of watching onscreen rape. Described by Sabine Sielke as the "rhetoric of rape," sexual violence often is utilized as a narrative device with which to talk about much broader issues.[7] The intensity of rape often underscores the seriousness of these other factors. Consequently, there is a tension between these wider concerns, and the reality of rape itself. For Wolfthal:

> Images of rape often involve other issues—political concerns, sexual desire, or ethnic, class and gender difference—and this complexity enriches our understanding of such depictions. But ... despite other layers of meaning, these representations are also about "real rape."[8]

Sexual violence in rape-revenge films is sometimes used to emphasize these adjoining issues. But there is no singular or consistent system, method or approach that unifies every single rape-revenge example. Again, in rape-revenge films, "diverse notions" of rape have "coexisted contemporaneously."

Confusion about the relationship between rape and its artistic representation is historically entrenched and existed long before screen culture. Wolfthal's argument responds to the privileging in art history of the tradition of "heroic" rape imagery, where heroes and gods who rape do so to indicate power in both Ancient Roman and Greek legends, later immortalized in canonical artworks from Renaissance Italy, including Titian's

The Rape of Europa (1562) and Botticelli's *Primavera* (1482). In *Against Our Will: Men, Women and Rape* (1975), Susan Brownmiller identifies recent examples of "heroic" rape in contemporary outlaw mythology, citing Hunter S. Thompson's writings on the Hell's Angels and the Rolling Stones. She identifies a pattern where representations of rape present perpetrators as "big men" at the expense of their women victims.[9] Both Wolfthal and Brownmiller emphasize that "heroic" rape imagery celebrates the rapist, with notably less attention paid to the victim.

These issues are not specific to the visual arts. As Trudy Govier suggests, "human societies develop legal systems and seek to establish the rule of law"[10] precisely to overcome the "exaggerated, unreliable and anarchic tendencies of personal revenge as a strategy of retribution."[11] That these systems are broadly considered so notoriously ill-equipped to deal with rape provides the premise of many rape-revenge films: a rape survivor (or her agent) takes justice into her own hands when the law proves incapable or unwilling to punish those responsible. Arguably, revenge is rarely more complicated than when triggered by rape. Writing about rape—even fictional representations of it—is a formidable task, considering the ideological minefield and deeply subjective and emotional responses the topic evokes. Past critics have approached the subject with more than the usual disclaimers that regularly accompany discussions about onscreen violence. As one of the only books dedicated to the rape-revenge film specifically, Jacinda Read's *The New Avengers: Feminism, Femininity and the Rape-Revenge Cycle* (2000) is essential reading on this subject. But her justification for examining only mainstream instances of the rape-revenge plot appears too readily dismissive of the broader issues at stake in the wider field of rape-revenge. Positioning her argument as an either/or response to the dependence of Carol J. Clover's *Men, Women, and Chain Saws: Gender in the Modern Horror Film* (1992) on horror, Read aims to rescue mainstream film from the status of rejected Other to the horror and exploitation titles of interest to Clover. Projansky's *Watching Rape: Film and Television in Postfeminist Culture* (2001) is one of the most exhaustive treatments of rape and its onscreen representation, and she identifies a "feminist paradox between a desire to *end* rape and a need to *represent* (and therefore perpetuate discursive) rape in order to challenge it."[12] In this sense, even the act of watching onscreen rape is ideologically loaded:

> Graphic representations of rape, at least for the moment in the text during which the rape appears, can be understood to express hatred for and violence against women and thus can potentially increase anxiety and discomfort for many spectators.... Paradoxically, even texts that explicitly articulate an anti-rape perspective can also inadvertently contribute to these backlash representations.[13]

The instinct to step away from the abyss where even the slightest suggestion that a woman's suffering is desirable or titillating is therefore both commendable and understandable. But at the same time, Tammy Oler's observation that "rape-revenge films are at once contributors to and reflections of real-world beliefs and attitudes about rape and violence"[14] presents a clear problem: if this is the case, then surely it is even more urgent that *all* images of rape (including the graphic ones) are placed under a critical microscope. The decision to *not* turn away from looking at the more vicious or exploitative examples of the rape-revenge category should not be taken lightly, and the legacy of Clover's work (discussed further shortly) provides strong precedence for the critical value of the nastier instances of rape-revenge.

Perhaps, however, there is a vital element missing when rape-revenge is examined in these terms: that of the filmmaker's own creative response to the material in question. Instructive here is talking to filmmakers directly. Peter Strickland's *Katalin Varga* (2009) follows its eponymous protagonist (Hilda Péter) after she is thrown out of her home by Zsigmond (László Mátray) when he learns he is not the biological father of their child, Orbán (Norbert Tankó). As the film unfolds, it is revealed that Orbán was conceived as the result of a rape at the hands of Antal (Tibor Pálffy). The film follows Katalin as she travels towards Antal to confront him, with tragic consequences. Aside from its exquisite pastoral landscapes and low-key, even slow tone, *Katalin Varga* is marked by the absence of a rape scene; rather the film's climactic revelation takes place on a relatively quiet boat trip where Katalin verbally accounts the assault to Antal and his wife. Strickland's thinking behind this setup and the experience that led to it reveals a great deal about how a specific filmmaker's creative vision and ideological drive are often inseparable:

> I was trying to see if by withholding visual information, the audience might compensate more in their heads. Paradoxically, we all know that words can sometimes have more impact than images. I remember a woman I was staying with in Sarajevo unexpectedly telling me about the siege back in 2003. I wanted to record her talking about local recipes and we misunderstood each other. It would've felt insensitive to ask about the siege, but maybe she assumed that was what most Western tourists wanted to know. Initially, I didn't understand why she was getting so distressed over a recipe, but then it dawned on me that she was recounting her experiences over those horrors. I didn't understand anything, but hearing the cracks in her voice and seeing her face affected me far more than the images of brutality on the news back in the '90s.[15]

He continues:

Hilda Péter (left) and Tibor Pálffy (center) on the set of *Katalin Varga* (Peter Strickland, 2009) (photograph by Marek Szold, courtesy Marek Szold and Peter Strickland).

When we shot the film in 2006, to feature a talking head was one of the most passé crimes against cinema, which made me want to be confrontational with it. To trap the audience with that kind of eye contact and not let them go. The crew could be quite rebellious due to their low fees and had no hesitation in telling me if something was rubbish. I remember some of the crew on the neighbouring boat complaining how boring the scene was, which put Hilda off. She was very sensitive to that kind of criticism and believed that what she was doing was boring. I had to really coax her into doing it and she managed to go into herself and ignore everyone and everything around her. We spent so long arguing that by the time we got round to filming, it started to rain midway through the take, which looked ridiculous (in a bad way) and unrealistic. I was about to call "cut," especially as we were running low on film rolls, only I could see Hilda was going even further into this reverie of hers. It almost looked as if she was in a trance and the best thing I could do was to stay out of her way. Not calling "cut" was the best decision I made on that film and the scene felt very powerful even though we had to dub it a year later after we lost the sound. When I wrote it, someone suggested I use flashbacks to the attack within that lake scene, but that would've undermined everything I wanted to convey.

Though diverging noticeably from Strickland's film—specifically in its representation of rape—Madeleine Sims-Fewer and Dusty Mancinelli's *Violation* (2020) is equally revealing in terms of *how* rape is depicted onscreen and the creative decisions behind those representations. Presented in a non-linear manner, *Violation* focuses on Miriam (played by co-director Sims-Fewer) who is raped by her brother-in-law, which leads to her torturing and murdering him. That both Sims-Fewer and Mancinelli have spoken openly about their experiences as sexual assault survivors intrinsically binds their creative decisions regarding the representation of rape to their own personal experiences of the trauma associated with sexual violence. In particular, the rape scene itself is remarkable for how it deviates from the typical way such scenes are shot; filmed in extreme close up it is difficult to see what is happening outside of the tight visual frame, a disorienting technique that places the audience in an affective relationship with Miriam herself who wakes up from a drunken sleep while the rape is happening. Like Miriam, we do not wholly understand what is occurring, while the tightness of the frame renders the sequence an uncomfortable, suffocating experience. As Mancinelli notes, "we had to refilm that sequence several times because we recognized really early on that it needed to be so intimate with these macro photography lenses, and so claustrophobic and fragmented … trying to capture that feeling of … shock."[16] Sims-Fewer continues this thought, describing it as being "like an out of body experience; you're just frozen, and there's nothing you can do but just observe yourself from outside yourself." For Sims-Fewer, it is this disorientation that leads to the desire for revenge. "Something that we talked about a lot with our own experiences is the idea of feeling so impotent in the moment and feeling so completely helpless and then that creating the anger later." She said, "So you go away and the longer space there is between the assault and the time passing, you just start to feel more and more angry with yourself and angry with the other person and angry at the situation because you weren't able to do anything." Listening to filmmakers themselves speak about why they film rape scenes in certain ways is a revealing window into the broad possibilities of representation, highlighting the importance of the creative decisions in shaping the audience's relationship to depictions of sexual violence.

The tendency to ignore the diversity of how rape scenes in women-centered rape-revenge films are shot and edited reflects a broader denial of the diversity that exists within the category as a whole, typified by Peter Lehman's declaration that "female rape-revenge films are a licensed form of violence in which a woman acts out male desires for the erotic satisfaction of a predominately male mass audience."[17] This not only does not apply to many rape-revenge examples, it falsely assumes that only men watch and enjoy rape-revenge movies (and, as is so widely assumed, that only men—until recently at least—have made them). As Oler points out, this is far from the case: many women watch and enjoy rape-revenge films, and thus, despite the "conventional wisdom" that encourages the rejection of rape-revenge as "nothing but misogynistic schlock designed to titillate male audiences," we can now safely say that "feminists and film critics alike now grudgingly recognize that the films are doing more complicated cultural work."[18]

There is something fundamentally harrowing in any filmic depiction of rape that aims to "make visually palatable such a horrifying event that bears no beauty whatsoever."[19] This is in part what I intend to address: are the pleasures found in watching these films—for both men and women—only able to be viewed as sadistic, misogynistic, or just "wrong"? More importantly, can we even collectively refer to them as "these films"? Are they really that unified a body of work? And if not, does diversity exist only between genre, era, budget or nationality, or is there a case for analysis to be splintered into a film-by-film basis? The problem with answering these questions in part lies in the very "unrepresentability" of the reality and trauma of rape itself—the inability to capture the magnitude of human suffering that results from sexual violence—that is the understandable source of so much critical discomfort. However, to avoid these questions avoids the problem that so many rape-revenge films seek to either consciously ignore or are so determined to address. As this book demonstrates, there is no singular, unified treatment of rape across the rape-revenge category. Rather, these diverse, broad and often contradictory films offer a multitude of representations of—and reactions to—sexual violence.

Approaching the Rape-Revenge Film

The rape-revenge film is popularly attributed to North American horror and exploitation cinema during the 1970s, where they flourished. This was partially due to an easing of censorship restrictions and a "mainstreaming" of public discussion about sexual politics that resulted from the high visibility of the anti-rape movement that formed a part of second-wave feminism's sweeping influence from the late 1960s. Andrea Dworkin and Catherine MacKinnon were the public faces of the antipornography movement, and they vocally argued that the pornographic representation of women could be held directly responsible for sexual violence in the real world; as fellow radical feminist Robin Morgan so famously claimed, "Pornography is the theory, rape is the practice." Widely considered as both an exhaustive treatment on the subject and one of the first feminist texts to reach bestseller status, Brownmiller's *Against Our Will: Men, Women and Rape* argues that "to simply learn the word 'rape' is to take instruction in the power relationship between male and females."[20] She explores how historical treatments of rape shaped contemporary attitudes to sexual violence. Writing that rape only became illegal because it was historically deemed a property crime between men, the legacy of this in rape-revenge cinema is broad and can be seen in films ranging from *'Gator Bait*, *Marlina the Murderer in Four Acts* (*Marlina Si Pembunuh dalam Empat Babak*, Mouly Surya, 2017), and Dick Lowry's 1981 television movie *Coward of the County* adapted from Kenny Roger's 1979 country hit of the same name. Brownmiller lays the foundations that view rape not only as an issue pertaining to women and femininity, but as equally significant to discourses about men and masculinity. There are, of course, other configurations of rape than male-against-female, but as Kimberly Peirce's devastating *Boys Don't Cry* (1999)—based on the real-life story of a transgender man who was gang raped—the biologically essentialist lines that separate "male" from "female" pale in comparison next to the viciousness of sexual violence itself. However, that so many of the most immediately recognizable instances of the rape-revenge film are predominantly structured around a male perpetrator and a female victim informs both this preliminary history and the book as a whole.

Representations of sexual violence offer a rich site of investigation for feminism because, as Lynn Higgins and Brenda Silver suggest, "rape and rapability are central to the very construction of gender identity and that our subjectivity and sense of ourselves as sexual beings are inextricably enmeshed in representations."[21] Tanya Horeck[22] and Projansky[23] note a tension between the intimate, personal crime of rape and the intensive public scrutiny placed upon the act that makes how it is represented crucial. From this perspective, representations of rape suggest a complex range of meanings that are far more expansive than those immediately associated with the trauma of "real" rape itself. Sielke captures this succinctly, observing that when "transposed into discourse, rape turns into a rhetorical device, an insistent figure for other social, political, and economic concerns and conflicts."[24] Projansky also identifies an allegorical aspect to onscreen rape, noting that it has become a method of invoking a broad range of discourses about other things: "Rape narratives are so common in cinema (and elsewhere) that they seem always to be available to address other social issues."[25] From rape-revenge that explore themes of class like *Nocturnal Animals* (Tom Ford, 2016) or race like *Avenged* (Michael S. Ojeda, 2013), contemporary evidence is not difficult to locate.

Rape as a narrative trope or plot device has a long history. For example, Mieke Bal has traced the structural and thematic utility of rape to the Book of Judges in the Bible, noting the ability of sexual violence to propel narrative.[26] Rhiannon Graybill suggests that Judges 4–5 can be read explicitly through the lens of the slasher film and rape-revenge.[27] Like Bal, Projansky, Read and Rikke Schubart emphasize rape as a transformative device within onscreen rape narratives.[28] Projansky observes in the case of horror and thriller films that "rape or the threat of rape [acts] as a fulcrum for a narrative about the transformation of a meek woman into a powerful independent woman who protects herself and sometimes her friends and family."[29] For Schubart, in rape-revenge films "rape is the initiation rite that pushes women from being 'soft' victims to becoming 'hard' avengers,"[30] while for Read the "rape-revenge film and feminism itself are perhaps better understood not in terms of authentic moments but as narratives of transformations."[31] Filmmakers themselves have sometimes responded critically to this trend; Jen and Sylvia Soska's *American Mary* (2012) avoids precisely this rape-makes-feminists arithmetic, amplifying the eponymous protagonist's feminist credentials long before she is assaulted. But even taking this diversity into account, at the very least there is ample evidence that supports Read's claim that "the rape-revenge cycle might usefully be read as one of the ways in which Hollywood has attempted to make sense of feminism and the changing face of heterosexuality in the post–1970 period."[32] In short, "the rape-revenge film can be seen to be attempting to make sense of feminism."[33] It does this, she claims, by opening and exposing the tensions and contradictions "between the (feminine) victim and the (feminist) avenger and the way in which films negotiate the transformation from one to the other."[34]

Read's analysis of rape-revenge launches from a preliminary rebuttal of Clover's influential *Men, Women, and Chain Saws: Gender in the Modern Horror Film*. Clover's understanding of rape-revenge as a sub-genre of horror allowed her examination of Meir Zarchi's original *I Spit on Your Grave* (1978) to add weight to her primary argument for cross-gender identification in the modern horror film. This argument contrasts with Laura Mulvey's notion of a sadistic and dominant male gaze, as established in her foundational essay "Visual Pleasure and Narrative Cinema" (1972).[35] For Clover, in the case of *I Spit on Your Grave*, "the only way to account for the spectator's engagement in the revenge drive is to assume his engagement with the rape-avenging woman."[36] She concludes, "The center of gravity in these films lies more in the reaction (the revenge) than the act (the rape), but to the extent that the revenge fantasy derives its force from some degree of imaginary participation in the act itself, in the victim position, these films are predicated on cross-gender identification of the most extreme, corporeal sort."[37]

While the legacy of Clover's book is undeniable, Read is not the first to challenge aspects of her argument. Both Klaus Rieser[38] and Tony Williams[39] question the "victory" of the female victim-heroes or "final girls"[40] in the films Clover has selected, suggesting that just simply "not dying" can hardly be considered any cause for feminist celebration. The reliance of horror studies on psychoanalysis (of which Clover's work is a key example) is also a source of debate. In his critique of Clover, Frank Burke suggests the dependence upon psychoanalysis "dehistoricize[s] by addressing films and their female characters in universalizing Freudian and post–Freudian terms, which makes representation only and always the reproduction of patriarchy/masculinity."[41] Andrew Tudor questioned the dominance of psychoanalytic approaches to horror, suggesting its deployment is more concerned with establishing itself as the dominant location for a singular, "genuine" film history that recapitulates the power of the critic (analyst) over actual meaning: "It is an inordinately reductive form of analysis, presupposing the overall credibility of a particular perspective and seeking to assimilate the widest possible range of cultural variation to those terms."[42]

Read's issues with Clover's treatment of rape-revenge film hinges primarily on text selection, and she argues that rather than being a subgenre of horror, rape-revenge is "a historically specific but generically diverse cycle of films."[43] For Read, the assumption that the rape-revenge is a subgenre of horror is not only inaccurate but ideologically loaded:

> Clover's feminist analysis ... depends on drawing a distinction between underground and mainstream rape-revenge films, a distinction that also translates into an opposition between feminist and feminine and that, therefore, again necessitates the exclusion of the latter. Thus, while the low-brow rape-revenge film is elevated to the status of a politicized avant-garde (consumed by male audiences), the mainstream version is implicitly analyzed within a framework that condemns mass culture as a feminized and, therefore, depoliticized culture (consumed by "normal," that is, mixed audiences).[44]

"Cultural texts tell several different stories," she continues, "in doing so it is not sufficient (as Clover does) to simply repress or disavow the presence of apparently contradictory or mutually exclusive stories, since it is in the very struggle between such stories that meaning is produced."[45] While this is certainly true, the eagerness with which Read approaches the act of "debunking" Clover blinds her to some degree to the same weaknesses in her own argument. Most immediately, while Read chooses films that support her argument of a "historically specific" element to the rape-revenge films that construct the cycle as she defines it, the rape-revenge film category is broader and more diverse than she gives credit. Read's view of rape-revenge as a narrative structure is convincing, but her determination to prove Clover and her dedication to horror "wrong" render her own text selection equally biased. While Read draws parameters around those examples she chose to examine—as much out of a practical necessity as I do here—both Yvonne Tasker[46] and Karen Hollinger[47] query why *Sleeping with the Enemy* (Joseph Ruben, 1991), *Batman Returns* (Tim Burton, 1992) and *The Last Seduction* (John Dahl, 1994) are privileged in a book on rape-revenge cinema. This is particularly poignant when considering so many more immediately identifiable non-horror titles such as Robert M. Young's *Extremities* (1986) and Lamont Johnson's *Lipstick* (1976) fail to gain but the briefest of mentions in *The New Avengers*. Even the book's cover is incongruous; as I discuss in Chapter Two, *Dirty Weekend* (Michael Winner, 1992) is a fascinating rape-revenge film, but despite its privileged position on the cover of Read's book, it receives little concrete analysis.

Does *The New Avengers* solidly examine the intersection of second-wave feminism and contemporary Hollywood cinema? Certainly. Does it convincingly demonstrate how the rape-revenge films are uniquely positioned to provide insight into this intersection? If the best examples to support this claim are *Batman Returns*, *The Last Seduction* and *Sleeping with the Enemy* (the last two Read herself admits only offer a "residual, rather than dominant deployment of the rape-revenge structure"[48]), then perhaps not. As Read says, "We are living in a culture in which ideas about feminism and its history are as, if not more, likely to be gleaned from popular culture than from reading feminist theory."[49] In this sense, Read's project was to look at the popular cinema of her present. As true as it may have been (and may still be) that we can learn "ideas about feminism and its history" from popular Hollywood films, we do not necessarily learn a great deal about rape-revenge when so many non–Hollywood "dominant deployment[s]" are rejected in favor of her more "residual" examples.

While no book can examine every single rape-revenge film ever made, to base an argument on the necessary exclusion of a bulk of those films does not appear to fully appreciate the value of the category. The theoretical "heavy lifting" can only be performed when its case studies are understood and identified for what they *actually* are, and how they fit into a bigger picture. This book surveys a sample of rape-revenge films that span genres and national and historical boundaries to emphasize that, in regard to the representation of sexual violence especially, "diverse notions coexisted contemperanously" and continue to do so today.

Cinema from Rape to Rape-Revenge

Like literature, myth and legend long before it, film has a rich tradition of exploiting rape. The Greek mythological figure of Philomela and Celtic queen Boudica are surely ancestors of cinema's women rape avengers. Rape-revenge features centrally in Shakespeare's *Titus Andronicus*, adapted to the screen as *Titus* in 1999 by Julie Taymor. Alex Cox's 2002 film *Revengers Tragedy* reimagined Thomas Middleton's 1606 Jacobean play of the same name, maintaining the latter's explicit engagement with rape and revenge. Despite the assumed low-brow nature of rape-revenge, literary adaptations are not rare: *Nocturnal Animals* was adapted from Austin Wright's novel *Tony and Susan* (1993), *Straw Dogs* (1971/2011) were inspired by Gordon M. Williams's *The Siege of Trencher's Farm* (1969), Janet Greek's *The Ladies Club* (1986) was based on the 1977 novel of the same name by Casey Bishop and Betty Black, *Big Driver* (Mikael Salomon, 2014) was adapted from Stephen King's 2010 novella of the same name, *Vengeance: A Love Story*

(John Martin, 2017) was based on Joyce Carol Oates's novel *Rape: A Love Story* (2003), *The House of the Spirits* (Bille August 1993) was based on Isabelle Allende's *La Casa de los Espíritus* (1982), and Carl Jørgen Kiønig's *Revenge for my Daughter* was adapted from Anne Holt's *Blessed Are Those Who Thirst* (1993). Despite the literary credentials of many of these authors, when adapted to the screen the highbrow/lowbrow tension between literature and film has held steadfast, Lili Pâquet's asserting that "rape-revenge narratives adapt to literature—whether fiction or memoir—as more nuanced and less reliant on the corporeal female body, as readers can empathise with the victim through narration that offers her perspective, rather than spectacle."[50]

Yet when moving to cinema, the deployment of rape—and of rape-revenge—does not support the claim that in cinema, sexual violence is deployed for spectacle alone. Additionally, it is a decidedly international phenomenon, as *Rashomon* (Akira Kurosawa, 1950) and *The Virgin Spring* illustrate—two revered art films that challenge the assumed lowbrow status of rape on screen. Hollywood cinema provides a useful starting place, as the deployment of rape motifs stretches back to early cinema. D.W. Griffith's *Birth of a Nation* (1915) is celebrated for establishing many of the defining formal features of the "Hollywood style," such as continuity editing, but these technical accomplishments pale next to its extremist right-wing political agenda. The Ku Klux Klan are painted as victorious superheroes who save the Aryan damsel-in-distress and her fellow downtrodden whites from the supposed rising ranks of liberated southern Blacks. Possibly by accident, possibly as a suicide, the young, white Flora Cameron (Mae Marsh) flings herself off a cliff when threatened by the advances of the Black soldier Gus (Walter Long). This, combined with the attempted rape of Flora's sister Elsie (Lillian Gish) by the mulatto leader Silas Lynch (George Seigmann), reveals white fears of miscegenation and equates interracial sexual activity with sexual violence.[51] Films of pioneering Black filmmaker Oscar Micheaux are important to acknowledge here, *Within Our Gates* (1920) reversing the racial politics of *The Birth of a Nation* by featuring a Black woman assaulted by a rich white man. In *Body and Soul* (1925), both rapist and survivor are Black, a legacy which in the case of rape-revenge specifically culminates in the final film of the groundbreaking Michael Schultz, *Woman Thou Art Loosed* (Michael Schultz, 2004).

By the early 1920s, rape and the cinema had also become inextricably linked in the popular imagination through the highly publicized trial of the comic Roscoe "Fatty" Arbuckle in the rape and murder of actor Virginia Rappe. Arbuckle was accused of a sexual assault so violent that it ruptured Rappe's bladder, leading to death. Despite facing three trials and being found innocent each time, Arbuckle's career was destroyed, and this scandal in part sparked the associations between Hollywood and questionable morality that made way for the rise of the censorship regulations implemented by Will Hays from the 1920s onwards. From then until the introduction of the Production Code in 1934 under the stern eye of Joseph Breen, this pre–Code Hollywood period still provided leeway for risqué subject matter (including rape) to be included in films produced in this context. It was during this period that some of the most notable depictions of onscreen rape appeared before this mode of censorship began to collapse in the 1950s.

Because of the appearance of rape and revenge individually from the earliest days of Hollywood cinema, it is perhaps futile to attempt to locate the precise moment when it intersected and turned into "rape-revenge." Regardless, there are key moments long before second-wave feminism that have been privileged at the beginnings of a loosely understood rape-revenge film history. For James M. Alexander, that moment was the

Swedish film *The Virgin Spring*,[52] while for Read it is *Johnny Belinda* (Jean Negulesco, 1948).[53] Laura L. Finley's emphasis on Anna May Wong's character Hui Fei killing of the man who raped her in *Shanghai Express* (Josef von Sternberg, 1932)[54] suggests that there is, however, evidence that rape-revenge has more specific pre–Code origins. A key figure is William A. Wellman, in whose films *Wild Boys of the Road* (1933) and *The Robin Hood of El Dorado* (1936) rape and revenge intersect either explicitly in the former or implicitly in the latter. Most intriguing of his films from this era and perspective is *Safe in Hell* (1931) which sympathetically tells the story of Gilda (Dorothy Mackaill), a secretary forced into sex work after have being "seduced" (implicitly raped) by her ex-boss, Piet (Ralf Harolde). Discovering the "affair," Piet's wife makes it impossible for Gilda to keep any job outside of prostitution. The film opens as Gilda is tricked into visiting Piet, believing him to be a legitimate client. A fight ensues, and Gilda accidentally kills him. She awakens the next morning to find her sailor boyfriend Carl (Donald Cook) returned from sea and tells him of her predicament. Deeply in love with Gilda, he hides her on a remote tropical island with no extradition laws. As the only white woman on an island filled with dangerous male criminals also in hiding, the film's title is explained: while Gilda may be safe from prosecution in the United States, as the island's executioner Bruno (Morgan Wallace) tells her, she is now "safe in hell." The degree that Wellman goes to emphasize the sexual threat Gilda faces on this island is remarkable: locked in her room (she keeps a chair under the doorknob for extra protection), at numerous times throughout the film the men in her hotel line their chairs up outside her door and stare at it for what is suggested to be hours. Like other rape-revenge protagonists, such as Thana in *Ms. 45* (Abel Ferrara, 1980) and Carla in *Naked Vengeance* (Cirio H. Santiago, 1985), for Gilda, sexual threat is everywhere.

Carl and Gilda marry in an informal wedding ceremony on the island before he returns to sea, and she vows to remain true to him. Despite the pressure and loneliness, Gilda keeps her promise. To her surprise, Piet comes to the island and tells her that he had faked his death as an insurance scam (he, too, escapes to the island to avoid extradition). Observing Piet's lecherous intentions toward Gilda, Bruno slips her a gun and tells her that despite their illegality on the island, he wants her to be safe. It is with this gun that she shoots Piet after he attempts to rape her again. There is a public court hearing, and her once-threatening hotel mates now rush to her defense to clear her name. Bruno tells her that even if she is released on the murder charge, he will insist she is prosecuted for possessing the very firearm that he supplied her with—he has set her up so that she is forced to become his sex slave. Rejecting this possibility, Gilda rushes into the courtroom and declares the murder of Piet was premeditated; and—as she expected—she is sentenced to death. The film ends as she says a brief farewell to Carl (not telling him of her upcoming execution) and then walks to the gallows defiantly, victoriously staring Bruno down.

Gilda's world is one where rape, sexual threat and domination are everyday phenomena. Like Thelma and Louise discovered over fifty years later in the context of their experience, what is effectively suicide remains for Gilda her only access to any kind of female agency. For Gilda, dying or killing are her only weapons against rape. While not quite a prototype of the rape-revenge films that became common in the 1970s, *Safe in Hell* complexifies the relationship between rape and revenge much more than more famous—and much later—rape films that feature elements of revenge, such as *Outrage* (Ida Lupino, 1950) and *Johnny Belinda*. More importantly, *Safe in Hell* also allows its story to be Gilda's and Gilda's alone; there is no man to save her (not even Carl), so she makes the only choice she feels she can in the circumstances. That her decision is so bleak not only underscores the futility of her entire experience, it also foreshadows the nihilism that permeates later rape-revenge titles like Craven's *The Last House on the Left*.

George Archainbaud's *Thirteen Women* (1932) is another pre–Code artifact that, while not explicitly focused upon rape in its construction of its woman villain's search for revenge, makes clear in the film's climactic confrontation that rape—and the absence of protection from it—lie at the core of her vendetta. The film follows vampish, "half–Hindi" Ursula (Myrna Loy) as she systematically terrorizes a group of women, actively encouraging their death. One of these women, Laura (Irene Dunne), attempts to escape from Los Angeles to New York by train in order to protect her son Bobby (Wally Albright). Ursula is also on the train and confronts Laura, who asks, "What has anyone done to make you so inhuman?" Ursula replies bluntly:

> Do I hear the very human white race asking that question? When I was twelve years old, white sailors … (*pauses*). Do you know what it means to be a half-breed? A half-caste in a world ruled by whites? If you're a male, you're a Coolie, and if you're a female, you're, well … (*pauses*). The white half of me cried for the courtesy and protection that women like you get. The only way I could free myself was by becoming white, and it was almost in my hands, when you, you and your Kappa society stopped me…. Six years slaving to get money enough to put me through finishing school, to make the world accept me as white, but you and the others wouldn't let me cross the color line.

Although Ursula dies soon after this conversation, to a contemporary audience Laura's defense that "we were young" is more difficult to accept than it may have been at the time of the film's production. According to Ursula, her status as a racialized Other resulted in an implied long history of rape and sexual abuse. Understanding the crucial role of her racial status in her inability to protect herself from sexual violence, Ursula's attempts to feign whiteness are thwarted by racist fellow students. In this light, the "thirteen women" are not only far from innocent, they are to some degree complicit in the acts of violence that Ursula suffered by refusing her "the courtesy and protection" of women like themselves. As continued in later films, ranging from *Ms. 45* and *Dirty Weekend* to *Positive I.D.* (Andy Anderson, 1986) and *Savage Streets* (Danny Steinmann, 1984), this model of agency for women is coded as vampish and overtly sexualized.

A cursory glance at films including *The Unpardonable Sin* (Marshall Neilan, 1919), *The Rogue Song* (Lionel Barrymore, 1930), *The Story of Temple Drake* (Stephen Roberts, 1933), *Gone with the Wind* (Victor Fleming, 1939), *My Name Is Julia Ross* (Joseph H. Lewis, 1945), *Ruby Gentry* (King Vidor, 1952), *The Blue Gardenia* (Fritz Lang, 1953), and *The Burglar* (Paul Wendkos, 1957) demonstrates that rape or attempted rape is not invisible in classical Hollywood cinema, and often has a key narrative function. There are films from this era that are significant for their particular articulation of rape trauma rather than their union of rape and revenge. Most famous of these is *Johnny Belinda*, which adopts the motif of the mute woman protagonist from *The Spiral Staircase* (Robert Sidomak, 1945), thus establishing the rape-survivor-as-mute motif that can be seen in films such as *Thriller: A Cruel Picture* (*Thriller: En Grym Film*, Bo Arne Vibenius, 1974), *Golden Karate Girl* (*Karateci kiz*, Orhan Aksoy, 1974), *Ms. 45*, *Savage Streets*, *The Demoniacs* (*Les démoniaques*, Jean Rollin, 1974), *Speak* (Jessica Sharzer, 2004), *Sweet Karma* (Andrew Thomas Hunt, 2009), and *The Seasoning House* (Paul Hyett, 2012).[55] *Johnny Belinda* follows a young doctor (Lew Ayres) sent to a small village in Nova Scotia where he meets deaf-mute farm girl Belinda (Jane Wyman). Inspired by her intelligence, he teaches her sign language and lip reading, and they develop a strong relationship. She is raped by local Locky (Stephen McNally) and soon discovers she is pregnant. Locky decides he wants custody of the baby, and Belinda shoots him when he tries to take the child. During the subsequent murder trial, Locky's young wife Stella (Jan Sterling) admits that Locky raped Belinda and that he was there to take her child. The film ends with Belinda's release, and she is romantically united with the doctor. While renowned as a key rape text from this period, in terms of Classical Hollywood cause and effect logic, the rape is crucial only in that it leads to the birth of the child that propels the narrative tensions between the men in the last half of the film. The sequence where Belinda gives birth is much longer than the rape scene and is a relatively joyous affair.

Less critically privileged is Ida Lupino's *Outrage*, identified by Pam Cook as "partly a rape-revenge story."[56] For Molly Haskell, Lupino's gender granted her no unique insight into female experience, and she argues that Lupino's hypersexualized star persona and the "masculinity" of her films render her as nothing less than a gender traitor:

> Lupino was tougher as an actress than as a director: the movies she made (*Hard, Fast, and Beautiful*, *The Bigamist*, *The Hitchhiker*) are conventional, even sexist; and in her interviews, like so many women who have nothing to complain about, she purrs like a contented kitten, arches her back at the mention of women's lib, and quotes Noel Coward to the effect that women should be struck regularly like gongs.[57]

Although *Outrage* does not rate even a passing reference in this dismissal, the film suggests a very different Lupino to that described by Haskell. Like *Johnny Belinda*, *Outrage*, too, offers institutionalized male intervention (again by a professional—this time a priest) as the "solution" to rape and its traumatic repercussions. The film's concluding scenes, where Ann (Mala Powers) returns to her parents and fiancé to lead a normal life, occur relatively suddenly and with a neatness that contrasts sharply with the film's earlier dedication to the nuance of Ann's experience. But it is the scenes in the film's first half that contain *Outrage*'s most powerful moments; unlike with *Johnny Belinda*, rape is not confined to a distant, historical past-tense, but happens in its contemporary moment, in the suburbs, to able-bodied girls with charming fiancés, nice parents and steady jobs. The randomness of the attack—an intense *film noir* sequence that highlights Ann's confusion, isolation and terror—provokes a lengthy analysis of the question "Why Ann?"—not only by the spectator and Ann herself, but later by her parents and the police investigating her case. The sequences when she is interviewed by doctors and the police, when she walks from her house to the bus stop for the first time after the attack, and when she returns to work, all go to painstaking extremes to demonstrate Ann's trauma (and is the ancestor to similar scenes in films like *The Accused*). Ann's decision to run away to another town is therefore justified. Lupino and Powers' combined efforts sympathetically illustrate Ann's desperation but never patronize her. The film's sympathetic alignment with Ann's experience is demonstrated stylistically throughout the film, most dramatically when a local boy propositions her at a church dance. Shown through extreme close-ups and abstract, subjective POV shots, her violent response to his attempted seduction is understandable.

Although limits of space restrict this book to feature film, rape and revenge has long intersected in series television on programs including *Simon & Simon*, *The Equalizer*, *Barnaby Jones*, *Dallas*, *Starsky and Hutch*, *Hawaii Five-O*, *Beverly Hills 90210*, *Home and Away*, *Law and Order: SVU*, *The Bold and the Beautiful*, *Coronation Street*, *Star Trek: The Next Generation*, *The Sopranos*, *This Is England '86*, *The Shield*, *Dexter*, *Veronica Mars*, *Dietland*, *Criminal Minds*, *Downton Abbey*, and *Sweet/Vicious*.[58] As early as 1955, the ethical complexities of avenging rape were the subject of the first episode of *Alfred Hitchcock Presents*, "Revenge." Vera Miles plays Elsa, the emotionally delicate wife of Ralph Meeker's Carl, who have together moved to a seaside trailer park while Elsa recovers from an unnamed trauma. With her husband at work, Elsa reclines outside her trailer to sunbathe, and a careful ellipsis jumps ahead to Carl returning home and finding Elsa almost catatonic, eventually telling him she had been raped by a travelling salesman (adhering to censorship restrictions at the time, her words are "he killed me," but it is unambiguously a rape). Seeing the man and pointing him out to her husband, Carl follows the man to his hotel room where he bludgeons him to death with a

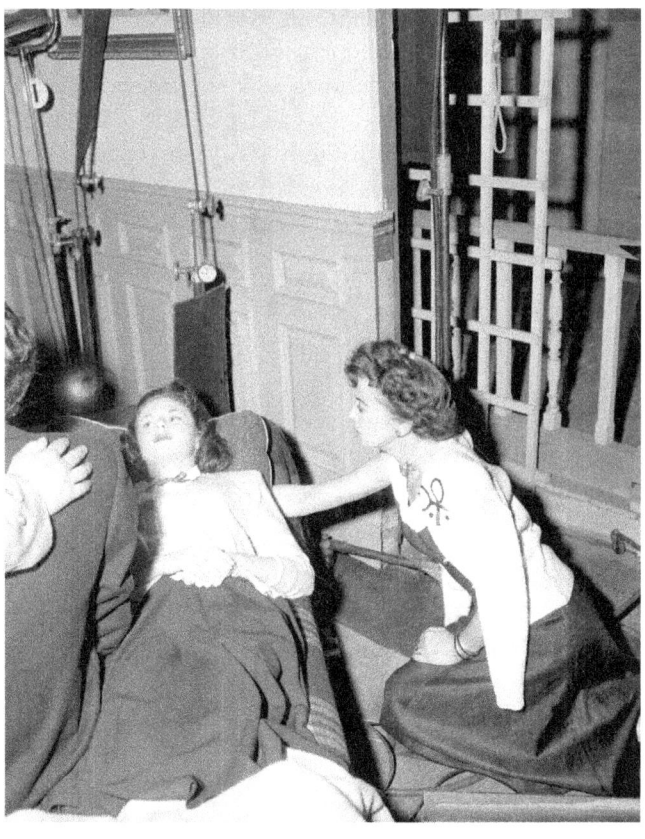

Director Ida Lupino (right) on the set of *Outrage* (1950) with Mala Powers who plays Ann Walton (Everett Collection Inc./ Alamy Stock Photo).

spanner off-camera. But the twist is revealed in the final moments when, leaving the scene of the crime to the sound of approaching sirens indicating Carl is soon to be arrested, Elsa sees another man on the street and identifies *him* as the rapist. The traumatized woman she her rapist everywhere, revealing the futility and moral hollowness of Carl's attempted vengeance. Far from a clear-cut justice fantasy, "Revenge" reveals the messy ethical terrain where the desire to avenge a rape can lead.

Six years later, Meeker appeared again in a film where cinema's long, complex, and often contradictory treatment of rape comes to light. *Something Wild* (Jack Garfein, 1961) is a bizarre and inescapably confronting love story about teenage rape survivor Mary Ann (Carroll Baker) and the man who holds her captive after he rescues her from a suicide attempt (Meeker) which also deserves recognition in rape-revenge history. Although the plot of the film is undeniably outrageous, the early scenes in the film of Ann's rape and immediate reaction afterwards are surprisingly sensitive. In particular, the scene where she sits on her bathroom floor and carefully cuts her ruined dress into tiny flushable pieces so her mother does not find out about the rape adds a depth to her experience that is still today both heartbreaking and poetic. The post-assault bathroom sequence is far from rare in contemporary rape-revenge films, but this small moment in *Something Wild* remains one of its most moving variations. "Revenge" and films such as *Outrage, Something Wild* and *Safe in Hell* offer—often despite themselves—brief yet powerful glimpses into rape trauma and suggest that the later rape-revenge configuration may stem from historical roots more diverse than previous treatments have acknowledged. This diversity can be identified even in the most well-known examples of the rape-revenge film, and this "rape-revenge canon" is the subject of the following chapter.

Chapter One

The Rape-Revenge Film Canon

To speak of a "rape-revenge film canon" may seem incongruous. Surely a phenomenon that writers such as Neil Fulwood have labeled as outright "seedy"[1] is not sophisticated or valuable enough to justify canonization. But in making an exception of Sam Peckinpah's *Straw Dogs* (1971) with his praise, Fulwood implies there may be some rape-revenge films that have been elevated above others—if not for their enlightened outlook, then at least for their notoriety. Janet Staiger argues that film canons form with ideological intent regarding what films are privileged, and which ones fall beyond critical and popular scope.[2] The rape-revenge titles regarding man-against-woman rape that have lodged most firmly in the popular imagination support this view; films as diverse as *The Accused* and *Thriller: A Cruel Picture* demonstrate just how broad the field is. The films in this chapter have garnered attention for their abilities to exemplify particular ideological representations of sexual violence and its relationship to retribution. But these films have by default been privileged above other titles—why, for instance, is *Ms. 45* still celebrated, while *Positive I.D.* is all but forgotten? As Jonathan Rosenbaum suggests, it is vital to treat "canon formation as an active process of selection rather than a passive one of reportage."[3]

While the word "canon" may imply a qualitative judgment, in this instance distinctions of taste have not been employed as a primary method of discernment. Rather, it is the ubiquity of these texts that have rendered them so commonplace in both critical and popular discourse concerning the rape-revenge film. With the mainstream and art-house examples, industry recognition in the form of awards and other accolades solidify the importance of some over others. The credible stamp of the auteur or the inclusion of identifiable stars also elevates some titles. But even in the case of exploitation or trash film cultures (what Jeffrey Sconce has referred to more holistically as "paracinema"[4]), there is a distinction to be made between celebrated cult films (such as, in the case of rape-revenge films *Ms. 45*, *Thriller: A Cruel Picture* and the original versions of *The Last House on the Left* and *I Spit on Your Grave*) and what Matt Hills calls "para-paracinematic" texts[5]: titles that fall outside the revered territory of cult cinema fandom. Once again—reflecting Diane Wolfthal's observations that in medieval and early modern art "diverse notions [of rape] coexisted contemporaneously"—these films are intriguing not only for what they share, but also for where they deviate.

Mainstream Rape-Revenge Films

Despite its sleazy reputation, the rape-revenge film has a relatively auspicious heritage. Winning the Academy Award for Best Foreign Language Film in 1961, Ingmar

Bergman's *The Virgin Spring*[6] was described by James R. Alexander as "the basic template" for the contemporary rape-revenge film,[7] and as Craven's *The Last House on the Left* and its many variants and remakes suggest, the plot has demonstrated remarkable longevity. Despite spawning a number of exploitation knock-offs (discussed in Chapter Two), *The Virgin Spring* is an art classic.

The Virgin Spring is adapted from the medieval ballad "Töre's Daughter at Vänge,"[8] dating from between the twelfth and fourteenth centuries.[9] Scriptwriter Ulla Isaksson combined different versions into her screenplay, creating the familiar plot: Karin (Birgitta Petterson) is the spoiled daughter of Christian parents Märeta (Birgitta Valberg) and Töre (Max von Sydow). Along with her pregnant, pagan foster sister Ingeri (Gunnel Lindblom), Karin embarks upon a journey to make a delivery to her church. After the two girls separate, Karin is raped and murdered by a group of goat herders. Unaware of Karin's relationship to Töre and Märeta, the goatherds arrive at Karin's family home in search of accommodation and employment. Märeta realizes that Karin has met with a nasty fate when one of the goatherds attempts to sell her a piece of Karin's clothing. Töre embarks upon his brutal revenge and murders the goatherds, and the next day Ingeri takes Töre and Märeta to Karin's body. Töre announces that despite his inability to understand God's actions, his faith remains unshaken and declares that he will build a church on the site of Karin's death. Symbolically, when he lifts her head, a spring of water miraculously appears—the "virgin spring" of the film's title.

The Virgin Spring is about Töre's journey of spiritual redemption, even though it stems originally from the rape and murder of his daughter. This crime provides a logical motive for Töre's vengeance, and therefore underscores the thematic punch of God's response and Töre's final revelation. Rape is not the subject of this film, but rather it acts as a narrative trigger that provokes a battle between Töre and his metaphorical demons. Crucially, however, this plot focus deviates substantially from the film's visceral impact: as the spectator witnesses her rape and murder in full, it is impossible to not be overwhelmed by Karin's suffering and the brutality of the event. So while the final impact depends on the transferal of this compassion for Karin's suffering at the hands of her attackers to the turmoil experienced by her vengeance-hungry father, whether that narrative force supersedes the impact of Karin's rape and murder is open for debate. The violence and cruelty of Karin's rape and murder supposedly corresponds with the intensity of Töre's bloodlust. In turn, this facilitates his spiritual conversion with the discovery of the "virgin spring." Ultimately, the power of the film does not stem from its narrative (the story of Töre's spiritual journey) or affective elements (Karin's rape and murder) alone, but rather from the tension between them.

While *The Last House on the Left* is *The Virgin Spring*'s clearest progeny, its influence reaches far beyond its plot synopsis. Most notable is its religious legacy: just in the rape-revenge canon alone, both *Thriller: A Cruel Picture* and the original *I Spit on Your Grave* include important scenes where their protagonists go to church before embarking upon their revenge. *Ms. 45*, with Thana as the fetishized, suspender-belt-wearing nun, makes this influence just as explicit, a legacy that continues in more recent rape-revenge exploitation pastiches such as *Nude Nuns with Big Guns* (Joseph Guzman, 2010), and *Run! Bitch! Run!* (Joseph Guzman, 2009). Unlike *The Virgin Spring*, these are obviously not "religious" films, but even to a secular audience these are powerful symbols: these are women who want God on their side and, in Thana's case, even suggest they are representing God. After *The Virgin Spring*, rape-revenge films become predominantly secular crusades. But, as more examples will continue to demonstrate, what they are crusading for—and how they do so—is diverse.

The Virgin Spring is not the only rape-revenge film to receive Academy recognition. As gang rape survivor Sarah in *The Accused*, Jodie Foster[10] won her first Oscar and freed herself from the "child star" label. Inspired by the true case of a 21-year-old woman gang raped on a pool table in Massachusetts in 1983, *The Accused* was as successful with the critics as it was at the box office. Taking the spectator on a relentless and often torturous tour of the legal humiliations rape survivors like Sarah must face—hospital examinations, police interviews, the identification of suspects, and the often cruel disappointments of the judicial process itself—*The Accused* is not set in the medieval past of *The Virgin Spring*, but in an environment readily identifiable as the "real world." But it is its status as a courtroom drama that has hindered its unanimous acclaim.

The film opens at the Mill Bar, a run-down dive in what appears to be a poor, industrial area. Sarah runs out of the bar screaming, clutching her ripped clothes to her body. A clean-cut young man (later identified as Ken, played by Bernie Coulson) calls 911 for help, saying a woman has been gang raped. Sarah is taken to hospital where she is examined and interrogated and meets the lawyer who will be prosecuting her case, Assistant D.A. Kathryn Murphy (Kelly McGillis in a role originally intended for Jane Fonda). Sarah returns to the Mill Bar with Kathryn and identifies her rapists, and Kathryn begins to build her case. Discussing it with male colleagues, and after negotiations with the defendant's attorneys, Kathryn agrees to a deal where they are charged with "reckless endangerment." Sarah, who suggests Kathryn only sees her as a "low-class bimbo," furiously interrupts Kathryn during a fancy dinner party, angered at having the charge of rape reduced to something as undefined as

Star of *The Accused* Jodie Foster at the 49th Annual Publicists Guild Awards Luncheon at the Beverly Hilton Hotel on 24 February 2012 (Kathy Hutchins/Shutterstock.com).

"reckless endangerment." Deeply traumatized, Sarah is pushed even further when she is harassed in a parking lot by one of the men who witnessed her assault. Snapping, she rams his car repeatedly. Kathryn visits her in the hospital and is affected by Sarah's accusation that "you did all my talking for me." An overnight research montage leads her to decide that she has a case to charge the spectators of the rape with criminal solicitation, and despite risking her own career in doing so, she proceeds with the case. Kathryn discovers Ken's identity through an arcade game he recorded his name as a winner on at the time of the rape, and despite facing pressure from his friend Rob (now in jail as one of Sarah's rapists), he testifies. Sarah tells her story in court, and when Ken appears the rape is shown as a flashback. The jury finds in favor of Kathryn and Sarah, and they euphorically leave the courtroom, where Sarah tells reporters, "I'm very pleased." In closing, statistics about rape and gang rape in the United States appear onscreen.[11]

Both Clover and Read agree that despite its reputation as a classic example of the rape-revenge film, *The Accused* is a relatively straightforward legal drama about rape. For Clover, the "revenge" component exists solely as it pertains to the judicial system. Although there is the possibility that the guilty parties may escape punishment, the film demonstrates that the law (personified in part by Kathryn herself[12]) is capable of correcting its own mistakes: "There is a sense in which the third party, the legal system, becomes the hero of the piece."[13] For Read, *The Accused* employs a rhetoric that has less to do with feminism than with a general sense of the dominant popular morality of the late 1980s in Britain and the United States.[14]

Clover's observation that "with *The Accused*, the rape-revenge drama hits Oscar level"[15] belies the influence of the film's greatest cinematic ancestor. *The Accused* finds its most immediate heritage in Otto Preminger's *Anatomy of a Murder* (1959), which, although it did not win, was certainly at "Oscar level," with its seven nominations (including Best Picture). It is difficult to define *Anatomy of a Murder* as a rape-revenge film for similar reasons as to why *The Accused* fits so uncomfortably—it is legal drama that explores how the legal process *responds* to rape, rather than focusing on rape as such. *Anatomy of a Murder* follows small-town lawyer (James Stewart) who defends a soldier (Ben Gazzara) after he murders a man for raping his wife (Lee Remick). To prove his client acted justifiably, Stewart's character must establish that the rape occurred. Aside from clear references to Preminger's film in *The Accused* (such as the centrality of a pinball machine to both rapes), both hinge heavily upon the low-class status and suggested promiscuity of the rape survivors, and their dramas play out through predominantly verbal re-enactments of the night in question. In its updating of *Anatomy of a Murder*, *The Accused* deliberately subverts its focus—while the earlier movie follows the trial from the perspective of the likeable, male defense attorney, *The Accused* invests in the rape survivor herself.

A less known but equally relevant ancestor to Kaplan's movie is William Dieterle's *The Accused* (1949), where Loretta Young plays a college professor who murders a student when he attempts to rape her. Both versions of *The Accused* deploy their title to emphasize the ambiguities that rape presents to clear-cut categories of guilt and innocence: who is the accused here? Yet that Kaplan's *The Accused* is so sharply attuned to Sarah's trauma and her struggle for agency undermines its central formal conceit. Superficially at least, *The Accused* is constructed to make the audience a "jury" themselves; by not seeing the rape until the end of the film, the audience is asked to sit in judgment on the case (Kathryn's closing summation is even shown from the point of view of the jury box). Thus, when Sarah says to Kathryn, "You saw me at the hospital. You think I asked for that?" she is asking the audience the same question. It is, of course, only tentative in its formal suggestion that the audience is required to make any significant judgment call; it is difficult to not wholeheartedly believe Sarah's version of events, if only because she is very much presented as the sympathetic "victim" in contrast to those on trial, including smug, rich college boy Bob (Steve Antin) and hostile Cliff (Leo Rossi). The catharsis this scenario allows hinges directly upon the guilty verdict that not only sends Cliff and the others who encouraged the rapists to jail but converts the previous charges of reckless endangerment to rape. This release is palpable in the final moments of the film, with its upbeat soundtrack heralding Sarah and Kathryn's victory as they leave the courtroom. The logic that allows the legal process to magically delete Sarah's trauma of sexual violence is encapsulated in Clover's accusation of the film's intrinsic "Pollyannaism."[16]

Regardless, what *The Accused* accomplishes that no other film in this book quite achieves is its ability to so aggressively address the notion of spectatorship itself in regard to rape and revenge. By placing its emphasis upon the act of *watching* rape (suggesting that it is equal to rape), the film aligns itself explicitly with Laura Mulvey's essay "Visual Pleasure and the Narrative Cinema." Mulvey claims that the gaze in classical Hollywood cinema is inherently male and sadistic, and that the act of looking is itself an act of violence. *The Accused* transfers this from the conceptual realm of film theory firmly into the domain of a legal melodrama, and it reiterates continually that the act of watching rape is just as criminal as rape itself. *The Accused* may not technically be a rape-revenge film in the same way that *Ms. 45* or *The Virgin Spring* are, but at the very least it presents a watertight case for the ethical complications inherent to *watching* rape-revenge.

For Clover, it is erroneous to credit *The Accused* with "mainstreaming" rape-revenge: that honor lies with *Lipstick* (1976), a film that firmly moved it away from the art film and exploitation circuit and into the domain of the popular.[17] Promoted heavily as a vehicle to launch the acting career of supermodel Margaux Hemingway, the film bombed commercially and critically. Paradoxically, it brought attention to Hemingway's fifteen-year-old sister and co-star, Mariel, who played the character of Kathy. That Margaux and Mariel—granddaughters of writer Ernest Hemingway—played sisters onscreen brought a degree of verisimilitude to the film, a motive reiterated by the fact that Margaux's character, Chris McCormick, was also a famous fashion model. The association between Margaux's famous visage (one that had been displayed on magazines from *Vogue* to *Time*) and the thematic exploration into the commodification of women's bodies so central to the film was no accident.

Developing a rape-revenge scenario with a mainstream audience in mind, *Lipstick* supports Clover's claim that most mainstream variants are concerned first and foremost with issues of justice and the law.[18] Even within the confines of what often boils down to a legal drama, however, there are still differing treatments and representations of sexual violence. While *Lipstick* shares its status as a courtroom drama with a range of mainstream rape-revenge films, in many senses it is the anti–*Accused*: while supposedly white-trash Foster finally achieves courtroom justice, in *Lipstick*, rich supermodel Chris has no choice but to get a gun and go vigilante in order to protect the (literal) sisterhood.

Lipstick is also significantly determined in its refusal to characterize its rapist as a two-dimensional villain. Peter Lehman has observed that "in some of these films nearly all the men are presented as sexually repulsive,"[19] but Chris Sarandon's performance as Kathy's music teacher proves a notable exception. As Gordon, before the rape he is utterly likeable: charming, funny and not difficult to look at. Great effort has been made to avoid Othering him as the villain before the assault; hugging his tape-recorder when he first meets his pupil's famous sister, if anything, Gordon is valued no differently from anyone else in the film before the rape.[20] To emphasize the fact that rapists can be people who seem otherwise ordinary—a notable distinction from the majority of rape-revenge films where rapists are often cartoonish villains—director Lamont Johnson divides the film's time relatively democratically between the intimate details of the lives of both Gordon and Chris before the assault.

This refusal to demonize Gordon beforehand means his moral status after the rape is based solely upon his violence towards Chris. Visiting her at home to play her his music, Gordon reacts with a sudden violent outburst when he suspects she is disinterested and patronizing. Kathy accidentally walks in on them during the rape and, confused, leaves quietly. With the support of her priest brother Martin (John Bennet Perry), Chris presses charges, with the assistance of prosecutor Carla Bondi (Anne Bancroft). The case collapses when the defense insists that Kathy's failure to call the police when she interrupted Chris and Gordon meant that it was consensual rough sex. Returning to modeling, Chris finds it difficult to readjust after the trial, and decides to take Kathy on a trip after one final photo shoot. Exploring the building where the studio is located, Kathy finds Gordon working on a musical performance; whereupon he chases and rapes her. Badly beaten and with ripped clothes, Kathy returns to Chris and tells her what has occurred. Wasting no time, Chris chases Gordon out of the building, grabs a rifle and shoots him dead in a parking lot. A brief voice-over at the end of the film announces that Carla wins Chris a "Not Guilty" verdict in the subsequent murder trial.

Lipstick balances two opposing explanations for Gordon's vicious attack. Firstly, it deliberately places it in the context of Chris' profession: the fashion shoot opening of the film alone establishes a link between using her to sell products and the implication of sexual availability. More specifically, her lipstick-stained mouth is formally disembodied and objectified. The courtroom scene allows this issue to be explicitly debated, giving Chris the opportunity to define her job: "I'm supposed to be what every woman wants to look like." Much of the film hinges upon the link Gordon's defense makes between Chris' job as a model, consumerism and sexuality: they argue Gordon cannot be held accountable for viewing her as a sexual commodity to be consumed because that is precisely what she encourages. Gordon appears to suggest this during the rape itself, where he forces her to wear lipstick in an attempt to make the rape as much about her (and her sexuality) as possible. He deliberately tries to eroticize the rape, despite the fact that it is an encounter fuelled only by his rage and sense of rejection.

It is this fury that defines the alternate (and true) motive for Gordon's attack. He uses rape to establish himself in a position of power. His defense that it is about Chris's sexuality is merely a distraction from the real motivations for his crime. When he first arrives at Chris' house, Gordon observes a photograph of her with the avant-garde musician Sean Gage. Gordon fixates upon this photo, visibly shaken by Chris' association as he explains how Gage rejected his earlier attempts at contact. The ambitious Gordon therefore had viewed Chris as another possible steppingstone to assist in his career, but when she wanders out of the room while his tape plays to talk on the telephone, his rejection (compounded by the earlier rejection of his idol, Gage) turns to violence.

Gordon's music is intrinsic to his motivation, and to demonstrate the point he even places his tape recorder at Chris' head while he rapes her. Carla identifies the importance of Gordon's music, and in her prosecution strategy she applies a moral value to it; playing his composition to the courtroom, she alludes that the experimental, "deviant" nature of the music itself can only reflect upon the ethical consistency of the man who composed it. But Carla's strategy fails for the same reason that arguments about Chris' modeling career also cannot provide an adequate motive. Neither Gordon's music nor Chris' photographs are the issue: the responsibility for Gordon's violent attack lies not in art, but in him and him alone. It is in this spirit that the film's memorable climax—as Chris runs through the parking lot in a floor-length red evening gown toting a shotgun—suggests that, in turn, no one else can be more responsible for a woman's right to safety than women themselves. The court does finally grant some justice for Chris, but without the fanfare of the similar sequence in *The Accused*. By the end of *Lipstick*, to celebrate the court victory seems pointless.

Despite the negative reception *Lipstick* received, another star vehicle a few years later won its leading performer much more acclaim than Margaux Hemingway. Based upon William Mastrosimone's stage play of the same name, *Extremities* surprised audiences and critics alike with its powerful lead performance by Farrah Fawcett. Although the film was far from a box-office hit, Fawcett herself was widely praised (as she had been for her performance as an abused wife in Robert Greenwald's 1984 telemovie *The Burning Bed*), and she was nominated for a Golden Globe Award for Best Actress in a Drama. As Marjorie, the film opens as Fawcett's character endures a frightening attempted rape in her car on her way home from work. After escaping, she receives little assistance or support from the police, and when she realizes her attacker, Joe (James Russo), has stolen her wallet with all of her personal information in it, she locks down at home. A week later Joe invades her home after her two flatmates have left for work. Desperate and frightened as he physically and psychologically tortures her, Marjorie fights back during another attempted rape and sprays insect repellent in his eyes. Tying him up with cords from household appliances, she crafts a makeshift cell in her fireplace with an old bed frame. Convinced from her earlier experience that the police will not believe her version of events, Marjorie digs a grave in her garden and decides that her only choice is to bury Joe alive. Her housemates return home before she can act, however, and the women debate the ethics of their situation in the film's remaining time. Joe attempts to turn the women against each other, but when he is finally forced by Marjorie to confess, the women agree to get the police.

Extremities still makes a remarkable impression. The film explores issues of justice and the failures of the judicial process to deal with sexual assault. "What should a woman do when the police let her down?" is not a rhetorical question, but a defining thematic concern, and a great deal of time is spent exploring the issues inherent in a variety of answers. The screenplay, also written by Mastrosimone, offered him the opportunity to plug some of the narrative holes in the original stage version. Embracing the ability to move the film outside of the housebound constraints of the stage, the attempted rape in Marjorie's car at the beginning of the film is an addition that provides tangible evidence of her belief that the police will not assist her. What in the play is a suspicion, in the film is an experience-based probability.

At the time, Fawcett was a familiar face as Jill Munroe in the hit TV series *Charlie's Angels*. This tough-girl legacy is effectively employed in *Extremities*. Initially, it makes Marjorie's escape from Joe after his attempted rape in her car plausible for intertextual reasons alone, but also demonstrates that even the *threat* of sexual violence has devastating consequences for a strong and successful female "superhero." The film is structured into two almost perfectly equal sections, the first allowing Fawcett to deliver her performance as the tortured, traumatized and terrified victim. Raw but never sensationalized, intense but never tacky, despite the democratic exchange of point-of-view camera angles between Marjorie and Joe, the sympathies of the spectator lie firmly with the former, and Fawcett deserves the praise she received for the role. But even before the broader ethical debates of the film's second half begin, it is clear that the scope of the film expands far outside the domain of rape alone. As an example of Joe's increasing cruelty, he mockingly demands that Marjorie cook for him. Sitting at her kitchen table and drinking beer, he jokes viciously, "I come home and you've got nothing to fucking eat?" This chilling reconstruction of this typical scene of domestic violence expands the scope of the film's thematic intent from rape specifically to a more general domain of the abuse of women (as well as providing a link to *The Burning Bed*).

The final half of the film begins suddenly, marked by Marjorie's successful counterattack as she symbolically sprays pest repellent in Joe's eyes. Despite appearing to be in control, however, Joe still considers himself in the position of power, belittling Marjorie and convincing her that the police will let him go because it is her word against his. After she locks him in his "cell," her housemate Terry (Diana Scarwid) returns home and is deeply shocked by what she sees. Close to denial, she sits at a table drinking and smoking while Marjorie digs a grave. When the third housemate, Patricia (Alfre Woodard), returns from her job as a social worker, the film shifts dramatically from its Joe/Villain vs. Marjorie/Victim binary and focuses instead upon the splintering of the three women (the "sisterhood"). It is here that *Extremities* packs its most explicit thematic clout, as it demonstrates that rape is not simply a "us vs. them" scenario. The film from this point hinges upon the assumption that there is no singular contingency plan for how to respond to violence against women.

It is here where the "extremes" of the film's title come to the fore. On one side is Patricia, the "bleeding-heart" liberal who represents a softly-softly approach. She is contrasted sharply against Marjorie's newfound militant vigilantism. Even in their appearance (Black Patricia, blonde-haired and blue-eyed Marjorie), these two women symbolize the polarized "extremes" offered within the ranks of feminism itself. The exclusion of Terry from this duality is of no small importance. Angrily exploding at Marjorie, Terry finally confesses that she herself was raped as a young girl, but was not as fortunate as to escape. She furiously describes her inability to do anything about it, her rage is directed at Marjorie as she tells her, "I'm not going to prison for you." The film contrasts these three positions—the vigilante, the liberal, and the rape survivor herself—until it reaches its resolution.

This conclusion is far from uncomplicated. That Marjorie's liberation and her ability to reunite with her female peers hinges so inherently upon Joe's confession means that he still maintains a position of power. Despite being physically restrained, Joe remains the primary agent of her liberation: if he chose not to confess, the three women would never have agreed to contact the police. The film emphasizes that it was *Joe's* choice (not Marjorie's) that determined the final outcome. This issue of male power transcends the film's diegesis. If the film feels conflicted, it is because the two primary male figures who created it—director Young and writer Mastrosimone—stood in direct opposition to each other regarding the ethical nature of revenge. While promoting the film, Young mentioned on numerous occasions the rape of his daughter when she was sixteen, and openly acknowledged this event as his primary motivation for making *Extremities*.[21] For him, it was absolutely not a rape-revenge story because Marjorie did not kill her assailant. As Edward Guthmann points out in the *San Francisco Chronicle*, however, this contradicts Mastrosimone, who noted in the film's press kit that he was "glad that I allowed Marjorie to act out a woman's intense feeling for revenge," and then cites an anecdote where a rape survivor who saw his play told him, "It's better to act and be killed … than to live with oneself as a coward." When Guthmann presented this information to Young, the director's response was clear: "I think that's a terrible statement: that's dangerous…. I wouldn't want to encourage anyone to act out of those kinds of reasons."[22] At stake in this discord is not only the ethics of revenge; even more arresting is how the foundations of the film's thematic core are reduced to debates between men about what the rape of women does and does not mean. In this light, *Extremities* can be seen to function as a discrete attack upon feminism as a whole, its conclusion firmly establishing that the issues the women raised were not ones able to be resolved by the women on their own terms. Consequently, the fracture within the sisterhood that the film so effectively exposed never adequately healed. An exploration of feminism itself, as much as it is anything else, *Extremities* is therefore far from the clear-cut example of the rape-revenge plot it is so often assumed to be. Its attack upon the factionalization of feminist discourse, and final reminder that it is men who hold the power (both diegetically and extradiegetically), render it just as disturbing—and as ideologically ambiguous—as more notorious rape-revenge movies.

If *The Accused* is the flipside of *Lipstick*, then *Thelma & Louise* (Ridley Scott, 1991) is the anti–*Extremities*. Where dramatic tension in the latter is as predicated in part on friction within female ranks, in *Thelma & Louise* even such small details as their shared accent and similar hair color places the emphasis firmly upon female solidarity. While popularly recognized as one of the most iconic of all contemporary rape-revenge films, that it deviates so substantially from what a rape-revenge film is more broadly considered to be seems little more than a passing observation next to its hefty cultural significance. Whether it is a rape-revenge film *per se* or not pales next to the way that this feminist fantasy captured not only the public imagination at the time of its release but garnered a slew of accolades for many of its key players, including an Oscar and Golden Globe for screenwriter Callie Khouri, and nominations for its director Ridley Scott and lead actors Geena Davis and Susan Sarandon.

Thelma (Davis) is a downtrodden, naïve housewife who flees her oppressive domestic situation to spend a weekend at a cabin with her assertive yet jaded friend Louise (Sarandon). Stopping at a bar on their way, Thelma is sexually assaulted in a parking lot by a man named Harlan (Timothy Carhart) whom she met during an evening of margaritas and line dancing. Louise rescues Thelma by pulling a gun, and when Harlan verbally abuses her, she kills him. Fleeing the scene on the assumption that the police will not believe their story, they are pursued by sympathetic policeman Hal Slocum (Harvey Keitel). Led by the dominant figure of Louise, the women aim to escape to Mexico, although Louise insists that they do so by bypassing Texas. Surprised and angry that his wife left him, Thelma's husband, Daryl (Christopher McDonald), assists the police and lets them tap his phone so they can trace her when she calls. Louise's boyfriend Jimmy meets the two women in Oklahoma, and, after delivering Louise's life savings per her request, proposes to her. Refusing, she emotionally bids farewell to him and is met by a bed-headed Thelma, who confesses to a sexually charged evening with hitchhiker JD (Brad Pitt). When Louise discovers that JD has stolen their money, she crumbles both physically and emotionally, leaving Thelma to take control of the situation. Thelma robs a store to get them money, and their journey leads them to the Grand Canyon. A phone call to Daryl's house enables the women's location to be traced, and they are pursued to the edge of a large cliff. In the film's famous closing scene, the women agree that they cannot return to their old lives, and—smiling and holding hands—they drive off the cliff in a final act of solidarity and defiance.

Much critical discussion surrounding *Thelma & Louise* appears unable to agree on whether Thelma's assault was a rape or an attempted rape. The film itself certainly provides enough evidence to support the former claim, if only through Thelma's own words when she tells Louise, "He was rapin' me!" The attack itself is far more explicit than the attempted rape in *Extremities*: Harlan hits Thelma hard, and as she struggles, both of their pants are pulled down as she lies face down and he forces himself against her. If there isn't penetration, then it is certainly close.[23] Perhaps more importantly, however, is the misconception that Louise kills Harlan for raping (or attempting to rape) Thelma. While she pulls a gun on him and threatens him, it is not until he verbally abuses the women as they walk away that she responds with violence. This does not mean that Louise was not prepared to respond to Thelma's assault with violence, but it demonstrates that she seeks liberation from a far broader notion of oppression and abuse than just this one act.

This broader threat frames the film's central enigma: what happened to Louise in Texas? This "Texas Question" (if it is a question at all—Louise's demeanor alone suggests that it is related in some way to the events in the parking lot) emphasizes the importance of the temporal divide between past, present and future. As the women embark upon their journey, there is a distinctive 1950s aspect to the mise-en-scène: both women are dressed in purity-defining white, Louise with a headscarf and cats-eye sunglasses, and Thelma in a cotton dress with a sweetheart neckline. Even Louise's retro convertible recalls this era, the car itself functioning at this early stage as a kind of "time machine" capable of taking the women back to before their respective confinements in unsatisfying marriages and unfulfilling jobs. Throughout the film their appearance becomes increasingly tomboyish: first to go are the white clothes, then the lipstick, and finally the bras. In this spirit, *Thelma & Louise* is undeniably a feminist fantasy. This is defined no more clearly than when they blow up the truck of a man who had been harassing them throughout their journey. The film is careful to steer clear of the construction of an "us vs. them" binary between men and women, as indicated by the significant presence of Harvey Keitel's compassionate Hal Slocum, who asks rhetorically at one point how many times Louise and Thelma are going to be "fucked over." And while there are many more grotesque and stereotyped images of regressive men—Daryl, the truck-driver, Harlan, even the policeman in Daryl's house who looks at pornography while he waits for Thelma to call—that the women themselves adopt a more masculine appearance acknowledges from within the diegesis that gender is far more fluid than these stereotypes suggest.

Thelma & Louise rejects the vision of feminism in the face of sexual violence as the splintered, fractured war depicted in *Extremities*. Rather, as they fly in slow-motion into the Grand Canyon, their story becomes an allegory for a very human desire for unity, friendship, respect and love, even if liberation comes at the expense of their own lives. Thelma and Louise are literally women pushed to the edge, not only by rape but also by the broader cultural tendency towards the oppression of women's bodies, voices and spirits. *Thelma & Louise* has earned its place in the rape-revenge canon if only for demonstrating that revenge is not the only option available in the pursuit of liberation.

The Exploitation Rape-Revenge Film

It would be unhelpful to reductively categorize rape-revenge films along a mainstream-progressive/exploitation-regressive divide and assume their politics can be so neatly delineated, as to do so ignores the complexity of films that at first may appear almost crassly simplistic. Demonstrating the complexities of rape-revenge, we can fruitfully look at binaries between justice fantasies and those which subvert or critique justice fantasies. Beyond the highbrow/lowbrow, mainstream/exploitation divide we find curious deviations that situate films like *The Accused* and *I Spit on Your Grave* in the former category, and *Ms. 45* and *Violation* in the latter. And yet, we need only think of the influence of the so-called "roughies"—vicious low-budget films whose production began in the 1960s, defined by Elina Gorfinkel as "narratives of male lust sublimated into violence or the excessive qualities of women that exhibit either socially inappropriate desires or sadistic impulses"[24]—to see why we may default to exploitation cinema when talking about rape-revenge film. Two giants of this exploitation filmmaking from this era, Russ Meyer and Herschell Gordon Lewis, both made films where rape and revenge feature, *Motorpsycho* (1965) in the case of the former, and *Just for the Hell of It* (1968) in the case of the latter. Rape-revenge roughies were not rare as evidenced by films like *The Girl Grabbers* (Simon Nuchtern, 1968), or those helmed by Doris Wishman, the queen of the grindhouse who flourished in this space, discussed further in Chapter Four.

For better or for worse, rape-revenge films are synonymous with exploitation cinema. This is demonstrated nowhere more powerfully than in the original *I Spit on Your Grave*, a film whose impact is still difficult to deny over thirty years since its original release. While other notorious examples of the British "Video Nasties" controversy[25] now seem dated by their crude and excessive special effects, the power of *I Spit on Your Grave* stems from its steadfast depiction of rape as ugly and terrifyingly brutal. In the United States, critic Roger Ebert famously decried the film as "sick, reprehensible and contemptible," citing it as a victory for gutter-minded perverts.[26] The attention Ebert's scathing attack brought to the film at the time of its release was ironically embraced by Zarchi called the critic one of "the best promoters ever"[27] Central to Ebert's attack was his contention that spectators are encouraged to identify with the rapists, exposing the film's fundamental misogyny. But for many contemporary critics—among them Joe Bob Briggs, Carol J. Clover, Philip Green, Marco Starr and Gary Crowdus[28]—*I Spit on Your Grave* is an unflinching, powerful, and, for some, even subversive meditation upon the reality of sexual violence. While Ebert claims the film glorifies the rapists, Clover argues that Jennifer is central: "Most of the action is registered from her vantage, and there is no doubt whatsoever that its sympathies lie with her."[29]

Released initially as *Day of the Woman*, the film is known more generally as *I Spit on Your Grave*, a riff on Boris Vian's revenge novel *I Shall Spit on Your Grave* (*J'irai cracher sur vos tombes*, 1946) and the Michael Gast 1959 film adaptation of the same name. Inspired by Zarchi's discovery of a beaten, naked rape victim on the street, the plot is simple. Jennifer (Camille Keaton) leaves the city to spend time alone in the country working on a writing project. What begins as ominous harassment by four local hooligans soon turns into an extremely graphic, violent and drawn-out gang rape. Jennifer recuperates enough from the initial physical trauma to go to church and pray for forgiveness for the response she has decided upon. One by one, she hunts down her rapists and kills them in a variety of gruesome and creative ways, including hanging, slicing up with a boat's propeller blade and—most notoriously—castration. Reducing the rape-revenge equation to its barest terms, the film ends the instant she has killed her final victim. That critical positions on the film have conflicted so dramatically suggests, at the very least, that Zarchi hit a nerve.

With its gritty 25-minute rape scene, the film has been released in a variety of different versions. In her assessment of the censored rape scene in the 2002 UK DVD release, Linda Ruth Williams observes, "The less seen of Jennifer's rape the better, one might think; but this may have the curious effect of making the revenge less defensible, since less of the rape is evident."[30] At the same time, any censoring of the revenge component (such as the notorious castration scene) simultaneously risks letting the rapists off the hook to some degree. The censoring of *I Spit on Your Grave* raises an important question: which is more upsetting to watch, the rape or the revenge? And who has the right to answer this? On whose behalf do they speak? In its uncensored version, the answers become no clearer, but here at least the film's raw central thematic conceit is at its most explicit: rape is brutal, unglamorous and unrelentingly cruel. The total absence of filmic poetry grinds our sophisticated emotional distancing skills to a raw, disoriented dust.

Claiming it as the first rape-revenge film where a woman avenged her own rape (rather than having an agent act on her behalf), Zarchi identified the influence of *I Spit on Your Grave* on movies including *The Accused*, *Thelma & Louise* and *The Girl with the Dragon Tattoo* (*Män som hatar kvinnor*, Niels Arden Oplev, 2009).[31] But cinema history has granted no contingency plan regarding how to correctly respond to a film quite like this one. Ebert attacked the audiences at his screening for laughing, but it can be argued in their defense that—awkward, confused and totally out of their film-viewing depth—they simply did not know what else to do. Even today, the blatant (and yes, sensationalized) depiction of human suffering in *I Spit on Your Grave* emphasizes how desensitized we are to glossier depictions of rape. Somewhere in those grueling 25 minutes is a lightning flash of empathy where we realize we are trapped, too—even leaving the cinema or turning off the DVD can't take back what we've already seen. Jennifer's rape leaves *us* powerless. *I Spit on Your Grave* moves the onus of trying to comprehend the brutal incomprehensibility of rape firmly onto the spectator.

The legacy of the original *I Spit on Your Grave* continues today, both explicit and suggested. While *Naked Vengeance* (Cirio H. Santiago, 1985) begins by establishing a diegesis not wholly dissimilar to Michael Winner's *Death Wish* (1974) and *Ms. 45*, Carla's (Deborah Tranelli) revenge includes an underwater castration and a motorboat sequence that acknowledges the influence of *I Spit on Your Grave*, itself perhaps inspired by the motorboat-heavy *'Gator Bait* that preceded Zarchi's film by four years. More overt references can be seen in the titles of films such as *I'll Kill You…. I'll Bury You…. I'll Spit on Your Grave, Too* (Thomas R. Koba, 2000), *I Spit on Your Corpse, I Piss on Your Grave* (Eric Stanze, 2001) and the rape-revenge parody, *I Spit Chew on Your Grave* (Chris Seaver, 2008). Donald Farmer's unauthorized sequel to *I Spit on Your Grave* was released in 1992 under a variety of names, including *Savage Vengeance*, *I Will Dance on Your Grave*, *I Will Dance on Your Grave: Savage Vengeance* and *I Spit on Your Grave 2: Savage Vengeance*. The inclusion of Camille Keaton appears to be the main connection between the two projects, although that she appears under an alias supports rumors that her involvement with the project was a far from positive experience.

Over thirty years after the original *I Spit on Your Grave*, Meir Zarchi took the role of executive producer on Steven R. Monroe's remake of his controversial 1978 movie. Although Zarchi was initially more partial to the idea of a sequel, he was both happy with and a major collaborator on the recent version. Just as Zarchi had based his original on his experience of discovering a beaten gang-rape victim on the street, Monroe too channeled his own personal experience into the project. In an interview with Sean Decker on the horror website *Dread Central*, Monroe discussed the effect the rape of his ex-girlfriend had on him at the time, admitting that "there were times when I saw him [the victimizer] and I wanted to take a baseball bat and bash his head in."[32] It was this intensity that both Zarchi and Monroe brought to the new project; Zarchi has said that when "Steven told me, 'Your movie pushed the envelope,' I told him that the remake should shove the whole mailbox."[33] The remake of *I Spit on Your Grave* includes many affectionate references to the original. The famous bathtub castration scene from the earlier version, for instance, is here adapted to a scenario where instead of being *in* the bath naked with her rapist, a fully dressed Jennifer instead ties him *over* the bath as she tortures him. But one of the most striking differences between the films is that while Camille Keaton's Jennifer used seduction and the promise of sex to catch her prey, Butler's Jennifer executes scenes of violence such as this in jeans and plainly cut tops. Unlike the rape-avenging Keaton, there are no floral bikinis for this Jennifer as she slices and dices her way through those who wronged her. Monroe has insisted that Jennifer's seduction of her rapists in the original was one of the major features he wished to change. Although Butler's Jennifer does not use her sexuality to seduce her rapists in the same way Keaton's does, it is still important to note that from the audience perspective at least, the new Jennifer is still "eroticized." In the bathtub scene in the recent version, for example, she wears simple, unisex-styled jeans and a long-sleeved t-shirt. But this top is thin and light-colored, allowing her erect nipples to be clearly visible at times. The rape scene is shot predominantly with hand-held cameras, and the slick editing and director of photography Neil Liks' polished digital imagery place it in a stylistic universe well beyond Zarchi's raw original. Less crude than aiming for an aesthetic of contemporary horror *vérité*, the 2010 *I Spit on Your Grave* is formally closer to *Cloverfield* (Matt Reeves, 2008) than the 1978 *I Spit on Your Grave* or Craven's *The Last House on the Left*. Obviously, the economic realities of releasing a film in 2010 are notably different to those at the time when Zarchi's film was originally released, and access to film production equipment is far greater than it was thirty years ago. One of the more interesting features of the remake is its awareness of these technological factors and the notion of mediatization Early in the film, Jennifer is videoed by Stanley (Daniel Franzese)—one of the rednecks who later rapes her—through her window. This camera also appears during the assault itself, where at times the perspective shifts to the rapist's "rougher" handy-cam footage. This articulates a sense of distance between the men and the action taking place before them, and also adds a degree of self-awareness to the film as a whole. This *I Spit on Your Grave* is consciously aware that it is at a literal technological distance from Zarchi's raw, rough original.

I Spit on Your Grave 2 (2013) saw Monroe return to the series, this film following the plight of a model called Katie (Jemma Dallender), resituating the franchise in the fashion world, thus recalling *Lipstick*, *Ms. 45* and *Photographic* (Timothy Whitfield, 2012). Set primarily in Bulgaria, like Levan Bakhia's *Landmine Goes Click* (2015), this Eastern European context implies through a soft racism an ambient corrupting regional force supposedly specific to this part of the world (Katie's sanctuary in the finale of *I Spit on Your Grave 2* is literally the U.S. embassy). While the first film in Monroe's series offered numerous intelligent twists on the original (specifically in terms of its inclusion of ubiquitous digital media technologies), *I Spit on Your Grave 2* was less critically engaging, Anton Bitel noting that "*I Spit on Your Grave 2* ends up being precisely the reprehensible, pointless piece of shit that Zarchi's original is often (wrongly, in my opinion) accused of being," as "it panders to the viewer's basest instincts without even once interrogating them, and presents revenge as something entirely unproblematic."[34] However, what Monroe failed to achieve with *I Spit on Your Grave 2*, R.D. Braunstein more than made up for with *I Spit on Your Grave III: Vengeance Is Mine* (2015). Returning Butler to the franchise as Jennifer Hills, the film maintains its generic thrills, but also expands the psychological landscape that drives Jennifer's desire for revenge, complicating and amplifying the dynamics by which her thirst for vengeance has turned her into something entirely monstrous. While rightly voicing disappointment with the second film in the series, Bitel champions its follow-up, stating, "Like the best revenge flicks, *I Spit on Your Grave 3: Vengeance Is Mine* foregrounds then interrogates its own fantasy, before punishing us with whatever moral conclusion we choose to draw." By returning to the original character from the first of Monroe's films in the rebooted series, Bitel celebrates it as the superior film of all three, noting "this is without question the best of the series, and a whole lot better than one might imagine."[35]

I Spit on Your Grave shows no signs of losing its cult appeal, demonstrated by Zarchi's own return to the franchise with 2019's *I Spit on Your Grave: Deja Vu*. This "déjà vu" relates not only to Zarchi's return, but to Keaton herself, again as Jennifer Hills. She and her daughter Christy (Jamie Bernadette) feature centrally, the story picking up from the original 1978 film and finding Jennifer and Christy tormented, tortured and—in Jennifer's case—murdered by the families of her original victims in the first movie. *Deja Vu* is an extraordinary demonstration of the insidiousness and futility of revenge; there is, as Jennifer learns—not just here but even when played by a different actor in the 2010 remake and *Vengeance Is Mine*—no foreseeable end to the cycle of violence and trauma outside of death itself. While satisfying on its own merits and pleasurable if only for the joy of seeing Keaton return to the role that made her so famous, the potency of *Deja Vu* emerges in and through the film's reflection on the broader themes of the series as a whole, as fractured as it may be. The cult legacy of *I Spit on Your Grave* has transcended the films themselves; the very title on one hand has become a general signifier of that which is forbidden, transgressive and taboo, but at the same time, doing so in a distinctly nostalgic frame. A case in point: the same year *Deja Vu* was released, Zarchi's son Terry directed the documentary *Growing Up with I Spit on Your Grave*, the family connection clearly seeking to validate the documentary's authority based on the rightfully perceived sense of reverence the film's fans hold for the original. Despite its surface attempts at objectively mapping out the controversies that entangled *I Spit on Your Grave*, *Growing Up with I Spit on Your Grave* is clearly not objective, as its very title suggests.

Another title caught up in the British "Video Nasties" scandal recently remade was Wes Craven's *The Last House on the Left*, described by its lead actor David Hess as "a quantum leap into an unknown area of screen violence."[36] The film launched the horror careers of two of the genre's biggest names, Wes Craven (who would go on to direct such infamous horror franchises as *Nightmare on Elm Street* and *Scream*) and Sean S. Cunningham (who directed the first of the *Friday the 13th* films). Having worked successfully on the Marilyn Chambers-fronted adult film *Together* (1971), Craven and Cunningham were given the opportunity to make a horror film, and *The Last House on the*

Left was born. John Kenneth Muir considers *The Last House on the Left* a "loose interpretation"[37] of *The Virgin Spring*, while for Michael Brashinsky, Craven's film was an attack on the very ideals upon which the earlier movie was based.[38] Teenager Mari Collingwood (Sandra Cassel) heads to the city to see a band with her friend Phyllis (Lucy Grantham) to celebrate her seventeenth birthday, taking a peace sign necklace that was a gift from her parents. During their search for marijuana, they meet Krug Stillo (David Hess), his son Junior (Marc Sheffler), Sadie (Jeramie Rain) and Weasel (Fred J. Lincoln). The group decides to smuggle the girls to Canada in the trunk of their car after they beat and rape Phyllis. Their car breaks down in front of the Collingwoods' house, where Mari's parents had been planning a surprise party for their daughter. While the police half-heartedly interview the Collingwoods about Mari's disappearance, Krug and his gang drag the girls into the woods where Mari is raped, and both girls are beaten, humiliated and eventually murdered. Pretending to be traveling salesmen, the gang seeks accommodation with the Collingwoods, unaware of their relationship to Mari. Mrs. Collingwood (Cynthia Carr) discovers Junior has the peace sign necklace they had given their daughter, leading her and Dr. Collingwood (Richard Towers) to the discovery of Mari's body. Crazed and grief stricken, the Collingwoods exact their revenge: Mrs. Collingwood seduces Weasel and orally castrates him. After Junior commits suicide, Dr. Collingwood attacks Krug with a chain saw, and Mrs. Collingwood slits Sadie's throat in their swimming pool. The film ends as the blood-covered Collingwoods grimly reunite while the dumbfounded police assess the carnage.

Though the basic plot is similar to *The Virgin Spring*, significant details are altered in *The Last House on the Left*. Aside from the increase in explicit violence, the most notable difference is the absence of any equivalent to Bergman's eponymous spring that signifies the redemption of the victim's father and provides his catharsis. Craven's film is therefore much darker, supporting Muir's observation that "the two plotlines differ most ... not in specific details or characters, but in religious convictions and overtones."[39] The updated location of *The Last House on the Left* to the contemporary United States of the film's production is even more pivotal. With the increasing realities of the Vietnam War encroaching upon daily life, for Brashinsky, Craven's film is "one of the first reactions to the defeat of the 1960s, coming from inside the generation that lost."[40] According to Adam Lowenstein's book *Shocking Representation: Historical Trauma, National Cinema, and the Modern Horror Film* (2005), *The Last House on the Left* articulates the looming reality of the death of the progressive ideals of the 1960s. With the hippie dream well and truly over, the film is set in a nihilistic world where there is little place for romantic idealism. While the graphic and drawn-out rape scene is essential in justifying the later revenge component of the narrative, it functions only as a narrative device with which to enter a wider examination of the issues affecting America at the unique time of the film's production.

The Virgin Spring and *The Last House on the Left* diverge not over the treatment of sexual assault as much as they do in regard to the morality of the revenge act by the victim's agents. While the 1972 film, unlike *The Virgin Spring*, may appear at first to have "no moral center,"[41] Craven's rejection of a happily-ever-after universe is an ethical statement in its own right. The message of *The Last House on the Left* may be bleaker than Bergman's, but it says much of the film's zeitgeist: revenge is futile and can only be rewarded with chaos and despair. In *The Last House on the Left*, violence begets more violence, and an assumption that "good" will triumph over "evil" is exposed as naïve. This is nowhere more apparent than in the film's climactic chain saw decapitation of the primary villain,

Krug Stillo, which occurs off-screen and is almost immediately replaced by the image of the shocked, bloodied Mr. and Mrs. Collingwood. This is where the melodramatic "payoff" would traditionally be situated, but any sense of victory is denied by the speed and impact with which it collides with the harsh realization that the Collingwoods are now killers themselves. *The Last House on the Left* demonstrates how rape-revenge narratives may actively collapse assumed ethical structures concerning right/wrong and heroes/villains from within. The brutal efficiency with which Craven and Cunningham depict this kind of ideological disillusionment is no doubt one of the primary reasons for the film's success, both at the time of its release and in regard to its longevity with cult audiences almost fifty years later.

As *The Virgin Spring* and *Last House on the Left* demonstrate, rape-revenge films run the gamut of cinematic artistry. This is nowhere clearer than in *Thriller: A Cruel Picture*, which demonstrates simultaneous levels of both aesthetic exquisiteness and an unflinching poverty of craftsmanship. Banned twice even in its liberal homeland of Sweden, *Thriller* shot into the public imagination when its protagonist's iconic eye-patch was referenced by Elle Driver (Daryl Hannah) in Quentin Tarantino's *Kill Bill* (2003/4). The more beautiful moments of the film—and the film *does* contain instances of genuinely breathtaking filmmaking—suggest the time director Bo Arne Vibenius spent working with Ingmar Bergman on *Hour of the Wolf* (1968) and *Persona* (1966) was not wasted.[42] But at the same time, *Thriller: A Cruel Picture* also exhibits moments of exploitation filmmaking at its most aesthetically, morally and intellectually bankrupt. This glaring paradox makes viewing the film an even more strange and confusing task than that entailed by almost all other rape-revenge films in this book.

The film begins with the carefree frolicking of a little girl playing in autumn leaves. Spun around in the

U.S. poster art for *Thriller: A Cruel Picture* (Bo Arne Vibenius, 1974) (Everett Collection, Inc./Alamy Stock Photo).

air by an elderly man, the scene turns from idyllic to ugly when interrupted by a close up of his contorted, grotesque face that—when combined with a shot of her crumpled, discarded dress—implies that the child has been raped. The police capture the unnamed man but the film cuts to Madeleine (Christina Lindberg) as a young woman, while two elderly female neighbors discuss how the assault resulted in Madeleine's muteness and that the perpetrator went unpunished. Dedicated to her parents and her life on their farm, Madeleine is encouraged by her father to take some time off and go into town. The fashionable young Tony (Heinz Hopf) picks her up after she misses her bus, and he takes her to a fancy restaurant. He invites her back to his apartment and drugs her. While she is unconscious, he announces in a telephone call that she is the fifth girl he has captured in this manner that year. When she wakes up, Madeleine is informed that she is now addicted to heroin and must work as a prostitute for him to keep receiving drugs. Pretending to be Madeleine, Tony writes unkind letters to her parents who, grief stricken, take their own lives. Tony's clients begin to arrive, and Madeleine scratches the eyes of the first one when he approaches her for sex. Tony retaliates by cutting out one of her eyes, requiring the addition of her famous eye-patch. After the discovery of her parent's death, Madeleine goes to church to pray and uses extra money she gains from raising her prostitution rates to learn karate, how to shoot and how to drive. Her abuse and drug use continues, but when her "colleague" Sally (Solveig Andersson) is murdered, Madeleine begins her revenge by tracking down her clients and killing them. Challenging Tony to a duel, she enacts an elaborate murder, and the film ends when he dies and she drives away from his corpse.

Thriller: A Cruel Picture's extreme reputation stems primarily from its graphic eye-gouging scene. The rumor that Vibenius used an actual corpse and that what the film showed was a real human eye being punctured with a scalpel became an integral part of the film's notoriety. While unarguably disturbing to a spectator with limited gore literacy, for those familiar with eyeball-heavy film violence (spanning from Luis Buñuel's 1929 film *Un Chien Andalou* to the work of Italian director Lucio Fulci) the scene is not particularly exceptional. Far harder to dismiss, however, is the hardcore pornographic inserts that feature in the uncensored version of the film. *Thriller: A Cruel Picture* is, of course, not the only film to fall under a broader "adult" rubric to incorporate rape-revenge elements. While it would be a major task that falls well outside of the parameters of this book to assess the wider application of rape in adult film, some of the more notorious rape-revenge examples from this era also include *Emanuelle's Revenge* (Joe D'Amato, 1975), *The Taking of Christina* (Armand Weston, 1976), *Terri's Revenge* (Zebedy Colt, 1976), *Forced Entry* (Shaun Costello, 1973) and Ann Perry's *Teenage Sex Kitten* (1975).

Even to spectators unfazed by hardcore pornography, films like *Thriller: A Cruel Picture* still prove to be an extremely difficult viewing experience. Although *Thriller*'s brief pornographic close-ups featuring explicit vaginal (and, at one point, anal) penetration are on their own non-violent, the context of their placement within the telling of Madeleine's story renders them profoundly violent indeed. In an interview with *Cinema Sewer*'s Jan Bruun, Vibenius is open about doing the film to make money, stating that he needed to recuperate financial losses from an earlier project and thus "decided to make the most commercial film ever made." On the inclusion of these hardcore inserts, he notes that they were only included to profit on the increasing "liberalization of porn in Denmark and Sweden"[43] at the time. Due to the inclusion of these hardcore inserts, *Thriller* far transcends the violent nastiness of the original versions of *I Spit on Your Grave* or *The Last House on the Left* by making it impossible to deny the directorial intent of making rape sexually titillating. In this sense, the pornographic inserts allow a significant conclusion to be made: their inclusion in such a bleak story is evidence that the filmmakers at least assumed there was a viable demographic who would watch a rape-revenge film for no other reason than the promise of the violent sexual degradation of women.

While it is impossible to transcend an analysis of *Thriller: A Cruel Picture* beyond the nasty commercial reality that its hardcore inserts belie, the crushing ugliness of these moments make the film's strengths even more conspicuous by comparison. As Vibenius himself puts it, "Looking back on it, it's a shitty film, but with interesting aspects to it."[44] Not the least of these is the performance of Christina Lindberg. Although in her mid–20s at the time *Thriller: A Cruel Picture* was made, Lindberg was making softcore films around this period that emphasized her youth, such as Joseph W. Sarno's *Swedish Wildcats* and Walter Boos' *The Swinging Co-Eds* in 1972, Torgny Wickman's *Swedish Nymphet* and Ernst Hofbauer's *Secrets of Sweet Sixteen* in 1973. Part of the decision to include these hardcore inserts no doubt stemmed from the fact that her fans at the time may have assumed an erotic aspect to her performance. But as the mute Madeleine (also called Frigga in the film), her ability to communicate her character's experiences without words is flawless. When her clumsy, pink-painted fingernails fumble with syringes and tourniquets, Madeleine's innocence is suffocating, and paralleled onscreen only by Natja Brunckhorst's performance as the title character of Uli Edel's *Christiane F* (1981). As Madeleine embarks upon her revenge, her silence becomes a weapon as she transforms into an enigmatic, determined vigilante. Far from impaired by her optical and vocal disabilities and twice-a-day heroin habit, Lindberg's Madeleine is capable of sawing off her own shotgun (a powerful metaphor for castration). Dressed similarly to Meiko Kaji's rape-avenging protagonist in *Female Prisoner #701: Scorpion* (Shunya Ito, 1972), Lindberg's performance as rampaging Madeleine is as nuanced, desperate and sympathetic as that of her Japanese counterpart.

Bookended by the immaculate formal symmetry of an approaching and departing police car, the film's stylistic strengths make it a cohesive whole. The slow-motion scenes where Madeleine attacks her victims, combined with its strange, delay-heavy soundtrack, grant the sequences an almost ethereal quality. As her hair, trench coat and the blood of her victims float through the air, this depiction of Madeleine evokes references to the work of Pre–Raphaelite painters such as John Waterhouse. These painterly comparisons do not end here: the use of color is strategically deployed as a moral indicator throughout the film. Madeleine's yellow-orange dress as a child in the film's opening moments is the same hue as Tony's lounge suite and the shirt of the first client she kills; this simple visual clue poetically reiterates the unrelenting grip of those childhood events upon her adult life. The film's concluding moments where Madeleine murders Tony in a significantly medieval manner is a sumptuous visual experience that marks a tonal and aesthetic chasm between scenes like these and the hardcore pornographic inserts in the first half of the film. No matter how beautiful and well-constructed other aspects of the film may be, these few strategically placed porn shots make the nasty intent of the movie inescapable. With its motives so explicitly embossed upon its sleeve, *Thriller: A Cruel Picture* is even more sadistic than its no-frills title suggests.

Abel Ferrara's *Ms. 45* stands out from many of its fellow exploitation titles because despite the panning it received upon its initial release, on the whole it has both fans and critics united in their view of it as one of the more ideologically sound offerings. Kier-La

Janisse—author of the groundbreaking *House of Psychotic Women: An Autobiographical Topography of Female Neurosis in Horror and Exploitation Films* (2012)—wrote upon the film's 2013 re-release that "declaring *Ms. 45* as the most integral film of this oft-maligned subgenre is not just a juicy soundbite, nor is it the result of a limited familiarity with what the genre has to offer," continuing that "another reason *Ms. 45* remains a singular classic of the genre is in its tragic depiction of self-sabotage…. *Ms. 45* bravely dares to accuse its wayward protagonist of being complicit in her own misfortune."[45] As I note in my 2017 monograph on the film for the *Cultographies* series, "the film's longevity lies in just how powerfully it reveals the trauma rape can have on its survivors."[46]

Set in Ferrara's signature New York City locale, *Ms. 45* opens in the fashion world, but unlike *Lipstick*, the glamor is almost instantly stripped away and the gritty industrial realities are exposed. Thana (Tamerlis), a young, mute textile worker, is shown standing behind sewing machines and ironing boards. Haunted by male harassment—both in the workplace and on the streets—she is raped by a masked stranger (played by Ferrara himself) on her way home from work, and then once again by a burglar when she arrives home to her apartment. Desperate, she fights her second assailant and kills him with an iron. Panicked and hallucinating more attacks, she cuts his body up, puts the pieces in her fridge and deposits in public rubbish bins one small garbage bag at a time. A young man who has been harassing women on the street notices Thana leaving a bag by a roadside. When he chases her down a dark alley to return it to her, she panics and shoots him. Deeply shaken, she returns home and vomits, but after the continuing harassment by her boss and strangers on the street, Thana becomes a vigilante, roaming the streets shooting men that harass women. Her murder spree climaxes at her office Halloween party, where, dressed as a nun, she shoots the boss whose constant attentions have caused her such trauma, and then shoots every man at the party she can see. Finally, a female colleague stabs her from behind at the same time the police and her landlady discovers her crimes.

Ms. 45 owes its success to its seamless application of its grander mythic and symbolic elements to its gritty, urban locale. For example, much has been made of Thana's name—in psychoanalysis, "Thanatos" is the term describing the death instinct or drive toward destruction.[47] Her muteness also compounds the mythic quality of her ordeal—it makes literal the taboo unspeakability of rape and personifies the inability to articulate the sheer scope of female oppression. But more specific to her own story, the texture of her silence structures the two "types" of Thana that dominates the film's action. For Thana the downtrodden, frightened victim, her silence represents her literal inability to speak up for herself. As *femme fatale*, however, Thana takes control, and her silence becomes a weapon—instead of a weakness, it enigmatically emphasizes the force of her physical presence.

The switch to these *film noir* aspects marks a distinct thematic as well as stylistic turn in *Ms. 45*. The night of Thana's rampage is dominated by Ferrara's hardboiled New York cityscape that perfectly suits her makeover (as well as providing a female counterpart to the New York City of *Death Wish*'s Paul Kersey). Costume becomes even more significant in the film's final scene, with the images of Thana as the iconic, gun-toting nun. Preparing herself for her final showdown with her lecherous boss (played by Albert Sinkys), Thana's subversion of *Taxi Driver*'s (Martin Scorsese, 1976) famous "Are you looking at me?" sequence in front of her bedroom mirror before she leaves her house perfectly captures her psychological state. Her shooting spree (shot in slow motion—perhaps another reference to *Thriller: A Cruel Picture*) falters slightly when she sees a man dressed in a wedding dress. Taken off guard, it is here that her friend and co-worker Laurie (Darlene Stuto) is able to stab Thana from behind. Genuinely stunned that violence is not so clearly demarcated along gendered lines (in terms of both victims and perpetrators), Thana dies in shock. It is no coincidence that it is a man in drag and a woman in a leotard tuxedo wielding a crotch-level, phallic knife that cause her downfall: Thana's assumption of an "us vs. them" scenario collapses with tragic results at these ambiguous sexual identities.

Or does it? The famous coda seems little more than a cute, tacked-on afterthought to raise the tone of the bleak action that has preceded it. Although it appeared that Thana had shot her landlady's little dog for being too nosy, not so: the final shot of the film shows him returned to his owner's door. But why name him Phil? Why not Spot? Rover? Fido? That the dog is given a human *male* name carries a powerful yet subtle suggestion that Thana's fears that men will return if they are not stopped may hold some merit. While Thana had successfully eradicated some dangerous men, the film implies in these final moments that even those that appear to have vanished have a way of returning. The return of Phil therefore marks Thana's failure while simultaneously justifying her fears. As the next section will discuss further, male aggression is not a solely female concern.

Masculinity and the Rape-Revenge Film

Straw Dogs (Sam Peckinpah, 1971), *Deliverance* (John Boorman, 1972), *Sudden Impact* (Clint Eastwood, 1983) and *Death Wish* (Michael Winner, 1974) in particular rate high on the list of well-known revenge films that feature sexual violence as a crucial element of their narrative. These films are best understood as exposing a specific subset of thematic concerns regarding the function and depiction of masculinity and male identity. While most rape-revenge films with male characters (be they victims or perpetrators) can be understood in some sense as engaging with ideas surrounding masculinity, some films obviously locate this as a greater source of fascination than others. For instance, while the original *I Spit on Your Grave* suggests a complex and competitive relationship between the group of men who gang rape Jennifer, it is her experience (of the horror and trauma of rape, and of the cathartic satisfaction of her revenge) that consistently remains the core of the film's interest. *Straw Dogs* also includes a group of men who attack a main female character, but it focuses primarily less on the relationship between the woman and her rapists than it does upon the relationship between these men and her husband. Put simply, in the women-centered rape-revenge films that are the primary source of interest to this book, the plight of a woman-in-a-man's-world is examined. But in this section, particular attention is paid to how rape-revenge articulates the experience of a man-in-a-man's world. These canonical rape-revenge films demonstrate that the narrative and thematic intersection of rape and revenge in these instances is just as complex as it is in women-centered rape-revenge.

As Clover notes, the city/country binary provides the thematic foundations for a number of rape-revenge films.[48] Whether set in rural or urban spaces, films such as *Straw Dogs*, *Deliverance* and *Death Wish* explore tensions between these spaces and what they represent, and how this impacts the construction of masculinity. *Straw Dogs* is renowned as one of Peckinpah's most notorious, violent and confronting films. Critical responses have generally agreed upon its supposed "caveman ethic of dominance by the strong"[49] and identify in it "reactionary sexual politics" that contribute to "a masculinist backlash against an emergent feminism."[50] For Clover, films such as *Ms. 45* and the original *I Spit on Your Grave* mark a distinct shift *away* from *Straw Dogs*' misogyny.[51] In his 2003 review of the DVD re-release of the film, Christopher Sharrett is scathing: "It is an unremittingly ugly work, a vision of a human zoo minus any of the sympathetic interest Peckinpah develops for the cruelest of characters in his major films."[52] Renowned for his personal leanings towards macho rebelliousness, Peckinpah himself espoused contradictory reflections on the film that at their worst did not help garner critical favor. Citing a remarkable interview in *Playboy* magazine, Stephen Prince quotes Peckinpah's notorious statement that "there are women and there are pussy … [Amy] is pussy under the veneer of being a woman." Here, Peckinpah states outright that Amy "asked for the rape."[53] But the film itself suggests that while there is certainly room to claim *Straw Dogs* as "tawdry," in no way is it "simple."

Straw Dogs is based on Gordon M. Williams' novel *The Siege of Trencher's Farm* (1969), its adaptation of the trope grimly serious, as American university academic David (Dustin Hoffman) receives research funding and moves to a house on the Cornish coast left to his British wife Amy (Susan George) by her father. A group of local roughs dominate the town and intimidate David from the outset. David is particularly sensitive, as one of the men, Charlie (Del Henny), is Amy's ex-boyfriend; although David teases her about it early in the film, it is clear he sees it as a genuine threat to their relationship. Regardless, David hires the men to repair the roof of their garage. It is here that their behavior becomes increasingly threatening. Beginning with the theft of Amy's underwear, it grows in seriousness to the hanging of her cat in their bedroom wardrobe, followed by the brutal rape of Amy by Charlie and Norman (Ken Hutchison). Desperate to avoid conflict, David attempts to immerse himself in his research and ignores the increasingly violent reality that surrounds him. At the film's climax he is finally forced into action and decides to protect village idiot and suspected pedophile Henry Niles (David Warner) from the drunken vigilantism of the gang after Niles is involved in the disappearance of local girl Janice (Sally Thomsett). David vows to take a stand and protect his home and Niles against the men, revealing Amy's conflicted loyalties between Charlie and David, and exposing her to a violent outburst by Niles. Defeating the gang in a lengthy bloodbath, David leaves Amy and drives smiling into the night with Niles by his side.

While the film is violent throughout, it is unsurprising that the brutal rape scene has been the source of primary attention. What begins as a clear-cut sexual assault by Amy's ex-lover morphs into something far different, as Amy's precarious relationship with both Charlie and David explodes onscreen in this complex, challenging sequence. David Andrews observes that semi-consensual rape in the cinema has a long history, stemming back to the 1920s, but it manifests most famously in this sequence.[54] While there is certainly nothing "ironic" about Amy's rape—Charlie holds Amy down to be sodomized by Norman in a sequence which contains none of the ambiguity of her interaction with Charlie—Andrews suggests Amy's assault by Charlie (for it is, at the beginning at least, undeniably a rape) is far more complex than the simple pleasure/displeasure or consent/refusal binaries that often dominates discussion of the scene. Unlike the notable area of child sexual abuse in movies, it is significant that few women-centered rape-revenge films function beyond the stranger-as-rapist paradigm, despite the fact that there is statistical evidence that victims commonly know their rapists.[55] Amy's past sexual relationship with Charlie surely means that the politics of this encounter (as rape: non-consensual) is going to be heavily influenced by their past sexual contact (as lovers: consensual). It is offensive to suggest that this by default results in semi-consensual rape: Charlie and Norman are *both* rapists. But is there the possibility that by turning a rape into something she *looks* like she is enjoying, Amy is somehow attempting to reclaim *some* degree of power in the situation, or at least is trying to protect herself from further harm, not just rape but other forms of violence?

This is an ethical hornet's nest, but this question exposes the ease with which so many critics (and, as mentioned above, the director himself) so smoothly sought to blame Amy for her own rape. Claims that she was "asking for it"—Sharrett literally calls her "slutty"[56]—ignores the differing relationships she has with the two rapists. Again, this is far from staking an uncomplicated or progressive claim for the sequence. As Linda Ruth Williams notes, the "scene is dense with outrageous implication," as the consequences of these distinctions are themselves of concern. Of the second rape, she says, "If this is 'bad' rape, then the first rape must have been 'good.' In the *Straw Dogs* discourse, rape is not necessarily negative—it all depends on who's doing it to you."[57]

Susan George's own experiences of filming *Straw Dogs* are vital in terms of Peckinpah's control over her body as an actor *Straw Dogs* was the film on which Peckinpah received the greatest creative freedom,[58] and the film is almost unanimously discussed in terms of his (masculine) control (the rapes were added to the film and did not appear in the original novel). Weddle provides an enlightening version of the film's production from George's perspective. She admitted that she was frightened of shooting the rape scene because she was unclear what it would physically demand of her. According to Weddle, she told Peckinpah she had previously lied about being happy to do it "because I wanted to get the role and the rape scene was in the picture, and now I'm not sure if I can do it." Using language that reflects the power relations in the scene in question, Peckinpah replied, "Well, you'll have to do it! I'm gonna make you do it!"[59] George quit the film but agreed to come back to the project after she convinced Peckinpah to shoot the scene on her terms. The implications of George's next comment to Peckinpah suggest that the violence in the final version was originally intended to be far more explicit:

> I propose to do it [show the violence of the scene] through my eyes. If I'm the kind of actress that you think I am, and the kind of person that you think I am, I think I can tell you everything with my eyes. If you focus on my eyes and my body movements, I promise you I will lead you down the road you wish to be lead down. I will make you believe every bloody moment of it.[60]

Peckinpah agreed, and the scene took a week to shoot. From this perspective, George paradoxically gained control of a scene where she loses all rights to her own body as Amy but reclaims some aspect as to how her body as an actor was depicted. This anecdote does not neutralize this challenging sequence but suggests that if Amy lost something here for women and how they are represented, then George as a performer may have reclaimed *some* ground.

At the intersection of George's experience in *Straw Dogs* lies the fact that as Amy, her body became a site for masculine power—both in the case of the rape sequence (a battle between Charlie and David for "possession") and with Peckinpah over how that rape scene should be shot. This is explicit in the film's promotional poster: beheaded and cut off from the waist down, an objectified Amy literally becomes the space where male-dominated conflict is enacted. The image of Amy's chest is the first shot of her in the film, and as Williams notes, "so textbook an example of fragmented femininity ... seems almost parodic."⁶¹ This image—in both the film and the poster—defines Amy's function, stripping away her agency not only as rape survivor but also as abused wife (which, in the face of David's psychological cruelty, she absolutely is). That function is simple: Amy exposes the failings of the men in the film. This is less an establishing shot of a subject than it is of both the central object and terrain over which the masculine tensions of the film will be fought.

From this perspective, the film's status as rape-revenge is further complicated. As Xavier Mendik observes, "The film's theme of a meek college professor reacting violently to the rape of his wife reveals an underlying ambivalence to female sexual liberation."⁶² But Amy never *tells* David about the rape; although it is perhaps obvious what has happened, his refusal to acknowledge it is yet just something else he is in denial about. The red herring is that Amy fires the last shot in the film, and the image of her with a gun aimed at Chris (Jim Norton) instantly evokes rape-revenge traditions. Chris undoubtedly traumatized Amy throughout the film (the first violation against her was when he stole her underpants), and his sadistic, high-pitched laugh remains one of the movie's most chilling features. But her actual rapists were Charlie and Norman; did David seek to avenge her rape against these two men? No—again, Amy never explicitly tells David she was raped, and he never acknowledges it (implying he, too, suspects she was "asking for it"). It is therefore noteworthy that it is *Charlie* who kills Norman: one rapist avenges the rape by killing the *other* rapist. By this point, Amy has attempted to leave with Charlie, a factor that David (and many critics) consider proof of her lack of character and betrayal. But that David responds by pulling her hair in exactly the same way Charlie had during the rape sequence exposes that *both* men are threats—from Amy's perspective, Charlie may simply be the "best of a bad lot," and that this "best" has previously raped her exposes just how diabolically low her opinion of David is (not to mention how grim her plight is in the world of *Straw Dogs* more generally).

These rape-revenge elements are complicated even further. Firstly, the whole reason Norman, Chris, Charlie and their gang go to David and Amy's farm that night is to get Henry Niles *whom they believe has raped Janice*. Again, we have rapists enacting vengeance against another suspected rapist. This paradox is even more explicit in the film's finale when David, after Amy's desertion when she tries to leave with Charlie, leaves her alone in a house full of corpses and instead drives almost romantically into the night with Henry—a man whom, even leaving aside his accidental killing of Janice and the rumors of his pedophilia, David *sees* attack Amy during the siege. This is David's terrifying victory, as the discovery of his masculinity frees him from the supposed shackles of women like Amy forever. After all of his repetitive accusations of Amy's childishness, he smiles as he is ultimately able to replace her with a manchild. The rape of a woman is not avenged in *Straw Dogs*, it is instead eradicated completely as an issue when David chooses instead the safety of his newfound masculinity in an all-male world.

Aside from relocating the action from Britain to the United States, there appears little to distinguish Peckinpah's film from Rod Lurie's 2011 remake of the original starring James Marsden and Kate Bosworth. An exception is the role that Amy plays in avenging her own rape; while in the original Charlie shoots Norman, in Lurie's version—supposedly an updating of the gender politics to remove the agent model of vengeance—it is Amy herself who kills him. As David Andrews argues, however, there is something hollow and superficial about this attempt to "fix" the gender politics of Peckinpah's original, due to what Andrews suggests is a basic problem with the ethical legibility of Lurie's efforts. Andrews notes of the rape scene that "in its quietness, Lurie's remade scene contains an emotional dynamic that is difficult to read." While Lurie wanted the scene to be understood as a repudiation of Peckinpah's scene (and broader world view), for Andrews there is a fundamental lack of clarity that this is in fact the case. Of equal concern to Andrews is the question of the revenge component of the equation. That there seems to be an implied progressive shift to allow Amy to be the agent of her own vengeance in her killing Norman, as Andrews shrewdly articulates, "that she focuses all her venom on Norman alone also suggests that she disliked the second rape more than the first." He continues, "This is a problem, for Lurie's rejection of Peckinpah's semi-consensual scene suggests that he views the two rapes as equivalent." Rather than a critique of Peckinpah's film, then, Andrews convincingly argues that it almost inadvertently does exactly the same thing, but in a different way: "The effect is to make it seem as if Amy views Norman, not Charlie, as her main antagonist, just as she does in the original."[63]

While *Straw Dogs* symbolically plays out its masculine dramas upon the site of femininity and "femaleness," the dominance of feminine bodies by masculine ones in *Deliverance* deletes the necessity of women characters almost entirely by gendering the site of the film's action—the fictional Cahulawassee River in the American South—as female. While Amy's body becomes a symbolic plane for *Straw Dogs*' masculine tensions to unfold, in *Deliverance* the metaphor is made literal: the setting itself is gendered "female" (the river often referred to as "she"). In this sense, one of the movie's most significant features is that there is, in fact, two feminized "victims" in the film, despite it having no main women characters.[64] Without an "actual" woman to expose the binary distinctions between male and female, Boorman instead relies on a hierarchy of masculinity defined by the men themselves—that it is "chubby," soft Bobby who is sodomized by the hillbilly mountain men is no coincidence. As Clover observes, "From such a man to an actual woman—from Bobby in *Deliverance* to Jennifer in *I Spit on Your Grave*—is but a short step."[65] In lieu of the absence of female bodies, new gendered Others rapidly take their place. "Rape is about inscribing macho-masculinity," notes Rikke Schubart on the film. "When women are not available, this is done on male bodies."[66]

Both Clover[67] and Schubart[68] acknowledge the influence of *Deliverance* upon the cycle of rape-revenge films of the 1970s and 1980s. While effectively an action film, the scope of its influence ranges well beyond generic boundaries. Despite being based on screenwriter James Dickey's 1970 novel of the same name, the film and book diverge in their treatments of violence and masculinity. In an interview with Michel Ciment, Boorman said:

> Philosophically, we had little in common. Dickey's beliefs are not unlike Hemingway's, especially the idea that one attains manhood through some initiatory act of violence. For me, the contrary is true: violence doesn't make you a better person—in fact, it degrades you.[69]

Rejecting the very myth of masculinity that the book celebrates, Boorman confidently focused on an individual's journey of self-discovery that—like many of his other films—results in what is more often than not an equally isolating discovery.[70]

Deliverance tells the story of a disastrous canoe trip down one of the last untouched rivers in northern Georgia by four middle-class Atlanta businessmen before the area is flooded to become a dam. The men represent different versions of urban masculinity: Bobby (Ned Beatty) and Drew (Ronny Cox) are the least experienced outdoorsmen of the group, manifesting initially in Bobby's brashness and Drew's naivety. Lewis (Burt

Reynolds) is the veteran camper of the group, described by Ciment as "fascinated to a near-fascist degree of notions of survival and courage and physical culture."[71] The film's central protagonist, Ed (Jon Voight), is somewhere between these groups—while having gone on trips with Lewis in the past, he finds it difficult at one point to shoot a deer, and struggles to accept Lewis' nihilistic view of urban living. After an initial tense meeting with "redneck" locals in the infamous "Dueling Banjos" sequence, the men begin their journey. Things take a turn when Ed and Bobby step off their canoe to get their bearings and are confronted by two "mountain men" who sodomize Bobby at gunpoint. Before Ed is assaulted, Lewis and Drew arrive, and Lewis shoots Bobby's rapist with an arrow. The other man flees, and the four men debate their next step: Drew insists they go to the police and confess, but the others outvote him and they bury the corpse. Returning to the river, Drew mysteriously falls out of the canoe (the others assume he has been shot by the second, escaped mountain man as vengeance). In the confusion, both canoes overturn, and the men are thrown around in the violent rapids. With Lewis badly injured, Ed takes control, and kills the man he believes has murdered Drew. The men sink both Drew's and the mountain man's corpses to the bottom of the river. After they return to civilization, the Sheriff (played by Dickey himself) is suspicious of their story, but without further evidence he releases Bobby and Ed, while Lewis remains in the hospital. After what appears to be a permanent goodbye from Bobby, Ed returns home to Atlanta but has a nightmare about a corpse rising from the bottom of the river.

Bobby's rape is both one of *Deliverance*'s most memorable scenes and one of the most iconic moments of 1970s American cinema It features little sound beyond the hooting rapists, the rustling of leaves and twigs, and Bobby's tortured cries and forced "piggy" squeals; but in the popular memory it is inescapably haunted by the earlier "Dueling Banjos" musical motif. Establishing the tune as the informal hillbilly horror anthem from that point onwards, its positioning at the beginning of the film (and the remarkable sequence where Drew and the unnamed local play the song together) emphasizes the importance of class in the movie. The rape scene itself is difficult to comprehend beyond distinctions between urban/rich and country/poor. As Schubart observes, "It's poor men's power over rich men's bodies."[72] For Clover, "city man may be rich, but he is also soft; and he is soft because he is rich. So soft that he is rapable."[73] The rape of Bobby is therefore only one skirmish in an ongoing class war. The rapists are not named in the film, but in Dicky's script are called "Bearded Man" and "Tall Man," as their identities are located firmly within the masculinity that they wield so mercilessly over Bobby, and with which they threaten Ed. This distinction between Ed and Bobby's experience is crucial to the film's thematic deployment of rape: like the book and script, the film privileges Ed's *witnessing* of Bobby's rape (through point of view and reaction shots) much more than it does Bobby's subjective experience. James F. Beaton describes the shots of Bobby themselves as contrasting sharply with the film's overall realist tone, calling it "a melodrama of disembodied eyes, mouths, and faces, a grotesque abstraction of the event."[74] This stems from how the rape appears not to Bobby or the rapists, but to Ed. He struggles not to look, yet he cannot look away, and Bobby's rape is constructed from his perspective as a horrific blur. After Drew's death, little (if any) time is spent on Bobby's trauma. Sally Robinson notes that after this point, this trauma manifests in Lewis' body more than anyone else's: confronted with the violent feminization of a male body through the rape of Bobby (a possibility that goes directly against his dearly held beliefs about masculinity), Lewis almost physically shuts down from the psychological trauma.[75]

Consequently, despite the narrative importance of the rape of Bobby to the film's action, it is not thematically central. In fact, the rape itself is one of the things that the men actively seek to hide. "The larger crisis the film explores has little to do with the rape," Robinson notes, as it "must be buried along with the male bodies that keep piling up in its wake."[76] It does not appear to be the rape of Bobby that Ed consciously seeks to avenge; rather, his goal is simply one of survival. But even this is ambiguous: was the man Ed killed on the top of the cliff *really* the second assailant? Was Drew *really* shot? That these questions are left open allows for the possibility that vengeance is Ed's motive, albeit subconsciously—he wants to hit back and needs a reason. But placing these ambiguities to the side, *Deliverance* still remains at its heart a rape-revenge film, one that merges the figurative with the literal. From this perspective, the rape of Bobby is considered an act of vengeance by the mountain men. As Clover suggests, "The chain does not begin with the mountain men's rape of Bobby in the forest; it begins with the city men's 'rape' of the landscape, the visible destruction of the physical habitat of the mountain people."[77] That this lies at the heart of one of the most famous rape-revenge films of all time is as significant as it is shocking, and, as shall be discussed elsewhere in this book, this is not the only instance where rape avenges a rape. It does, however, expose the troubling mechanics of masculinity that seeks to privilege urban, middle-class white men by Othering women and the lower classes through a language of sexual violence.

A similar binary between city/country is central to *Death Wish*. This distinction is again ideological. The tensions between these two spaces mirrors the tensions that define masculinity under threat, a threat that manifests through the rape of feminine (if not female) bodies. For reasons not wholly disconnected from director Michael Winner's own widely known right-leaning political beliefs, many contemporary considerations of *Death Wish* still share a view typified by Vincent Canby upon the film's release as "a bird-brained movie to cheer the hearts of the far right-wing."[78] Like many rape-revenge films, these sorts of interpretations hinge upon notions of identification: whose story is this, and what does it being told from their perspective mean to the film's ideological position? These debates therefore center on how the main character, Paul Kersey, is constructed. So closely is actor Charles Bronson associated with the role of Kersey that even in academic treatments of the film, the character is referred to not only as "Charles Bronson's character," but also often at times just as "Charles Bronson."[79] Bronson had what Charles Laughton once described as "the strongest face in the business,"[80] and this hypermasculine image established a star persona of a tough man capable of violence only when pushed. Bronson had displayed these features earlier in *Chato's Land* (1972), another rape-revenge film Bronson and Winner made together. It is *Death Wish* and its numerous sequels, however, that firmly established Bronson's macho star persona.

Adapted from Brian Garfield's 1972 novel of the same name, *Death Wish* centers on liberal architect Kersey, whose worldview changes dramatically after his wife Joanne (Hope Lange) is murdered, and his daughter Carol (Kathleen Tolan) is raped and left catatonic after a home invasion by a group of muggers. Sent by his employer to Arizona for a change of scene after Joanne's funeral, Kersey befriends Ames (Stuart Margolin), who reminds him of the legacy of the American Western tradition and gifts him with a gun. Kersey returns home, where an attempted mugging pushes him too far, and he establishes himself as the anonymous avenger the media dubs "The New York Vigilante." Deliberately baiting thugs solely to annihilate them, Kersey becomes a popular sensation that inspires others to fight back. Officials, however, are disturbed by the Vigilante's success in reducing the number of crimes because it appears to validate his tactics and urge Detective Frank Ochoa (Vincent Gardenia) to eradicate the mysterious figure without martyring him. Ochoa discovers Kersey's identity and quietly relocates him to Chicago. The film's final shot suggests that Kersey's vigilante days may be far from over, and hints at the longevity of a franchise that would see another four installments between 1982 and 1994.

Death Wish was shot on location in New York City in the winter of 1974, and the bleakness of the primary urban location contrasts dramatically with the film's two idyllic, non-urban spaces (the tropical Hawaii at the film's opening, where Kersey and Joanne holiday, and rural Arizona). This tension speaks of a return to another kind of America for New Yorker Kersey, one that dominant readings of the film suggest is overtly regressive. For Canby, *Death Wish* "raises complex questions in order to offer bigoted, frivolous, oversimplified answers."[81] Michael Ryan and Douglas Kellner suggest the film predicted the shift in America from the liberalism of the 1960s to the conservatism defined by the reign of Ronald Reagan, paying particular attention to Ames, noting, "The vehicle of his [Kersey's] conversion is a Sunbelt rightist, the social type that would indeed take over from the liberals in the eighties as the dominant social policy voice in the country."[82] As Mendik adds, "*Death Wish* appeared to strike a chord with an increasingly militant and reactionary white, middle-class seventies America."[83] Mendik emphasizes the importance of economics and class tensions to the film: one of the muggers tells Joanne before she is murdered that he "hates rich cunts," and Kersey's first attack is symbolically not with a gun, but with a sock full of coins. From this perspective, Mendik argues that the ambiguous ethical space that is supposed to distinguish Kersey from the street criminals he rallies against—a distinction that right-wing readings of the film view as crucial—is deliberately framed by economics and class. In this light, *Death Wish* may suggest that the only thing that makes Kersey a "hero" and not one of the thugs against whom he rallies is the fact that they are poor and he is rich. For Mendik, that Kersey is alienated from his social group—not only at parties, but ultimately forced to leave New York altogether—is the film's internal way of complicating the ethical status of a protagonist whom most critics tend to read as an intended hero.

Winner himself argued the identification of Kersey as a hero is a misreading of the film. Citing the mood at the time of the film's production as one heavily dominated by the disillusionment accompanying Watergate and the Vietnam War—where, as he described it, "Camelot had changed into a Hieronymus Bosch painting"[84]—he maintained that the rules of identification had necessarily changed:

> It is certainly not intended as a fascist picture.... If you see ... a picture about a man who becomes a killer and society applauds him, it does not mean the filmmaker applauds him. We are saying that there are certain things this man does which strike a gut reaction to which you are sympathetic; but if you applaud him, you're obviously applauding the same sort of violence he's out to perpetuate himself.[85]

The film's politics therefore hinge upon how the spectator is positioned in relation to the film's key actions, and this is nowhere clearer than in the scene where Joanne is murdered and Carol is raped. While not as explicit as many of the rape scenes discussed in this book, the painting of Carol's buttocks with red spray paint provokes a deeply visceral sense of shock and horror. The film makes literal the idea that female bodies are nothing but spaces for male expression, to be defaced with graffiti like on a brick wall. Carol's rape is shown primarily from Joanne's perspective, but as she dies only moments later, her maternal perspective is not privileged. Rather, both Joanne and Carol—through the former's actual death and the latter's symbolic one—do little more than narratively provide Kersey with a reason to seek vengeance.

While Eli Roth's 2018 remake avoided the shocking rape sequence that made the original so notorious, that the rape in Winner's *Death Wish* is solely there to justify the intensity of this vengeance stands as fact, regardless from which side of the political divide one chooses to read the ethical validity of that vengeance. Like other Winner films that demonstrate a continuing interest in the intersection of rape and revenge—such as *Chato's Land* and *Dirty Weekend*—rape is once again narrative rather than thematic. But both *Death Wish* itself and the critical discourse that surrounds it are of significance to an analysis of rape-revenge because of its melodrama of masculine morality, of how male bodies attempt (and perhaps fail) to "play out" distinctions between right and wrong, right and left, and hero and villain. If this is ambiguous in *Death Wish*, it is spelled out spectacularly in the opening scene of J. Lee Thompson's *Death Wish IV: The Crackdown* (1987). Here, a woman walks to her car in a deserted parking lot and is attacked by three men. Kersey interrupts the attempted rape, shoots two of the men and chases the third after he escapes. Finally cornering him, Kersey shoots and bends over the body of this third man and removes the stocking from his head to reveal the rapist's identity. Underneath the stocking, Kersey discovers his own face. Cutting to a shot of him waking up in a sweat, this sequence is revealed to be a nightmare that makes explicit Kersey's greatest fear: that the line that separates those capable of rape and murder and the self-appointed vigilantes who so violently and ruthlessly seek to avenge it is not as clear as he had assumed.

Sudden Impact (1983) shares *Death Wish*'s focus upon the relationship between masculinity and the often-hazy distinctions between justice and vigilantism. Parallels between the two films were not uncommon at the time of *Sudden Impact*'s release[86] (both films were widely considered part of the "right cycle" of films from this era). William Beard, however, observes that the heroic image of masculinity—personified by "Dirty" Harry Callahan—aspired to a much more poetic, even mythic, level than Bronson's Kersey.[87] Like Kersey, Callahan's now-iconic image of masculinity was linked to its star's intertextual persona. Returning Clint Eastwood to the screen after a seven-year break in the role of Dirty Harry, *Sudden Impact* is not only the sole film in the series directed by Eastwood, but it also contained the line so famously associated both with Dirty Harry and Eastwood himself: "Go ahead, make my day." Ironically, the film proved to be the most financially successful of all the Dirty Harry titles,[88] despite the fact that Eastwood had previously stated he would not return to the series[89] (Sondra Locke—Eastwood's partner at the time and *Sudden Impact* co-star—has suggested that his motives were purely financial after the lackluster box office performance of *Honkytonk Man* and *Firefox* the previous year[90]).

Structurally, *Sudden Impact* focuses upon two concurrent stories. The first follows conflicted policeman Callahan as he struggles to balance his idea of justice with those deemed acceptable within the parameters of the law, while the second concerns artist Jennifer Spencer (Locke), who seeks to find and kill those involved in the rape of her and her sister (who, like *Death Wish*'s Carol, also became catatonic after the assault) ten years earlier. Callahan and Spencer's stories intersect when the former is punished for unruly behavior and sent from San Francisco to the fictional town of San Paulo to investigate the murder of George Wilburn (Michael Maurer), one of Spencer's victims. Initially ignorant of Spencer's involvement, Callahan and Spencer establish a sexual relationship while each focuses on their missions. The film reaches its climax after Spencer has killed the majority of her and her sister's rapists, and is captured by Mick (Paul Drake), the remaining assailant and leader of the first rape, in the same amusement park where the initial assault took place. Spencer fights back, but Mick and his two lackeys restrain her and attempt to rape her again. Callahan rescues Spencer at the last minute, and Spencer believes Callahan will turn her over to the police. Instead, she is surprised when he frames the now-deceased Mick for her murders. Protected by Callahan's story, the film ends as the couple walk away from the amusement park together.

Considering Eastwood is one of the most revered living contemporary American directors today, revisiting reviews of *Sudden Impact* from the time of its release is an odd experience. While a box office success, critical responses were dismissive and often outwardly hostile, the *Los Angeles Times*' Kevin Thomas describing it as an "exploitation picture at its most nakedly manipulative."[91] Canby was no more complimentary, stating, "The screenplay is ridiculous, and Mr. Eastwood's direction of it is primitive,"[92] while for Gary Arnold of the *Washington Post*, it was "obviously cuckoo," as he dismissed Callahan himself as an "indomitable, reactionary fantasy figure."[93] Peter Stack at the *San Francisco Chronicle* offered a rare take on the film at the time as something more sophisticated, noting in particular its black humor.[94] Even with the benefit of hindsight, however, some elements of the film are still far from palatable. As Deborah Allison indicates, the character of Ray Parkins (Audrie J. Neenan)—a two-dimensional evil lesbian who set up the rape of Spencer and her sister, her characterization spawned by "misogyny and homophobia"[95]—makes the film impossible to wholly rescue retrospectively. So extreme is the depiction of Parkins that Allison agrees with Stack, identifying a turn against the realism of the earlier Dirty Harry films and other crime films of the era towards something more self-consciously theatrical and postmodern.[96] To be fair, the "evil" lesbian stereotype in rape-revenge is hardly unique to *Sudden Impact* and can be found centrally in *Red Sonja* (Richard Fleischer, 1985), *Girls Against Boys* (Austin Chick, 2012), and although not a revenge film, Caryn Krooth's *Jaded* (1998) features a woman who is sexually assaulted by two other women.

Callahan's deadpan machismo can thus be understood as competing with—rather than complimenting—Spencer's vampish female avenger. *Sudden Impact* pitches the two types of rape-revenge—the male-lead vengeance trope, where a man takes revenge as an agent for a woman survivor, and the trope where a woman is the agent of her own revenge—directly against each other. The film's original script did not initially include Callahan, as *Sudden Impact* was intended as a star vehicle for Locke alone.[97] Certainly the film's generous emphasis on her story echoes these origins, with some critics even christening her "Dirty Harriet."[98] When these two models of rape-revenge are pitched against each other, a surface reading of the plot suggests Callahan's version emerges victorious. After all of her tough girl posturing and successful annihilations, Spencer ultimately needs to be "rescued" by a male hero who arrives in the nick of time. But formally, the image of Callahan's arrival can be read very differently. When Callahan's silhouette is shown against the bright lights of the deserted amusement park, the iconic image of Dirty Harry and his absurdly phallic oversized gun is drenched in irony. While he is there to "rescue" Spencer, that he is coded so heavily as a *film noir* villain marked by such excessive masculinity in this shot articulates Spencer's predicament: she is still at the mercy of men (it was, after all, *Callahan's* decision to not report her to the police). This image in *Sudden Impact* thematically carries the same disturbing message contained within the opening scene of *Death Wish IV* four years later: whether he is there to rape you or save you, women are still dependent on men. While far from progressive (particularly in its depiction of Ray Parkins), *Sudden Impact* suggests in this single shot that there is only a thin line between the hypermasculinity defined by Callahan and Kersey, and the type of behavior they so self-righteously seek to eradicate.

This section has focused upon the function and depiction of masculinity and how it relates thematically to rape and revenge. What remains untouched thus far is how each of these examples refers in some way to the generic construction of the Western. Ciment regards *Deliverance* as an "updated Western in which the director turns a number of American myths on their head,"[99] while Alan Casty considers *Straw Dogs* explicitly in how it re-adapts the structure and conventions of the Western but eradicates the "romantic dignity" of its predecessors.[100] Bill Harding views *Death Wish* as an updated Western,[101] a claim supported by the fact that iconic Western actor Henry Fonda turned down the script before Winner and Bronson became involved.[102] The relation to the Western is even more obvious in *Sudden Impact*. Eastwood, of course, had established his career with a range of Westerns as both an actor and director before the Dirty Harry films appeared, and his image as a readily identifiable Western protagonist undeniably influenced how audiences read Harry Callahan at the time of the film's release. The next chapter explores how genres like the Western have accommodated the rape-revenge trope, and once again proposes that rather than presenting a unified treatment of rape, across this and other genres, rape-revenge films are diverse and often contradictory.

CHAPTER TWO

The Rape-Revenge Film Across Genres

Rape and revenge appear across a range of generic frameworks, and while the first chapter has sought to examine the most well-known rape-revenge films, the rest of this book will demonstrate that broad, diverse and often contradictory treatments of sexual violence exist well beyond this loosely-defined canon. This chapter explores both the diversity and potential complexity with which rape and revenge can appear in horror and the Western, as well as other genres where they may not necessarily be expected. Take comedy, which is surely tonally inappropriate for such a serious subject. At the heart of the rape-revenge comedy lies the controversial question, "can rape jokes be funny?" As Rebecca Solnit wrote in 2015, there are complexities to the power dynamics within rape jokes that contain the *potential* at least for subversion:

> That rape jokes aren't funny was an axiom assuming that rape jokes are at the expense of the victim.... People then drew a distinction between punching down (mocking the less powerful) and punching up (aiming at the privileged, the status quo, maybe even striking blows against the empire). The rape joke as it then existed was all about punching down.[1]

For Solnit, women comics of the caliber of Tina Fey and Amy Schumer making fun of (now convicted, then alleged) rapist Bill Cosby "marks the rise of feminist comedy in the mainstream and the weakening of rape culture. There is no more clear changing of the guard than this."[2] Solnit's observations—and the implication that rape jokes can be not only feminist, but funny when they mock the perpetrator—are useful for approaching a number of films that at first glance are overwhelmingly offensive simply by virtue of being so seemingly tone deaf to joke about such a horrific subject.

Looking for the intersection of rape and revenge in comedy can lead to surprising places. While by no means a rape-revenge film per se, Spike Jonze's *Being John Malkovich* (1999) illustrates the various ways that sex, violence and vengeance can intersect. Craig (John Cusack) locks his wife Lotte (Cameron Diaz) in a cage so he can "be John Malkovich" in order to have sex with Maxine (Catherine Keener). Maxine believes she is having sex with Lotte in Malkovich's body, when in fact Craig has used violence against Lotte to procure sexual penetration with Maxine. When Maxine discovers the truth, she and Lotte enact their revenge against Craig, and the film ends with the two women romantically united as Craig is punished. The women seek revenge against him as punishment for his decision to use violence to gain sexual penetration. Although certainly far from what is readily identifiable as a rape-revenge plot, this example suggests that rape and revenge may intersect and co-exist in film far more elastically.

Even without a revenge component, filmic comedy rape may also appear as the source of incongruous hilarity. The most cursory survey offers a diverse range of titles that include rape or attempted rape in some way, including *Pretty Woman* (Garry Marshall, 1990), *Sixteen Candles* (John Hughes, 1984), *Switch* (Blake Edwards, 1991), and *Revenge of the Nerds* (Jeff Kanew, 1984). Revisiting the latter film in a #MeToo context, the director of *Revenge of the Nerds* clearly regretted the scene in question, noting, "it's not excusable. If it were my daughter, I probably wouldn't like it."[3] But it is in the terrain of black comedy where rape-revenge has proven richest. While recent examples of rape-revenge themed black comedies include *Big Bad Wolves*, *Three Billboards Outside Ebbing, Missouri*, and *Promising Young Woman*, an earlier and far more explicit intersection of rape-revenge and comedy can be seen in Michael Winner's darkly satirical *Dirty Weekend*. The film returned its director once again to the terrain of rape-revenge after *Death Wish* and *Chato's Land*. *Dirty Weekend* is based on Helen Zahavi's controversial novel of the same name, a book that garnered comparisons to Bret Easton Ellis' notorious *American Psycho* (1991) that was released in the same year. Winner co-wrote the script for this black comedy with Zahavi, and the film was as controversial as the novel when released (it was banned by the British censor on video for a number of years). After a series of humiliations at the hand of her uncaring and promiscuous boyfriend in London, mousy bella (Lia Williams) moves to Brighton on the British seaside for a new beginning. Despite the superficial festivity of her new surrounds, Bella discovers—like so many of her female rape-avenging comrades—that sexual threat encircles her. A neighbor aggressively stalks her, and the policeman who comes to her assistance is equally as menacing. As the threats from her stalker become increasingly more disturbing, Bella awakens one morning and declares that she's "had enough." She visits a psychic who deliberately provokes her and, handing her a knife, tells her: "You hold the answer in your hand … murderer or victim, take your pick." From this point onwards, the new *femme fatale* Bella takes control. She finds her prey is not difficult to locate, as her world is riddled with revolting, aggressive and violent men, some of whose excessive repulsiveness borders upon the comic (like Michael Cole's sadistic academic Norman, or David MacCallum's sleazy dentist Reggie). That it is not until late in the film that Bella is actually sexually assaulted seems neither here nor there—the threat has been constant, and she makes it clear from the film's opening moments that it is only a matter of time before verbal threats take physical form.

There is nothing "funny" about *Dirty Weekend* or its subject matter, but the bleakly sarcastic tone of its narrator throughout the film culminates in a strangely detached, bitterly ironic victory as she leaves Brighton to continue her rampage against misogynists. *Dirty Weekend* is a corrupted fairy tale from the outset, beginning with the protagonist's voiceover declaring, "This is the story of Bella, who woke up one morning and realized she'd had enough." Narrating her own story in the third-person, Bella exists outside of herself, and the film suggests that she, too, watches herself go through the "motions" of rape-revenge along with the spectator. Feminist responses to the book were divided but tended not to stray far from Elizabeth Wilson's dismissal of it as "repellent." The fact that Michael Winner directed the film tended to render its ideological status as an open-and-shut case (Winner, as she puts it, is "not exactly well-known for his feminist credentials"[4]). While the film is doubtlessly as exploitative as the book upon which it is based, and the director has a history of making rape-revenge films deemed "problematic" at best (in terms of their gender politics), there is, regardless, something refreshing about Lia Williams' performance as such a self-aware protagonist. The sarcastic knowingness of her voiceover implies that she is fully aware of the rape-revenge traditions that she now participates in. Whether audiences find this as amusing as Bella is open for debate, but there is no doubt that she herself finds it the source of great humor.

Another black comedy—this time with a horror twist—is *Teeth* (2007), which tells the story of Dawn (Jess Weixler), who the film introduces as a young child in a wading pool on the front lawn of a suburban house near a nuclear power plant. Her mean stepbrother Brad shares the pool with her, and after a series of harassing comments he exposes his hand from below the water to reveal his bleeding finger. Moving forward to the present day, Dawn is a key figure in her high school's Christian Abstinence movement, but after meeting the attractive Tobey (Hale Appleman) she finds her vow of chastity challenged. With her feelings reciprocated, Tobey and Dawn kiss at a deserted swimming area. Tobey's arousal intensifies, and when Dawn asks him to stop, he rapes her. To Dawn's surprise—as much as his—Tobey is castrated as he penetrates her. Shocked at what has happened, Dawn's research leads her to believe she has teeth in her vagina. She seeks the advice of a gynecologist to confirm her diagnosis, and she severs his fingers when she senses an inappropriate pleasure on his behalf during her internal examination. Returning home, she finds her ill mother dying on the floor of their house while her brother (John Hensley) has sex with his girlfriend and ignores her mother's condition. With her mother in the hospital and close to death, Dawn turns to her friend Ryan (Ashley Springer) and consents to have sex with him. Initially, as the act is consensual, Ryan is not castrated. But when Dawn realizes he had placed a bet on her willingness to have sex with him, she engages him in coitus once more and this time castrates him with her vaginal teeth. In the film's climactic scene, she confronts the lecherous and selfish Brad, and—knowing that he had always been sexually attracted to her—she seduces him. At the same moment that Brad remembers that the cause of his cut finger in the film's opening scene was a bite from Dawn's vagina when he molested her in the wading pool, Dawn castrates him as an act of revenge for her mother's death. The film concludes as Dawn hitchhikes out of town. She is picked up by an elderly man who demands sexual payment, and Dawn looks toward the camera. Like *Descent* and *Straightheads* (discussed shortly) *Teeth* finishes with a look toward the audience. Here, however, the intent is comical: "Oh-oh!" Dawn seems to be thinking, "Here we go again!"

Teeth was not the first rape-revenge film to center on the concept of vagina dentata; at the very least, *Penetration Angst* (Wolfang Wolfgang Büld, 2003) pre-dated it by four years. In *The Monstrous Feminine: Film, Feminism, Psychoanalysis* (1993), Barbara Creed has noted that "the myth about woman as castrator clearly points to male fears and fantasies about the female genitals as a trap, a black hole which threatens to swallow them up and cut them into pieces." Additionally, it "also points to the duplicitous nature of woman, who promises paradise in order to ensnare her victims."[5] Creed offers a range of metaphorical and literal instances of vagina dentata in pre–1993 horror films that support her central claim of a dominant "monstrous-feminine." Re-evaluating Laura Mulvey's identification and analysis of a sadistic male gaze that dominates the cinematic apparatus, Creed contends that while "the presence of the monstrous-feminine in the horror film speaks to us more about male fears than about female desire or feminine subjectivity … this presence does challenge the view that the male spectator is almost always situated in an active, sadistic position and the female spectator in a passive, masochistic one."[6]

Creed's theory about vagina dentata and the horror film comes to life in *Teeth*, which presents the flip side to the male fears of castration and feminine duplicity that vagina dentata represents. Dawn's ability to punish her rapists at the point of penetration is presented as a blackly comic feminist fantasy. Perhaps unsurprisingly, this raises some complications for *Teeth*. While many critics praised its sense of fun and Jess Weixler's natural and sympathetic portrayal of Dawn, Lichtenstein's undeniable talents for getting an ironic laugh in many instances overshadow the simple fact that Dawn is horrified as much—or even more—by her *own* body as she is by the sexual assaults themselves. Yes, her biting vagina is a rape-avenging weapon, but the rapes themselves do not appear to be so much her real problem as the fact that her vagina has teeth *at all*. Consequently, that the one time that Dawn consents and finds sex pleasurable goes so horribly wrong renders her discovery of sexual pleasure as tainted. As Kyle Buchanan points out, considering the film seems to support Dawn's sexual awakening (many of its funniest scenes are those that openly mock the abstinence ideals at the start of the film), that the one time Dawn is able to enjoy sex turns into yet another scene where she is forced to castrate means that "for a movie that purports to celebrate female sexuality, scenes like that really bite."[7] Dawn's look-to-camera in the film's final scene implies that she is reconciled with both her unusual talent and its particular utility in protecting herself against sexual predators. While Buchanan and my distaste for *Teeth* appears to be anomalous,[8] that this reconciliation comes with an acceptance of herself as "the monstrous-feminine" and at the expense of her being able to enjoy sex in its own right, however, renders *Teeth* far from uncomplicated.

Castration appears more explicitly thanks to an enormous pair of scissors in Sam Ashurst's astonishingly original 2020 rape-revenge black comedy, *A Little More Flesh*. The setup is as simple as it is effective; the film's main character is a filmmaker called Stanley Durall (James Swanton on camera, with Ashurst providing Stanley's voice uncredited) who we almost solely hear off-camera as he records an audio commentary to accompany a home entertainment release of his controversial first film, *God's Lonely Woman*. We learn early on the reason for this controversy; the two women who appeared in the film— Candice Embers (Hazel Townsend) and the star of *God's Lonely Woman*, Isabella Dotterson (Elf Lyons, who co-produced the film with Ashurst)—would die by suicide, clearly as a result of horrendous sexual harassment and abuse. In both Candice and Isabella's case, this culminates in rape; statutory rape in the case of 14-year-old Candice who Stanley seems to disgracefully interpret with shocking casualness her sexual relationship with the film's adult cinematographer, and in the case of Isabella, a gang-rape at the hands of two dangerous non-professional actors Stanley hired for the film and explicitly instructed to assault Isabella for the film's climactic scene. As a character study, Stanley is a masterful demonstration of someone being given enough rope to hang themselves. Here the film is fascinating—among many other reasons—for the way it subverts his authorial voice even as it literally drowns out that of the two women he drove to suicide. Stanley's commentary runs the gamut of casual sexism to outright violent misogyny and it is his own words that paint him as such a thoroughly monstrous figure. As he dominates the surface of the film, the revenge component manifests more formally as Isabella and Candice appear in brightly colored, abstracted flashes with increasing frequency throughout the film, haunting Stanley and *God's Lonely Woman* itself until the final scene where Isabelle appears—finally able to speak. With her impressively large scissors, Isabella avenges both her and Candice's rapes that drove them to their early graves as Stanley is forced from the recording booth into the movie *God's Lonely Woman* itself, appearing in the very barn where Isabella was raped.

Chapter Two. The Rape-Revenge Film Across Genres   59

Bedeviling their abusers: Candice (Hazel Townsend, left) and Isabella (Elf Lyons) look off-screen at the cinematographer and director of *God's Lonely Woman* in *A Little More Flesh* (Sam Ashurst, 2020) (courtesy Sam Ashurst).

A Little More Flesh is both very funny and politically powerful, largely because the humor stems from Stanley's repulsiveness, oblivious to how repugnant he is. Ashurst and the bulk of his collaborators (except for Swanton) came from a comedy background, so the comic element was not incidental. "I'd researched the laughter impulse, and discovered some people believe laughter originated as a fear response, as a noise that acted as a warning when confronted with shock or surprise," he said.[9] For Ashurst, while the audio commentary format was a creative response to budget limitations, and the headlines about Harvey Weinsten at the time he was developing his project reminded him of his mother and her stories of working as a model and an actress in the 1960s and 1970s (some of Isabella's experiences at Durrell's hands—such as being spiked with LSD—were based on his mother's lived experience). In an earlier version of the story, Ashurst saw the roles being reversed between Stanley and Isabella, where "the director would get pushed into the film, where he'd be tortured at length, and she would take over the commentary, to take charge of her own story." Lyons, however, was unmoved by this suggestion, telling Ashurst, "Nah, I just want to cut his cock off." Instantly recognizing the eloquence of this gesture in the context of the film, Ashurst agreed. Yet to make this so effective, it was important that Stanley's monstrosity was carefully developed. For Ashurst, it was essential to make him "someone you could almost feel sorry for in those early stages, because he's so pathetic, before he fully reveals himself." Although far from a standard rape-revenge film, Ashurst very much considers *A Little More Flesh* as being in dialogue with the trope. "I really do believe that rape-revenge films can be a positive force for good," he said. "No right-minded person is pro-rape, obviously, but some people don't think about it as much as they should. I wanted this film to be a weapon against some of my audience, and catharsis for the rest…. For me, the most powerful rape-revenge films deliver extreme discomfort, to represent trauma." This tension between catharsis and discomfort lies at the heart of both *A Little More Flesh* and, for Ashurst, rape-revenge more broadly: "The more extreme one is, the more powerful the other can be. I wanted to play with that balance, through the filmmaking itself."

Not all rape-revenge comedies are as dark as *Teeth*, *A Little More Flesh*, or *Dirty Weekend*, of course, as demonstrated in exploitation parodies like *I Spit Chew on Your Grave* and *Mother's Day* (Lloyd Kauffman, 1980). Despite the seriousness of the subject matter, it is hard to not recognize the blatant attempts at bringing levity to both of these films: the humor in *Mother's Day*, for example, stems from the hyperactive viciousness of its "mother" figure, who provokes her hillbilly sons into their violent crimes against the film's female protagonists. Configuring the rape and revenge in direct relation to this controlling matriarch, one of these women murders "mother" in the movie's climax by suffocating her with a pair of giant inflatable breasts. Films such as these demonstrate how broadly rape-revenge has been applied to a range of exploitation sub-genres.

Once a sensitivity to the presence of rape-revenge structures begins to develop, even the antics of the Warner Bros. skunk Pepé Le Pew can be seen to regularly cross the line between seduction and assault. On most occasions, Penelope Pussycat clearly does not enjoy his sexual advances, squirming desperately when he holds her tightly, and running away. But there are a few instances where the tables are turned. In *Little Beau Pepé* (Chuck Jones, 1952), Le Pew joins the French Foreign legion in order to recover from an unspecified heartbreak. On duty, he neglects his post when he sees Penelope Pussycat and attempts to woo her. During his pursuit of the terrified cat (she is repulsed by his terrible odor), Le Pew reflects on what he considers the typical female "no means yes" attitude to romantic contact: "You know, one of the mysteries of my life is why a woman runs away when all she really wish is to be captured." At the end of the cartoon, however, the situation has been reversed. In order to seduce her, Le Pew makes a concoction of exotic perfumes and douses himself in it, causing her to instantly fall in love with him. It is now Le Pew who is terrified and struggling, as she chases him across the desert. "Why is it whenever a man is capture by a woman," he asks rhetorically at the end, "all he wants to do is get away?" He also learns a similar lesson in how distressing unwanted and aggressive sexual attention can be in *For Scent-imental Reasons* (Chuck Jones, 1949).

As Le Pew indicates, even as children the rape-revenge template can be allegorically softened to present mature material in a child-friendly way. Robert Stromberg's 2014 Angelina Jolie vehicle *Maleficent* is a clear example, adapted from the 1959 Disney feature *Sleeping Beauty*, itself inspired by Charles Perrault's classic version of the fairy tale, *La Belle au bois dormant* from 1528. Jolie plays a powerful yet tragic dark fairy whose mission to protect the Moors where she lives are overtaken by a desire for revenge after a violent, vicious betrayal, leading her to curse the young princess whom she later discovers is the key to peace returning to the troubled kingdom. The violent act that has such a transformative impact on Maleficent is her being drugged and having her wings cut off by a lover who betrayed her. Jolie made clear that "we were very conscious, the writer [Linda Woolverton] and I, that it was a metaphor for rape,"[10] which thus by default frames her vengeance as fitting firmly—albeit allegorically—in rape-revenge terrain. This element was not missed by critics, cleverly referenced in the title of William Bibbiani's review of the film, "I Prestidigitate on Your Grave."[11] Aside from Jolie's metaphorical foray into rape-revenge, many big-name women stars have appeared in more overt rape-revenge films, such as Isabelle Huppert in *Elle* (Paul Verhoevenn, 2016) and *The Bedroom Window* (Curtis Hanson, 1987), Demi Moore in *Mortal Thoughts* (Alan Rudolph, 1991), Jennifer Lawrence in *Red Sparrow* (Francis Lawrence, 2018) and Helen Mirren in *The*

Good Liar (Bill Condon, 2019). That all these films are thrillers should not suggest all rape-revenge films in this genre have instant multiplex appeal. While garnering passing mentions by both Carol J. Clover and Jacinda Read, *Positive I.D.* (Andy Anderson, 1986) is long overdue for recognition as one of the more intelligent and subtle deployments of the rape-revenge trope and deserves a reputation equal to Ferrara's *Ms. 45*. Suburban housewife Julie (Stephanie Rascoe) is still deeply traumatized by a rape that occurred before the film began (the rape is never shown), and the opening scenes focus upon her pain and inability to return to a normal life with her devoted but frustrated husband, who is attracted to a female family friend. The film begins a year after her rapist has been put in jail and focuses explicitly upon Julie's difficulties connecting emotionally with those around her—until one day by accident she realizes that she can establish an entirely new identity. Thrilled that Julie is beginning to show some enthusiasm, her husband is unaware that she is building an elaborate new life as the sexy and sophisticated Bobbie King. It is not until "Bobbie" pulls the trigger on her rapist that the spectator is fully aware that her activities have been anything more than post-trauma catharsis: the viewer is excluded from her revenge strategy until after the fact.

The result of this is as simple as it is effective: Julie forces the spectator to understand her emotional process of trauma and recovery *independently* of her wish for vengeance. Julie's desire to be "someone else" is shown very clearly to be separate from her plan for vengeance, as she starts changing her identity be*fore* she hears her rapist is being released. This is made even more apparent at the film's conclusion, where—now totally alienated from her family—she adopts another disguise and leaves her old lives (as Julie and Bobbie) behind her. *Positive I.D.* is unusual (although not alone) in that it is a retrospective rape-revenge film: it is only exposed as a rape-revenge plot after the key acts of vengeance are executed. Until that moment, the ethical questions the film raises are solely to do with the details of Julie's attempts to rebuild her life and—literally—to reconstruct a post-rape identity. The sympathy and compassion for Julie's situation, combined with the fact that the revenge component itself is almost incidental when placed next to this complex emotional portrait, renders *Positive I.D.* one of the more insightful (and underrated) efforts regarding rape trauma, identity and the search for female agency.

Rape-revenge films have even found their way into superhero films, such as cult favorite *Robot Ninja*—made by 19-year-old J.R. Bookwalter in 1989—with even Marvel getting in on the act with *The Punisher: Dirty Laundry* (Phil Joanou, 2012) and the Netflix series *Jessica Jones* (2015–2019). Rape-revenge is an enduring motif across action cinema more broadly such as in films including Sig Shaw's 1985 film *Sudden Death* (whose very title indicates the influence of *Death Wish* and *Sudden Impact*), *Deadbeat* (Harry Kerwin, 1977), *Swift Justice* (Harry Hope, 1987), *High Kicks* (Ruta K. Aras, 1993), *Vigilante* (Aash Aaron, 2008) and *For the Sake of Vicious* (Gabriel Carrer, Reese Eveneshen, 2020). Again, big name actors join Eastwood in *Sudden Impact* and Bronson in *Death Wish* in rape-revenge action films, such as Jason Statham in *Wild Card* (Simon West, 2015), Nicolas Cage in *Vengeance: A Love Story*, and even Sylvester Stallone in the action-western *Rambo: Last Blood* (Adrian Grünberg, 2019). Not all rape-revenge action films concern male protagonists, as demonstrated by Kathy Long's appearance in *The Stranger* (Fritz Kiersch, 1995), cult action star Cynthia Rothrock's *Angel of Fury* (David Worth, 1992), and of course *Blue Steel* (Kathryn Bigelow, 1990) starring Jamie Lee Curtis.

Beyond these rare examples, rape-revenge action films predominantly feature male agents acting on a woman's behalf. The title of *Law Abiding Citizen*, for example, refers to Clyde Shelton (Gerard Butler), a family-loving everyman who deploys an elaborate, high-tech system of vengeance not only against the man who raped and murdered his wife and young daughter, but against the prosecutor (Jamie Foxx), the legal system, and ultimately the entire society who allowed the rapist and killer to go unpunished. The film begins with the invasion of Clyde's family home and the allusion to the rape and murder of his wife and child (shown from Clyde's perspective, he passes out before the details can be shown). Clyde's revenge frequently delves into torture-porn aesthetics, and much of the film's action hinges upon complicated, tech-based torture. In many ways *Law Abiding Citizen* is little more than a standard crime thriller, but Butler's performance as Clyde adds *gravitas* to his many speeches concerning the failure of the law (referring to it at one point as "this broken thing"). Perhaps inescapably, Clyde is punished for taking the law into his own hands, but the supposed victory of the legal system is bitterly framed, particularly as Foxx's prosecutor Nick seems ambivalent at best about the initial crime committed against Clyde's family. On the whole, *Law Abiding Citizen* departs little from male-centered rape-revenge traditions where men act as agents of vengeance for violence committed against female loved ones. This places the ethical logic of the film within the traditions regarding rape as a property crime between men rather than acknowledging the subjective trauma of the female experience of sexual violence.

On the flip side, the centrality of women to action-based rape-revenge films is perhaps nowhere more visible than in girl gang rape-revenge films. Grindhouse classics such as *Black Alley Cats* (Henning Schellerup, 1973) and *Rape Squad* (Robert Kelljan, 1974) feature another popular variation, the rape-avenging girl gang. In the latter, a group of women, unsatisfied with police treatment after they are assaulted by a serial rapist known as the "Jingle Bells Rapist" (named after the song he makes his victims sing during the attacks), band together to form an action group. Initially, the women seek legitimate avenues of resistance and establish a 24-hour rape counseling hotline, but they soon find more aggressive techniques are required and they turn to vigilante tactics. The "Jingle Bells Rapist"—who, with his hockey mask, looks suspiciously like the cult horror figure Jason Voorhees as he appeared in Steve Miner's 1982 film *Friday the 13th: Part III* onwards—is beaten to death at the end of the film after he attempts to assault the key five members of the "rape squad" for a second time. The girl gang avengestress motif continues in later films, including *The Ladies Club* (Janet Greek, 1986), *Lethal Woman* (Christian Marhnam, 1989), *Blood Games* (Tanya Rosenberg, 1990), *A Gun for Jennifer* (Todd Morris, 1996), *Tomboys* (Nathan Hill, 2009), *Bound to Vengeance* (José Manuel Cravioto, 2015), and *Revenge Ride* (Melanie Aitkenhead, 2020). Recalling *Extremities,* the most fascinating thing about many of these films are the fractures that occur among the women as they negotiate their ethics in the face of a preliminarily shared goal or, how they struggle to get other survivors on side and join them. Ashley C. Williams stars in the eponymous role of Matthew A. Brown's *Julia* (2014), the singular aspect of the film's very title revealing a deliberate tension in the film between individual and collective action. After being drugged and gang-raped in the film's opening moments, it is apparent that Julia is experiencing a much longer trauma here implied to be connected to sexual assaults preceding this one. Under the guidance of Dr. Sgundud (Jack Noseworthy), Julia joins a rape-avenging cult of women who steadfastly follow their mentor's instructions for supposedly therapeutic benefit, castrating and murdering the men who have raped the women in the group. However, when Julia goes freelance—avenging her own rape on her *own* terms, outside the ritualistic and significantly male-controlled regime—she is considered an enemy of the group, and Dr. Sgundud prepares to kill her also. Saved by the vampish Sadie (Tahyna Tozzi) who originally got Julia involved with the group, Julia kills not just Dr. Sgundud but Sadie also before leaving the film as she began: a lone wolf. *Julia* presents no vision of solidarity for women if it is dominated by the patriarchy, here personified in the figure of Dr. Sgundud himself. It is, she discovers, merely exchanging one form of violent masculine oppression for another, failing to free her from the suffocating, traumatic restraints of rape culture.

W.A.R.: Women Against Rape (Raphael Nussbaum, 1987) is particularly worthy of note here in that the serial rapist who assaulted many of the women is revealed at the film's conclusion to be one of the policemen assigned to investigating the case. This alone renders *W.A.R.: Women Against Rape* as one of the more intriguing girl gang–centered rape-revenge films. If anything, the movie clearly articulates the connection between the literal violation victims suffer at the hands of rapists and the continuing symbolic violation received by an unsympathetic legal system. But rapist policemen are not rare in rape-revenge films, featuring in films as diverse as *Macon County Jail* (Victoria Muspratt, 1997), *I'll Never Die Alone* (*No moriré sola*, Adrián García Bogliano, 2008), *Twilight Portrait* (*Portret v sumerkakh*, Angelina Nikonova, 2011), and *Even Lambs Have Teeth* (Terry Miles, 2015). In *Ravage* (Teddy Grennan, 2020), the rape survivor is not only hounded by men who are friends with the local police, but the entire film is framed as an interview in a hospital with a disbelieving police officer who dismisses her story as the ravings of a "bat shit crazy" opioid addict.

Rape and revenge are also not uncommon in blaxploitation films, although as Novotny Lawrence indicates, even this label must be understood as having cross-generic reach.[12] On its own, revenge is not an uncommon theme in blaxploitation, as demonstrated in titles such as *Black Sister's Revenge* (Jamaa Fanaka, 1976), *J.D.'s Revenge* (Arthur Marks, 1976), *Ghetto Revenge* (Wendell J. Franklin, 1971) and *Avenging Disco Godfather* (J. Robert Wagoner, 1979). Examples such as *Black Caesar* (Larry Cohen, 1973) and *Black Heat* (Al Adamson, 1976) also illustrate how rape has been deployed in this context, while rape and revenge intersect most visibly in films like *The Black Gestapo* (Lee Frost, 1975) and *Foxy Brown* (Jack Hill, 1974). As Stephane Dunn observes, the union of blaxploitation and rape-revenge has a clear historical context, as "the tough, sexy, avenging black woman personified in *Coffy* and *Foxy Brown* emerged during a period that the B-grade rape and revenge films appeared amid the second-wave feminism of the 1970s."[13] However, it is not only Black women who seek vengeance for rape in this context. Robert A. Endelson's *Fight for Your Life* (1977) plots its "races at war" intent clearly, as a Black family are terrorized by a group of escaped prisoners consisting of a Caucasian, Hispanic and Asian man. When his teenage daughter is raped, the father can take no more and exacts his violent and spectacular retribution. One of the more unusual blaxploitation revenge tales involving sexual violence is *Soul Vengeance* (Jamaa Fanaka, 1975). Here, a Black man survives a beating and attempted castration by white policemen and seeks revenge upon his release by—among other things—strangling a man with his penis. While these films are notable for their diversity, even in such outrageous examples as *Soul Vengeance*, it remains clear that sexual violence and rape is coded in specifically racial terms, becoming a "metaphor for racial power and relations."[14]

Continuing this focus on race, of note here is the video for Rihanna's "Man Down" (2011). Running at just over five minutes in length, it opens with Rihanna shooting a man in a busy train station, with the song beginning as the imagery cuts to a flashback from the previous day. Although she begins smiling and frolicking outside with friends, the action moves to a nightclub that evening where she is sexually assaulted by a man she flirts with but explicitly communicates no interest in having sex with by shaking her head "no" before she leaves. Regardless, he follows her, making the reason for her shooting the "man down" clear as he rapes her in an alley. For Debra Ferreday, the question of race is inextricable from the meaning of the "Man Down" music video:

> What is radical about this depiction of rape, then—albeit a radicalism that was not recognised by many feminist commentators in the mainstream media—is the way it twists the spectator's expectations of the traditional music video. By showing a scene of feminine display culminating not in the consummation of heterosexual romance, but in violence, the viewer is made uncomfortably complicit with the gaze of the rapist. The video hence problematises the violent relations of looking in which black women's pleasure is subject to hostile and violent scrutiny.[15]

As such, for Ferreday "Man Down" "can be read as an act of symbolic revenge against the very regimes of surveillance that produce women's bodies as responsible for the violence they are assumed to engender."[16] For Janell Hobson, the video is closely tied to Rihanna's star persona, particularly at that moment which was so linked to the famous photograph of her injuries resulting from an assault by her then-partner, Chris Brown. In terms of the "Man Down" video then, for Hobson "it is almost as if Rihanna, in the wake of her abuse and the release of the photo of her battered face, has had to engage in a different type of 'dissemblance' to protect her vulnerability and to counter the debilitating image of the 'abused black woman,' who does not make a sympathetic victim." Hobson continues, "black public discourse has reduced the issue to gender stereotypes: either one supports Rihanna against the 'black brute' that Chris Brown had become, or one supports Chris Brown against the 'angry black woman' who must have provoked his batter."[17] Likewise for Ferreday, "Man Down" must be seen through the lens of Rihanna's Blackness, arguing that "Rihanna's work constitutes a protest at the framing of victimhood in which shame 'sticks' to the body of the rape victim, and especially to the bodies of victimized women of colour."[18]

The ubiquity of rape and revenge becomes even clearer when examining a number of perhaps equally surprising music videos and music-related films. Rape and the musical might seem an incongruous fit until one recalls that Stanley Donen's jaunty 1954 golden era musical *Seven Brides for Seven Brothers* is famously based on the Roman myth of "The Rape of the Sabine Women." From David Fincher's music video for Aerosmith's "Janie's Got a Gun" (1989) to Lana Del Rey's "Ride" (Anthony Mandler, 2012), "Man Down" is far from unique as a rape-revenge music video, although the specificity of Rihanna's broader celebrity status make it a profoundly effective example. More lighthearted are the full-length versions of Lady Gaga's music videos "Paparazzi" (Jonas Åkerlund, 2009) and "Bad Romance" (Francis Lawrence, 2009) which present the pop star in narratives where she avenges attempted rapes. For Gaga, the "Bad Romance" video is about the "tough female spirit,"[19] and in this clip she is captured by the Russian Mafia and auctioned off in a sexy routine to the highest bidder. Gaga approaches the buyer as he waits for her in bed, but it explodes into flames as she sings in the foreground. The video ends with her wearing a firework-shooting bra as she lies victoriously next to his burnt skeleton. "Paparazzi" opens as Gaga and her boyfriend (played by Alexander Skarsgård) make out on a balcony. When Gaga sees a photographer, she urges her boyfriend to stop but he does not (she realizes that he has set up the scenario and is in cahoots with the photographer). They struggle as her boyfriend continues to fondle her, and when she hits him he pushes her off the balcony. Recovering from her physical injuries, the music video concludes when Gaga poisons him and is arrested with great media fanfare. "Paparazzi" was followed in 2010 by the sequel video "Telephone" (also directed by Åkerlund). It follows Gaga's time in jail and her subsequent escape with pop singer Beyonce, as the two women drive off in the "pussy wagon" from Quentin Tarantino's 2004 rape-revenge–tinged film *Kill Bill Vol. 1*.

Rape-revenge and music have intersected in feature films, too. In 1981, Dick Lowry's made-for-television adaptation of the 1979 hit Kenny Rogers song "Coward of the County" overtly incorporated a rape-revenge element into its story of the eponymous coward Tommy (Frederic Lehne) whose girlfriend Becky (Largo Woodruff) is gang raped by the menacing Gatlin brothers in response to Becky choosing Tommy over Jimmy Joe Gatlin (William Schreiner). The film's climax finds Tommy joining forces with his until-then pacifist uncle the Rev. Matthew Spencer (played by Rogers himself) in the bar brawl that avenges the rape, proving to the community at large that Tommy is, in fact, no coward. If the rape of Becky sounds incidental, that is because it is. While the rape itself is only implied, the film still features surely one of the most tone-deaf creative decisions in any rape-revenge films ever made—even among more explicit exploitation examples—in the scene where Becky and Tommy reunite after the bar brawl. "It's an unfortunate thing what happened," Tommy tells her as she attempts to give voice to her trauma, "but it didn't just happen to you alone; it happened to both of us." Becky readily accepts this and is magically "cured"; *The Coward of the County* is not her story, after all, and rape is deployed here as a mere plot device to trigger Tommy (and his uncle's) long-held pacifism, making a "man" of him. At the end of the film Tommy victoriously leaves Becky to join the World War II effort which is aggressively signposted throughout the film as the idealized end game for any true patriotic American man.

An altogether different rape-revenge film finds another popular musician at its center; Madonna's notorious first feature film role in *A Certain Sacrifice* by Stephen Jon Lewicki, filmed in 1979 but released in 1985 to profit on the international success of her groundbreaking *Like a Virgin* album. *A Certain Sacrifice* was released in the same year that Madonna made her mainstream cinema debut in Susan Seidelman's *Desperately Seeking Susan*, but while the latter playfully experiments with Madonna's signature wild, carefree "bad girl" star persona at the time, her character Bruna in *A Certain Sacrifice* takes this stereotype to the extreme. Following an unpleasant protagonist called Dashiel (Jeremy Pattnosh), he leaves home and hooks up on the streets with sexually liberated, polyamorous Bruna who has a penchant for sadomasochistic roleplay and lives with a "family of lovers." The film's drama largely follows Dashiel and Bruna's journey towards monogamy, culminating in Bruna being raped in a diner where she and Dashiel are eating. Unlike the aggressively sexualized sadomasochistic group sex scene with Bruna and her lovers earlier in the film, the rape is shown off camera, and it is the image of the broken, distraught, disempowered Bruna that communicates the brutality of the assault compared to the assertiveness with which we had previously seen her engage in consensual sadomasochism. Teaming up with Dashiell and her "family of lovers," the group seduce the rapist and in an indescribable crescendo, Madonna's future fame as a musician seems to be somehow foreshadowed by a revenge sequence that takes place on stage during an elaborate rock band performance. Tied up on stage, the torture of the rapist is literally turned into an on-stage spectacle, the song itself even referring to the rape of women as the scene culminates in a bloody choreographed attack of the rapist himself. The film ends as Dashiell and Bruna make love, continuing the ritualized aspect of the revenge scene as he coats her with what we assume is the blood of the rapist himself.

While broadly synonymous with exploitation and horror, the fact that there is also such a large number of made-for-television rape-revenge movies clearly made with an intended women audience demographic in mind is also worthy of consideration. As Maria Bevacqua has noted, "Beginning in 1972, movies, documentaries and specials produced for television increasingly focused on rape,"[20] coinciding with the growth in public interest in feminist issues alongside the rise of second-wave feminism. In 1974—the same year that Susan Brownmiller's *Against Our Will: Men, Women and Rape* achieved blockbuster status—NBC screened the groundbreaking *A Case of Rape*, directed by Boris Sagal. *Bewitched*'s Elizabeth Montgomery stars as Ellen, who is raped after a night school class. Deciding against reporting the crime to the police or even to her husband, she is soon raped again by the same man, and this time badly beaten. Reporting the second attack, the attention lavished in this movie upon the lack of sympathy of her husband, the police and the legal system in general is generous. As her lawyer tells her at one point, "Never try a rape case unless your victim is a 90-year-old nun with at least four stab wounds." *A Case of Rape* includes no revenge-coded catharsis—that he is found "not guilty" for Ellen's assaults and is shot during an attempted rape of another woman is presented as far from a victory for Ellen. To emphasize this point, the film ends with Ellen divorcing from her emotionally estranged husband. Two years later, another unlikely sitcom star appeared in a TV movie concerning rape, this time more explicitly concerned with rape and vengeance. *Revenge for a Rape* (Timothy Galfas, 1976) stars Robert Reed (familiar to contemporary audiences for his role as Mike Brady in the zeitgeist-defining *The Brady Bunch*) as an inept sheriff in this made-for-television *Deliverance* adaptation. Replacing *Deliverance*'s four men with a heterosexual couple, the rape victim is female, and it is the man who acts as agent for her revenge. Ultimately, however, *Revenge for a Rape* lacks the complexity of *Deliverance* and is little more than a simplistic melodrama.

Rape-revenge TV movies were not confined to their supposed 1970s heyday,[21] of course, with the '90s in particular featuring additions to the category such as *Settle the Score* (Edwin Sherin, 1989), *The Rape of Dr. Willis* (Lou Antonio, 1991), *A Mother's Revenge* (Armand Mastroianni, 1993), the aforementioned *Coward of the County* and *No One Could Protect Her* (Larry Shaw, 1995). So popular was sexual violence as a motif in TV movies from this era that it had even been labeled the "season of rape."[22] One of the many sophisticated engagements with rape-revenge from this category, *No One Could Protect Her* centers on Jessica (Joanna Kerns) and the emotional fallout she suffers after being raped by a home invader. Jessica struggles both with rape trauma itself and with an additional sense of neglect as her well-meaning husband becomes increasingly determined to avenge her rape. His crusade, however, renders him absent to her, both literally and metaphorically. She does not want a vigilante as much as she wants a supportive, caring husband, and the film presents a sensitive portrayal of their relationship as much as it does the more sensational hunt and capture of the rapist himself.

Moving towards the more fantastic terrain of horror cinema, it is worth acknowledging that science fiction movies such as Douglas Cammell's *Demon Seed* (1977), *Inseminoid* (Norman J. Warren, 1981) and *Breeders* (Tim Kincaid, 1986) are all based around sexual violence, and Ernest D. Farino's science fiction film *Steel and Lace* (1991) hinges on a strong rape-revenge plot. Here, a successful young pianist, Gaily Morton (Clare Wren), is viciously gang raped by a group of yuppie real estate developers, lead by the corrupt

Daniel Emerson (Michael Cerevis). When they are found not guilty at trial, a devastated Gaily takes her own life in front of her roboticist brother Albert (Bruce Davison) by throwing herself off the roof of a building. Five years after her death, Albert builds a cyborg "Gaily" and systematically sends her out to kill the rapists as he watches remotely in his lab via a camera he has installed in her. The courtroom artist from Gaily's trial, Alison (Stacy Haiduk), becomes interested in the murders, and her investigation leads her to the cyborg "Gaily," who (with traces of the real-life Gaily's personality becoming more dominant) is becoming increasingly unsure of her brother's orders and lured to the idea of Alison as a potential friend. When Albert asks the cyborg "Gaily" to kill Alison, she defies him. After the execution of Emerson on a rooftop when Albert overrides Gaily's personality, police surround Albert and the cyborg Gaily. Repeating the real Gaily's death, the cyborg Gaily suicides by throwing herself over the edge of the building, this time taking her brother with her.

While aspects of *Steel and Lace* are inescapably problematic (particularly its highly glamorized gang rape scene), the film features the curious incorporation of two types of rape-revenge film. It plays off the tension between a woman seeking to execute her own vengeance with the idea of a man exacting vengeance on the woman's behalf. But where *Sudden Impact* contrasts these two figures through the characters Harry Callahan and Jennifer Spencer, *Steel and Lace* combines that struggle within a single cyborg entity. It *looks* like it is Gaily who acts out the revenge, but it is cyborg "Gaily" acting under the orders of her brother. Consequently, *Sudden Impact*'s battle for narrative supremacy between Spencer and Callahan in *Steel and Lace* becomes a battle over the body of Gaily herself in a *Frankenstein*-like tension between creator and creation.

Peter Lehman bases his discussion of *Steel and Lace* on its assumed male audience, specifically in regard to issues of male spectatorship demonstrated in Albert's watching of the murders committed by the cyborg Gaily.[23] While Lehman is right to note the film's fascination with male spectatorship, it is with a great deal of self-aware dark humor that it makes literal the notion of female bodies as a conduit for male spectatorial pleasure. There are strong elements of black comedy in the film: the chest-propeller blades which the robotic Gaily uses to execute her first victim are as grimly absurd as the scene in *Mother's Day* where Mother is suffocated with giant inflatable breasts. But when Lehman states that the film's "narrative structure makes clear that the seeming female revenge takes place entirely in the service of male desire,"[24] he does not fully acknowledge the fact that plot-wise the film focuses much more on Alison's investigation and Gaily's personality as it struggles in a synthetic body. Both the narrative propulsion and the film's spectacular and often absurd key action scenes rely on the two women much more than they do on the rapists or Albert. To focus only on Albert inflates his centrality and dismisses the core relationship between the film's two female characters, which is pivotal to its climax. There is also a deliberate ambiguity between the two versions of Gaily in the film—the cyborg Gaily commits almost all of her murders in disguise, and it is of note that those disguises are not always necessarily female (one memorable moment shows a supposed male investigator growing breasts as "he" peels off his mask to reveal the cyborg Gaily underneath). Ultimately, the cyborg Gaily is deliberately constructed as a space where Gaily's personality and Gaily's physical form (symbolically controlled by her brother) battle for ownership. The body itself is thus for Albert a kind of perverse technological vengeance doll, and it is against this that Gaily struggles. For obvious reasons, *Steel and Lace* may not readily lend itself to a progressive reading, but to ignore its self-conscious black humor and dismiss the central female-driven narrative misses the fact that in the generic context of science fiction, rape-revenge is often ideologically less clear-cut than has previously been credited. Films such as *Steel and Lace* and those mentioned previously demonstrate the ease with which rape-revenge crosses generic boundaries beyond its assumed realm of horror and the Western.

Westerns and Rape-Revenge Film

Rape-revenge was established as a convention of the Western long before it became synonymous with horror. As Read has observed, rape and revenge in the Western are not just "standard motifs ... they are intimately connected,"[25] a claim supported by films ranging from *The Bravados* (Henry King, 1958), *Chato's Land*, *For a Few Dollars More* (Sergio Leone, 1965), *Kid Vengeance* (Joseph Manduke, 1977), *Hannie Caulder* (Burt Kennedy, 1971), *Last Train from Gun Hill* (John Sturges, 1959) and *The Hunting Party* (Don Medford, 1971), to name but a few. Rape and revenge also manifest in the Western in ways that exist well outside what is most instantly recognizable as a rape-revenge structure. For example, while rape-revenge assumes violence is sought to avenge a rape, in *High Plains Drifter* (Clint Eastwood, 1973) the film's protagonist rapes a woman as part of his revenge.[26] Rape is an inescapable part of the Western environment, as demonstrated in a range of movies, including *Hud* (Martin Ritt, 1963) and *The Outlaw Josey Wales* (Clint Eastwood, 1976). Associations between rape and the American frontier in popular screen cultures find literary heritage in nineteenth-century captivity narratives, whose influence upon the Western cannot be underappreciated. Captivity narratives have also influenced contemporary rape narratives beyond this generic context, including the rape-revenge category more broadly.

The basic structure of the captivity narrative concerns the rescue of "helpless" maidens who have been kidnapped by "natives" at the last possible moment by a "hero." Commonly, this "hero" is rewarded through marriage. For James R. Lewis, the nineteenth-century captivity narrative was intended to either entertain or titillate audiences, or to function as propaganda.[27] Just as the function of rape shifted between entertainment and propagandist captivity narratives, so too did its representation. Those designed to entertain frequently contained "unconsummated threats" of rape, whereas "consummated rapes usually characterized propagandistic literature designed to evoke moral indignation."[28] These narratives were primarily structured in terms of the relationship between the virtuous victim and the villain, and this frequently indicated the primary function of the narrative itself. For Lewis, the ethical articulation of heroes, victims and villains were a crucial part of how the entertainment-focused captivity narratives functioned; but in propagandist captivity narratives, the role of the hero was often deliberately less clear. "The motivation behind captivity propaganda is to involve the reader—to inspire the reader to take up the role of the heroic avenger," he states. As a consequence, this allowed

> male readers of captivity literature [to identify] ... not only with the sexy violence of the hero, but that they also [though usually not consciously] participated imaginatively in the sexual violence of the hero's shadow self, the villain. The guilt aroused by relishing sexual sadistic fantasies could be subsequently purged when the rescuer slew the villain.[29]

This tradition is examined in rape-revenge films that reference Westerns—most notably, in the beginning of *Death Wish IV: The Crackdown* and the ambiguous shot of Harry Callahan at the end of *Sudden Impact*, discussed in the previous chapter.

From *King Kong* (Merian C. Cooper and Ernest B. Schoedsack, 1933) to *The Last of the Mohicans* (Michael Mann, 1992) to *Taxi Driver* (Martin Scorsese, 1976), the legacy of captivity narratives in cinema is strong. Part of its adaptability is the constant reassessment of the ideologies that lay behind the structure, which suited perfectly the wave of revisionist Westerns from the 1960s and 1970s. For Elliot Gruner, modern captivity narratives seek to titillate as they mimic morality tales. Contemporary filmic instances of captivity, he suggests, reduce the impact of rape, as it is little more than a generic requirement of the captive's story:

> Surviving rape or sexual assault is an essential trial which the female captive must face. Such moments of cinematic rape are so persistent that the rape of the female captive has become an assumption, an assumption that negates male responsibility for the crime since such a scene has come to be accepted as inevitable.[30]

From this perspective, the abduction, captivity and implied rape of Debbie (Natalie Wood) in John Ford's *The Searchers* (1956) drives the narrative, as it provides Ethan (John Wayne) and Martin (Jeffrey Hunter) a motive for the "search" of the film's title. The film's power lies in its ability to expose the redundancy of these male "searchers," mirroring threatened white masculinity in a period rocked by the Civil Rights movement. Barbara Mortimer suggests that *The Searchers* re-adapts the conventions of the captivity narrative to speak not of a distant past, but as a coded response to the U.S. Supreme Court's decision in 1954 that segregation in public schools was unconstitutional.[31]

Linda Colley's observation that "captivity narratives have been persistent, protean, profusely distributed over time and often downright plebeian"[32] manifests nowhere more distinctly than in the rape-revenge category. While *Death Wish*, *Sudden Impact*, *Deliverance* and *Straw Dogs* may most immediately demonstrate how closely rape-revenge and the Western sit more generally, the genre—be it produced in an American or non–American context—is littered with references to captivity narratives. While some of these seem to enforce the racist assumptions of the captivity narrative, others appear to subvert them, demonstrating (again) that diverse and often-contradictory treatments and attitudes toward rape can exist at the same time. In terms of rape-revenge films set in the present day, they almost always present as a drama between Whites. Read has noted an absence of Black rape avengers,[33] while Philip Green has stated, "To my knowledge, there has never been a rape-revenge film in which the victim was black and the rapist(s) white."[34] This may in part stem from the fact that "deliberate interracial rape" is uncommon: as one statistic suggests, "88 percent of victims are the same race as the perpetrator."[35] This is not to say that interracial rape is totally absent in rape-revenge film, and Green has since been proven wrong in the rare cases where this does happen: *Descent* (Talia Lugacy, 2007), *Chaos* (David DeFalco, 2005), *A Time to Kill* (Joel Schumacher, 1996), *The Perfection* (Richard Shepard, 2018), *Fight for Your Life* and *Rape Squad*, to name but a few. Of note here, however, is just how diverse these films are in terms of budgets, intended audiences, production contexts, and representations of sexual violence.

Westerns are commonly set in a historical past-tense, so while they sometimes function as symbolic metaphors for contemporary issues (such as in *The Searchers*), there is still some diversity in their treatments of race and rape. *Chato's Land* features a Bronson playing a First Nations man searching for vengeance after white settlers rape his wife. In *Black Jack* (Gianfranco Baldanello, 1968), a gang hires a First Nations man to rape and scalp the sister of the gang's leader, and the film follows the gang leader's retaliation.

Richard C. Sarafian's *The Man Who Loved Cat Dancing* (1973) stars Burt Reynolds as a man on the run from the law after killing the man who raped and murdered his First Nations wife. *The Animals* (Ron Joy, 1970) follows the story of a woman who is nursed back to health by an Apache chief after she is gang raped, and the chief assists in her search for vengeance. Even the adult film *Sweet Savage* (Ann Perry, 1979) plays with captivity narrative traditions in its focus upon the rape of a First Nations girl as punishment for embarking upon a relationship with a white man, and her brother's search for revenge. First Nations politics is not specific to the western rape-revenge film, of course, as seen elsewhere in the horror movie *Avenged*.

The influence of the captivity narrative and its treatment of race transcend the generic borders of the Western. The brazenly "plebeian" original version of *I Spit on Your Grave* references captivity narrative traditions, and as both Joe Bob Briggs[36] and Clover note, "When we hear Johnny and his friends … whooping in the forest outside Jennifer's house at night, we must recognize the trope of the restless natives."[37] Upon closer analysis, *I Spit on Your Grave* responds to the four defining anxieties of the captivity narrative as outlined by Barbara Mortimer. It evokes "a primal fear of physical danger" in the threat of physical violence against Jennifer; the four rapists exhibit a clear and distinct "fear of unrepressed sexuality, especially female sexuality"; the men also inflict their violence upon Jennifer more to perform for each other, indicating "cultural doubt or self-questioning"; and the absence of a non-diegetic soundtrack combined with the minimal dialogue in the film speaks directly to an "anxiety of silence, a tension between what is said and not said."[38] *I Spit on Your Grave* does not simply mimic the structure of the captivity narrative, but reconfigures it. From this perspective, Mortimer's description of how certain character types function within captivity narratives is crucial:

> The hunter is ambiguous in that he inhabits a middle ground between the Indian's "world" (associated with the wilderness and uncultivated nature) and the white woman's "world" (associated with Christianity and civilization). In the captivity narrative, he must use this position between two opposing worlds on behalf of civilization, even though the latter will ultimately destroy the conditions of his own way of life. Thus, the hunter's importance lies in his role as a mediator between two opposing categories, "civilization" and "savagery."[39]

Zarchi's *I Spit on Your Grave* expands this scenario and exposes its flaws by making the hunter and victim one and the same in the figure of Jennifer. In doing so, the lines between "civilization" and "savagery" become murkier. With this allusion to traditional captivity narratives, *I Spit on Your Grave*—not dissimilarly to *The Searchers*, although an aesthetic and reputational chasm away from it—acknowledges a redundancy in the structure, while at the same time acknowledging its influence.

In rape-revenge film, the sexual threat so often implicit to "captivity" is obviously joined by notions of vengeance. Again, in the Western there is a strong heritage of revenge, identified in Will Wright's foundational treatment of the genre's popular "vengeance plot." In *Sixguns and Society: A Structural Study of the Western* (1975), Wright suggests that this particular Western trope had little box-office impact before 1949 and demonstrates a blurring of the ethical legibility of the classical plot that dominated the genre between 1931 and 1955. "Unlike the classical hero who joins society because of his strength and their weakness," he observes, "the vengeance hero leaves society because of his strength and their weakness."[40] From his analysis of *Stagecoach* (John Ford, 1939), *The Man from Laramie* (Anthony Mann, 1955), *One-Eyed Jacks* (Marlon Brando, 1961) and

Nevada Smith (Henry Hathaway, 1966), Wright identifies a number of key features that typify this vengeance plot:

1. The hero is or was a member of society.
2. The villains do harm to the hero and to the society.
3. The society is unable to punish the villains.
4. The hero seeks vengeance.
5. The hero goes outside of society.
6. The hero fights the villains.
7. The hero defeats the villains.
8. The hero gives up his special status.
9. The hero enters society.[41]

This vengeance plot is marked by an ideological shift in the Western hero from the classical plot. In these films, "society is no longer dependent upon the hero for survival, and he is no longer directly involved with it," Wright observes. "Rather, he is directly involved with the villains through his desire for revenge."[42] In a rape-revenge context, this is illustrated in *The Bravados*. The film follows Jim Douglas (Gregory Peck) on his mission to track down and execute the four men he believes raped and murdered his wife. Having been on their trail for six months, the film opens with Douglas' arrival in a town where the men, now captured by the law, are to be executed. He meets his religious ex-girlfriend Josefa (Joan Collins) and soon discovers that the four prisoners have escaped from jail and taken local woman Emma (Kathleen Gallant) hostage. Douglas returns to his hunt, and the first man he finds is Alfonso (Lee Van Cleef), whom Douglas kills despite his victim's denial that he had ever seen Douglas' wife when shown her portrait. Soon thereafter, Douglas finds and kills a second man. The two surviving prisoners happen across the cabin of Douglas' neighbor, John (Gene Evans), whom they kill, and Bill (Stephen Boyd) rapes Emma. Douglas tracks Bill to Mexico, where again he shows him the portrait of his wife; like Alfonso, Bill also denies having seen her. Furious, Douglas kills him as well, and then pursues the last of the group, Lujan (Henry Silva). Lujan's wife knocks Douglas unconscious, and with Douglas now his prisoner, Lujan asks why they have been so viciously pursued. Here, Douglas discovers the four men whom he so mercilessly hunted were, in fact, innocent of the rape and murder of his wife; the crimes were committed by his neighbor, John, whom the gang murdered earlier. Shattered, Douglas cries out "Oh God!" and returns to the church in town to confess. Reunited with both Josefa and with the Church, the joyous townsfolk celebrate the demise of the gang as Douglas realizes that his desire for vengeance blinded him to basic Christian morality.

While *The Bravados* ticks all of the boxes for Wright's Western vengeance plot, from a rape-revenge perspective it deviates in a number of important ways. Firstly, it is a clear reversal of what would later become a common motive for revenge—in films like *Death Wish* and *Sudden Impact*, the male agent exacts his vengeance explicitly because the law is unsatisfactory. But in *The Bravados*, it is Douglas' attempts at justice that prove initially futile—the law plans to execute the gang after Douglas had spent six months trying to find and kill them himself. Secondly, the broader thematic message of the film actively undermines the self-righteousness of Douglas' moral agenda. That its protagonist is driven so aggressively to seek revenge blinds him to the basic issue of the men's guilt for his wife's rape and murder. But it is not only Douglas who neglects this essential fact: the spectators are forced to question their own ethical assumptions also. But revenge is still executed upon the film's rapists, albeit inadvertently: John is punished for his crimes against Douglas' wife, and Bill's suffering is emphasized so as to punish him for raping Emma. In contrast, Lujan—with his sick child and devoted wife, and the fact that he is the messenger of truth for Douglas—is presented as comparatively innocent. The spiritual revelation at the film's conclusion (one that foreshadows that of *The Virgin Spring*'s Töre a few years later) therefore feels slightly too little, too late. While a necessary part of Wright's vengeance plot, Douglas' return to society pales next to the thematic intensity of the fact that he was so off target in his search for vengeance in the first place.

Not all rape-revenge Westerns adhere so closely to Wright's vengeance plot. Read argues that Westerns with a female avenger reconfigure the relationship between rape and revenge as presented in rape-revenge films where a man acts as an agent for a violated woman. The latter tends to treat rape as a property crime between men. As Kate Millett describes it, "Traditionally rape has been viewed as an offense one male commits upon another—a matter of abusing 'his woman.'"[43] For Susan Brownmiller, rape was a crime that one man committed against the "property" of another man, and the establishment of rape as a criminal offence therefore "entered the law through the back door."[44] This manifests in the Western rape-revenge film (and rape-revenge films more generally) as a male avenger who responds to the "theft" (rape) of a man's "property" (woman). Most commonly, says Read, this is a wife or fiancée, but the diversity of these relationships adds to the potential variety of the trope. A brief survey offers a range of significant instances that support this diversity. *Rancho Notorious* (Fritz Lang, 1952) concerns the rape of the protagonist's fiancé, and

Poster for *The Bravados* (Henry King, 1958) featuring Gregory Peck. © 20th Century-Fox Film Corp. (Everett Collection, Inc./Alamy Stock Photo).

films including *The Bravados, His Name Was King* (Giancarlo Romitelli, 1971), *Cole Justice* (Carl Bartholomew, 1989) and *Cut Throats Nine* (Joaquín Luis Romero Marchent, 1972) involve the rapes of wives and girlfriends. Sisters are also popular victims, as demonstrated in examples like *Black Jack, I Want Him Dead* (*Lo voglio morto*, Paolo Bianchini, 1968), *The Long Cavalcade of Vengeance* (*Lunga cavalcata della vendetta*, Tanio Boccia, 1972) and *Django Does Not Forgive* (*Mestizo*, Julio Buchs, 1966). Even mothers are not spared, as in *Death Rides a Horse* (*Da uoma a uomo*, Giulio Petroni, 1967) and *Kid Vengeance*, where a young Leif Garrett avenges the rape and murder of his mother. Other films demonstrating the diversity of the rape-revenge Western include *The Man with a Shotgun* (*Sandanju no otoko*, Seijun Suzuki, 1961), *Hot Spur* (Lee Frost, 1968), *Red Hill* (Patrick Hughes, 2010), *Brimstone* (Martin Koolhoven, 2016), *Wind River* (Taylor Sheridan, 2017), *Marlina the Murderer in Four Acts* (Mouly Surya, 2017), and *Flatland* (Jenna Bass, 2019). Even the Sylvester Stallone vehicle *Rambo: Last Blood*—while ostensibly an action film—adheres to the rape-revenge western tradition, following the abduction, drugging and forced prostitution of Rambo's business partner's granddaughter by a Mexican drug cartel. While Rambo rescues her, she dies of a forced drug overdose, thus forcing Rambo into a showdown with the cartel's leaders.

Read claims that second-wave feminism provided a new context for rape and revenge to be understood in the context of the Western, and in examples such as these, "rape is not a crime against women … [but] a crime whose social resonance to a patriarchal society is symbolized through the villains' robbery."[45] Just as other genres focused on women avenging their own rapes, so similar patterns emerged in the Western.[46] Read's analysis of this type of female-centered Western rape-revenge film focuses on *Hannie Caulder* and *Handgun* (Tony Garnett, 1983), and considers how the shift to a female-centered vengeance narrative responds to Wright's vengeance plot. For Read, these films suggest a shift from a male vs. female binary, to a more conceptual feminine/private vs. masculine/public one; and "these films engage with and attempt to make sense of some of the more sophisticated and complex debates and oppositions put on the agenda by feminism" during this period.[47]

Female-centered rape-revenge Westerns superficially assume a rejection of women as male property. Women are not objects to be fought over, but rather active agents seeking to right a wrong committed against them. The supposed autonomy of *Hannie Caulder*'s title character is suggested through her dress alone, as she spends much of the first part of the film in a poncho and fedora highly reminiscent of Clint Eastwood's loner protagonist in *A Fistful of Dollars* (Sergio Leone, 1964).[48] Hannie (Raquel Welch) is raped and her husband murdered by the Clemens Brothers (played by Ernest Borgnine, Jack Elam and Strother Martin), who happen upon their remote home after a failed robbery. Shattered, Hannie meets bounty hunter Luther Price (Robert Culp), who is sympathetic to her situation and teaches her the skills necessary for her revenge. She develops romantic feelings towards Price during her training, and the Clemens Brothers continue their often comically inept criminal endeavors. Despite Price's ethical protestations, Hannie insists on carrying out her vengeance, and the Clemens Brothers kill Price when he attempts to hand them over to the sheriff before Hannie can locate them. With her desire for revenge now even stronger, she confronts one brother in a whorehouse and another in a perfume shop, and swiftly executes them. Hannie tracks the final brother to a prison, but her skills fail her. She is saved at the last moment by a mysterious man in black who had appeared earlier in the film, and he shoots the final rapist dead. The film's final shot shows Hannie riding back to town with the last corpse alongside the mysterious man, implying that she is now a bounty hunter herself, and suggesting a future romantic involvement with the stranger.

While placing a woman at the center of a Western rape-narrative may suggest a step forward in its inherent rejection of the "woman as male property" tradition, *Hannie Caulder* as a whole forbids such a simplistic reading. On the one hand, Hannie succeeds in gaining her revenge without losing her femininity—as Read notes, Hannie does not need to choose between a male (aggressor) and female (victim) identity, but rather she renegotiates gender difference by reprogramming notions of femininity itself to suit her needs.[49] On the other hand, this model of femininity is hypersexualized, and the very presence of superstar Welch herself (who spends much of her onscreen time half-naked) makes the film's desire to titillate inescapable. Even more challenging is the emphasis throughout the film upon the comic and bumbling ineptness of the Clemens Brothers. Verging frequently on slapstick, they are not presented as evil or dangerous, despite their violent assault of Hannie and the murder of her husband. In the pursuit of her vengeance, Hannie is therefore not required to demonstrate skill or strength as such, but merely to prove that she is not as hopeless as they are. Read notes that the only places where Hannie is successful in her attempts to kill the Clemens Brothers is in spaces coded as feminine—a perfume shop and a brothel—where "heterosexual femininity is traditionally reproduced and transformed."[50] Beyond these spaces, men are still a necessity—she needed Price to train her, and she needed the mysterious man in black to save her at the film's climax.

For Read, female-centered Western rape-revenge films such as *Hannie Caulder* and *Handgun* support her broader argument that the rape-revenge narrative structure seeks to articulate the tensions between feminism and femininity. While set in contemporary urban Texas, her selection of *Handgun* as her second case study illustrates this point well. As she indicates, the film explicitly relies upon Western mythology and character types.[51] Issues of genre aside, *Handgun* is a remarkable film for a variety of reasons, first and foremost as it concerns a date rape. In perhaps a surprising number of rape-revenge films, rapists are commonly either strangers or distant acquaintances. As Lisa M. Cuklanz has noted, in screen fictions "date and acquaintance rape will never lend themselves to the moral clarity of violent stranger rape ... stranger rape is clearly non-consensual [whereas] date and acquaintance rape are more ambiguous, especially if weapons and physical violence are not involved."[52]

Handgun follows Kathleen (Karen Young), a teacher who relocates to Texas to take up a position at a high school. At a party she meets lawyer Larry (Clayton Day), a gun-collector with a roving eye and a penchant for Westerns. The two begin a tentative relationship, but after-dinner drinks one evening turn into a refused sexual advance, and Larry rapes Kathleen at gunpoint. Lying in bed next to the frightened and devastated Kathleen, Larry embarks upon terrifying, intimate chatter completely inappropriate to the situation. The audacity with which he begins to smoothly psychoanalyze what he perceives as her frigidity demonstrates just how dangerously unhinged he is. With little help from the police, her lawyer and a priest (who tells her to forgive and pray for her rapist's soul), Kathleen cuts her long hair short and joins Larry's gun club. She spends a large portion of the film developing her firearm skills in front of an increasingly nervous Larry. At the film's climax, Kathleen lures Larry out to the deserted gun club at night, where she shoots him with a tranquilizer, then dumps his body in front of the courthouse. Showing him humiliated and humbled in the hospital, the film ends as Kathleen returns to school, smiling and victorious.

Kathleen's story is rich with references to the Western. The high school musical performance of *Seven Brides for Seven Brothers* that opens the film acknowledges the heritage of rape in frontier mythology, and at one point she even asks Larry explicitly if he sees himself as John Wayne or Alan Ladd. As Jacob Knight observes, "When asked whom his favorite movie star is early on, Larry replies, 'John Wayne—he's a real man, not like these faggots they have on TV now.' This may be the ultimate summation of *Handgun's* worldview when it comes to those who make up this bullet-riddled cabal. Pacifists are pussies. The gun is God. Women submit." Knight continues, however, that "Kathleen's embracement of this 'man's world' attitude is the ultimate subversion of its tenets. She turns the tables on its members and ensures that nobody will ever touch her again…. Tony Garnett actually embraces a woman protagonist and her mission to transform her trauma into the domination of a culture itself, not just the chastisement of her aggressors."[53] Kathleen is a woman who has been forced to take action in what the film suggests is specifically masculine terrain. This is emphasized in the lengthy sequences of Kathleen's training under the watchful eye of an all-male peer group; and what in many films would be swiftly communicated in a rapid-cut montage sequence here takes up a large amount of screen time. The matter-of-fact nature of both her approach to training and her trainer's approach to her reiterates the shift from feminine to masculine. The final image of Kathleen in the film marks a return to a new kind of femininity that she has negotiated on her own terms.

Despite *Handgun's* obvious engagement with the Western, there are other female-centered Westerns concerning rape and revenge that more immediately encourage comparisons with *Hannie Caulder*. The 1976 spaghetti Western *The Belle Starr Story* is a case in point. Originally helmed by director Lina Wertmüller, who departed the project after only a few days and Piero Cristofani took over directing duties under the shared alias Nathan Wich. Wich. This was an adaptation of the real-life female outlaw's life story that—like *Belle Star* (Irving Cummings, 1941), *Court-Martial* (George B. Seitz, 1928), *Belle Star's Daughter* (Lesley Selander, 1946) and *Montana Belle* (Allan Dwan, 1952)—showed little interest in historical accuracy. *The Belle Star Story* opens during a poker game where Belle (Elsa Martinelli), dressed in men's clothing, plays and drinks at a table of men in a saloon. The enigmatic bandit Blackie (George Eastman) takes Belle on one on one, and when he asks her to use her own body as the stakes, she throws the game and ends up alone with him in a bedroom. Even from these early stages, their relationship is volatile and passionate. Their first encounter darts between intense passion and violence on both their parts, and Belle has flashbacks to images of sexual violence throughout. Telling Blackie that the only man who ever tried to have sex with her is now dead, Belle explains to Blackie through flashbacks how her reputation as an outlaw began. Belle—then Mirabelle—befriended a man called Cole in Missouri who was a lost childhood friend. Teaching her how to shoot and galvanizing what Belle saw as a solid friendship, the two form a gang and undertake to steal horses. Belle's excitement at the news that her Uncle Jonathan had arranged a marriage fades at the discovery that the man is old and ugly, and the marriage was only to assist her uncle's political career. She runs away to stay with Cole, but soon hears that her uncle had raped her servant Rappica and used his position to set her up to be hanged. Belle takes Cole's gun to save Rappica and murders her uncle. On her return, Cole is furious that he was left without a weapon, and he attempts to rape Belle—this time, it is Rappica who rescues Belle. The second half of the film returns to the present, where Belle and Rappica become involved in a jewel heist, and Belle's relationship with Blackie becomes increasingly hostile. Although seemingly now enemies, Belle saves Blackie from being tortured, and at the end of the film the couple agree that their love-hate relationship "will always be like this." Rape and revenge are key elements of *The Belle Starr Story* that actively pertain to Belle's struggle for autonomy in an overwhelmingly violent, male-dominated world. That an on-again-off-again relationship with the volatile Blackie is the best the film can do to reach a romantic conclusion highlights how damaged Belle is in terms of her relationships with misogynistic and aggressive men.

Al Adamson's *Jessi's Girls* (1975) is also readily identifiable as a Western in terms of its surface iconography and features not one but four women at the core of this female-centered rape-revenge story. Director Adamson is a familiar name to trash film fans and was a prolific director during the 1960s and 1970s when he produced low-budget movies, predominantly in the horror genre. Despite featuring his signature high dose of nudity and sex, *Jessi's Girls* is a useful point of comparison to *Hannie Caulder*—upon whose mainstream success it shamelessly seeks to profit—for a variety of reasons, particularly in regard to its treatment of female agency. The film opens on a happy young Mormon couple, Jessica (Sondra Currie) and Seth (Rigg Kennedy), in their covered wagon as they relocate from Utah to Arizona. They are hijacked by a group of five men who murder Seth and rape Jessica. Believing she is dead, they leave the traumatized woman to heal her wounds and bury her husband. An elderly man called Rufe (Rod Cameron) takes Jessica into his house, nurses her back to health and teaches her how to shoot. Deciding upon revenge, and knowing she needs assistance in her mission of revenge, Jessica intercepts a wagon carrying three female prisoners being transported for trial, and the women form a gang. From here, the film focuses upon the politics between the women as they support the now masculinely-dressed "Jessi" in her search for vengeance. The film's exploitative intent is impossible to escape, and much of the movie hinges upon softcore sex scenes (including an explicit and ugly gang rape scene) and Russ Meyer–style girl-fights. But unlike Hannie, Jessi was at least able to kill her rapists outside space marked as specifically feminine, and she did not need male assistance to do so. The exploitative and graphic nature of *Jessi's Girls* make it one of the nastier female-centered rape-revenge Westerns, and while only brief, its rape scene is so violent that it draws comparisons to the much lengthier sequence in the original *I Spit on Your Grave*. The all-girl Western perhaps reached the peak of its public visibility in the 1990s with Jonathan Kaplan's *Bad Girls* (1994), a film about a group of prostitutes who team up to avenge a range of gender-based injustices, including attempted rape. Kaplan did not receive the same accolades he did with *The Accused* only a few years earlier, despite returning to the familiar terrain of gender and violence. *Bad Girls* is marked by a radical shift not only in generic focus, but also in its campy tone. Referring to documentation from this earlier imagining of the film that was to have been directed by Tamra Davis, for Christina Lane, "the Davis version would have commented unrelentingly on the women's lack of agency by framing them in relation to phallic power … a specifically male power that must be forcefully wrested back into women's control."[54] Regardless of how Davis's film may have differed from Kaplan's, once again it is clear that a broad range of attitudes about rape can co-exist in film, even within the generic confines of the Western. The same is also true of the horror film.

Horror and Rape-Revenge Film

The assumption that movies depicting violent and graphic scenes of rape belong to the horror genre makes sense in terms of semantics alone: rape is horrifying, it is *horrible*. Remembering her earliest traumatic horror film experience, filmmaker Karyn Kusama cited the little-known rape-revenge film *Buster and Billie* (Daniel Petrie, 1974), recalling, "That scene of that rape, which felt very much like you were with her and her horror of the experience, was incredibly transformative for me, and wasn't strictly horror. But I experienced it as my first horror memory."[55] It is therefore unsurprising that films containing graphic depictions of rape encourage a generic approach, if only in order to quarantine such conceptually difficult material in an attempt to isolate it as a dark curiosity or a monstrous abnormality. As Read has convincingly argued—and has been illustrated in this chapter thus far—to consider rape-revenge only as a subgenre of horror risks misidentifying its diversity and broader cultural significance. At the same time, however, to dismiss horror altogether because of this ignores what is an undoubtedly important element of rape-revenge, one well deserving of critical investigation. Horror cinema is useful to an analysis of rape-revenge film if only because of horror's particular treatment of the body. Linda Badley notes that that "horror's language is somatic, communicating on a preliterate, subconscious level."[56] Horror predominantly occurs through, on and around bodily spaces, and is often predicated upon bodily harm (or, at least, the threat of bodily harm). The frequent and excessive focus in the horror film upon visceral bodies emphasizes its defining generic sense of the theatrical and the fantastic, and a heightened awareness of physicality both on the screen and within the spectator themselves.

Linda Williams has argued that post–*Psycho* (Alfred Hitchcock, 1960), horror has been riddled with "sexually disturbed but entirely human monsters."[57] In this sense, it is little surprise that the genre's sexual predators who most immediately attract critical attention are those with a psychological make-up most closely resembling "real-life" perpetrators. While literal rape is not rare in horror—as demonstrated by its presence in texts ranging from *Cannibal Holocaust* (Ruggero Deodato, 1980) to *Hollow Man* (Paul Verhoeven, 2000)—its metaphorical presence is even more expansive. Most immediately, the ubiquity of symbolic rape in horror is critically understood through the phallic nature of the knife, a weapon frequently employed in slasher films in particular. For Clover, "knives … are personal, extensions of the body that bring attacker and attacked into primitive, animalistic embrace."[58] This symbolic relationship between knife and phallus predates feminist film criticism, Diane Wolfthal identifying a historical precedent in both art and literature with the dagger and sword as stand-ins for the penis and phallic male power.[59] From this perspective, films including *Psycho*, *Peeping Tom* (Michael Powell, 1960) and *Halloween* (John Carpenter, 1978) can be situated in critical debates about rape and horror, as the violence in these examples can be understood as violent and penetrative in a more general sense. But in the case of rape-revenge specifically, there are more direct examples that can be discussed, including films such as *Pigs* (Marc Lawrence, 1973), *Deadly Virtues: Love.Honour.Obey* (Ate de Jong, 2014) and *Wildling* (Fritz Böhm, 2018), as well as the many other films explored in this section.

This section will consider both supernatural horror and examples grounded in a less fantastic realm. Of the latter category, the most notorious examples today still surely include Wes Craven's *The Last House on the Left*, which, while itself an adaptation of Bergman's *The Virgin Spring*, has spawned a number of explicit and implicit remakes.

As will be discussed further, despite what is often a clear attempt to profit from the success of Craven's film, these *Last House* knockoffs demonstrate that rape can be treated in a variety of ways even across films that share similar plot elements. This shift from the rape-revenge ultraviolence of the original versions of *The Last House on the Left* and *I Spit on Your Grave* towards a slasher aesthetic can be identified in a range of films including *Nail Gun Massacre*, *Cherry Falls* (Geoffrey Wright, 2000), *Silent Bloodnight* (Elmar Weihsmann and Stefan Peczelt, 2005), *Romina*, and *Initiation* (John Berardo, 2020). *Demented* (Arthur Jeffreys, 1980) begins with the violent gang rape of Linda (Sallee Elyse). Despite the fact her rapists are imprisoned, Linda has ongoing hallucinations of men invading her home and attacking her. Compounding her situation is her unfaithful and increasingly hostile husband, Matt (Harry Reems, under the alias Bruce Gilchrist). While earlier in the film it is clear that Linda has imagined the home invaders, it becomes increasingly difficult to tell what is real and what is imagined. When four local teens break in and one attempts to rape Linda, she snaps and murders him with a meat cleaver. She then dresses in sexy lingerie and one by one kills the remaining teens—poisoning one and even castrating another with piano wire. It is only when her husband returns from an evening with his mistress to tell Linda he is leaving her that it becomes clear the teen (and Linda's revenge) was not imaginary. The final moments of the film show him uncovering the bed sheets to discover a corpse, as he turns to find Linda coming at him with the meat cleaver.

Demented wears its slasher film intent on its sleeve—that the rapist teens all wear Halloween masks (one even says "trick or treat"), combined with the construction of each killing as a hyper-stylized, elaborate murder vignette, make this abundantly clear. The rape-revenge elements are therefore troubling, as the "demented" of the title obviously refers to Linda herself, who is presented throughout the film as alternating between clingy, hysterical, shrill, seductive, and murderous.[60] Openly disinterested in her trauma beyond how it propels her transformation into a slasher-style killer, the film's emphasis upon its gore shots again highlight its true sub-generic allegiance. This must not be assumed to be the case with all slasher-imbued rape-revenge films, however. Jim Hemphill—director of the 2005 film *Bad Reputation*—is explicit in where his inspirations for his rape-revenge project lay:

> It didn't start with me thinking, "I want to make a rape-revenge movie." It started with me wanting to write a movie about sexual double standards and hypocrisy, and with wanting to exert a kind of artistic revenge on a real-life situation, which was a gang rape that occurred in Orange County not long before I made the film. This group of high school guys got a girl drunk or drugged, I don't remember the precise circumstances now, and then gang raped her and videotaped it—and then the girl was smeared in all the usual ways, accused of "asking for it" and all that nonsense. I think the guys did end up going to jail, but at the time I was reading about the case in the paper it looked like they were going to get off because of their parents' influence—one of them was the son of a sheriff—and I was just infuriated. I wanted to kill these guys, if not literally then in a fictionalized narrative, and once you start thinking that way the rape-revenge genre starts to become an obvious container in which to pour the story.[61]

Bad Reputation is driven by the powerful and commanding performance of Angelique Hennessy. She plays shy, bookish Michelle, a teenage girl with a mean-spirited, alcoholic mother, who finds refuge in her studies. Flattered and excited when popular Aaron (Jerad Anderson) invites her to a party, Michelle's evening becomes a nightmare when he drugs her with a spiked drink and gang-rapes her with his friends Jake (Mark Kunzman) and Steve (Chris Basler). Aaron's jealous ex-girlfriend Debbie (Dakota Ferreiro) and her friend Heather (Kristina Lauren) discover the passed-out Michelle, and in a fit of jealous rage they tape her to a tree in Aaron's backyard and write "slut" on her forehead "to teach this slut a lesson." Debbie's friend Wendy (Danielle Noble), who has earlier spoken kindly to Michelle, tries to stop them, but is told there will be social consequences for her if she does so. Devastated by both the rape and the consequent harassment by Debbie and her friends, Michelle returns to school and is subjected to a systematic barrage of teasing, humiliation and abuse as she is branded the school slut—not only by fellow students but also by the hostile and lecherous school counselor whom she visits, seeking assistance. Reaching the end of her tether, Michelle decides to convert her weakness into her strength, and returns to school dressed sexily in a micro-mini, knee-high-boots and a see-through top, while seductively sucking a lollipop. One by one she seduces and kills her rapists, then Debbie and Heather, until the film climaxes with a final confrontation between Wendy and Michelle. Although Wendy finally kills Michelle, she feels sorry for her, and Wendy gently holds Michelle's hand as the latter lies dying.

As both a filmmaker and a critic for prestigious publications including *Film Quarterly* and *American Cinematographer*, director Jim Hemphill's film literacy has been amply demonstrated. Thus, despite its budgetary restraints, the first half of the movie in particular delivers with remarkable clarity and sensitivity the story of Michelle's trauma, both during the night of the rape itself and in the intolerable aftermath as she is terrorized at school. Hemphill has flagged Emily White's book *Fast Girls: Teenage Tribes and the*

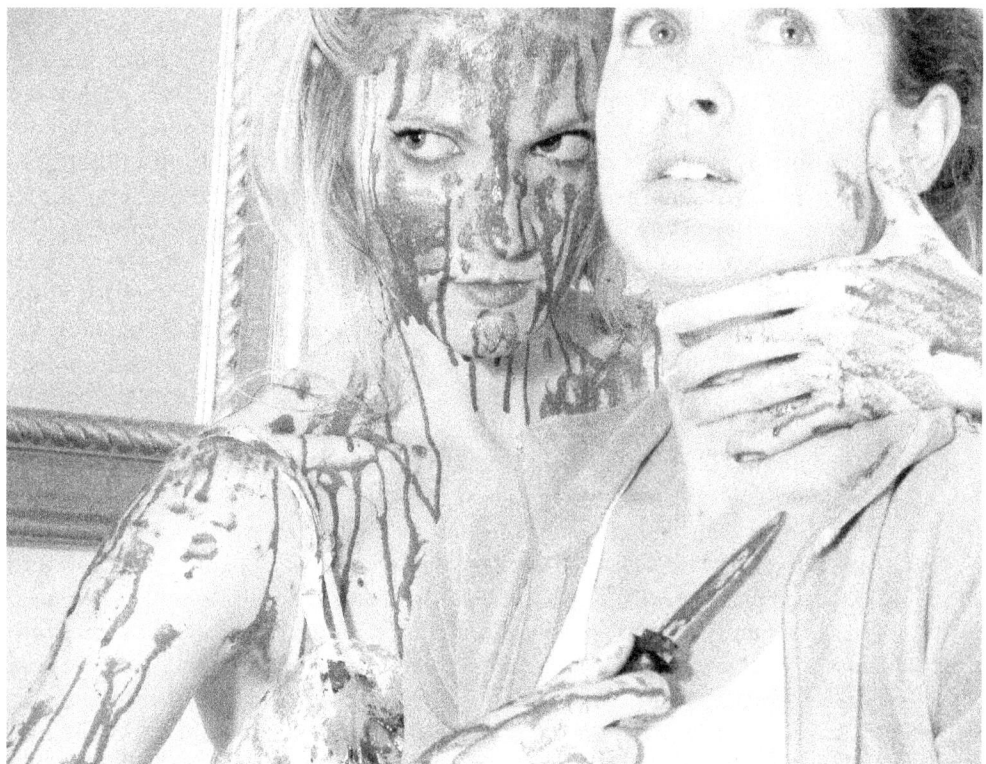

Michelle (Angelique Hennessy, left) and Wendy (Danielle Noble) in *Bad Reputation* (Jim Hemphill, 2005) (photograph by Evelyn Sen, courtesy Jim Hemphill).

Myth of the Slut (2002) as a central influence, particularly in regard to the "high school slut" figure, and Hemphill even includes a scene where Michelle bludgeons one of her rapists to death with a copy of Carol J. Clover's *Men, Women, and Chain Saws: Gender in the Modern Horror Film*. That she does so after anally raping him with a handful of pencils does suggest a less than purely theoretical engagement with Clover's arguments, but fifteen years after the film's initial release there is a certain power to the undeniable crudity here that makes knowledge—explicitly feminist knowledge—a kind of weapon in and of itself. Largely, this is due to the specific context of *Bad Reputation* as a horror film per se. For Hemphill, it is the tension between the conservative and progressive potential of the genre that makes it such a powerful tool to speak to politics, gender politics included:

> Horror is such an interesting genre, because it has a strong conservative element to it, but in the hands of someone like Wes Craven or John Carpenter or George Romero it can be so transgressive and radical, and that's the kind of horror I've always responded to—the kind of horror that really attacks the status quo with relish.

"Part of the way you fight against conservatism is to make people uncomfortable," Hemphill continues, "and few things are more uncomfortable to explore on screen than rape."

Not all rape-revenge films must explicitly contain rape, and nowhere is this clearer in contemporary film than Quentin Tarantino's *Kill Bill Vol. 1* (2003) and *Death Proof* (2007). Renowned for his signature gleeful intertextuality, Tarantino's films are not so much artifacts that exist alongside the exploitation films he celebrates, as they are instead a "theme park ride version"[62] of those texts. *Kill Bill Vol. 1*, for example, may not be a rape-revenge movie as such—although the Bride does kill the men who raped her while she pretended to be in a coma early on in the film—but it references them heavily, most notably with Daryl Hannah's eye patch nod to Christina Lindberg in *Thriller: A Cruel Picture*, and the reconstruction of *Lady Snow blood* in the final showdown between the Bride (Uma Thurman) and O-Ran (Lucy Liu). *Death Proof* engages even more explicitly with rape-revenge traditions. As Tarantino's "road rage opus,"[63] *Death Proof* is divided into two stories about Stuntman Mike (Kurt Russell), an outwardly pleasant but deranged and sadistic stunt driver who torments women on the road with the indestructible car of the film's title. The first part begins as three female friends—Arlene (Vanessa Ferrite), Shanna (Jordan Ladd) and "Jungle Julia" (Sydney Tamiya Poitier)—visit a number of bars to celebrate Julia's birthday. Stuntman Mike follows the women to The Texas Chili Parlor, where he approaches the women and flirts with Arlene. The up-until-now pleasant Stuntman Mike then offers a stranded Pam (Rose McGowan) a ride home, but once in his car he becomes insane and sadistic and drives the car recklessly. With no safety harness, Pam is violently hurled around the cabin until she dies (he tells her that the car is "death proof," but only in his seat). He then locates Arlene, Shanna and Jungle Julia on a deserted road and crashes into them, deliberately causing their deaths, which are shown in graphic detail. At the hospital, Sheriff Earl McGraw (Michael Parks) voices his suspicion that Stuntman Mike deliberately caused the girls' deaths and believes there is a sexual motivation behind the crime. Being unable to prove it, however, he resigns himself to making sure that Stuntman Mike does not commit the same act in Texas again.

The movie then restarts some time later. Again, it opens with three women, Lee

(Mary Elizabeth Winsted), Abernathy (Rosario Dawson) and Kim (Tracie Thoms), who all work in the film industry. Stuntman Mike sees them at a convenience store, where he tickles Abernathy's feet, and he follows them as they pick up New Zealand stuntwoman Zoe (played by Zoe Bell as herself—Bell was Uma Thurman's stunt double in the *Kill Bill* films). Zoe directs her friends to a farm where there is a vintage Dodge Challenger she wishes to test drive. Leaving Lee as collateral with the car's owner, Kim drives the car with Abernathy as a passenger as Zoe crawls onto the moving car's hood to play "ship's mast": She intends to stand on the speeding car's hood while hanging onto two belts coming from inside the vehicle. With Zoe in this dangerous position, Stuntman Mike appears and torments the women during the film's lengthy action climax. The tables are turned on his violent harassment of the women when they decide to return the attack. The women cause his car to crash, and Zoe, Abernathy and Kim beat him mercilessly as the film ends.

Considering *Death Proof* does not include scenes of rape or attempted rape as such, it is therefore perhaps surprising how explicitly it references rape-revenge traditions. *Death Proof* is unambiguous in its linkage of sexual violence with vehicular homicide (both attempted and otherwise). In the first part of the film, Sheriff McGraw makes it clear that he views Stuntman Mike's behavior as "a sex thing," observing to a colleague that the sexual nature of the crime stems from the erotics of the car crash, with its "high velocity impact, twisted metal, busted glass, [and] all four souls taken at exactly the same time." Later in the film, as Kim, Zoe and Abernathy chase Stuntman Mike and seek their revenge, this is explicitly sexual: "Fuck this bastard," they declare, and Kim mockingly says, "I'm the horniest motherfucker on the road!" Tarantino has openly acknowledged the influence of Clover's writing about the "final girl" in the slasher film on *Death Proof*'s first half in particular,[64] but its specific reference to rape-revenge stems from its reconstruction of the memorable scene from the Australian rape-revenge movie *Fair Game* (Mario Andreacchio, 1986). In terms of the logic of the Tarantino universe and how the film responds specifically to *Fair Game* in particular, it is clear that much thought has gone into its reversal of the earlier film's vision of the relationship between women, cars and violence. Tarantino's description of *Fair Game* captures the excessiveness of the image, and it is in light of such an impact that his reconstruction of the scene (this time with Zoe Bell as the "human hood ornament" instead of Cassandra Delaney) can be re-thought in terms of rape-revenge. Sharing a monster-car-as-male-sexuality metaphor, *Death Proof* reconfigures *Fair Game*'s gender relations. In the Australian film, the woman is strapped to the front of the car as an act of sexual violence, symbolizing her complete powerlessness in the face of male aggression, power and misogyny. But in *Death Proof*, Zoe not only asserts her power over the car and finds pleasure in doing so, but ultimately rejects the notion of the car as being an inherently "masculine" object at all. She chooses to play "ship's mast" voluntarily, and Stuntman Mike's intrusion seeks to control the activities that she may find pleasurable. The relationship between Stuntman Mike and these female protagonists is therefore more than a case of the latter seeking revenge for thinly disguised metaphorical sexual violence. It is about them reconfiguring the entire symbolic language of gender in relation to car culture, so commonly ascribed as a masculine domain. Just as *Death Proof* reworks ideas, motifs and themes from the earlier *Fair Game*, so too even more explicitly can we see in the legacy of *The Last House on the Left* (itself inspired by Bergman's *The Virgin Spring*) the scope for differing treatments of rape even in examples sharing a similar plot is both broad and fascinating.

Last Houses on the Left (and Right)

The influence of the original *The Last House on the Left* is illustrated nowhere more obviously than in the vast number of films whose names so clearly seek to imitate it. While the title of Wes Craven's film itself may owe a debt to John Sturges' rape-revenge Western *Last Train from Gun Hill* (1959), movies such as *Last House in the Woods* (Gabriele Albanesi, 2006) and *Last House on Hell Street* (Robin Garrels and John Specht, 2002) are just two recent examples that demonstrate the longevity of the original's notoriety. During the 1970s in particular, sexually violent exploitation film from around the world was often re-branded with *Last House*–sounding titles in the United States in order to profit upon the theatrical success of Craven's movie. Mario Bava's *Twitch of the Death Nerve* (1971) was re-released in the United States as *The Last House on the Left, Part II*; Aldo Lado's *Night Train Murders* (1975) was released at different stages as *Second House on the Left*, *The New House on the Left* and *Last Stop on the Night Train*, the Turkish film *Ugly World* (*Çirkin dünya*, Osman F. Seden, 1974) was released as *Last House in Istanbul*; Enzo G. Castellari's *Sensitivita* (1979) was released as *Last House Near the Lake*; *Death Weekend* (William Fruet, 1976) was released as *Last House on the Lake* and Pasqueale Festa Campanile's *Hitch Hike* (*Autostop rosso sangue*, 1977) was at one point released as *Hitchhike: Last House on the Left* (this latter film even starred David Hess). Other movies—such as Roger Watkins' *Last House on Dead End Street* (1977)—were U.S. productions that deliberately employed titles mimicking Craven's title. There were even whispers at one stage of an official sequel to the 1972 *The Last House on the Left*, rumored to star David Hess again and to be directed by Danny Steinman (who would go on to make the rape-revenge film *Savage Streets* with Linda Blair in 1984).

One of the first manifestations of *The Last House on the Left*'s influence is the low-budget exploitation film *Wrong Way* (Ray Williams, 1972). To those unfamiliar with grindhouse aesthetics, *The Last House on the Left* may appear to be as crude as cinema production can get, but when compared to *Wrong Way* it demonstrates moments of genuine artistry. If the rape and revenge depicted in the original versions of *The Last House on the Left* and *I Spit on Your Grave* have been critically deemed to be more complex than its raw production values suggest, *Wrong Way* demonstrates that this is by no means the norm. While it spends ample time on the depiction of its ghastly and vicious rape sequence, its story is inexplicably interrupted with an irrelevant side story before any revenge component is fully established.

Regardless of its incoherence, its debt to *The Last House on the Left* is clear—not only because of its shockingly realistic and lengthy rape scenes that stand in notable opposition to the softcore pantomime-style romps of earlier "roughie" films, but also in its basic story. Its plot elements are only loosely established and flagrantly directionless, but *Wrong Way* tells of two teenage girls, Nancy and Kathy (played by Laurel Canyon and Candy Sweet), who are picked up by a group of men when their car breaks down in the woods. The women are viciously brutalized for over twenty minutes in a sequence as lengthy and harrowing as the gang rape in the original *I Spit on Your Grave*. The girls are then abandoned in the woods, where they stumble upon yet another group who appear as equally intent on rape (the leader of this group tells them he will make the girls "sexual beasts"). While the film provides no explanation as to why it leaves the girls' story at this point, these two sequences are intercut with scenes that show one of the girl's fathers calling the police, who later discover the girls' underwear in the woods. While the last section of the film deviates to a new, unrelated story and does not return to the girls, these similarities between *Wrong Way* and *The Last House on the Left* are surely not coincidental.

More explicit homages to Craven's film were soon to follow. For cult audiences, Aldo Lado's name is most immediately associated with slick *gialli* like *Short Night of Glass Dolls* (*La corta notte delle bambole di vetro*, 1971) and *Who Saw Her Die?* (*Chi l'ha vist morire?*, 1972). And while demonstrating a sharp increase in its nasty depictions of sexual violence, Lado's *Night Train Murders* does not lack the impact of these other films. Superficially, the basic plot of *Night Train Murders* diverges only slightly from *The Last House on the Left*, moving the action to the train of its title. The primary difference lies in the politics of the attackers—Blackie (Flavio Bucci) and Curly (Gianfranco De Grassi) are loutish, but they do not appear to become dangerous until they fall under the influence of a wealthy, sexually-dominant older woman enigmatically called the Lady (Macha Meril). It is she who encourages them to rape and murder the two girls, and earlier she even offers one of the girls to a passing businessman who was spying on them (he eagerly accepts the offer to rape her). The inclusion of the Lady radically shifts the message of *Night Train Murders* from *The Last House on the Left*: in Craven's film, it is a case of the poor Krug and Co. *versus* the wealthy Collingwoods. But in Lado's film the poor (Blackie and Curly) are under the *control* of the bourgeoisie. *Night Train Murder*'s Mrs. Collingwood equivalent, Mrs. Stradi (Marina Berti), does not join in her husband's vengeance, and, in fact, she repeatedly begs him to stop. Unlike *The Last House on the Left*, this therefore provides a voice of reason from within the film's own diegesis. Professor Stradi (Enrico Salerno) chooses to ignore her, and in doing so suffers the consequences of his actions. This presents another binary relationship absent in Craven's original, this time between a self-policing middle-class (Mrs. Stradi) and an out-of-control middle-class (Professor Stradi). The result of this tension is made devastatingly apparent in the film's final shot: as Professor and Mrs. Stradi survey the carnage in stunned silence, the Lady joins them. In doing so, she aligns herself with the devastated parents rather than with the murdered Curly and Blackie. It is implied that Professor and Mrs. Stradi do not know—and never will—that it was the Lady who masterminded the rape and murder of their daughter. The Lady gets away with it not because she is innocent, but because she is rich and can therefore socially align herself with the family she has just destroyed.

Last House on the Beach (*La settima donna*, Franco Prosperi, 1978) is another Italian film whose title was changed for release in the United States to profit from Craven's earlier movie. Combining the nunsploitation subgenre with rape-revenge, the film deviates plot-wise from *The Last House on the Left* substantially but arrives at a similar ethical conclusion. Florinda Balkan stars as Sister Christina, a nun who has taken five teenage schoolgirls to a deserted beach house to rehearse a production of Shakespeare's *A Midsummer Night's Dream*. Only moments into the film the house is invaded by a group of violent thugs. These men are thieves who have just escaped a failed heist, and in between reading William Faulkner's 1931 novel *Sanctuary* (upon which Stephen Roberts' notorious 1933 rape film *The Story of Temple Drake* was based) and bickering among themselves, they spend the bulk of the film terrorizing and torturing the women. The rapes range in intensity, length and stylistic treatment, but one of the more gruesome and bizarre instances is shot entirely in slow motion, with the leader of the gang wearing a full face of make-up. When one of the girls is murdered after being raped with a large wooden stake in the film's most harrowing scene, the god-fearing nun puts her cross aside and executes two of the invaders. The surviving invader confronts Sister Christina in the garden, and the remaining girls beat him to death with garden rakes and shovels as they rescue her. The final image focuses on the shattered and disillusioned Sister Christina as she turns her head away from the violence before her.

Last House on the Beach lacks the shocking eloquence and impact of Craven's *The Last House on the Left*, but while it deviates from that film's storyline substantially, it shares its same message in this final shot. Although there is no doubt that Sister Christina's vengeance was understandable according to the logic of the film, it is problematized when she realizes with terror that not only has she herself become a violent monster, but that she also has taught her students—for whose spiritual as well as physical care she was responsible—that violence is acceptable. Like the Collingwoods, she realizes that she too has become a monster. *Last House on the Beach* sharply contrasts with *Trip with the Teacher* (Earl Barton, 1975), another teacher-and-schoolgirl-themed rape-revenge film. Unlike the Italian film, Barton's movie concludes with the surviving girls happily embracing their smiling female teacher. *Last House on the Beach* is substantially darker than films such as this, and therefore closer in tone to Craven's *The Last House on the Left*.

Ruggero Deodato's *House on the Edge of the Park* (1984) aspires to a more explicit homage to *The Last House on the Left*, as demonstrated by both its title and the casting of David Hess as the villain. The film begins as Alex (Hess) rapes and murders a woman whose car he forces off the road in New York City. Later, Alex is shown preparing for a night out with Ricky (Giovanni Lombardo Radice) at the garage where they work. Their plans are interrupted when sophisticated Lisa (Annie Bell) and her boyfriend arrive with a broken-down car and casually invite them to a party. Increasingly frustrated with the guests' behavior, Alex loses his temper and beats up a male party guest, then rapes and tortures many of the women. These scenes take up the bulk of the film and culminate in a lengthy, graphic scene where he mutilates a woman with a razor. The guests finally find a gun and shoot Alex in the genitals, telling him that the entire event had been planned as a way to avenge the rape of the woman at the beginning of the film, who was the sister of one of the guests. Mirroring Sadie's death at the hands of Mrs. Collingwood in *The Last House on the Left*, Lisa and her guests push Hess' Alex into the pool to bleed to death. Aside from this shot, the film's treatment of rape and revenge is casual in contrast to Craven's original, as the guests half-heartedly debate the ethics of their vengeance.

Italian directors such as Lado and Deodato were not the only ones interested in expanding *The Last House on the Left* universe. In 2005, an American film set out to resurrect Craven's original film with hopes of shocking a new generation of filmgoers. Directed by David DeFalco, *Chaos* was made in 2002 but was not released until 2005 in the United States. Its association with *The Last House on the Left* was explicit, despite the creators' denials (probably stemming from legal issues). The plot is almost identical, the film poster overtly referenced the promotional material for the original, and it is even rumored that David Hess had initially intended to star in it. Like the original *I Spit on Your Grave*, *Chaos* is noted for provoking the ire of film critic Roger Ebert, who gave the film a rare zero stars and asked, "Is it admirable for filmmakers to depict pure evil? Have 9/11, suicide bombers, serial killers and kidnapping created a world in which the response of the artist must be nihilistic and hopeless?"[65] For Ebert, there were two key issues that separated Craven's original from DeFalco's remake: the violence is undeniably more vicious and explicit in the latter, and the different endings of each film carry different moral messages. In terms of the latter, it is difficult to deny that the ending of *Chaos* is both arbitrary and silly and speaks more of a project stuck for what to do than it does of any profound thematic intent. In Craven's film, the Collingwoods dispatch Krug and his gang, only to be left stunned at their actions as the police arrive. But in *Chaos*, a confusing and illogical sequence of events has its Mr. Collingwood character, Leo (Scott Richards), turning a gun on Chaos (the Krug character, played by Kevin Gage), only for Leo to be shot by a racist policeman who disapproves of his interracial marriage. Leo's wife, Justine (Deborah Lacey), then shoots the policeman, and Chaos kills the second policeman and then Justine herself. The film ends with Chaos' survival, thus turning Craven's reflection on the nature of violence into a melodramatic battle between good and evil, where the latter wins out.

Both this ending and its extreme and excessive depictions of sexual violence expose *Chaos'* indifference to the central themes of *The Last House on the Left*. Although even today the violence in Craven's film is shocking and brutal, that its intensity is so inherently connected to its broader thematic intent is undeniable. In *Chaos*, however, because the conclusion does not aim to provide any concrete message beyond a simplistic "the world is full of bad people" message, the function of violence also changes. It is precisely because of this that its revolting scenes of rape and torture are exposed as little more than manifestations of a creatively challenged and regressive adolescent mind. In particular, the scene where one of the victims' nipples is cut off and she is forced to eat it is juvenile, misogynistic and disgusting in equal measure. As Eric Somers notes, the DVD extras to the film feature DeFalco referring to himself on numerous occasions as "the director of the most brutal film of all time,"[66] thus showing he was propelled more by "bad-ass" posturing than a desire to present a deep or complex social critique.

Despite all of this, however, *Chaos* offers at least one significant point of interest that makes it unique among most of the films in this book and demonstrates that even the most idiotic text can be worth examining. Craven's Mari is replaced in *Chaos* by Emily, who has a Black mother and a White father. The film thus raises a range of issues about race, rape and power absent in the original. *Chaos* does not deal satisfactorily or progressively with these issues by any means, but it is worthy of note that Justine's suspicions that there are racist motivations for the police's indifferent response to their missing person report are confirmed when one of the policemen goes on a vicious rant against interracial relationships to his colleague as they leave to investigate. The film does not make it clear, but it appears to be this racism that leads the policeman to shoot Leo in the film's hasty conclusion. It is in relation to race that *Chaos almost* finds itself capable of making some kind of statement in what is otherwise no more than an unsophisticated and misogynistic *Last House on the Left* knock-off. That its violence is so glaringly functionless beyond stoking the director's desire to be "the director of the most brutal film of all time," however, renders this potential line of investigation underdeveloped at best.

Less critically abhorred than *Chaos*, Dennis Iliadis' 2009 remake of *The Last House on the Left* (one of the rare adaptations of Craven's film to use the same name) also goes to great lengths to deflect its thematic meaning far from that in the original. In *Chaos*, Justine and Leo fight not out of a desire for vengeance, but for survival. In the 2009 version, the same can be said up to a point of its equivalent couple, Emma Collingwood (Monica Potter) and her husband John (Tony Goldwyn)—at least until after they commit their first murder. The major difference between the original and this remake is that Mari (Sara Paxton) does not die: the gang believe they have killed her, but she manages to return home where her father, a doctor, performs emergency surgery. It is Emma and

John's desire to get their daughter to proper medical care (not to mention their own survival) that propels them to remove Krug and his cohorts. This changes, however, after John and Emma assault Krug's brother, Frank (Aaron Paul). Face-down in the sink, it is clear that they have disabled him as a threat, but as John turns on the garbage disposal near Frank's arm, his eyes light up with joy and offers the first concrete moment where revenge trumps survival as a driving force behind his actions. The motivation for the Collingwoods' violence alternates between these two points for much of the rest of the film: it is often unclear if they are fighting because they are trying to remove obstacles to getting their daughter to safety, or if they are simply on a vengeance-fuelled rampage. If it is the latter, there is the added complication that this automatically means they are opting to indulge their desire for vengeance *over* helping the badly injured Mari. In the conclusion, where John paralyzes Krug and blows his head up in a microwave, the ethical complication is that Mari is waiting to leave for medical attention; instead of rushing to get her help, her father instead chooses to execute this gruesome and elaborate torture. The film tries to gloss over this fact by intercutting John's revenge with footage of the family leaving on the boat, skewering the linear logic of how these events had to have chronologically unfolded.

The family that leaves on the boat includes Krug's son, Justin (Spencer Treat Clark), whose role in the 2009 remake also deviates substantially from the original. In the first film, the Collingwoods discover the gang is responsible for Mari's death by accident, but here Justin deliberately provides them with the clue. The film's climactic face-off is between the father figure from each group, John and Krug, and it is Justin who provides the resolution. He attacks Krug, and although Krug stabs him in retaliation, this distraction allows Emma and John the opportunity to finally subdue Krug. This violent showdown is between two families, led by men, who fight over a son figure. Despite Mari's key presence in the film, this son figure is crucial to the 2009 remake. As an addition to Craven's story, the Collingwoods in this version had recently lost a son, and Justin's role as surrogate is foreshadowed by Emma's earlier affection for him (referring to him gently as "sweetheart" and "honey"). Unlike the earlier film that finds the Collingwoods standing alone and shocked at the monsters they have become in order to combat monsters, here the ending is notably more positive and hopeful, if somewhat conservative when compared to the original. Explicitly reaffirming dominance of the middle-class nuclear family—mother, father, daughter and the new "son"—it is this reconstituted family that leave the weaker, poorer and now dead Krug, his brother and his lover Sadie (Riki Lindhome) behind.

The 2009 *Last House on the Left* is also coded much more explicitly as a horror film than the 1972 version, suggesting it is responding more to current genre conventions than it is seeking any particular political statement. The remake loyally adheres to genre conventions, particularly with its use of ambiguous point-of-view shots and its suspenseful hide-and-seek vignettes. The bulk of the film's action in and around the Collingwood house takes place at night—during a thunderstorm, no less—and this also demonstrates that this remake is "genrefied" as much as it is gentrified by its high budget and slick production values. Despite this, the rape scenes in particular are undeniably nasty, and to a contemporary audience the shock value would surely be as intense as that of the original at its time of release. There is, of course, graphic violence beyond the vicious attacks on the girls: the scene of Krug's head being microwaved, for example, recalls horror classics such as David Cronenberg's *Scanners* (1981) and Brian De Palma's *The Fury* (1978). The violence in the film does not adhere solely to this Krug vs. Collingwood trajectory, however, which suggests that there is a desire on the part of the filmmaker to get as much gore in as possible. This is most apparent in the two home surgery scenes—firstly of Frank's nose being put back into place and stitched up, and then of John tending to Mari's bullet wound and removing blood from her lungs—shown in lingering detail and shot in close-up with vivid sound effects.

The most obvious shift towards a more generic horror structure, however, manifests in the "final girl" elements of Mari's character that are absent in the original. In 2009, Mari is not interested in drugs and argues against it (although she finally succumbs). She fights back consistently throughout her attack; she deliberately lures Krug to her parents' house as a way of possibly getting help; and Krug himself even observes at one point that she is a "cool customer." The film celebrates Mari's determination to survive, and the fact this Mari lives and the 1972 one does not inadvertently act as condemnation of the earlier version. The 2009 Mari was a fast swimmer and could get away (she was still shot, but only in the shoulder). But the 1972 Mari was physically unable to escape, and thus her "punishment" was death. Sara Paxton's Mari in the recent *The Last House on the Left* is not killed, and this presents the possibility that she herself was able to enact her own revenge, a dramatic act that would have significantly moved the film from being a rape-revenge film where her parents act for her, to one where the raped woman seeks vengeance on her own behalf. Although her survival should have made this likelihood a possibility, the film does not explore this option. Rather, it opts for what in contrast is a surprisingly old-fashioned scenario, where the climactic scene of violence takes place in what effectively feeds into traditional views of rape as a property crime dispute between men. As mentioned above, that this property dispute is as much about the son as it is the raped daughter is of significant concern.

The 2009 remake also denies Emma the satisfaction of killing on her own. The best she can do is either assist (as with Frank and Krug) or come to John's rescue (as in the bathroom with an unnecessarily topless Sadie). Emma is not the only incapacitated woman in the Collingwood family in this new version. The depiction of Mari after Krug and his gang leave her (assuming she is dead) is a clear genre-marker, as she climbs out of the dark water at night to stumble home *Creature from the Black Lagoon*–style. This depiction of her as vacant monster continues throughout the rest of the film. Mari is not so much a rape survivor as she is the walking dead, whose only function is to provide her parents (specifically, her father) with a motivation for violent and spectacular vengeance. Even in the scenes where John performs emergency surgery on their living room coffee table, Mari's face is mostly turned from the camera. It is less about *her* reaction and trauma than it is the *impact* her traumatized body has on her father. While Mari's survival seems more dependent on her function as a plot device with an unspoken near-supernatural ability to survive, rape-revenge has ventured more concretely into the realms of the supernatural long before these more recent examples.

Supernatural Rape-Revenge Film

Like film more generally, supernatural horror rape-revenge movies do not present a unified treatment of rape. These stories function within the realm of the fantastic, and thus may stretch the limitations of Earth-bound feasibility. By appealing to spectatorial awareness that their events can only occur within the fictional world of the film's diegesis, these movies offer new perspectives on rape that would seem illogical or absurd in other contexts. As one of the many acts of violence (and threats of violence) that riddle the genre more broadly, rape appears across a vast range of supernatural horror films. Even the most cursory survey offers a range of examples that encompass *Rosemary's Baby* (Roman Polanski, 1968), *Night of the Demon* (James C. Wasson 1980), *Evil Dead* (Sam Raimi, 1981), *The Hills Have Eyes* (Wes Craven, 1977/Alexandre Aja, 2006), *Baby Blood* (Alain Robak, 1990), *Jack Frost* (Michael Cooney, 1996), *Dead Girl* (Marcel Sarmiento, 2008) and *Contracted* (Eric England, 2013). When approached with a particular eye towards the intersection of rape and revenge, there is again a variety of ways in which vengeance and sexual violence are represented in the context of supernatural horror in films including *Ghost of Chibusa Enoki* (*Kaidan chibusa enoki*, Goro Katano, 1958), *Kuroneko* (Kaneto Shindo, 1968), *Ghost with Hole* (*Sundelbolong*, Sisworo Gautama Putra, 1982), *Carnival of Souls* (Adam Grossman and Ian Kessner, 1998), *Gothika* (Mathieu Kassovitz, 2003), *Bloodrayne* (Uwe Boll, 2005), *Dorothy Mills* (Agnès Merlet, 2008), *Wicked Lake* (Zach Passero, 2008), *The Twilight Saga: Eclipse* (David Slade, 2010), *Mirrors 2* (Victor Garcia, 2010), *Avenged*, *Rings* (F. Javier Gutiérrez, 2017), *Black Christmas* (Sophi Takal, 2019), *I Am Lisa* (Patrick Rea, 2020), *Amulet* (Romola Garai, 2020), and *Evangeline* (Karen Lam, 2013).

Returning to an earlier film, however, we see this is hardly a new fascination in supernatural horror. Sidney Furie's *The Entity* (1981) may be one of the most memorable, a movie that documents the serial rape of suburban mother Carla Moran (Barbara Hershey) by an invisible ghost. There is only one visible body in the room during these attacks as she is violently restrained and assaulted by an invisible adversary throughout the film. Beyond the supernatural specificities of its plot, *The Entity* resembles films like *The Accused* and *Lipstick* in crucial ways. In these films, the rape survivor must contend both with post-rape trauma and the unsatisfactory nature of the institutional treatment of their circumstances. Here, Carla is caught between both her supernatural abuser and the male-dominated world of science. She shares her frustration at the latter with the spectator, for while neither they nor Carla can see the face of her rapist until the end of the film, both are forced to look at a slew of unbelieving (mostly male) doctors and psychiatrists who dismiss her experience as a manifestation of repressed childhood trauma. Although a team of paranormal investigators are soon involved to prove her claims, Carla's is as much a showdown between her and the rapist ghost as it is a battle between believing and non-believing scientists and doctors who are predominantly men.

Significantly, that the rapist is a literal monster deletes any possibility of "his" vindication. The film's battle is not between victim and perpetrator, but between survivor and the system. The narrative is therefore firmly focused upon Carla's relationship between the two factions that seek to confirm or deny her claims. *The Entity* echoes Norman Bryson's observation that "attacker and victim are almost the least privileged to speak about rape, and even when accounts and confessions are forthcoming they are usually elicited and publicized by authorities with a stake in the wider melee."[67] Ultimately, Carla's revenge is not necessarily against the eponymous and vague "entity" that raped her, but rather against the psychiatrists, psychologists and other doctors that dismissed her claims. Carla's body becomes not only the site of her initial trauma, but a battleground between two scientific approaches that, while distinct, are both still coded as primarily masculine.

The fantastic possibilities of invisibility more recently came to the fore in Leigh Whannell's *The Invisible Man* (2020) which reimagines H.G. Wells' original 1897 novel as a vehicle to explore domestic violence in all its intersecting manifestations: physical, psychological and sexual. Like Carla in *The Entity*, Elisabeth Moss's Cecilia is tormented by an invisible masculine force as she desperately seeks to escape from her abusive partner, a powerful scientist who has total control over her life. Faking his death, he uses an invisibility suit to gaslight her, continuing his abuse into his seeming afterlife. Any attempt to rebuild her life or make new relationships is destroyed by the unseen abuser, the desperate Cecilia eventually framed for murder and appearing to everyone as unquestioningly guilty. While eventually exposing the truth behind the plot to destroy her, Cecilia's journey provides a powerful tour of the multifaceted ways that domestic violence can occur. Of these, reproductive abuse is explicitly mentioned; believing she had successfully been able to hide the fact that she was taking the contraceptive pill, Cecilia discovers not only that her partner was aware of this and had, it is implied, replaced them with a placebo, but when she falls pregnant it is assumed that marital rape was the cause, taking place while she was in a heavily drugged sleep. After making his presence clear to her, Cecilia's abusive partner uses the unborn baby—conceived through rape—as a way of maintaining control over her.

Rape manifests in a different way in the supernatural rape-revenge film *Stir of Echoes* (David Koepp, 1999). Based upon the novel of the same name by cult horror author Richard Matheson, of *I Am Legend* (1954) fame, *Stir of Echoes* concerns a psychic link established between a teenage girl who was raped and murdered and buried in the walls of a deserted house, and a later male tenant. The girl supernaturally bestows a subjective understanding of her traumatic experience upon the male protagonist, and she encourages him to act as an agent for her vengeance. This male protagonist is Tom (Kevin Bacon), who has his psychic abilities accidentally unlocked at a party one evening where his sister-in-law Lisa (Illeana Douglas) hypnotizes him to show that her belief in the supernatural is not unfounded. Planting a post-hypnotic suggestion that he be "more open-minded," her demonstration is more effective than she intended, and Tom becomes highly susceptible to strange and violent visions in his house that he does not understand. As these hallucinations become more vivid, Tom begins to lose his grasp on reality—much to the concern of his wife, Maggie (Kathryn Erbe). His obsession continues to grow, and Tom is inexplicably driven to start digging up the garden of their rental property. When this search is fruitless, he begins demolishing the house itself as he searches under floorboards. In a hidden wall cavity in the basement, he discovers the mummified corpse of Samantha, a girl he earlier discovered had gone missing—this information was conveyed by Samantha's sister Debbie (Liza Well), whom Tom's psychic son Jake (Zachary David Cope) had lured to the house earlier in the film. The discovery of the body triggers a vision where he sees Samantha raped and murdered by a group of local teenage boys whose fathers are Tom's close friends. When Tom confronts these fathers about Samantha's rape and murder, they threaten to silence Tom and Maggie until one of the men has a flash of conscience and kills his accomplice before Tom and Maggie can be hurt. Samantha's body is finally buried, and the family prepare to move out of the house. As they drive away for the final time, Jake continues to hear voices from the houses they pass. This final scene suggests all houses have secrets like the one Tom just uncovered.

Stir of Echoes received many positive reviews at the time of its release, but it was unavoidably compared to the blockbuster *The Sixth Sense* (M. Night Shyamalan, 1999), another supernatural horror film that also featured a young boy who had a psychic connection with the dead. When considering the raw mechanics of the plot itself, however, the young boy's abilities are only of secondary concern to how they intersect with Tom's relationship with Samantha. On a preliminary viewing, the film may not immediately appear to be concerned with rape and revenge as these factors only become apparent when revealed through Tom's climactic vision after the discovery of Samantha's body. There is, however, strong evidence suggesting the film holds sexual violence and issues of power and control at its core from very early on. In fact, having sex is what triggers Tom's first vision outside of those images that he saw under hypnosis. Maggie and Tom have sex after they return home from the party, but flashes of first-person images of violence interrupt Tom's enjoyment. This includes the striking image of a female hand clawing at a floor until her fingernail is ripped off. Tom asks Maggie to stop having sex because he is so shaken, but she ignores him until he physically removes her. She asks him what is wrong, to which he simply replies that it was "weird."

Stir of Echoes flags issues of consent early on (Tom asks Maggie to stop, but she does not do so immediately), and gender identification also becomes increasingly more complex as the film continues. This culminates in the final vision where Tom's face morphs into Samantha's: he literally becomes her, thus allowing him to see and experience the rape and murder from her perspective. The scene is cruel and violent, and much of it is shown from Tom/Samantha's first-person perspective. Despite the intensity of the moment, there is little actual suspense—after all, the spectator and Tom both know that Samantha does not survive, so that when she is finally killed and the screen slowly turns black, the poignancy of the tragedy manifests stylistically as well as narratively. After the climactic action sequence where those both guilty of the crime itself and of covering it up are finally subdued, Tom sees Samantha finally leave the house. In this vision, she zips up her jacket, smiles, walks along the street away from the house, and then vanishes into what can assumed to be a less traumatic afterlife than that experienced behind his basement wall. Tom has brought Samantha justice and freed her spirit, but to do so Samantha found it necessary to show him rape through her own eyes and make him understand what it *felt* like. Employing the conceptual freedoms that supernatural horror allows, *Stir of Echoes* constructs a generically plausible scenario where rape trauma can be effectively communicated and resolved. In perhaps the darkest element of the film as a whole, the film's stylistic self-referentiality—typified most forcefully in the hypnosis sequences where Tom imagines himself sitting in a movie theater—knowingly suggests that this mode of resolution is one that strictly exists within the realms of cinematic fantasy. *Stir of Echoes*' idea of having a female rape victim control the body of a man in order to exact her revenge provided the basis for Joe D'Amato's *Frankenstein 2000* (*Ritorno dalla morte*, 1991). Also called *Return from Death*, the work of trash auteur D'Amato (aka Aristide Massaccesi) lies as far from the mainstream credibility of David Koepp's *oeuvre* as can be imagined. As mentioned in Chapter One, *Frankenstein 2000* was not D'Amato's only venture into rape-revenge territory; but unlike the adult film *Emmanuelle's Revenge*, this film returned him firmly to the generic domain of horror. *Frankenstein 2000* tells the story of psychic yet neurotic Georgia (Cinzia Monreale), who, with her son Stefano (Robin Tazusky) and husband, lives in an Austrian resort town run by the powerful Mr. Hoffner (Maurice Poll). Hoffner's son is part of a teenage motorcycle gang who terrorize Georgia. When Hoffner's private security company refuses to investigate their attempted rape of Georgia, the gang embark upon a more successful assault during a home invasion where they attack Stefano also. With Georgia in a coma and Stefano hospitalized, the private security officers are able to frame Georgia's handyman, Ric (Donald O'Brien), for the crimes. Ric is brought to the hospital to do an experiment in an attempt to jolt Georgia out of her coma. He tells her he loves her, and the two establish a psychic connection. That night, Hoffman's private security officers murder Ric in an attempt to quash further investigation by the police. The catatonic Georgia psychically reanimates Ric from her hospital bed and sends him on a vengeance-fuelled killing spree to gruesomely murder her attackers. Once they have been dispatched, "Frankenstein" Ric has a taste for blood and soon appears to act beyond Georgia's wishes, attempting to kill her husband. When Ric threatens Stefano, Georgia jolts out of her coma, screaming and distressed, stopping her heart and therefore killing Ric. In the final scene her heart monitor reactivates. Her reign of terror, it is suggested, has yet to end.

Despite its obvious rape-revenge influences and eponymous homage to Mary Shelley, *Frankenstein 2000*'s ancestors include Lucio Fulci's *Ænigma* (1987) and the Australian horror film *Patrick* (Richard Franklin, 1978), the legacy of the latter most famously manifesting in Tarantino's *Kill Bill Vol. 1* as the comatose Bride lies spitting in her hospital bed. *Frankenstein 2000* also reverses many elements of *Steel and Lace*, where instead of a man controlling the reanimated body of the murdered rape victim in order to enact vengeance, it is a woman who controls the reanimated body of a murdered man for the same reason. The inability to act that female rape survivors often face is expressed literally through Georgia's comatose state; but far beyond a man acting as her agent to replace her, here she controls and directs that agent (at least up until the film's conclusion). With his long and illustrious career as one of the most notorious European sleaze merchants of the 1970s and 1980s, D'Amato's *Frankenstein 2000*—while surprisingly tame next to films like *Emanuelle in America* (1977) and *Porno Holocaust* (1981)—makes no attempt to disguise its exploitative intent (the attempted rape scene is even intercut with close-ups of the horror film posters on the wall of Georgia's office to make explicit its intended association with commercial horror film). At the very least, however, the film offers an alternate treatment of the relationship between the immobilized rape survivor and the men that seek vengeance on their behalf that dominates many other rape-revenge films. *Frankenstein 2000* may be far from progressive, but it does provide a useful point of comparison for rape-revenge films that do not question the often-problematic scenario where men act on a woman's behalf.

A male agent of vengeance is employed in a more traditional manner in Alexandre Aja's 2013 film *Horns*, adapted from Joe Hill's 2010 novel of the same name. Daniel Radcliffe plays a distraught young man called Ig who has been falsely accused of the rape and murder of his childhood sweetheart, Merrin (Juno Temple). Embodying the figure of evil that those in his community see him as, Ig literally sprouts horns which grant him the ability to garner unfiltered honesty from those with whom he communicates. This allows him to uncover the true culprit of Merrin's rape and murder; his lawyer and best friend Lee (Max Minghella) who had not only defended Ig in his legal battle against these false allegations but had outwardly supported Ig's relationship with Merrin since they first met in church as children. What is so fascinating about *Horns* from a rape-revenge perspective is that while rape is so often an addition to a murder—often to add a bit of a sensationalism—here, the rape is Lee's *primary* goal, the murder an almost incidental by-product. Secretly in love with Merrin, Lee long harbored fantasies that she was in love with him, a belief seemingly confirmed when Merrin turns down Ig's marriage proposal.

Unbeknownst to Ig or Lee, Merrin is dying of cancer and her rejection is intended as a way of providing a buffer for the pain Ig would feel from losing her. Misconstruing Merrin's actions as a sign of her love for him, Lee reacts violently when her true motivations are revealed, raping and then murdering her. Upon discovering the truth, Ig confronts Lee and in the ensuing fight commands the overly phallicised snake companions that have accompanied him through his strange journey to execute Lee, forcing themselves down his throat in an unsubtle replication of oral rape. Ig dies, having embraced his dark side to avenge his lover's death, where, in the film's final moments, he is seemingly reunited with Merrin in the afterlife, her character appearing as the embodiment of feminized purity. The film's ending consolidates Merrin's secondary status within the narrative in which her character is barely granted a distinct personality, let alone her own agency: her function is symbolic, and nothing more.

Although more clearly a low budget and ostensibly "trashier" film, Dusty Nelson's *Necromancer* (1988) in contrast sees a return to a more complicated representation of femininity in a film where it is the rape survivor herself—not a male agent as in *Horns*—who enacts her own vengeance. From a horror perspective, it offers little of the hyperactivity of many of its more celebrated genre stablemates, despite its inclusion of so-called scream queen Liz Kaitan (here listed as Elizabeth Cayton). While far from being a progressive or sophisticated reflection on the nature of rape and its representation, *Necromancer* allows insight into the broader construction of rape-revenge through its particular merger of sexual violence, vengeance and the fantasy of the supernatural. The film follows the story of Julie (Kaitan), who is raped in a university theater one evening by a group of classmates. The rapists have discovered that despite having a current boyfriend—the eligible musician Eric (John Tyler)—Julie had a previous sexual relationship with drama professor Charles (Russ Tamblyn). Her rapists believe Julie will not report the assault out of fear her attackers will reveal her secret past.

Feeling trapped, Julie seeks advice from a female friend who finds a mysterious advertisement in the local newspaper offering vengeance for a price. The two girls visit Lisa (Lois Masten), a mysterious woman with supernatural powers who was shown at the beginning of the film murdering another female client. Not taking Lisa or her ad particularly seriously, Julie accepts her offer but is thrown by the intensity of Lisa's demonic ritual where a vengeance demon is called forth. Although laughing about it afterwards, Julie becomes increasingly concerned as her rapists begin to disappear. The revenge killings are executed by a Julie look-alike who dresses sexily and seduces each man before turning into a gruesome monster and killing them (often through genital mutilation). Once these initial targets have been dispatched, Lisa (appearing as Julie) continues to murder any man who angers Julie, including Charles (who tries to blackmail Julie into re-establishing their sexual relationship) and even Eric when they have an argument. The climax of the film occurs in Eric's bedroom when the two "Julies"—Julie herself and the vengeance demon Lisa, who takes the physical form of Julie—meet in a violent confrontation. As they look and dress identical, it is difficult to tell them apart, and while it appears "good" Julie has won, the final shot shows Lisa's silhouette at her window, laughing. The closing title card features a quote ascribed to Edgar Allan Poe: "I am safe—I am safe—yes—if I be not fool enough to make open confession!" Vengeance demon Lisa has successfully murdered Julie and permanently replaced her.

While stylistically unsophisticated, the rape scene in *Necromancer* occurring on a stage suggests a self-referential awareness of the performative nature of the crime as it appears on film. Rapist Paul (Stan Hurwitz) is "performing" masculinity—not for Julie, but for his accomplices Allan (Shawn Eisner) and Carl (Edward A. Wright). The reflexivity demonstrated within this sequence indicates the film's awareness of itself as a construction. Julie is raped at knifepoint under a giant glitter ball with dramatic colored lighting, thus emphasizing the contrived, theatrical nature of the film as a whole. Paul, Carl and Allan even wear Halloween animal masks during the attack, again reiterating the "staginess" of the sequence while simultaneously underscoring the primal, animalistic nature of their violence. *Necromancer* is even more noteworthy, however, in its division of Julie into two separate entities. While rape survivor and rape avenger are usually either the same person (the woman herself) or divided between the rape survivor and (commonly) a male agent who acts on her behalf, *Necromancer* finds a third option via the fantastic possibilities of supernatural horror. By dividing Julie into "good Julie" and "bad Julie" (vengeance demon Lisa in the form of Julie), the former retains her humanity and avoids any of the nastier ethical complications that arise for many of the other rape avengers in this book. This does not render the film problem-free—that "bad Julie" is ultimately victorious over "good Julie" does more than tick the generic box for a conclusion with a bitter twist. As "good Julie" herself tells her friend when she first witnesses her doppelganger in action, "I saw her ... me ... it!" That it is *her* fury that provokes the monster (it is made clear earlier in the film that the only way to neutralize "bad Julie" is for "good Julie" to forgive) implicates her in many ways in the gory murders. *Necromancer* makes explicit the difference between *desiring* revenge and acting it out, and its construction of two different versions of the central protagonist bring a spectacular element to this conceptual tension.

The spectacle of rape that *Necromancer* so explicitly references is the primary reason for its deployment in Jean Rollin's *Demoniacs* (*Les Démoniques*, 1974). While French horror from this period never quite achieved the international cult status of Italian offerings, Rollin is undeniably one of France's key figures in the genre. Films such as *The Living Dead Girl* (*La Morte vivante*, 1982), *The Grapes of Death* (*Les Raisins de la mort*, 1978) and *Fascination* (1979) still figure largely in the Eurohorror canon. Rollin's work is marked by his signature and often-breathtaking visual poetry and shows little interest in concrete narrative beyond how it supports his defining cinematic style. Part horror, part art film and part softcore erotica, Rollin's films are heavy on both gore and exposed female flesh, and this intersection of sex and violence manifests often in his films as rape scenes. As the title *Rape of the Vampire* (*Le Viol du Vampire*, 1968) demonstrates, Rollin is not shy about deploying rape for its exploitative value, and in *Demoniacs* it is used specifically in a rape-revenge context.

While the plot is loose, *Demoniacs* follows a group of "wreckers"—Captain (John Rico), the sadistic and beautiful "she-wolf" Tina (Rollin regular Joëlle Coeur) and two others—who trick ships into coming too close to land and then plunder the cargo when they are incapacitated. In keeping with the pirate traditions to which the film lovingly pays tribute, pillage is often accompanied by rape, and when two unnamed blonde women (Lieva Lone and Patricia Hermenier) stagger on shore from one of these wrecks, the gang attack them and believe they have left them for dead. Celebrating later at a bordello in a local village, the drunken Captain has a vision of the two dead girls and is terrified. One of the prostitutes, Louise (Louise Dhour), has "second sight" and tells the Captain and his accomplices that tonight the spirits will seek their vengeance. Unsure if the girls are dead or alive, the wreckers return to the shore to dispatch them either way, but the girls manage to escape to the nearby ruins of a church that the locals believe is cursed. Here they meet a strange female clown (Mirelle Dargent)—whose inclusion typifies Rollin's surrealist inclinations—who takes them to the tomb keeper. Realizing that the girls are unable to speak (yet another instance of the rape-survivor-as-mute motif that spans across films including *Ms. 45* and *Thriller: A Cruel Picture*), the tomb keeper tells a mysterious man (Miletic Zivomir) of the girls' arrival. The girls sacrifice themselves in return for the power to enact their revenge against the wreckers. In Rollin films, of course, "sacrifice" translates to sexual submission, and much screen time is dedicated to the softcore erotics of this transaction. Although bestowed with supernatural abilities, the girls do not succeed in their attempted revenge and only manage to kill one of the four. The gang capture them, tie them to the skeleton of a shipwrecked boat and rape them again before the girls are drowned in the rising tide. Driven mad at his destruction of innocence, the Captain kills Tina and his remaining ally before he himself is drowned while attempting to rescue the girls.

So strong is Rollin's dedication to surrealism that this brief sketch of the already hazy narrative drastically undervalues the intense stylization of the film. *Demoniacs* is visually stunning, and many of its key scenes offer images that are both breathtaking and confrontational iconographic subversions, such as the sequence where the two girls attack Tina with falling religious statues. The rape-revenge elements exist solely as a canvas for Rollin's unique visual flair. Beyond its obvious deployment as exploitative titillation, *Demoniacs* has little interest in either rape or revenge thematically, nor does it pretend to. Rape is depicted very casually in the film, but unlike the bulk of supernatural rape-revenge horror films, here the supernatural elements are not only narratively inconsequential, but they also provide no benefit to the women who have been granted that power. Partially, this is because they choose to stay with the female clown who had helped them recover when she was injured in a confrontation with the gang at the cursed ruins; the girls chose friendship and loyalty over their own bloodthirsty desire for revenge. When the newly empowered girls confront the captain in the bordello or Tina in the ruins, however, they are still unable to kill them. In fact, the only member of the gang that dies appears to do so more because of his extreme drunkenness than any action taken by the girls. Their hearts do not appear to be into the idea of revenge, and this reinforces the Captain's revelation at the film's conclusion that they are innocent and pure. The bare threads of narrative that string Rollin's stunning imagery together in *Demoniacs* make it a difficult film to present in terms of its deployment of rape and revenge. But along with many of the others discussed in this chapter, *Demoniacs* demonstrates that rape-revenge manifests in film from across the globe to a variety of ends and in a range of generic contexts.

The same is true of Banjong Pisanthanakun and Parkpoom Wongpoom's Thai 2004 horror blockbuster *Shutter* and Masayuki Ochiai's 2008 remake, which shares the same basic plot as the original. In the original Thai film, Jane (Natthaweeranuch Thongmee) and her boyfriend, photographer Tun (Anada Everingham), hit a woman on the road one dark night and drive away. In the Hollywood film, Jane (Rachael Taylor) and her new husband Ben (Joshua Jackson)—also a photographer—hit a mysterious woman on the road on their arrival in Japan, where they have moved for Ben's work (unlike the Thai couple, Jane and Ben get out of their car to investigate but do not find a body). Both couples soon begin to be haunted by strange events, and the mysterious woman begins to appear in photographs. Jane in each film decides to investigate and is introduced to the notion of spirit photography. As they look further into it, they receive clues in photographs that lead to the identification of the woman: In the Thai film it is Natre (Achita Sikamana), and in the Hollywood film it is Megumi (Megumi Okina), the ex-girlfriends of Tun and Ben, respectively. Their partners (who are also tormented by the appearance of the ghosts) tell the two Janes that Natre/Megumi were possessive and inexperienced in love and took their break-ups badly. In each film Jane therefore believes that a jealous, spawned lover is haunting them. But the couples continue to be tormented, particularly ben and Tun when they discover that their best friends (who also knew Megumi and Natre) have died in strange and violent circumstances.

Both Jane and Ben and Jane and Tun journey to Megumi and Natre's homes and learn that the respective women had committed suicide. After putting their bodies to rest, they believe their hauntings will end. Returning to what they hope is a normal life, Jane in both films unthinkingly gets some photographs developed that lead her to the discovery of visual evidence (film in the Thai version, and a camera's memory stick in the Hollywood one) of Natre and Megumi being raped by ben and Tun's friends, and that Ben and Tun photographed each assault. Devastated, the women confront their partners who defend themselves by claiming their friends forced them into it, and that they did not realize that their harassment of Natre and Megumi would escalate into sexual violence. Disgusted and horrified, both women leave their partners. A furious and frantic Ben and Tun take photographs with a Polaroid camera to try and locate Megumi and Natre in their homes, and it is only when they drop the camera and it accidentally takes a photo of themselves that they discover the women are clamped around their necks, explaining the two men's mysterious neck and shoulder pain that had been mentioned throughout the film. The final shot of each film shows Ben and Tun hospitalized in psychiatric institutions after having seriously injured themselves trying to remove the vengeful spirit from their bodies. A reflection in the window of each hospital room shows Megumi and Natre still in place, sitting on Ben and Tun's shoulders.

Despite Taylor's claim that the U.S. remake of *Shutter* has "very cerebral aspects to it,"[68] the film made little impact critically or at the box office, with both filmgoers and reviewers widely dismissing it as an unimaginative rehash of the earlier film. The Thai version—which was a financial phenomenon and one of the most successful Thai films to date—for some may appear to simply rehash the same terrain as J-horror success stories such as *Ringu* (*The Ring*, Hideo Nakata, 1998) and *Ju-on* (*The Grudge*, Takashi Shimizu, 2000). Despite condemning most of the movie as a pedestrian Asian genre entry, Jamie Russell identifies its rape-revenge elements as its strongest feature. "Once it shows its hand," he says, "*Shutter* transforms into a supernatural footnote to the rape-revenge cycle, a kind of *I Spit on Your Grave* from beyond the grave." He continues, "While much of its running time insipidly retreads other movies, its final reel is dark enough to be memorable after the credits roll."[69] The subgeneric alchemy that converts both versions of *Shutter* from being horror films about the returned spirit of a spawned lover to being more explicitly supernatural rape-revenge films "from beyond the grave" is where each film gains the impact of its twist ending.

The two films deviate in a small but crucial way regarding their overall treatment of rape and revenge, however. In the Thai film the image of Tun in the hospital room is shown from Jane's perspective. But in the Hollywood film, Ben's identical predicament is not shown from Jane's perspective, simply because she is not there. Thus, when Jane in the Hollywood *Shutter* walks out on Ben at the discovery of his grotesque involvement in Megumi's rape (an attack that led to her suicide), her decision is final—there is no chance of reconciliation with a man involved in such a revolting act. But in the Thai film, Jane is there. This does not necessarily imply reconciliation between her and Tun, but, more than in the Hollywood version, it suggests that her severing of ties with Tun is not as complete as American Jane's is with Ben. Combined with the fact that the Thai film implies that Natre's motivations for harassing Tun do have at least something to do with her romantic obsession with him, Thai *Shutter*'s Tun seems to come out slightly less ethically scathed than Hollywood *Shutter*'s Ben, despite both of them physically ending up in identical places.

CHAPTER THREE

The Rape-Revenge Film Around the World

As has become apparent in the last two chapters, any suggestion that rape-revenge films are specific to the United States in the 1970s or to any single genre neglects a range of intriguing texts. Accordingly, this chapter seeks to examine international manifestations of the rape-revenge movie more closely; both in nation-specific contexts, but also how rape-revenge themes and motifs flow across national borders. It is undeniable that the popularity of North American rape-revenge films during this period had a strong influence on global production, but as the examination in the last chapter on *The Last House on the Left* adaptations demonstrates, the production of these films often transcends national borders. This chapter seeks to map the various configurations of rape and revenge that have appeared in cinema across different countries at different periods to demonstrate both its scope and diversity. To do this, fourteen short case studies provide a brief overview of how rape-revenge has manifested internationally, in countries including Argentina, Australia, Britain, Canada, Denmark, France, Germany, Hong Kong, India, Japan, Korea, Spain, Sweden, and Turkey. From the outset, it must be emphasized that these are not the only countries that have produced noteworthy examples of the rape-revenge film. Additionally, there is no suggestion that every single rape-revenge film in these particular national contexts will be examined, and in many instances it is not the most well-known examples that are explored. Rather, attention will focus on those movies that demonstrate the broad range of ways in which rape and revenge have intersected on screen.

Before embarking upon these case studies, the very task of cross-cultural analysis—particularly in an area as sensitive as sexual violence—raises as many questions about the cultural subjectivity of the critic as it does the texts they seek to examine. E. Ann Kaplan's reflection on the nature of cross-cultural analysis notes that the task is "fraught with danger," as "we are forced to read works produced by the Other through the constraints of our own frameworks/theories/ideologies."[1] In her exploration of Chinese cinema, she describes a scene from *Girl from Hunan* (Xie Fei and U Lan, 1986) that a Western critic would view as a rape scene but asks if a Chinese audience would read it the same way. This leads her to pose a series of important questions: "How is rape conceptualized in China? Does the definition of rape vary from culture to culture? Is rape acceptable as representation but not socially? Are we driven to undesirable relativism in such cross-cultural comparisons?"[2] Consequently, to assume that the "gaze" (a notion central to Western feminist film studies) or "social phases," such as modernism and postmodernism, apply to Chinese cinema is reductive.[3] With this in mind, this chapter does not seek to directly address Kaplan's questions as such, but it acknowledges them from the outset. The analyses that follow do not necessarily transcend the serious issues that surround cross-cultural analysis, but at their core they do not seek a singular or ultimate "meaning" of a particular film.

To narrowly restrict any film—including rape-revenge cinema—into singular, nation-specific contexts of production, while effective in the case studies that make up the bulk of this chapter, also risks denying the impact of transnational flows of influence (as seen most readily perhaps in the long reach of Swedish films like *The Virgin Spring* and *Thriller: A Cruel Picture*, for example), but also the practical realities of filmmaking in a production sense. While explicitly set in a pre-pandemic London where questions about the Brexit process, the London Bridge terrorist attacks and funding cuts to the NHS riddle the screenplay, the seemingly very British rape-revenge film *Feedback* (Pedro C. Alonso, 2019) is in fact a Spanish/U.S. co-production. And while the "Indonesian-ness" of Mouly Surya's rape-revenge western *Marlina the Murderer in Four Acts* is embedded in the cultural richness of the film, the director was explicit in her desire to speak beyond that specific culture in her film; "Usually Southeast Asian films that speak about these specific cultures use a very documentary approach to get the authenticity," Surya says. "Whereas I wanted to make it more universal in a way—so the audience can feel that this is a classic story that could happen anywhere."[4] Perhaps most famously we find Iranian filmmaker Asghar Farhadi's *The Salesman* (2016), an Oscar winning deconstruction of the rape-revenge trope that is built heavily around a strong intertextual reference to Arthur Miller's 1949 stage play, *Death of a Salesman*. Following a young couple who move into a new apartment, *The Salesman* centers around the sexual assault of the wife while the husband is out by a man believing the apartment is still occupied by a sex worker, just like the woman who had lived their previously. As her husband grows increasingly obsessed with tracking down the rapist, Farhadi presents a profound exploration of guilt and retribution; circling all of this like an ambient haze is the presence of violence against women, not only against the wife herself (although we do not see the rape), but the slow-dawning revelations of abuses the previous tenant also must have endured. While a film made by one of Iran's most acclaimed filmmakers, his privileging of *Death of a Salesman* seeks aggressively to break down national boundaries, opening his film up to a transnational dialogue and resulting in a movie that, like *Marlina the Murderer in Four Acts*, speaks in a more universal way to human experience.

A similar desire to explore a more universal truth lay at the heart of Peter Strickland's *Katalin Varga*. A British director making in a film in Romania with mostly Hungarian dialogue, it steadfastly refuses to be locked down to a specific national context, reflecting the broader internationalism of the filmmaker's practice and worldview. For Strickland, "the script was always set in a patriarchal culture even before I decided which country to shoot in."[5] He continues:

> I wrote the script in English in some mythical, "nowhere" land and once I found actors and locations, I tailored the writing to that place. I wasn't making any comment on Romania specifically even though the film is set there. That kind of patriarchal community can be found everywhere.

In a production context, however, for Strickland the international nature of *Katalin Varga* is nothing new and echoed the transnationalism of filmmakers such as Luis Buñuel or Jess Franco. "There was confusion as to the film's nationality upon release," he continued. "It could be British because of its writer/director and financing, Romanian because of its location or Hungarian since it mostly stars ethnic Hungarians in Transylvania and is in the Hungarian language apart from three small scenes where Romanians speak in Romanian or when a Hungarian speaks Romanian to a Romanian." For Strickland, the question of national specificity denies the reality of the broader context within which the film was made. "I've never really been that bothered about these things and always saw European culture as something much more all-embracing, especially now, in the face of Brexit." He added, "I'm half-British and half-Greek and never really agonised over my identity even though there are huge differences between those two cultures." Accordingly, while this chapter is structured along nation-specific lines, the following analyses seek to highlight the transnational aspects of rape-revenge as much as articulating geo-political issues that in some important cases are crucial to critically engaging with certain films most fully. But this is not an either/or scenario, again underscoring the diversity of rape-revenge.

Hilda Péter on the set as the title character in *Katalin Varga* (Peter Strickland, 2009) (photograph by Marek Szold, courtesy Marek Szold and Peter Strickland).

Argentina

Reflecting on the atrocities that have marked the histories of so many South American countries, it is perhaps unsurprising that rape-revenge cinema has proven a rich terrain to process specific national traumas while, at the same time, giving a diverse array of filmmakers rich if somewhat challenging material with which to creatively engage. Lucio A. Rojas's shocking 2017 Chilean rape-revenge horror film *Trauma* remains an extremely graphic and unambiguously distressing reflection on the scars the Pinochet regime left on the national psyche, flagged by the fact that the film—although largely set in 2011—explicitly begins in 1978 during the military dictatorship. In Guatemala, Jayro Bustamante's 2019 *La Llorona* utilizes the folkloric figure of "the weeping woman" and reimagines it as a ghostly revenge tale against a barely disguised stand-in for real-life dictator Efraín Ríos Montt. Bustamante and co-writer Lisandro Sanchez are clearly driven by undisguised fury over the genocide that stains that country's history, executed over a 36-year period and which saw the rape of over 100,000 women.[6]

But it is from Argentina where some of the most powerful South American rape-revenge films hail. From the introduction of sound in the early twentieth century, Argentina flourished as a key producer of South American cinema. It produced a wide range of films, including several relevant to this study of rape-revenge. To foreign audiences, Argentina is marked by its violent and dramatic recent history, political corruption and the struggles of its people against oppression. Perhaps unsurprisingly, rape-revenge has provided an opportunity for some filmmakers to reflect upon this history. Juan Carlos Desanzo is familiar to non–Argentinean audiences for biopics, including his Oscar-nominated movie *Eva Peron* (1996) and his fictional treatment of Argentinean writer Jorge Luis Borges in *Love and Fear* (*El amor y el espanto*, 2001). His earlier rape-revenge film *The Search* (*La busqueda*, 1985) arguably lacks the sophistication of films such as these, but it shares an intensity that marks the director's broader oeuvre. *The Search* was made in the early 1980s after a particularly strict period of censorship during the mid– to late 1970s. Because of this, its focus on corruption, abuses of power and a broader sense of uncertainty appears in some way to reflect the political climate around the time of its production.

The film follows the story of Patricia (Andrea Tenuta), a wealthy, happy teenage girl who witnesses her mother's sexual assault and her father's murder at the hands of a vicious gang. The criminals place a fake advertisement in the local paper to sell Patricia's father's Mercedes and rob and hold hostage all the potential customers who come to inspect the car. The violence inflicted against Patricia's family is not the sole intent of the home invasion, but rather these acts are deployed as both a system of control and as punishment for trying to escape. After the surviving family members are released, Patricia descends into furious rebellion as her brother, now catatonic, is hospitalized. Adopting a party-girl lifestyle, she meets massage parlor owner Mónica (Luisina Brando), an older woman who takes Patricia under her wing and gives her a job in her establishment as a waitress. Devastated at the discovery of Patricia's new life and the increasing tension and hostility between them, Patricia's mother commits suicide. Further outraged, Patricia continues to investigate the leader of the gang who traumatized her family, and discovers he is a criminal who demands protection money from Mónica (she also witnesses his influence over the police earlier in the film when he facilitates Mónica's release after a raid at an illegal party). Through work, Patricia identifies the gang leader's brother, who was also involved in the violation of her family; she meets him outside of work in the guise of a romantic rendezvous and kills him. This provokes the gang leader into another home invasion, this time with the intention of punishing Patricia for killing his brother, but Patricia murders both the remaining gang members (including the leader himself and her boyfriend Juan-Carlos, whom she discovers used her to gain information about her household in order to set up the initial crime). The film ends when Patricia and her younger brother, now fully recovered, are happily reunited via Mónica.

The most immediately striking feature of *The Search* is how it separates Patricia's trauma from her later desire for revenge. It is her mistreatment of her mother that leads to the latter's suicide, thus exposing a degree of selfishness to Patricia's trauma-fuelled rebellion. Despite the surface of the film having dated stylistically, there is a strong sense of verisimilitude in the troubled girl's behavior. Unlike many of the avenging women in this book, Patricia is not driven by a clear desire for revenge, nor is the plotline able to be neatly divided into distinct categories of rape and revenge. So severe is her trauma that such systematic reasoning is well beyond her capabilities. While it is certainly a story of transformation, Patricia's evolution—that follows her desertion of the family (driving her mother to suicide) to a return to the family, albeit with Mónica now as the mother figure—does not so neatly adhere to her search for vengeance against the men whose violence so dramatically changed her life. Rather, she floats around in a state of directionless fury until the opportunity for revenge finds her. Patricia's actions lead directly to her mother's suicide, and this prevents the spectator from completely aligning with Patricia (particularly considering it was the mother—and not Patricia—who was sexually assaulted earlier in the film). It is this precise irrationality of Patricia's behavior, however, that makes her story so compelling. Her final victory over the men who destroyed her family was never her intended goal, but it was ultimately what was required to provide her passage to a new life with her reconstructed family of her brother and Mónica.

Made over twenty years later, *I'll Never Die Alone* (*No Moriré Sola*, Adrián García Bogliano, 2008) offers another example of the Argentinean rape-revenge film. *I'll Never Die Alone* and *The Search* offer useful points of comparison, separated as they are by the internationally recognized wave of New Argentinean Cinema that began in the 1990s and includes the work of directors Alejandro Agresti, Daniel Burman, Juan José Campanella, Pablo Trapero and Lucrecia Martel. *I'll Never Die Alone* is brazen in its alignment with North American exploitation film traditions. There is evidence, for example, that the film is an intentional homage to the original *I Spit on Your Grave* in particular: its rural setting, its minimal use of dialogue, its outdoor rape scene followed by a second period of violence inside a nearby cabin, and its editing (like the earlier film, it too features many shots of a long duration). But *I'll Never Die Alone* deviates from Zarchi's film crucially in its intense stylization, positioning it as an homage to this era of exploitation alongside the work of directors Robert Rodriguez, Quentin Tarantino and Rob Zombie rather than with Zarchi himself. The film's arty composition, digital effects and sophisticated soundtrack render it more a love-letter to *I Spit on Your Grave* than an updating of it.

I'll Never Die Alone begins with four young female friends driving through the La Plata region, where they see the barely-alive body of a young woman on the side of a road. Seeing the men responsible for her injuries, the girls place the body in their car and head to a local village for help. Despite their efforts, the woman does not survive, and at the local police station they discover that the men responsible are policemen out of uniform. They file a report about the dead woman with the uniformed, lower-ranking policeman and seek to flee the area quickly. Their attempts are unsuccessful, however, and the senior policemen capture them, raping and torturing the girls in the nearby bushland, killing one of them. After this lengthy and brutal sequence, the girls help each other to dress and attempt to find help. They happen across a wooden cabin, but here again are discovered by the out-of-uniformed police. Another of the girls is killed here, and the uniformed police officer whose suspicions had led him to the cabin is also killed by his superiors. Shattered, the two surviving girls mobilize their fury and seek vengeance against the men who raped them and murdered their friends. One perpetrator has his nose graphically removed and is beaten in the head repeatedly with a hammer; one is strangled with barbed wire and then buried alive; and the final man is shot and left to be eaten by wild animals. Like *I Spit on Your Grave*, the end credits roll almost immediately as the last rapist is dispatched.

Recent Argentine rape-revenge films include *The Silent Party* (*La Fiesta Silenciosa*,

Diego Fried and Federico Finkielstain, 2019) and *Scavenger* (*Carroña*, Eric Fleitas and Luciana Garraza, 2020), and while the examples offered here are not intended to be the final word on rape and revenge in Argentinean cinema, that both *I'll Never Die Alone* and *The Search* explicitly feature rapists and murderers who are either policemen or have influence over the police appears to be far more than mere coincidence. Although neither of these films make explicit references to broader Argentinean political history, considering the state-approved violence that marked Argentina during the 1970s and early 1980s, it is significant that both these films feature corrupt, sadistic and violent men with links to the state. The military dictatorship during this period was marked by its use of rape and torture, and these films, whose villains are either government-sanctioned officers of the law or criminals that have control over such officers, cannot help but reflect upon this period of recent Argentinean history. While a surface reading of both films may initially suggest attempts at dehistoricizing sexual violence, the category of rape-revenge itself offers a strong thematic framework with which to consider the intersection of fiction and the real. This is nowhere more apparent than in *The Search*, when Patricia tells one of her victims, who asks about her family: "Mine got murdered in the war. What war? I'll tell you—there are many wars." Here, the intersection of the private sphere and her personal experience of violence is linked openly with the public and the political. This does not mean all Argentinean rape-revenge films after the so-called Dirty War must be assumed to be explicitly engaging with this period. However, that these two films in particular so deliberately construct their malevolent forces as being explicitly linked to a corrupt state is surely significant.

Australia

Colonized by the British in the late 1700s as a penal outpost, the proud "wild colonial boy" mythology that plays such a major part in the construction of white Australian identity renders the use of rape in Australian national cinema of little surprise. Rape in these films frequently translates to gang rape, and gang rape is often treated as the dark side of culturally celebrated notions of "mateship" and male friendship. Alice Aslan outlines the long history of gang rape in post–Invasion Australia, beginning with the abuse of First Nations women by Anglo-Australian officials, and culminating with a seemingly never-ending stream of modern-day news stories about male sports teams sexually assaulting female fans.[7] Two well-known contemporary Australian films in particular focus on issues of male friendship and loyalty in the context of gang rape and murder. *Blackrock* (Steven Vidler, 1997) marks the feature film debut of Oscar-winning actor Heath Ledger, who plays one of a group of teenage surfers accused of raping and murdering a local girl, and thus putting their friendship with central protagonist Jared (Laurence Breuls) to the test. Starring Toni Collette, *The Boys* (Rowan Woods, 1998) also focuses on a gang rape and murder, as it documents the events leading up to the involvement of three brothers in a vicious and unprovoked attack. Both *The Boys* and *Blackrock* were closely linked to famous real-life cases—the 1989 rape and murder of Leigh Leigh in Newcastle, New South Wales in Blackrock, and the infamous 1986 Anita Cobby case in *The Boys*—adding a sense of verisimilitude to each film. Together, these two movies place the mechanics of male bonding and masculinity under the microscope. They explore the notion of "mateship" that is so inherent to white Australian identity, and, through these extreme and disturbing narratives, expose their gender politics as deeply problematic.

Like *The Boys*, a group of rapist brothers also lie at the core of *The Proposition* (John Hilcoat, 2005). Written by acclaimed musician and author Nick Cave, *The Proposition* shifts the generic structures of the Western to a specifically Australian context, as the notion of the "frontier" easily adapts to the Australian outback of the late 1800s where the film is set. The movie begins after the rape and murder of the Hopkins family, assumed to have fallen victim to the notorious Burns Brothers gang. In *The Proposition*, rape and revenge intersect and deviate so randomly and chaotically as to effectively collapse the structural integrity of rape-revenge films like *Ms. 45*, or the original versions of *I Spit on Your Grave* and *The Last House on the Left*. Violent and powerful, the haphazard and undecipherable turmoil that rules this vision of the Australian outback is precisely the worst-case scenario that other Australian films concerned with rape and revenge hint at but struggle to resist. This is nowhere clearer than in *Shame*, another popular Australian film that has also drawn explicit comparisons with Western traditions. The film's title is commonly read as a deliberate reference to George Stevens' famous Western *Shane* (1953), encouraging interpretations that suggest a conscious gender reversal of the male stranger who arrives in a town to restore order.[8]

Shame begins with the arrival of Asta (Deborra-Lee Furness), a black-leather-clad city barrister, in the rural Australian town of Ginborak. Forced to stay in town as she awaits the arrival of a part to repair her motorbike, Asta befriends the Curtis family, whose daughter Lizzie (Simone Buchannan) has been gang raped by a group of local youths. These boys—one of whom is the son of the town's powerful and rich matriarch, and owner of the meatworks that employs much of the town, Mrs. Rudolph (Pat Skevington)—terrorize the town and its female inhabitants, while the local police adopt a dismissive "boys-will-be-boys" attitude. As her relationship with Lizzie and her family solidifies, Asta mobilizes both the Curtises and many of the town's other oppressed women to take a stand, leading Lizzie to press charges against the boys who raped her. Released on bail, the angry gang attack Lizzie's house one night, abducting her grandmother and badly beating her father. Asta and Lizzie manage to escape, and Asta takes the girl to what she believes is the security of the police station while the police (and a furious group of women from the town) find Lizzie's grandmother—whom the boys had attempted to rape—and detain most of the boys again. They realize too late that Lizzie has been left alone, however; in the time they are searching for her grandmother, the two lead boys abduct Lizzie in their car. Struggling to get free of the speeding vehicle, Lizzie opens the door and falls to her death. Still searching for Lizzie, Asta attacks one of the boys who mockingly feigns ignorance as to her whereabouts. Lizzie's body is soon discovered, and the police sergeant barks accusingly at Asta, "I hope you're bloody satisfied." One of the women answers for her and says, "No, we're not satisfied, not by a long way." The film ends on a still image of Asta's sad, defeated face.

While referencing the Western, *Shame* is also a deliberate subversion of traditional rape-revenge structures. It adapts the "agent" model of rape-revenge—where one person acts on behalf of a raped woman—but undermines its effectiveness and exposes its ethical weaknesses from the outset. While her intentions are good, the likeable and intelligent Asta feeds the raped girl post-feminist responses to rape, insisting that Lizzie should learn self-defense so she can "stick up for herself." Lizzie appears to identify only too readily how little this advice has to do with her own experience of rape ("What if there's six of them?" she asks a dumbstruck Asta). For Lizzie the issue is less about feminism than it is about class. At one point, she even tells Asta, "You must be rich ... you're not careful"; in her world, poor country girls get raped, and rich city women get to talk about it. In the face of Lizzie's death, Asta finally understands how futile her advice has been in the context of the very real class and gender issues that victimized Lizzie all along. As a rape-revenge story, Asta's plight is exposed as being fundamentally disconnected from Lizzie, despite her good intentions. Asta attempted to empower Lizzie by granting her the legal, physical and emotional artillery she assumed the girl needed, without consideration for Lizzie herself. The price for this misfired feminist vengeance fantasy was Lizzie's own life. For Kathi Maio, Lizzie's death is crucial in the film because—while bleak—"it is closer to the uncomfortable truth of women's lives."[9] But for Rose Lucas, the film is far more problematic: despite Asta's tomboyishness, the film appears to argue that gender inequality is inescapable and a simple fact of life. "Despite the horror and disgust engendered by the narrative," she says, "the film has offered no way out of the debilitating gender stereotypes of active male and passive female, as its bleak conclusion envisions no viable options for resistance to sexual attack."[10] This may be true for Lizzie, but as Asta climbs aboard her motorcycle and rides out of town, the film implies that there *are* options—but only for women who can afford them. Unlike Lizzie, bourgeois Asta (who can afford her feminist ideals) at least has the option to simply drive away.[11]

Fair Game (Mario Andreacchio, 1987) also concerns a town whose central industry is turning kangaroo meat into pet food. In *Shame*, a clear parallel is drawn between the cheap, processed meat that the rapist's family's factory produces and the bodies of the women who work there. In *Fair Game*, this symbolism is taken even further. In this film, a group of three hunters are introduced in the opening sequence speeding through the bush in a customized "ute" (Australian slang for a coupé utility vehicle), shooting kangaroos. They have trespassed on the property of the film's female protagonist, Jessica (Cassandra Delaney[12]), who runs a wildlife sanctuary on her property, where she is left to fend for herself while her partner is away. Even in its opening moments the film makes it explicit that in the world of *Fair Game*, masculinity is aligned with machines, while femininity is aligned with nature. The three men's determination to control nature through monstrous masculinity is demonstrated by the fact that they name their car "the beast"—they grant an animal-like quality to this machine in an attempt to construct an even playing field so the hunt can be considered a "fair game." From their perspective, reducing this hunt to a "beast" versus beast scenario—car against kangaroo—renders it less a slaughter than a competition where only the fittest will survive. That the men poach kangaroos to turn into pet food acts as a clear threat to Jessica, because her alignment with nature in their eyes also makes her the "fair game" of the film's title.

The three hunters—Sunny (Peter Ford), Ringo (David Sandford) and Sparks (Garry Who)—become increasingly enraged by Jessica after she attempts to press charges against them for trespassing, and their mild harassment evolves rapidly into an all-out attack. Jessica begins to realize the seriousness of her predicament when she awakens to find photographs of her sleeping nude stuck to her refrigerator door, and she spends a terrified night alone in her house waiting for further attacks. When the men awaken to find she has turned their weapons into an elaborate sculpture, they capture her and stage the film's most notorious, shocking and memorable feat: stripping her half-naked, they gag Jessica and tie her to the front of their car, then proceed to drive around in the scorching Australian sun until she collapses, humiliated and suffering from exposure. Despite being left for dead, she gets her revenge, before limping away with her beloved dog. Referenced heavily with its woman-as-human-hood-ornament motif in Quentin Tarantino's *Death Proof* (2007), the film's legacy is perhaps more famous than the original film itself.

The centrality of cars and machines mark the film's most obvious predecessor as *Mad Max* (George Miller, 1979), another vengeance-centered Outback action film. With its futuristic dystopia, *Mad Max*'s monstrous car culture is explicitly referenced in *Fair Game*, where Jessica's vision of a natural, "feminized" and harmonious Australia is placed in direct opposition to the "masculinized" world of violence and machines. This is amplified even further in Miller's 2015 film *Mad Max: Fury Road*. Set in the action franchise's signature dystopian future, Miller here links the abuse of women with the destruction of the environment, building a desert-patriarchy where water is more precious than gold and hoarded by the villain of the piece, Immortan Joe (Hugh Keays-Byrne), a dictator-king who keeps young women like breeding cattle, to be raped and forced to procreate. Toxic masculinity is not merely a metaphor in *Fury Road*, it is a disease that plays out on the corrupted bodies of broken men, corrupted both morally and physically by the desire for power. Yet while it is Max's name who still takes the title of the film (here played by Tom Hardy), its core is Charlize Theron's warrior woman Furiosa who fights for the emancipation of enslaved women and the rebirth of a near-destroyed environment. The two elements that the film sees as inextricably entwined as the oppression of women and environmental collapse are both resultant of toxic masculine power. To amplify Miller's focus on the film's gender politics, it was widely reported at the time of *Fury Road*'s release that Eve Ensler who developed the influential feminist play *The Vagina Monologues* in 1996 was a consultant on the film, working with key players on how to represent women and trauma.

Not all Australian rape-revenge films feature women protagonists, however. Writer, producer and director Steven Kastrissios' *The Horseman* (2008) blends the rough plot outline of Paul Schrader's *Hardcore* (1979) with a distinctly Australian vision of raw, masculine aggression. The film's title evokes apocalyptic overtones through the four horsemen from the Book of Revelation in the New Testament, while also prompting associations with Australian outback mythology in the figure of the drover who can tame wild horses, typified in Banjo Paterson's 1890 poem "The Man from Snowy River." *The Horseman* follows the story of a Brisbane man Christian (Peter Marshall) whose teenage daughter Jesse (Hannah Levien) died of a heroin overdose. He is anonymously sent an adult movie called *Young City Sluts 2* that shows a heavily drugged Jesse having sex with three men. Determined to seek vengeance for her death, Christian tracks down those involved in the production and distribution of the tape and slaughters them as he gains information regarding the location of other participants. Along the way he picks up the young hitchhiker Alice (Caroline Marohasy), and the two develop a strong relationship. Through Alice, Christian begins to come to terms with his guilt and grief regarding his daughter's rape and death. As the film's chilling climactic sequence unfolds, this revelation has arrived too late, and he cannot undo the inevitable consequences of his actions. Both he and Alice suffer horrifically for his decision to take justice into his own hands.

Despite its gritty look and its intense depiction of male-against-male violence, as a rape-revenge film, *The Horseman* shows little violence against women at all, even though such violence is at the heart of the narrative. There is a short clip of *Young City Sluts 2* shown early in the film that implies Jesse is drugged and forced to have sex, but in this brief clip Jesse herself is not naked, and there is little physical contact actually shown between her and the men. Later in the film, Alice struggles with a group of men, but again the violence against her is implied and happens off-camera. This should not suggest that this is a tame or gentle film by any means, however, and its depiction of Christian's revenge is graphic and disturbing. Peter Marshall's performance as the coldly determined Christian flawlessly depicts a man destroyed by his daughter's rape and death, and although not sympathetic as such, his reactions are believable and convincing. *The Horseman* is a harrowing view of contemporary Australian masculinity, but its impact spans far beyond its country of production. In terms of its brutality and final chilling message regarding the futility of vengeance, *The Horseman* is arguably the closest any filmmaker has yet to come in equaling Craven's original *The Last House on the Left*. Earnest, tragic and ferocious, *The Horseman* does not allow its audience the distancing luxury of irony. It is a difficult and intelligent film that deserves recognition well beyond the cult audiences that have already embraced it.

There are many more Australian rape-revenge films, as diverse examples such as *Acolytes* (Jon Hewitt, 2008), *Vigilante, Tomboys, Wasted on the Young* (Ben C. Lucas, 2010), *The Book of Revelation* (Ana Kokkinos, 2005), *Defenceless: A Blood Symphony* (Mark Savage, 2004), *Red Hill, The Day of the Broken* (Simon J. Dutton, 2014) and *Killing Ground* (Damien Power, 2016) demonstrate. Missing here—perhaps surprisingly for some—is Jennifer Kent's controversial *The Nightingale* (2018), a powerful, award-winning film that despite undeniably featuring acts of rape and revenge that are central to the narrative and thematic propulsion of the story, also include a range of other affronts to its vengeance-seeking woman protagonist, such as the gruesome murder of her baby and husband. Kent on this point is unambiguous; "I don't think it is a rape-revenge film," she has stated bluntly. Emphasizing the film's central journey that finds an Aboriginal man and an Irish woman forming an unlikely bond, for Kent, "this is a film about love in a very desperate time, and we live in desperate times."[13]

While *The Nightingale* will also be discussed briefly in Chapter Four, it was not the only Australian film to be critically discussed in relation to rape and revenge released in 2018. Directed by David Barker, *Pimped* is a notable entry into Australian films that fall under a rape-revenge umbrella precisely because of how far it shows the creative and thematic elasticity the trope can allow. Ella Scott Lynch plays two characters in the film; Rachael Montrose, a vampish femme fatale, the personified (yet imaginary) id of Sarah Montrose. Sarah is a controlled, intelligent woman who, with Rachael's encouragement, decides to pick a random man up in a bar for a one-night stand while her husband and daughter are away from home. Sarah however comes undone after the man she consents to having sex with, Lewis (Benedict Samuel), swaps out mid-coitus without Sarah realizing it as she is facing away from him, only to discover Lewis has let his friend Kenneth (Robin Goldsworthy) take his place. Rich and arrogant, this is one of a series of sexual games between him and Lewis, the latter just as arrogant and yet financially dependent on Kenneth whose hospitality he relies upon to live his ideal lifestyle. The title of the film therefore alludes (among other things) to what Lewis's role is as a man who procures women for the unattractive Kenneth. After Sarah murders Kenneth with a golf club once she realizes what has happened during her consensual encounter with Lewis, Sarah, Lewis (and Rachael, too, although the latter is unseen by Lewis) work through both the practicalities and ethics of what should be done, disposing of Kenneth's body until Lewis's depravity becomes so extreme that Sarah murders him, too.

Alongside films like *Black Rock* (Katie Aselton, 2012), *Pimped* deliberately reflects

Ella Scott Lynch in *Pimped* (David Barker, 2018) (courtesy Playground Films).

a reality rarely scene in rape film where consent is rendered far more complex than the more ubiquitous "stranger in an alley" assault scenario. Collectively these films are important because they hinge on the often-unspoken fact that consent may not be clear cut, but that does not render a rape any less of a rape because of it. Here, Sarah engages in sex with Lewis, not Kenneth, and their switching places is unambiguously done so without her knowledge or consent. Combined with her violent reaction to this discovery that results in her murdering Kenneth (and her later murder of Lewis), it is surely a rape-revenge film, and yet not in the way that is traditionally understood. As Barker recalls, the film's premise was based on what he assumed was an urban legend until he and Mentor discovered several similar cases that had been documented in Sydney in real life. Much of the effectiveness of the film hinges on how the rape scene itself was portrayed—seen from Rachael's perspective, while on paper how Sarah may not realize Lewis and Kenneth have switched places, the way that the scene is carefully put together means that as the audience, we too are just as confused as Sarah. "Even though the character of Rachael, as the primary POV, is essentially one of the unreliable narrator, the act of rape was something that we wanted to make sure remained in the realm of the real," said Mentor.[14] "The clash between the event with the already established schismatic Rachael, needed to be reflected with brutal rawness. David captured an extra layer by creating a dreamlike quality to the sex and consequent rape scene, juxtaposed with the sharper imagery of her first act of revenge." For Barker, much of the scene's success stemmed from the intuitive experimentation of Marianne Khoo, who when cutting the scene "went off script and started cross-cutting heavily between Sarah lost in desire and Rachael dancing, building to a point where the sensory climax meets the monster reveal. In that one scene, I feel it encapsulated much of our approach to the film: the idea of a personal schism in reaction to a warped and indecent reality." At the heart of this warped reality again lies the unorthodox, thoughtful and sensitive approach to the nuances of consent, working against the grain of how it is typically represented in cinema. "The issue of consent in this scenario is muddied by that there is both consensual and non-consensual sex," affirms Mentor. "One thing that was clear as we worked on the script was that the moment the line was crossed between consensual and non-consensual sex became a trigger for everything that follows. It is the major inciting incident that pushes the character and thus the content to extremes." Adds Barker, "There's a complexity to the rape experience, on a number of levels. Aspects of desire and pleasure within a conflicted woman, the abuse she experiences, creates this strange mix of abstraction and reality. The internal and the external. Yet, both are driven by their own truth." It is this question of truth that drives *Pimped* and makes it such an important and wholly original donation to the rape-revenge film category. While in many ways highlighting its abstraction through formal style and the figure of Rachael herself, Barker and his collaborators Mentor, Khoo and of course Lynch herself speak to a truth about the complexities of consent that far more literal—and famous—films fail to do.

Britain

Rape appears in many well-known British films also, as most notoriously demonstrated by films such as *No Orchids for Miss Blandish* (St. John Legh Clowes, 1948), *A Clockwork Orange* (Stanley Kubrick, 1971), *The Baby of Mâcon* (Peter Greenaway, 1993) and *Naked* (Mike Leigh, 1993). While the British rape-revenge film may be most immediately associated with Peckinpah's *Straw Dogs* (an American-British co-production set in Cornwall), Sidney Hayer's *Revenge* (1971) stars Joan Collins stars as the stepmother of a family whose young daughter has been raped and murdered. The family capture the man they believe responsible and hold him captive in the basement of their pub. When the family reach a point where they believe they may, in fact, have the wrong man, their moral collapse has occurred already (the peak of horror being a scene where Collins' Carol is raped in front of the captured man by her violent and frustrated stepson). "Video Nasty" *House on Straw Hill* (James Kenelm Clarke, 1976) also incorporates a rape-revenge sub-plot in its broader tale. Here, Linda (Linda Hayden) seeks revenge against a sexually sadistic author Paul (Udo Kier) for stealing her husband's work which resulted in the latter's suicide. While taking a job as Paul's secretary—part of her own vengeance scheme—Linda is raped at gunpoint in a field by two local thugs. But—stroking the barrel of the shotgun in a heavily eroticized manner—she gains control of the weapon, and fatally turns it against her rapists.

While there is no shortage of British rape-revenge films—including *Killer's Moon* (Alan Birkinshaw, 1978), *Lipstick and Blood* (Lindsay Shonteff, 1984), *Tyrannosaur* (Paddy Considine, 2011), *The Seasoning House*, *Amulet*, and *Dirty Weekend*—rape-revenge also appears as a central narrative mechanism in films that are not broadly considered as part of rape-revenge history, such as Mike Leigh's *Get Carter* (1971). While the film largely follows Michael Caine's legendary character Jack Carter's investigation into the death of his brother, just over an hour into the film he watches a pornographic film called "The Teacher's Pet" that he discovers his teenage niece—who is likely Jack's biological daughter—was forced to star in. The impact the porn film makes is not communicated to us through this film-within-a-film itself, but rather through a sequence of intense close ups of Jack's face as he moves through a series of intense emotions: shock, pain, sadness, and finally enormous anger. Beating the woman who showed him the film, he demands to know who was responsible for her involvement; while Jack was already on a mission to find his brother's killer, the discovery of his "niece's" forced participation in a porn film pushes him over the edge, his vigilante mission spiraling out of control until it ends with his famous death on a beach in the film's finale.

Rape-revenge continues to be a site of interest for British filmmakers, as demonstrated in Dan Reed's 2007 film *Straightheads*. The film stars Gillian Anderson in the first feature directed by documentary maker Dan Reed, and his unflinching treatment of the rape-revenge material is compelling viewing. The film opens as 23-year-old Adam (Danny Dyer) is installing surveillance equipment in the London apartment of the glamorous and professional 40-something Alice (Anderson). After some preliminary flirting, Alice invites Adam to a sophisticated party in the country that evening. Here, they have sex in a garden, and, on the drive back to the city, Adam tells Alice it has been the greatest night of his life. Caught up in the excitement of the moment, Adam mindlessly heckles a passing car. This unthinking act backfires, however, when Alice crashes her car, and both she and Adam are violently assaulted by the men whom Adam had previously mocked. Adam is viciously beaten, and Alice is gang-raped on the hood of her car in a powerful sequence. This is followed by a detailed study of Adam and Alice's mental and physical injuries as they return to Alice's apartment in the city to recover. During this period, Alice sees one of the rapists near the house of her recently deceased father. Deciding upon revenge, she demands Adam join her, and they begin to track down the other men. While Adam is less convinced that revenge is a good idea, Alice's desire for vengeance is strong, and she arms herself with her father's sniper rifle and shoots the dog of one of the rapists. This man, Heffer (Anthony Calf), has a troubled daughter called Sophie (Francesca Fowler), who looks for the dog. Although Alice is moved by the girl's plight, she continues her plan of revenge against Sophie's father. Adam's behavior becomes increasingly confused, and he attempts to rape Sophie in her bedroom after Alice forces him to break into Heffer's house to install surveillance equipment. With Adam's wiring well and truly askew, he is further confused when Alice rejects his new brutal and aggressive persona. Adam retreats angrily into the forest and returns to discover that Alice has confronted Heffer in his house. She has learned that on the night she was raped, Heffer diverted his friends' attention onto Alice to stop them from raping Sophie. Unmoved, Alice ties Heffer to the kitchen table and anally rapes him with her rifle. Shocked by her own actions, Alice flees and picks up Sophie who she sees walking aimlessly along the road. Back at Heffer's house, Adam does not share Alice's realization of the futility of vengeance and continues on his rampage. He shoots the two other rapists who arrive to see Heffer. After the last man is dispatched, Adam walks towards the camera, staring at the audience directly.

The few critics who paid any attention to *Straightheads* remained largely ambivalent. Derek Elley sums up the typical critical response, stating it "has no message about either random violence or the ethics of revenge. But as a gritty genre exercise—rather than a slice of socially aware cinema—*Straightheads* pretty much works."[15] Much of the ambivalence towards the film no doubt stems from its more excessive moments, particularly the sudden and unexpected scene where Alice rapes her rapist with the rifle (an act as shocking as it is "faintly ridiculous"[16]). As Anderson herself has pointed out, however, the attention on the last rape seemed to distract attention from the vicious first rape.[17] In terms of the nuts-and-bolts mechanics of representing sexual violence on film, this earlier rape is worthy of note.

As this book has demonstrated, rape can be formally represented in a variety of different ways. What *Straightheads* does, however, is relatively unique. As the bashing of Adam precedes Alice's rape, the film focuses on that preliminary act in gory, visceral detail. It then only briefly shows the beginning of Alice's assault. The result of this is what can be best described as "intensity-by-association": it is assumed, by proximity alone, that Alice's rape is *at least* as violent and horrific as Adam's beating. This is solidified even further by the following scene, which shows Alice sitting on a nearby tree stump the next morning with her back to the camera. As Adam approaches her, she stands up, and it is only when she stumbles (and blood is shown running down her leg) that the ferocious brutality of her assault is confirmed. Arguably, however, the care and consideration taken in the execution of this opening rape is not repeated in the "revenge rape" that Alice executes at the film's conclusion. Clumsy, graphic and sadistic, the "faintly ridiculous" nature of this assault to some degree undermines what had taken place previously. This is not to say that rape-*as*-revenge can only be critically understood in this way; mirroring the broader arguments of this book, there is a diverse range in which this configuration has been adapted. Rape-as-revenge is a notable trend particularly common in contemporary rape revenge films like *One Way*, *Straightheads* and *Descent*, and as will be discussed shortly, also appears in *The Girl with the Dragon Tattoo* and the *I Spit on Your Grave* remake.

In retrospect, *Straightheads* hinges thematically on Adam far more than it does on Alice. He is a young man destroyed by both the violent assault on his body and his proximity to Alice's rape and consequent emotional and psychological fallout. He does not share her vengeful drive, her experience, her income, or her intelligence, and consequently—as a newly-formed couple forged in the fire of random and extreme violence—his very notion of masculinity is guided by what he views as Alice's dominant hand ("You're so soft!" she tells him at one point when he attempts to smoke marijuana to cope with his physical and emotional distress). Consequently, when Alice begs Adam to stop the violence after she has raped Heffer, he is confused and angry because she had previously encouraged him to be more aggressive and vengeful. Simply, he turned to violence because Alice wanted him to. Adam struggles to articulate his trauma, and he looks to Alice for guidance, but she has her own emotional issues to contend with. By the end of the film, Adam resorts to violence with an almost child-like characteristic: "Shut up!" he tells Alice. "You've had your fucking go!" When Adam collapses the imaginary fourth wall and looks directly at the camera, he acknowledges the "presence" of the spectator with a cool yet accusing glare. Blurring the ethical distinction between "victim" and "villain" Adam's concluding gaze openly accuses the audience of being a willing participant through *our* act of spectatorship in the actions that preceded it.

Canada

To those familiar with the often-surreal climate of sexual violence in the work of David Cronenberg, to claim that Canada has produced some of the most confrontational images of sexual violence in film comes as little surprise. Despite a film industry that stretches between Montreal, Vancouver and Toronto, much critical treatment of the Canadian film industry focuses upon the long shadow cast by the dominant cinema of the neighboring United States. Not only does Canada appear to hemorrhage talent to its southern neighbor at a rapid rate, but many films are also criticized for lacking anything uniquely "Canadian." But, as films as diverse as *Class of 1984* (Mark L. Lester, 1982), *Sweet Karma*, *7 Days*, the late Ryan Nicholson's *Gutterballs* (2008) and *Hanger* (2009), *American*

Mary, and *Violation* suggest along with those discussed further here, Canada has its own rich, diverse history of rape-revenge films. William Fruet had already explored rape in 1972's *Wedding in* White which won the Best Feature Film gong at the 1972 Canadian Film Awards, but it was *Death Weekend* (1976) which set the precedent for Canadian exploitation rape-revenge films. As a classic example of 1970s B-grade "Canuxploitation," *Death Weekend* has retrospectively developed a cult audience beyond the lackluster response it garnered upon its initial release. While A.H. Weiler from the *New York Times* politely rejected the film as being "a good deal less than meets the eye,"[18] Clive Denton at *Cinema Canada* was less restrained in his declaration that it was no less than "an ugly, vicious, and downright shitty movie" and "mean-spirited garbage."[19] Recently, defenders of the film have argued for its status as a Canadian *Straw Dogs*,[20] and certainly in terms of its form and tone (as well as a few specific plot parallels), the suggestion holds some merit. But while granting it an air of legitimacy through comparisons to Peckinpah's film, this association simultaneously acts to highlight *Death Weekend*'s lack of "Canadian-ness"; even at the time of the film's release, Denton countered such defenses by asking, "Can't we be first in anything?"[21]

Set in the deserted Ontario countryside, the film opens with dentist Harold (Chuck Shamata) driving in his expensive sports car to his country house with model Diane (Brenda Vaccaro). A car enthusiast, Diane takes over the driving duties, and almost immediately a car full of threatening thugs challenges the couple to a race, led by the ominous Lep (Don Stroud). After a lengthy action sequence, Diane outsmarts and outdrives the group, leaving Lep furious and humiliated by what he sees as a direct insult to his masculinity. When she arrives at the materialistic Harold's house, Diane discovers that his intentions are far from wholesome: he admits to lying to her about having a house party that weekend, and confesses it is only the two of them on the deserted property. She is furious when he asks her to pose nude for some photographs; but unbeknownst to her, he has already taken naked pictures of her through a two-way mirror installed in the bathroom. Before she has the opportunity to leave, however, Lep and his gang invade the house, and their threatening attitude collapses into violence when Lep rapes a terrified Diane when she attempts to run away. Lep makes it clear that the rape is motivated not only by his desire to repay her for his earlier humiliation on the road, but also as a direct attack on Harold. After the rape, Lep realizes that Harold is so materialistic that he cares only for his property. At this discovery, Lep and his gang gleefully destroy Harold's house with a baseball bat, smashing pianos and shattering toilet bowls. It is only when faced with the destruction of his material possessions that Harold reacts and runs to get his gun. Lep overpowers him easily and takes the weapon, then chases Harold outside into the night. Left inside with the rest of the gang, Diane is raped again but this time manages to fight back and slashes her assailant's throat with a piece of broken mirror. Escaping outside, she continues her violent revenge as she drowns and burns to death the two other gang members, leaving only Lep. Discovering the dead body of Harold in a car, she pushes it aside as she attempts to escape but is pursued by a gun wielding Lep. In the film's climactic finale, she runs Lep over and kills him, leaving her in a brief slow-motion moment of shock before the end credits roll.

Released in the U.S. as *The House by the Lake*, *Death Weekend* played at theaters alongside a film similarly focused on rape and revenge, *The Last House on the Left*. But where Craven's film placed thematic attention on issues of class and the ethical ambiguities of revenge itself, Fruet's film is concerned primarily with the struggle between men to assert their masculinity, and the violent consequences that women who get in the way may be exposed to. In *Death Weekend*, sexual threats come at Diane from Harold as well as from Lep and his gang, and by constructing her host as a malevolent force from the outset, the film avoids simplistic class-based binaries. Here, *all* men are potential rapists, and all men are enemies. Consequently, there is an indistinct yet always present suggestion of inevitability to Diane's experiences. The way that she glazes over or is presented in slow-motion at crucial moments adds a feeling of "not quite there-ness," implying that she is in some way opting out of the reality of her circumstances because she simply does not know what else to do. Even the revenge component of the film seems somewhat lackluster next to comparative scenes in other movies—rather than actively relishing her vengeance, Diane seems to be merely tying up administrative loose ends. Although all the men in the film that had tormented her so brutally—including Harold— are dead by the end of the movie, the catharsis that so often accompanies such a conclusion is notably absent here, while also lacking the powerful ambivalence of the original *The Last House on the Left*. Fruet had hoped that *Death Weekend* would herald a return to the earlier successes of his career, but the critical rejection of the film prevented such an outcome.[22] With two well-known American actors in its leading roles, this may have partially stemmed from a view of the film as yet another Canadian-produced movie pandering to a commercial U.S. audience. But in terms of how the film functions as an example of the rape-revenge film so popular during this period, *Death Weekend* is strangely neither-here-nor-there. Despite solid performances and competent execution, the movie appears to dance unsatisfactorily around some interesting thematic terrain without ever seriously acknowledging it.

Denys Arcand's *Gina* (1975) sees rape and revenge merge in an even more explicitly Canadian context. As one of the key figures of contemporary Canadian cinema, Arcand's name is internationally associated with Québécois cinema, with films such as *Jesus of Montreal* (1989), *The Invasion of the Barbarians* (2003) and *The Decline of the American Empire* (1986). *Gina* begins with a shocking sequence of a woman being beaten and abused by a group of men as the title character (played by Céline Lomez) looks on indifferently while eating breakfast cereal. The central male figure tells the woman that, as an employee, she is to fulfill her work duties as a striptease dancer and not pursue external transactions while working for him. While never called a pimp, the viciousness with which he chastises the woman—and the fact that he takes money from her purse to compensate him for his perceived trouble—suggests this is effectively his role. Gina interrupts the violence only when she believes it is getting out of control, and while she blots the beaten woman's nose with a tissue, the "boss" asks her if she can replace the girl as a dancer. Gina agrees and catches a train to the Québécois town of Louisville. Simultaneously, the film introduces a team of four documentary filmmakers traveling from Montreal to Louisville to make a documentary about the textile industry. A supervisor from the National Film Board makes it clear to them that their project is controversial, but the four men are determined to continue production. In between the lengthy periods of the film that focus on the progress of the documentary—including interviews with local townsfolk (mostly women and the elderly) about how their lives have been affected by the poor, exploitative working conditions of the town's cotton factory—Gina establishes an informal friendship with the film crew. They hang out, smoke marijuana, go ice-skating, and accept a challenge to a game of pool with two burly snowmobile-riders, who are humiliated when Gina and her partner easily beat them.

The crew attend Gina's striptease performance at the hotel with the hard-working factory employee Dolorès (Frédérique Collin), whom they had previously interviewed. The evening becomes uncomfortable when the two men whom Gina and the film crew had earlier beaten at pool turn up with their snowmobile riding gang. The gang sexually harass and intimidate Gina before, during and after her performance. Refusing the advances of the gang's leader, Gina says goodnight to the film crew and retires to her room, where the gang—all fifteen of them, including women, and all wearing their brightly colored balaclavas, parkas and helmets—break in and viciously gang rape her. The deeply traumatized Gina showers and drinks gin, calming herself for the walk to a phone booth where she calls her "manager" who turns up at the hotel the next morning with a group of heavies. The film crew are unaware of what has happened to Gina and do not understand why she suddenly does not wish to talk to them. They face their own crisis, however, when they are informed that the owner of the textile factory has persuaded the National Film Board to cancel the documentary project, barring the crew from the premises of any textile factory in Canada. After the crew pack up and return to Montreal, Gina follows the leader of the snowmobile gang around town, while her manager locates the gang's headquarters. That night he and his associates surprise the gang at their base—an abandoned ship on a frozen river—and beat them with baseball bats and chains. Three snowmobile riders manage to escape, but Gina (who is waiting in a car outside) sees them and pursues them in a fast-paced action sequence that climaxes with the final rapist being fed through a woodchipper. The film finishes by showing what has happened to its central protagonists: Gina boards a plane to Mexico, the film crew happily shoot a television program about a crime of passion in Montreal and smiling Dolorès finally marries her fiancé.

At first glance, the juxtaposition of the textile documentary story with Gina's rape-revenge tale may seem incongruous, but the behind-the-scenes details of the film's production allow insight into how Arcand unites these two narrative threads to create his overall impact. Long before his status as a credible auteur was established, Arcand had a reputation within the Canadian film industry as "an unbankable trouble-maker,"[23] a political agitator whose Direct Cinema–imbued documentary work focused on controversial subject matters. Like the filmmakers in *Gina*, he, too, worked with the National Film Board, and had a documentary about textile production shut down. Arcand began filming *Cotton Mill* (*On est au cotton*, 1970) in 1968, and while the film finished shooting in 1970, broader nervousness about artists and radicals during the October Crisis led to the cancellation of the project. The National Film Board considered the film to be unreasonably biased and banned it, garnering Arcand a reputation as a "champion of free speech."[24] According to Pierre Veronneau, *Gina* began solely as a rape-revenge film, and Arcand later added the autobiographical aspects to emphasize his broader social critique.[25] Generic references to the Western have been identified in the film,[26] and in terms of its narrative structure, construction of a "frontier" space, and in particular the narrative-propelling function of a woman's rape as the cause of male confrontation, this association makes sense.

But in its bringing together of the textile documentary storyline with Gina's rape-revenge story, *Gina* also looks explicitly at industrial exploitation and the abuse of workers in all its guises, and frames rape in a broader picture of corruption, inequality and unfair work practices. The film focuses on the economic exploitation of a range of workers—particularly of factory workers like Dolorès and the elderly man interviewed by the documentary crew; the staff and unhappy wife of the man who runs the hotel;

sex industry workers like Gina herself; and the unnamed woman whose beating was so graphically depicted in the film's opening moments. As an outraged Gina explains to her "manager" after their arrival in Louisville, "I've been pushed around before, but never like this." There is an implication that while she understood that the type of already nasty sexual harassment she faced before the rape was part of the job, to be gang-raped by fifteen people is an occupational hazard she was unprepared for. The vengeance sequence where Gina mows down some of her rapists is privileged as the film's climactic moment and draws parallels with the many rape-revenge films that were finding success in the United States during this period. To some degree, this supports criticisms of the film in Canada at the time of its release as "attempting to copy the 'American way.'"[27] While there is certainly this transnational aspect to the film, this grossly neglects how specifically Arcand's broader social critique of Canada (and Quebec in particular) manifests itself in *Gina*. This is nowhere clearer than during the rape scene itself, as the Canadian national anthem plays in the background while Gina is viciously assaulted. The act of rape is therefore explicitly tied to an entrenched system of exploitation and abuse that, to Arcand at least, was intrinsic to the nation itself.

Denmark

To separate Nordic countries as I have done here in the case of Denmark and Sweden denies the often closely interwoven nature of production in this region. Regardless, there are key texts from these two national contexts specifically which demand precise focus. This is not, however, to deny the existence of rape-revenge films made in other countries in the region; in Norway, rape-revenge films include *Revenge for My Daughter, The Whore* (*Hora*, Reinert Kiil, 2009), and *Revenge* (Kjersti G. Steinsbø, 2015) while in Finland, films tackling the subject of sexual violence and rape culture more generally can be seen in movies ranging from *The Milkmaid* (*Hilja maitotyttö*, T.J. Särkkä, 1953) to the all-woman directed anthology *Force of Habit* (*Tottumiskysymys*, 2019). In some cases, films from Nordic countries—like elsewhere—may to the foreign eye at least lack any indicators of their cultural specificity outside of surface markers such as language and settings, such as the supernatural rape-revenge film *Room 205* (Martin Barnewitz, 2007). This tale of a ghost of a woman who died by suicide after a violent gang rape in her dorm room follows the spirit's escape after a new student accidentally cracks the mirror, releasing the ghost who undertakes a supernatural killing spree of the dorm's current tenants, punishing the living for her tragic fate. Thematically focused on bullying, *Room 205* is an entertaining horror film that incorporates rape-revenge elements, but appears to reject any cultural specificity to both Denmark itself or the region more broadly.

Denmark specifically, however, is an important country to consider in regards to its relationship to sexual violence and how it is represented on screen, with a number of reports indicating that the country has the largest prevalence of rape and sexual violence in Europe.[28] So great is his international success that Lars von Trier is virtually synonymous with Danish cinema, which in recent years has been complicated both by allegations by pop star Björk (the star of his 2000 film *Dancer in the Dark*) of sexual harassment against the director, but also wider allegations that sexual abuse had riddled the culture of his production company, Zentropa.[29] His 2003 film *Dogville* does not remain untouched by such a legacy, with von Trier on the record for suggesting that the scene in the film where lead actor Nicole Kidman wore a dog collar gave him "personal pleasure."[30] Although von Trier's *Dogville* appears to less consciously engage with rape-revenge traditions, there are enough narrative and thematic elements present to easily place it in this category. To boil its plot down to its barest narrative bones, it is the story of a woman who destroys an entire town for raping and tormenting her. In typical von Trier style, the manner in which this story plays out is far more complex than this skeletal synopsis suggests. Narrated by John Hurt, the film is divided into nine separate chapters that tell "the sad tale of the town of Dogville." Frightened and beautiful stranger Kidman's Grace wanders into the remote eponymous town in the Rocky Mountains of the United States seeking protection from ominous gangster figures that are searching for her. Under the strong recommendation of Tom Edison, Jr. (Paul Bettany), the townspeople agree to let Grace stay in Dogville, and at Tom's suggestion, she offers herself to do a variety of tasks for the town's residents as a sign of good will. As Tom and Grace fall in love, their happiness is disrupted when police visit Dogville and post a notice that says Grace is a dangerous woman wanted for her involvement in a number of bank robberies. Because of the added dangers involved in letting her stay in Dogville, the townsfolk cut her pay but increase her workload.

There is a distinct turn in Grace's treatment about an hour into the film. What begins as veiled discomfort and mistrust towards her escalates rapidly into rape and cruelty, until—after trying to escape Dogville (and being raped as punishment)—a large heavy wheel is chained to Grace via a collar around her neck. All the men in the town participate in the regular rape of Grace except for Tom. Upset that she still refuses to have sex with him (their romance was unconsummated), Tom decides to notify the gangsters who were looking for Grace of her whereabouts. The gangsters arrive, and Tom tells them magnanimously that he cannot accept a cash reward, but his understanding of the situation changes when it is revealed that the gang's leader (played by James Caan, referred to only as the Big Man) is Grace's father. After Grace and her father have a lengthy discussion about the ethics of violence, punishment and goodness, Grace announces, "I want to make the world a better place…. If there is any town this world would be better without, this is it." At her order, the town is burned to the ground, and all of Dogville's residents (except for the dog) are shot. She shoots Tom at point blank range, telling her father, "Some things you have to do yourself."

Sexual violence or gendered power struggles are not uncommon in von Trier's films, typified by *Dancer in the Dark* (2000), *Breaking the Waves* (1996), *Antichrist* (2009), *Nymphomaniac* (2013) and *The House that Jack Built* (2018). The man once described as "the P.T. Barnum of modern cinema"[31] has often met with accusations of misogyny—both in his films themselves and in regard to his alleged mistreatment of Björk during the making of *Dancer in the Dark*. In *Dogville*, von Trier attempted to distance himself from such claims by stating, "I would say that these characters are not so much females as they are a part of me. It's very interesting to work with women. They do my character well. I think that they portray me in a good way."[32] The film also received criticism for its perceived anti–Americanism, with its view of small-town ethics read as especially judgmental (particularly in respect to its concluding use of David Bowie's song "Young Americans" as it shows vintage photographs of poor Americans). These accusations von Trier also dismissed,[33] and as Jack Stevenson has noted, the film can just as easily be considered a response to the political climate in his own country (during the period of the film's production, von Trier had expressed vocal outrage at "a general swing of Danish politics to the right"[34]).

At first glance, such debates pale in comparison to *Dogville*'s most striking immediate feature—its stark, minimalist formal construction. Inspired by the theater of Bertolt Brecht, the film is shot in a large empty space with only white chalk-drawn outlines and writing on the floor to denote spatial boundaries. While there is some furniture, not all props are provided (the gooseberry bushes tended by Lauren Bacall's Ma Ginger, for example, are indicated simply by the word written on the floor where the plants should be). Von Trier chose this striking stylistic approach to place more emphasis upon the characters themselves, but at his bluntest there is an implication that the shock of such a formal choice stems from his love of provocation: "There's a black floor, it takes three hours, nothing happens, the outcome is terrible. Nobody should say that they were not warned."[35] In light of such a challenge, von Trier's utilization of a basic rape-revenge structure should be considered par for his broader authorial course. While the film is rarely discussed in such terms, Bryant Frazer offers one of the few instances that link *Dogville* to rape-revenge explicitly, noting that it "plays like the ultimate rape revenge flick—it's as if the ghosts of Bess from *Breaking the Waves* and Selma from *Dancer in the Dark* are wandering through Dogville, too, having come to kick some serious fucking ass."[36] But despite its obvious structural crossover with rape-revenge traditions, can Grace's total destruction of Dogville be so easily understood as the kind of pop feminist victory that Frazer suggests? The discussion Grace has with her father before she decides to annihilate Dogville places her decision in a far more complex conceptual terrain that concerns not only ethics and subjectivity, but also, more opaquely, the issue of Grace's survival in her life after Dogville. As Caroline Bainbridge suggests, Grace's circumstances at the end of the film are far from "happily ever after":

> Once again, Grace is left no room in which to exist as a subject on her own terms—her choice in the ending of *Dogville* is a stark one: she must either bear the brunt of rejection by the father or inflict punishment on those who have treated her so badly in order to properly enter the symbolic domain of paternal law and take up her properly feminized position. Grace's decision at the end of the film is arguably as much about survival as the one she makes at the beginning.[37]

Despite the undeniable catharsis granted through Grace's demolition of the town that raped and tortured her, this act, too, can be considered a symbolic negotiation as she enters into yet another complex gendered power relationship with her father. Just as Grace offered to do chores for the people of Dogville as a sign of good will, so too her annihilation of the town at the film's conclusion may be seen as a sign of good will towards her father (according to his own ethical logic, at least). Consequently, like many of the rape-avenging women in this book, Grace's spectacular and climactic moment of violent retribution against her abusers is far from a simplistic victory or defeat in the broader context of her status as an abused and victimized woman.

France

The cinematic movement referred to as the "New French Extremity" offers one of the most immediately recognizable instances of contemporary rape-revenge film. But revenge tales more generally have a strong history in French cinema, as demonstrated by auteurist offerings such as Claude Chabrol's *The Beast Must Die* (*Que la bete meure*, 1969) and, of course, one of the most famous female avenger films of all time, François Truffaut's *The Bride Wore Black* (*La Mariée était en noir*, 1968). Following in this tradition, a series of French rape-revenge films were produced during the 1970s and 1980s alongside the more widely discussed American rape-revenge cycle.

Rape-revenge films from this period demonstrate the variety of ways that sexual violence and vengeance were conceptually configured during this period. *The Old Gun* (*Le vieux Fusil*, Robert Enrico, 1975) is set during World War II in occupied France, where a disillusioned surgeon attempts to hide his wife and daughter from the Nazis and seeks revenge when he discovers they have been raped and murdered. Jean-Louis Trintignant had already appeared in Philippe Labro's 1971 rape-revenge film *Without Apparent Motive* (*Sans mobile apparent*), before he would co-star with Catherine Deneuve in *Act of Aggression* (*L'agression*, Gérard Pirès, 1975). This film addresses the potential futility of revenge in a rape-revenge context. Based on Montreal-based writer John Buell's novel *The Shrewsdale Exit* (1972), Pirès' film focuses on a man's frustrations after the law is unable to satisfactorily respond to the rape and murder of his wife Hélène and daughter Patty after a gang of motorcyclists terrorizes them. While the novel's focus is primarily upon the ethical turmoil of the male protagonist as he rallies against the motorcyclists he believes responsible, the film is distracted by what becomes its central area of interest—the blossoming romance between Paul (Trintignant) and his sister-in-law Sarah (Deneuve). Both these actors were considered sex symbols at the time, explaining perhaps why the emphasis of the film shifts from the rape and murder of Paul's wife and daughter to some degree. However, the deployment of a rape-as-seduction motif during their courtship exposes Pirès' ambivalence towards rape. After Sarah's arrival, Paul gets drunk and attempts to sexually assault her when she takes him back to his home to sober up. Her response to his announcement that he wants to "ball" her, and his subsequent violent pursuit around the house constructs it as an attempted rape as she screams at him, "You want to do to me what they did to Hélène!" In the world of *Act of Aggression*, rape is apparently only a problem if it involves murder. That Sarah ends this scene by taking off her wedding ring, stripping and saying to Paul, "Come on, I dare you!" indicates that rape here is merely part of a broader ritual of seduction that both Paul and Sarah seem both familiar and comfortable with.

Because the spotlight is placed more on Paul and Sarah's relationship than it is on Paul's vengeance—combined with the fact that rape itself is dismissed from within the diegesis as being serious only when associated with murder—the intensity of the film's climax is substantially weakened. Paul finally finds himself in a position to enact his revenge upon the three motorcyclists when it is revealed that they did not rape and murder Hélène and Patty after all. While they were responsible for the initial assault that drove Paul off the road, it was, in fact, André (Claude Brasseur), a man whom Paul had believed was an ally in his search of the motorcyclists, who was responsible. The revelation that he had attempted to kill the wrong party should have provided the source of the film's thematic clout about the ethical haziness of revenge, but in this context at least, this message is potentially complicated by a romance problematically constructed through the equating of rape with seduction. *Act of Aggression* is hardly alone on this front, however, and seduction as the modus operandi of the rape-avenging woman has a widespread and diverse application, seen everywhere from pedophile-hunter revenge film *Hard Candy* (David Slade, 2006) to the seductive Indian grandmother in Devashish Makhija's *Ajji* (2017).

Six years before *Act of Aggression*, René Clément cast a pre–*Chato's Land* and *Death Wish* Charles Bronson in the rape-revenge thriller, *Rider on the Rain* (*La Passager de la pluie*, 1969). Unlike *Act of Aggression* and Bronson's latter rape-revenge offerings, *Rider on the Rain* focuses primarily on the experience of its female rape-surviving protagonist, the young and naïve Mellie (Marlène Jobert). Far from *Act of Aggression*'s ambivalence about rape, Mellie's assault and the complications that arise—both from the trauma of the rape itself and from the fallout after Bronson's mysterious Colonel Dobbs arrives to investigate the whereabouts of the rapist she has murdered—are presented sympathetically. Predominantly, the story is mostly told from her subjective perspective—if not literally through the deployment of first person camera angles, then certainly in its focus on her emotional state and feelings of guilt, fear, anger and confusion. Dobbs' ethical position is ambiguous right up until the end of the film, but despite Mellie (and the spectator's) inability to decide if he is working for or against her, the two develop a platonic bond. It is her relationship with Dobbs (and his final decision to keep her secret about both her rape and the murder of the rapist) that finally grants her the maturity to accept the flaws in her life, forgiving her unfaithful yet jealous husband, and her loving but bitter and passive-aggressive mother.

One Deadly Summer (*L'Été meurtrier*, Jean Becker, 1983) places a woman rape-avenger at the center of a rape-revenge film that gained great commercial and critical success in France at the time of its release. Set in a rural French town during the mid-1970s, *One Deadly Summer* follows the story of young and beautiful Elle (Isabelle Adjani) in her attempts to avenge the rape of her mother by three men in Italy in the 1950s that led to her own birth. Elle moved to the village with her still traumatized mother and a disabled man whom she knew as her father. Elle's relationship with both parents is tumultuous and complicated, as a confronting scene where her mother breastfeeds her adult daughter suggests. The adoptive father's disability is widely believed to have been caused when he fell off a ladder, but a flashback later in the film demonstrates Elle's long-term psychological frailty, showing her as a teenager beating him violently with a shovel after she reads a sign of affection as an inappropriate sexual advance. Both Elle and her mother demonstrate disappointment and disrespect for the adoptive father's inability to seek vengeance for the mother's rape, so Elle accepts this undertaking herself in the belief that the death of the rapists will allow her family life to return to how it was before she found out the truth about her origins. Elle does so by seducing and becoming engaged to naïve fire fighter Pin-Pon (Alain Souchon), the son of one of the men she believes responsible for her mother's rape. Discovering that Pin-Pon's father is dead, Elle vows to destroy his whole family. Elle's grasp on sanity weakens further after the wedding, and she discovers that her adoptive father killed the rapists many years ago but did not tell anyone in order to avoid punishment. Shattered by the news that her plan for vengeance was futile—and, more significantly, that the death of the rapists did not lead to a return to her earlier happier family life—Elle has a mental collapse and regresses to her nine-year-old self. Deeply in love with Elle, Pin-Pon finds her list of potential victims and decides to continue Elle's plans of vengeance as a sign of devotion. Although knowing Elle had been mentally unstable for a long time, the film ends as Pin-Pon shoots two innocent men. This plot synopsis fails to capture the eloquence with which Becker presents what may at first appear to be familiar rape-revenge terrain. Like *The Bravados* and *Act of Aggression*, *One Deadly Summer* can be understood as a failed rape-revenge narrative in the sense that the person who has chosen to pursue a path of vigilante revenge is ultimately foiled. But its cinematic family tree expands well beyond sex comedies, melodramas and films more typically thought of as rape-revenge, adhering to a tendency in Adjani's filmography for playing complex yet unstable women.[38] *One Deadly Summer* may be best understood as weaving together many generic, conceptual and thematic threads to create a final, crushing impact. That it grafts these disparate elements so securely to a rape-revenge framework demonstrates the potentially centrifugal force of rape-revenge more generally.

And then, of course, is the so-called "New French Extremity," a phrase coined by James Quandt in 2004 in his review of Bruno Dumont's *Twentynine Palms* (2003), observing "the growing vogue for shock tactics in French cinema over the past decade" and a "recent tendency to the willfully transgressive."[39] Films such as *Martyrs* (Pascal Laugier, 2008), *High Tension* (*Haute Tension*, Alexandre Aja, 2003), *Frontier(s)* (*Frontière[s]*, Xavier Gens, 2007), *Trouble Every Day* (Claire Denis, 2001) and *Inside* (*À l'intérieu*, Julien Maury and Alexandre Bustillo, 2005) all involve sexually-themed violence to some degree. But it is *Baise-moi* (Virginie Despentes and Coralie Trinh Thi, 2000) and *Irréversible* (Gaspar Noé, 2002) that have earned the reputation for being two of the most controversial rape-revenge films made in recent years.

Noé is also no stranger to controversy and has actively engaged with the rape-revenge traditions to present his notorious vision of violence and retribution. With a reputation for shocking and extreme cinema confirmed by his debut feature *I Stand Alone* (*Seul contre tous*, 1998)—a film Nadine watches on a television in her apartment at the beginning of *Baise-moi* in a nod to Noé—the elements of rape and misdirected vengeance that appear briefly in his earlier movie take center stage in *Irréversible* (2002). The blistering formal conceit of the film is immediately apparent in the first few seconds of the opening credits, in which the words scroll backwards, beginning with the copyright information that normally ends a movie. Less than a minute in and the angle of these reversed credits begins to skew so much so that when the film's title is revealed, it is not only backwards but on its side. From the outset, *Irréversible* seeks not only a temporal reversal in its structure, but to turn a whole range of assumptions on their side. Played in reverse—starting with the last scene of the story and working its way toward its introduction—the film begins with violent revenge, is followed by a rape, and then focuses on the acts leading up to the rape. In this context the rape is inevitable for no other reason than it has already happened when the film begins.

Opening with Philippe Nahon as the Butcher—the same character he played in *I Stand Alone*—*Irréversible* deliberately places itself in the same sexually violent, racist and homophobic universe of Noé's previous film, giving those familiar with the earlier work some idea of the intensity of what is to follow. But even with that warning, the shift to a vicious assault in the seedy underworld of The Rectum (a gay S&M club) is deeply shocking. Although the characters have yet to be identified, Marcus (Vincent Cassel) and his friend Pierre (Albert Dupontel) are shown leaving the club, with Pierre in handcuffs and Marcus being driven away in an ambulance. Cutting back to the scene that took place previously, Marcus and Pierre search for a man called le Tenia ("The Tapeworm," played by Jo Prestia), who has viciously raped and beaten Marcus' girlfriend, Alex (Monica Bellucci). Marcus mistakenly identifies a man as le Tenia and has his arms broken, but Pierre interrupts before Marcus is raped and graphically beats the culprit's skull in with a fire extinguisher (in doing so, it can be linked to a diverse range of films like *Night of the Sunflowers*, *The Bravados*, and *Act of Aggression*, where mistaken identity results in the wrong person being punished for a rape). Again, there is a dramatic cut to the previous scene, and Marcus and Pierre discover that Alex has been brutally raped and is in a coma, even though in the film's chronology thus far that event has yet to happen. Marcus and Pierre are encouraged by a group of strangers who observe the scene to take justice into their own hands. Marcus and Pierre make enquiries as to the rapist's identity and steal a taxi to go to The Rectum. Next, Alex is shown leaving a party where Marcus is drinking and flirting with other women. She tries to get a taxi but fails and instead walks through an underground tunnel, where she sees le Tenia beating a transvestite. She interrupts them, and le Tenia turns his attack on Alex, embarking on a lengthy and violent sexual assault. The film then cuts to Pierre, Alex and Marcus traveling to and arriving at the party, followed by an earlier scene which focuses on Marcus and Alex happily discussing her possible pregnancy after they have had sex (when Marcus leaves, she does another test and confirms her condition). The final scene of the film—and the first scene of the story—shows a blissful Alex lying in the sunshine in a park, ironically reading J.W. Dunne's *An Experiment with Time* (1927) as young children play happily around her.

While this book has so far illustrated the diversity of how the rape-revenge trope has manifested, when played in linear order, rape-revenge films tend to share a basic structural trajectory. Generally, a film begins with a rape (or an attempted rape), and that rape will often be followed by an act of revenge (or an attempt at revenge). Even if the specific details of what will happen around those two key points of action are up for grabs in terms of who/how/where/when/why, on a fundamental level there is a preconfigured raw structural blueprint in place for audiences with even the barest familiarity of it, despite its myriad possible variations. By reversing this process from rape-revenge to revenge-rape, however, the bulk of *Irréversible* that occurs *after* Alex's rape is by contrast almost banal. Because the film has its two climactic acts of violence in the opening section of the film, everything after these events grants the spectator a strange sense of amnesia. As Noé himself has joked, the film actually has a "happy ending"[40] because of this structural subversion, but the impact of the film's two opening scenes of extreme violence load that "happy ending" with bitter irony.

The rape scene in *Irréversible* is arguably unchallenged in its visceral intensity, shown in an unedited single nine-minute-long take where for the first time in the film the camera is held statically (a sudden stylistic contrast to the wildly roaming camera that dominates the film up until that point). This change in camera movement effectively "locks" the spectator in place, the synthetic illusion of movement so aggressively constructed up until then abruptly halted for dramatic and grotesque affect. While few can dispute the intensity of this grueling scene, its ideological status is less clearly defined. For Noé himself, that the scene is at no point shot from the subjective perspective of the rapist automatically vindicates it from claims of glorifying rape.[41] But Elvis Mitchell maintains that Alex's flimsy dress and her decision to walk into a dangerous area mean "Mr. Noé is inadvertently saying that she's inviting the rape."[42] Nick James agrees, suggesting that the dress sexualizes her and therefore "undermines [the film] … as sincerely feminist," especially considering that the scene itself is "lit like a strip club."[43] Even more striking, however, is the sheer *length* of the scene itself—through its sudden rejection of the flamboyant editing and cinematography strategies that mark the film up until that point, this suffocatingly long take implies that *Irréversible* has moved into a real-time domain as it unflinchingly focuses upon the ferocious attack. While by no means *vérité* as such, the sheer impact of this dramatic temporal shift combines with the graphicness and viciousness of the scene to make it one of the most horrifying and memorable rape scenes ever committed to film.

Noé has noted that Sam Peckinpah's *Straw Dogs* was the first film he ever walked out of because of its shocking impact.⁴⁴ There is no doubt that he consciously sought to engage with the issues surrounding the rape-revenge film and its traditions, and Mark Kermode offers the most well thought-out reflection of the relationship between *Irréversible* and the broader rape-revenge category. Considering it in some part to continue the legacy of the original *The Last House on the Left*, Kermode suggests that Noé's film "is a realization of Wes Craven's dream of recreating a movie in which violence is seen as a wholly corrupting force, reducing everyone to their basest level." He continues:

> The true meaning of the film's title lies ultimately in its depiction of the damage of violence as being utterly irreversible, suggesting that (contrary to generic law) a rape-revenge movie can only have a genuinely happy ending if you play it backwards … it is Noé, with his unashamedly simple and derivative narrative device, who manages most succinctly to reveal this basic truth without betraying the visceral thrills for which his audience are ultimately paying.⁴⁵

The idyllic image of a maternal Alex that ends the film may seem a clichéd, even reactionary vision of female contentment, but despite its ideological nuances, it is a lot more ambiguous than the supposedly "victorious" rape avenger who appears in the final scenes of less controversial films such as *The Accused*. As Kermode notes, this stems not so as much from *Irréversible*'s depiction of rape, as from its narrative *placement* of it. Both *Ms. 45* and the original *The Last House on the Left* end with their protagonists either dead or forever sunk in an ethical quagmire, trapped by their own self-righteous lust for vengeance. The reversal of the rape-revenge story ultimately concludes in a celebration of a past that both rape and revenge destroys any possibility of returning to (hence the film's opening and closing statements, "Time destroys all things").

While not as explicit as *Irreversible*, Paul Verhoeven's *Elle* (2016) approaches the intersection of rape and revenge with an equally experimental eye, notable for being one of the very few films in the category that hinges explicitly on the rape of an older woman. The film begins with Michèle (played by iconic French actor Isabelle Huppert who was in her mid–60s at the time) being raped by a masked home invader, and as the film progresses her responses to the assault are as unconventional as Michèle's own broader life story. The daughter of a notorious mass murderer who has built a career as a successful videogame publisher, she casually tells her closest friends about the rape during dinner at a restaurant before beginning a consensual sexual relationship with her neighbor whom she later discovers was the masked assailant. To begin with, revenge (or at least, self-defense), is on her mind as she shops for weapons, but as her relationship with her assailant continues, *Elle* turns into an increasingly complicated film about force, consent and autonomy. When her son discovers the couple together at the end of the film in what looks to his eye like a sexual assault, he kills the rapist; whether Michèle staged this or whether it takes her by surprise is seemingly deliberately hazy. For Anne Billson, "Paul Verhoeven's *Elle* is one of the few rape-revenge films to take a more nuanced approach, digging into Isabelle Huppert's inscrutable and sometimes even comical reactions in the aftermath of her brutal assault by a masked home invader."⁴⁶ Revisiting the film after the Weinstein allegations and later conviction, Billson notes that in *Elle*, "the subsequent relationship she forms with her rapist foreshadows some of the questions asked of #MeToo accusers. Why didn't she go to the police? Why did she go on to have consensual sex with her attacker? And how 'consensual' was it anyway? Huppert ultimately gets her revenge, but the extent to which she herself engineers it is left ambiguous." While undeniably and deliberately provocative, *Elle* is as transgressive and unconventional as Michèle herself, and to deny or question her agency or liberty to respond to her circumstances how she sees fit is a challenge both Verhoeven and Huppert unhesitatingly turn back on the audience ourselves.

Germany

It is sadly unsurprising that rape was deployed in the broader anti–Semitic Nazi propaganda films that flourished during the Third Reich, seen nowhere more brazenly than in Veit Harlan's notorious 1940 film *Jud Süß*. A hate film ostensibly disguised as a historical drama, the film showed the rise of a stereotypically "evil" Jewish character who uses force to oppress his subjects in a variety of ways, including one of the film's most famous moments where he rapes a woman, clearly cast as the embodiment of supposed Aryan purity. In the postwar context, *A Degree of Murder* (*Mord und Totschlag*, 1967) stands as a fascinating bookend where rape and revenge provide a narrative framework through which to process questions about guilt, shame, and culpability. Even by today's standards, Schlöndorff's adaptation of Günter Grass' *The Tin Drum* (1982) stands as one of the most vicious depictions of the trauma of World War II from a German perspective, and much of its intensity hinges upon its deployment of sexuality and violence. Beyond the context of twentieth-century war, rape has featured in German cinema more broadly, be it in Fritz Lang's powerful *M* (1931) or Éric Rohmer's adaptation of Heinrich von Kleist's 1808 novel of the same name, *The Marquise of O* (Die Marquise von O, 1976). Regardless, *The Tin Drum* remains perhaps the most widely recognized offering from the New German Cinema. This period, spawned in the 1960s as a conscious step away from the increasing exposure of German audiences to American cinema, and inspired in part by the French New Wave, brought the work of such noted directors as Rainer Werner Fassbinder, Wim Wenders, Werner Herzog and Schlöndorff to the attention of international audiences. These films, noted for their art-house aesthetics and humble budgets, were predominantly government funded and provided a platform for launching—perhaps ironically—the Hollywood careers of three of these auteurs (except for Fassbinder, who died in 1982). According to Aristides Gazetas, the New German Cinema was marked by a collective interest in "the political and social situation arising from the postwar American Occupation," and these films were generally "preoccupied with questions of sexual identity, paranoia and disillusionment within a radical left-wing political framework."[47] In regards to rape in particular, its place in the German cinema's vision of the war would become explicit in films such as Helma Sanders-Brahm's *Germany, Pale Mother* (*Deutschland, Bleiche Mutter*, 1979), which follows a woman's postwar experience that includes her rape by enemy soldiers.

It is in this context that Schlöndorff's second film, *A Degree of Murder*, is worthy of note, due to its particular configuration of rape and revenge. As the follow-up to his impressive debut *Young Törless* (*Der junge Törless*, 1966), *A Degree of Murder* did not achieve the critical nor commercial acclaim of its predecessor, despite featuring a soundtrack (now lost) by Rolling Stones founder and musician Brian Jones, and being retrospectively hailed by Fassbinder as one of the top ten best films of the New German Cinema.[48] Sharing a similar focus on meandering urban hipsters as *Blow-Up* (Michelangelo Antonioni, 1966), *A Degree of Murder* is loosely structured and is largely dedicated to capturing a zeitgeist. Young waitress Marie (Anita Pallenberg) has a fight with her drunk ex-boyfriend Hans (Werner Enke) one night in her apartment, and she shoots him after he beats and attempts to rape her. Confused and panicked, she meets Gunther (Hans Peter Hallwachs) at the café where she works and confesses her story, begging for his assistance. In need of the cash that she offers for his services, he agrees and follows her to her apartment, where the two discuss their plans, drink coffee and have sex. Gunther borrows a car from the garage where he works, and he and Marie roll Hans' body up in a rug and place it in the car. With Gunther's friend Fritz (Manfred Fischbeck)—with whom Marie also becomes romantically involved—they drive to the country and dump the body near an autobahn construction site. After visiting Fritz' mother, they return to the city. In what is assumed to be some time later, Marie is shown working in the café happily, but the final shot of the film shows the discovery of Hans' body by construction workers.

The film consists of a parade of vignettes that only barely pertain to the central narrative: drinking in cafés and bars, hanging out in pinball arcades, shopping, and—most of all—talking, driving and arguing. Generically, *A Degree of Murder* features elements of the road movie and the black comedy that revolve around its central crime story of Marie's murder of the man who attempted to rape her. Hans-Berhnard Moeller and George Lellis describe it as less a genre film than an "anti-thriller" that "operates with *topoi* of the crime film but shows ambivalence about following the rules of the genre too closely."[49] Nowhere is this demonstrated more clearly than in the film's opening sequence, where a laughing Marie, Gunther and Fritz playfully chase each other around with a gun near the autobahn as the credits roll. It is as an "anti-thriller" that Moeller and Lellis suggest *A Degree of Murder* functions as a precursor to films such as Quentin Tarantino's *Pulp Fiction* (1994) in its postmodern, pop-culture-influenced approach to quotation and style.[50]

By comparing *A Degree of Murder* to *Thelma & Louise*,[51] Moeller and Lellis also tacitly acknowledge that it is a part of rape-revenge film history. Both *The Tin Drum* and Schlöndorff's later film adaptation of Margaret Atwood's 1985 Booker Prize-winning novel, *The Handmaid's Tale* (1990) demonstrate a continued fascination in the director's *oeuvre* with the relationship between sex and power, an interest that also manifests in *A Degree of Murder*. On the one hand, in its wandering, lighthearted tone, the assault and attempted rape of Marie early in the film can be taken as an almost insignificant act with little function outside of providing the barest of plot devices to propel the rest of the film. On the other hand, there is something unspoken and undeniably powerful within the constant flashbacks to the attack that Marie experiences throughout the film. She rarely articulates her trauma verbally, and the memories appear to strike her almost randomly—while they are driving or playing foosball. This more long-term trauma is suggested when she finally returns home after burying Hans'—seeing a photograph of Hans next to her bed, she screams hysterically. It may be a stretch to identify *A Degree of Murder* as a parable of postwar German guilt and trauma, but there is something poignant about Marie's inability (and through their association in disposing of the body, Fritz's and Gunther's also) to deal with the reality of their situation. As they cling desperately to a business-as-usual lightheartedness, despite the overwhelming seriousness of the events that lead them to this point, it is impossible to not reflect on the post-war context.

Not all German rape-revenge films share such prestigious heritage. Despite Eckhart Schmidt's position as a renowned writer and a figure in the West German punk movement during the 1970s, his New Wave movie, *Loft* (1985) is barely remembered outside of Germany. Drunk on its own neon aesthetic, *Loft* follows the bourgeois young couple

Raoul (Andreas Sportelli) and Raphaela (Rebecca Winter), who go to an art exhibition in *Loft*'s dystopian future to find a place to have sex. They are confronted by a violent pack of punks who, furious that the couple have ignored the art, torment them in a violent outburst of class rage. The rape and torture of the couple provokes a naked Raphaela into a vicious retaliation, depicted through a series of ultra violent sequences, including the graphic stabbing of one of the gang in the testicles with a knife.

Unlike *Loft*, the work of director Uwe Boll has been far from forgotten, and he is widely celebrated as a "love-to-hate" figure in contemporary genre film production. Boll is known mostly for his videogame-to-film adaptations (although he has directed non-videogame-inspired movies) and for what is popularly viewed as his cynical manipulation of German film funding policy.[52] His 2005 U.S.-German co-production *BloodRayne* typifies the type of genre film for which Boll is now notorious. Based on a computer game of the same name, the film follows the story of Rayne (Kristanna Loken), a "dhampir" (half human, half vampire) who is told by a fortune teller that she was conceived when her mother was raped by the King of the Vampires, Kagan (Ben Kingsley). The film follows Rayne through her search for vengeance as she gains allies along the way, until she finally confronts Kagan and kills him in her mother's name.

Another recent German-American rape-revenge co-production is *One Way* (Reto Salimbeni, 2007). Til Schweiger plays Eddie, a successful advertising executive, whose engagement to Judy (Stefanie von Pfetten), the daughter of the head of his agency, positions him to become a partner in the company; but despite this, Eddie cannot quell his promiscuity and continues to have affairs. Because of this, he prides himself on not having slept with his shy and mentally unstable colleague Angelina (Lauren Lee Smith), and tells her that the platonic nature of their relationship has provided the solid foundations for their deep friendship. However, when their colleague Anthony (Sebastian Roberts)—Judy's brother and the son of the firm's head—rapes Angelina, Eddie is placed in a difficult position. Anthony has evidence of Eddie's infidelities and blackmails him into testifying against Angelina's character in court. Anthony is freed because of Eddie's testimony, and Angelina must face an added humiliation on top of her already severe trauma. In retaliation, she announces to the court that she and Eddie were, in fact, lovers, and this—combined with Judy's already serious suspicions of her fiancé's unfaithfulness—leads Judy to break up with him. Eddie loses his job, and that evening gets in a fight with Anthony in a nightclub. After he leaves, a disguised Angelina drugs and seduces Anthony, luring him to a deserted location where she handcuffs him to a car, sodomizes him with a strap-on dildo, and shoots him dead. The nun who is caring for her provides a false alibi when the police begin to investigate, and this leads the police to arrest Eddie for Anthony's murder. Although Angelina tells Eddie that she murdered Anthony, Eddie does not tell this to the court during his trial out of fear that Angelina would commit suicide if placed in prison. Despite it appearing that Eddie will face life in prison for a crime he did not commit, at the last moment Judy takes the stand and provides him with an alibi, adding that she had not come forward sooner out of loyalty to her family. But, she declares, she has had enough: Anthony had raped her when she was fifteen years old, and she was not prepared to further lie to protect his honor. The film ends with a tentative reunion of Eddie and Judy, as a smiling Angelina catches a taxi to the airport to begin a new life elsewhere.

If *One Way* seems overly complicated, it is. Initially, the film suggests that its particular take on the rape-revenge structure was to focus on the transferral of the notion of rape as a property crime between men into a corporate setting. This comparatively lucid idea rapidly vanishes underneath a frenzy of other less well-thought-out elements. Most striking of these is the figure of Eddie, who embodies the film's strangely off-kilter moral compass. Despite the visceral intensity of the rape scenes themselves (firstly, of the gang rape of Angelina as a teenager, then Anthony's horrendous attack, and finally her retaliatory assault in the car before she kills him), they are all but forgotten next to the dominant focus upon Eddie's infidelities and the effect it has on Judy. It is in this sense that the film appears to be feebly attempting to offer a "what would you do?" ethical conundrum that falls flat because Eddie is neither likeable nor enigmatic. It is never clear why he cheats on his loving fiancée, for example, and his weakness and greed are rarely presented as general human frailties as much as they are the actions of a selfish, sleazy misogynist. He therefore appears less as an anchor for the plot than yet another revolting man who uses women, be it for personal satisfaction, business reasons, or both.

Even more troubling is the depiction of Angelina herself. While Lauren Lee Smith's outstanding performance should place her as one of the more sympathetic instances of the rape-avenging female, the ideological ambiguity of her character makes her difficult to celebrate. The film opens in a rural scene where four rednecks gang-rape a young teenage girl, but they are interrupted by a man Angelina later calls "the Black General" (an older, Black man in a military uniform) who shoots the rapists. Most immediately, this scene's explicit referencing to the original *I Spit on Your Grave* (and, later, the clear homage to *Lady Snowblood* [Toshiya Fujita, 1973] when Angelina kills Anthony) expose *One Way*'s conscious engagement with rape-revenge traditions.

The problem with the "Black General," however—aside from the film's determination to hold a non-white character responsible for the violent tendencies of a white one—is that he's not real. Angelina has severe mental issues, and she herself understands that she must take anti-psychotics to keep the "Black General" away. While there is no doubt that her rape by Anthony is real, the film is ambiguous about whether the gang rape she swears happened when she was fifteen actually occurred or was a figment of her deranged mind. It is, in part, this supposed "false" rape accusation that frees Anthony (along with Eddie's damning testimony). The film never addresses Angelina's background properly, and by painting her both as dangerously insane and as a woman with the potential to make false accusations of rape, the film is inadvertently hostile to her experience, despite the remarkable efforts of Smith to bring the character to life. It is unclear how the departure of Angelina on an airplane to begin a new life can be seen as any kind of victory for her; that it took Judy's admission of rape for her story about Anthony to be believed renders her just as powerless as ever. *One Way*'s inability to address the complex issues that it sets up pushes it far too close to a "blame the victim" treatment of rape, because Angelina's actions are explained not because she was viciously violated and then denied justice because of male corruption, but simply because she is "crazy."

Hong Kong

For Sally Stockbridge, rape is so pervasive in Hong Kong cinema that it is a "dominant trope."[53] For audiences outside Asia at least, rape and revenge in Hong Kong film merge most readily in the U.S.–Hong Kong co-production *Enter the Dragon* (Robert Clouse, 1973). This film was by no means unique in its deployment of rape and revenge in a Hong Kong kung fu context—for example, Shaw Brothers films such as *The Kiss of*

Death (Ho Meng Hua, 1973) and *The Intimate Confessions of a Chinese Courtesan* (Yuen Chor, 1972) were both action films that focused upon rape and revenge. But as Bruce Lee's final film, *Enter the Dragon* launched his iconic status as the face of Hong Kong action film internationally, bringing that country's kung fu cinema to a new audience. Bruce Lee stars as Shaolin martial artist Lee, who is invited to a martial arts tournament on an isolated island by the enigmatic Han (Kien Shih), who had defied the laws of Shaolin and was expelled in shame. Lee is engaged as an undercover agent for British intelligence to investigate Han's involvement in drugs and the sex trade. Before he leaves on his mission, Lee's father tells him that one of Han's assistants, O'Hara (Robert Wall), was responsible for the death of Lee's sister: when she realized that O'Hara was going to rape her, she suicided by stabbing herself in the stomach with a shard of broken glass. As the plot unfolds, Lee is finally forced into battle with both O'Hara and Han himself, and glass plays a symbolic part in both battles as a reminder of his sister's fate. At the film's conclusion, Lee ultimately defeats both men because of his Shaolin training.

The most vivid and notorious depictions of rape in Hong Kong cinema—and manifestations of rape-revenge—appear in the "Category III" films. In 1988, a three-tiered ratings structure was introduced, where Category I status was granted for films intended for all ages, Category II pertained to films not suitable for children, and the infamous Category III was applied to films restricted to adult audiences of 18 years and over.[54] According to one account, by 2001 Category III films accounted for up to 25 percent of Hong Kong film production,[55] and it was applied to such notorious films as *Sex and Zen* (Michael Mak, 1991) and *Naked Killer* (Wong Jing, 1992). While Andrew Grossman narrows Category III film down to ten major subgenres (of which rape-revenge is one),[56] Darrell W. Davis and Yeh Yeh Yueh-yu contend the films are far too diverse and varied to allow such a reading. Instead, they offer three broad conceptual categories: "Quasi-pornographic films" (because actual hardcore pornography was banned outright), genre films (particularly thrillers, gangster films, and horror), and "pornoviolence,"[57] the latter of which would include rape-revenge. These rape-revenge examples include movies like *Her Vengeance* (*Xue mei gui*, Ngai Kai Lam, 1988), *The Wrath of Silence* (*Chen mo de gu niang*, Frankie Chan, 1994), *The Lady Punisher* (*Tung chong 2 mung*, Cheung C. Law, 1994), *Daughter of Darkness* (*Mie men can an zhi nie sha*, Kai Ming Lai, 1993), *Crazy Emperor* (*Gu ben su nu zhen jing*, Hsiang-Yung Mai, 1993), *Windflower* (*Mi shi jin gu 12 xiao shi*, Wei-An Chen 1994), *Naked Poison* (*Shou xing xin ren lei*, Man Kei Chin, 2000) and *Water Margin: Heroes' Sex Stories* (*Shui hui chuen ji ying hiu sik*, David Lam, 1999).

As Linda Ruth Williams has indicated, the extreme depiction of often highly glamorized sexual violence that openly suggests that it is possible for a rape victim to enjoy their assault has caused the banning of many (if not most) of the Category III films that depict rape in countries like the United Kingdom.[58] Perversely—although perhaps not surprisingly—this has added a broader cult value to these movies for audiences in countries whose dominant treatment of rape is strikingly different from that depicted in films like the *Raped by an Angel* series (1993–2003), for example. These hugely popular Hong Kong Category III films began with *Raped by an Angel* (*Xiang Gang qi an zhi qiang jian*, Wai-keung Lau, 1993), followed by *Raped by an Angel 2: The Uniform Fan* (*Keung gaan 2: chai fook yau waak*, Aman Chang, 1998), *Raped by an Angel 3: Sexual Fantasy of the Chief Executive* (*Keung gaan: Oi yau waak*, Aman Chang, 1998), *Raped by an Angel 4: The Rapists' Union* (*Jiang jian zhong ji pian zhi zui hou gao yang*, Jing Wong, 1994) and *Raped by an Angel 5: The Final Judgement* (Billy Tang, 2000). Most of these films share a similar rape-revenge structure: a rape survivor (or group of survivors) mobilizes to seek vengeance against the man (or men) who raped them. The depictions of rape in this series are notable for their glossy eroticism and the focus upon the supposed "pleasure" of the victim.

The final *Raped by an Angel* film was directed by Hin Sing "Billy" Tang, who attained earlier notoriety for his representation of rape and revenge in *Red to Kill* (1994). As one of the most famously seedy Category III films, it has been described as a "sincerely atrocious … perversion,"[59] "a foul monument to depravity,"[60] and "perhaps the most vile exploitation film about rape ever made."[61] *Red to Kill* opens from the first-person perspective of its central rapist and killer as he walks down a shadowy, *noir*-like corridor and abducts an unidentified woman in a red satin dress. He viciously murders her and then rapes her nude corpse. This sequence is intercut with a social worker, Ka Lok Cheung (Money Lo), as she visits a frantic woman who throws herself out of her apartment window with her young son. Shaken by this event, Ka Lok tries to resign but is sent on another job, where she meets Ming-Ming, a teenage girl who loves dancing and who lives with an intellectual disability. Ka Lok tells Ming-Ming that her guardian has died in a car accident, and she takes the girl to live in the Social Welfare department's sheltered workshop and hostel, run by Mr. Chan (Ben Ng). While at first upset, the sweet and charming Ming-Ming adapts to her new life and develops a close relationship with Ka Lok, who also becomes her dance instructor. At the same time, the murders, rapes and attempted assaults continue, and are often shown again from the first-person perspective of the perpetrator. Revealed to be perpetrated by Mr. Chan himself, these attacks are triggered when he sees a woman (or, at one stage, a young female child) wearing red (the primal scene explaining this is shown in flashback, where his promiscuous, red-wearing mother murders his father when he catches her with another man). Neighbors of the shelter demand that the "crazy" ward be moved for their safety, but Mr. Chan and Ka Lok insist they are not dangerous and are simply "idiots." Both Mr. Chan and Ka Lok are moved by Ming-Ming's kindness to her peers, but when Ming-Ming performs a dance in a red dress, Mr. Chan is unable to control himself. In a lengthy, explicit and revolting sequence, he viciously beats and rapes her but does not kill her. The scene showing her trauma immediately following the rape is no less gratuitous: as she showers, her breasts and genital area are shown in medium and close-up shots that are frequently detached from the rest of her body. As she frantically cuts off her own pubic hair with a straight razor, she slashes her genitals until she draws blood in a scene almost as disturbing as the rape sequence itself.

Ka Lok discovers the traumatized Ming-Ming, and they take Mr. Chan to court. In a brief courtroom sequence, Mr. Chan is found not guilty because the judge—swayed by the defense lawyer's suggestions that Ming-Ming seduced Mr. Chan but was not mentally cogent enough to be able to understand consent—rejects the case and releases him because he believes Ming-Ming is not capable of providing useful testimony. Mr. Chan continues to terrorize the now-shattered Ming-Ming, and begins to harass Ka Lok, the latter realizing the importance of red to Mr. Chan when Ming-Ming reacts badly to a red t-shirt. Although she dresses up seductively in red and approaches Mr. Chan in a bar (causing him to pour ice down his underpants in a rare comedic moment), she does not act to subdue him. Instead, he confronts Ming-Ming and Ka Lok at the shelter, and, announcing repeatedly to the women, "I must fuck you to death," he attempts to rape Ka Lok. Ming-Ming becomes hysterical and rips her clothes off as she begs him to stop, beating him with shoes and plastic trays. The two women fight Mr. Chan, who at one point is stabbed in the chest with fluorescent tubes and in the eye with a flower stem.

Such attacks, however, do not curb the intensity of his violence. Once he has subdued Ming-Ming, Mr. Chan returns his attention to Ka Lok. She seductively lures him towards her on a saw bench, and in a graphic climax she kills him by cutting his head in half. The film ends in Ming-Ming's hospital room, where Ka Lok and Ming-Ming's friends weep and beg her to recover. She does not, and she dies as the film's credits begin to run.

While the plot outline of *Red to Kill* may seem shocking enough, it does not begin to credit the levels of depravity that have garnered this film its notoriety. Its graphic and confronting rape sequences are compounded by the gut-churning addition of Ming-Ming's status as someone living with an intellectual disability (it is, as an aside, not the only rape-revenge film to do this; Elmar Weihsmann and Stefan Peczelt's 2005 Austrian film *Silent Bloodnight* includes this same element). Very little has been critically written on this film, no doubt for these reasons alone—surely, of all the films in this book, *Red to Kill* is one of the few instances that are simply beyond comprehension. The compelling work of Julian Stringer on Category III films presents a useful critical framework to consider a film such as this. While certainly not aiming to "rescue" or celebrate movies like *Red to Kill*, he provides an historical context in which their production makes sense. As Stringer explains, Category III films produced in Hong Kong in the lead up to the handover of the island from the British back to Chinese sovereign control on 1 July 1997, can be understood as manifesting an "extreme pessimism and an alarmist mentality"[62] of a dystopian future, and thus "such representations of eroticism and cruelty can be read as the death dance of a wicked, economically decadent city."[63] He also notes that as Category III films engaged with working-class audiences (who cannot afford to go to the more expensive cinemas that play Hollywood films), these movies at this time spoke directly to the fears of the future many people faced:

> To put it bluntly, many of the people who work on the films, and certainly those who view them, are the ones least able to act on any possible desire to migrate from Hong Kong, or at least to be financially "safe" after 1997. At the same time as the genre is careful not to include material that could cause political problems later on, it also speaks in a direct way to the people who will most be affected by reunification. The core Category 3 audience does not share the same pleasures as the arthouse demographic because its future is more limited in possibility.[64]

Although Stringer does not discuss *Red to Kill* specifically, that it depicts government officials such as Mr. Chan and the judge in his rape trial as vicious and corrupt representatives of the state is of no small note. Even more noteworthy is the significance of the color red—representative of communism as a whole—in Mr. Chan's behavior. During Ming-Ming's rape, for example, he explicitly flags the color as the cause for his violence, with statements such as "Why do you wear red clothes?"; "I hate red most of all!"; and "You know I hate red." Mr. Chan's hatred of red and its association with his incomprehensible and sickening violence can therefore be linked to broader fears about the impending "red" Chinese control as outlined by Stringer. Regardless of the historical specificity of this film to its era of production, however, even among all the films surveyed for this book, *Red to Kill*'s brutality and impact stand apart.

India

The Hindi film industry in India—informally referred to as "Bollywood"—is today renowned as one of the most commercially successful and productive in the world outside of Hollywood. With a reputation for producing song-and-dance romances and action films, Hindi cinema is often dismissed by "Westerners and Indians alike as an example of the worst escapist excesses of postcolonial capitalism."[65] But as Gregory D. Booth has argued, such assumptions disregard the fact that Hindi films continue many cultural and literary traditions that existed before cinema. He identifies the origins of two of the main female character types of the Hindi epic film within the major ancient Indian Sanskrit epics. Along with the "chaste, long suffering example of Sita in the Ramayana," he also discusses the "determined, revenge seeking model of Draupadi" from the Mahābhārata.[66] In their cinematic form, these Draupadi figures commonly populate martial epics and are "often depicted as divinely inspired or, as actual (but temporary) manifestations of, such militant female goddesses as Durga and Kali."[67] The avenging female appears beyond the martial epic, and in particular is notable in the context of Hindi rape-revenge films like renowned director B.R. Chopra's *The Scales of Justice* (*Insaf Ka Tarazu*, 1980), *The Revenge* (*Pratighat*, N. Chandra, 1987), *Damini* (Rajkumar Santoshi, 1993), and *You Have My Heart* (*Hamara Dil Aapke Paas Hai*, Satish Kaushik, 2000). But this is just the tip of the iceberg; so abundant are Indian rape-revenge films that they even have their own Wikipedia page, which, as of November 2020, features a list of 66 films. The representation of women as a "social issue" to be "solved" can be traced back to the early days of Indian popular cinema[68]; and in the 1980s in particular the figure of the tragic/romantic woman began to be visibly overtaken by the popularity of a female equivalent of the angry male "anti-hero"—these women are provoked (often by rape) to take violent action.[69]

Rape was an issue of much public debate leading up to and during this period, provoked by highly publicized and controversial cases concerning teenage girl Mathura, which began in 1974, and, later, the Maya Tyagi case in 1978. In both instances these women were gang-raped by police, and women's groups protested voraciously when the two policemen in the former case were found "not guilty." The Mathura case in particular can be seen to have inspired the foundational Hindi avenging woman film *The Scales of Justice*, which was released at a period of rising vocal feminist sentiment. This discourse mobilized around the vigorous public debate regarding how to implement and legislate the necessary updating of rape laws that cases such as these indicated were so grossly out of date.[70] For some Indian feminist critics at the time, films such as this were merely exploitative attempts by the commercial film industry to profit from contemporary scandal.[71] But later feminist critics do not dismiss *The Scales of Justice* so easily, and Jyotika Virdi celebrates the fact that it "truly centers on the woman's narrative."[72]

The movie begins with a woman screaming as a hand (off-camera) rips her sari. She runs behind a frosted screen, and there is a silhouette of her being raped. Another man's shadow interrupts them and fights the rapist off the woman, and the rapist is stabbed. Cutting to a courtroom, a military man wearing many medals defends himself against a murder charge by saying that just as he kills to protect "Mother India," so too he must protect Indian women. After the title sequence that runs over various close-ups of a Lady Justice statuette, a beauty pageant introduces the film's central character, Bharti (Zeenat Aman), a beloved "beauty queen" and fashion model with many fans, including the wealthy businessman Ramesh (Raj Babbar). Bharti is happily engaged to Ashok (Deepak Prasher) and lives with her young sister Neeta (Padmini Kolhapure). Ramesh attempts to befriend Bharti, Ashok and Neeta, and throws Bharti a fancy birthday party where he gives her an expensive-looking necklace. Soon after, he goes to her apartment and is let in by Neeta before she leaves for school. He shows Bharti photographs from the birthday party and attempts to give her a portrait he has painted. However, Bharti is distracted by a phone call from Ashok, which infuriates Ramesh. He beats her, mocks her, drags her around her house by her hair and finally ties her up on her bedroom floor and rapes her. There is little nudity, and the intensity of Bharti's trauma is vivid as she cries and screams. Neeta comes home and discovers Bharti and Ramesh; Neeta escapes, upset but unseen.

The devastated Bharti tells Ashok what has happened, and she decides to press charges, despite the warnings of her sympathetic female lawyer (Simi Garewal) that "for the woman, a rape trial is no less a rape." Although Ramesh admits to his defense lawyer that he raped Bharti, a vindictive attack upon Bharti's character is launched in court that depends heavily upon associations between her job as a fashion model and an assumed looseness of morals (at one point he even suggests that she is a prostitute). In this lengthy courtroom scene, he declares, "I object to the presence of women like this in our society." After Neeta is called to the stand and coerced into giving ambiguous testimony, Ramesh is found not guilty. Bharti is humiliated, loses her career, and breaks off her engagement with Ashok. With both her and Neeta suffering from damaged reputations, they move to another city. About two years later, Bhati now has a job as a typist. Neeta has learned to type and attends a job interview, only to find her potential boss is Ramesh. In another torturous scene, he locks the girl in his office and terrorizes her, forcing her to strip and then raping her also. When Bharti discovers her traumatized sister, she gets a gun, goes to Ramesh's office and shoots him at point-blank range. Again, Bharti finds herself in court facing the same male lawyer and the same male judge, and she delivers a lengthy speech in which she makes it clear that the legal system had neglected her and facilitated Ramesh's death. So moved are the lawyer and the judge by her speech and Neeta's powerful tale of abuse at Ramesh's hands that the judge not only finds Bharti not guilty but resigns. The film concludes as Bharti and Ashok are reunited, joined by his conservative family who finally accept her.

If the plot outline of *The Scales of Justice* sounds familiar, it is because it is almost identical to that of Lamont Johnson's *Lipstick* (1976). These similarities come down to the shared fact that both films even depend upon an extratextual association between its lead female characters and their status as famous glamor icons (just as Margaux Hemingway was a famous supermodel, so Zeenat Aman had won the title of "Miss Asia" in 1969[73]). But to dismiss *The Scales of Justice* as merely a color-by-numbers remake of an American film grossly undervalues the specificity of the film to Indian culture at that particular historical moment. When Bharti announces to the court, "I wish the eyes of the law would open to the blood to see how the mistakes of the law are making beasts of men," it is near impossible to not recall the details of the Mathura rape trial and the debates it provoked. Unlike many Indian feminists at the time who decried the rape scenes in *The Scales of Justice* as exploitative and directed squarely at a sadistic male audience,[74] Virdi disagrees and notes that while "protracted," the rape of Bharti in particular "conveys nothing but pain, horror and naked male aggression."[75] But the film's conclusion in particular offers a number of areas of concern. Most obviously, that Bharti is suddenly deemed "acceptable" enough to return to both her fiancé and his conservative, middle-class family, combined with the resignation of the judge, situates the film firmly in the realm of fantasy, despite its earlier attempts (particularly during the court scenes) to add a sense of believability to Bharti's experience. Even more troubling, as Virdi suggests, is Bharti's declaration that "women are temples": By situating women less as human beings whose rights have been violated and positioning them as sacred objects (returning them to a patriarchal goddess/

slave binary), the film contradicts many of its central arguments about the urgency to treat women precisely beyond such binaries.[76]

In 1985, Ashok Roy released *Phoolan Devi*, an action film depicting the life of the legendary outlaw figure of the same name who was assassinated in 2001 at the age of 37. Outside of India however, the most immediately recognizable version of this particular intersection of rape and revenge in Indian cinema is surely *Bandit Queen* (Shekhar Kapur, 1994). The film was celebrated at international film festivals such as Cannes, and launched director Kapur's Hollywood film career, reaching its peak with the Oscar-winning biopics of Elizabeth I of England, *Elizabeth* (1998) and *Elizabeth: The Golden Age* (2007). *Bandit Queen* opens as the adult Phoolan Devi (Seema Biswas) announces to the camera from behind bars, "I'm Phoolan Devi, sisterfuckers!" It then cuts to 1968, when as an 11-year-old (Sunita Bhatt), the lower-caste Phoolan Devi is forced into an early marriage where she is beaten and raped by her husband. She runs back to her family but is sexually harassed by the local Thakurs and beaten for fighting back. Later, the police rape her, and she realizes early on that justice will not be afforded to her through conventional means. Kidnapped by a group of bandits, she is repeatedly raped by the leader of the group until Vikram (Anil Sahu), a lower-caste member of the gang, has enough of seeing her abused and shoots the leader. Vikram and Phoolan Devi fall in love and turn the gang's attentions to stealing from the rich in order to provide assistance to the poor. During this period she also locates her husband, the man who raped her as a child, and beats him to death with the butt of a rifle while he is tied to a tree. Sympathetic to the men that tormented Phoolan Devi, fellow Thakurs Sri Ram (Govind Namdeo) and Lala Ram (Sitaram Panchal) betray the couple, and Vikram is murdered. Phoolan Devi is captured, gang-raped and beaten while chained to a shed. When she recovers, she forms a new, vengeance-seeking gang with Man Singh (Manoj Bajpai). Together, they raid a city and steal valuables to give to the poor. They return to the village where she was gang raped and execute twenty-four members of the upper caste in a massacre. Because of Phoolan Devi's fame and celebrated status among the lower castes, the police decide that killing her will simply martyr her, so after brutally killing most other members of her gang, they force her to surrender. The film finishes with text announcing her release from jail in 1992, two years "after a government of lower castes came to power in the state of Uttar Pradesh." However, while Sri Ram died in an episode of gang violence while he was imprisoned, Lala Ram was still alive at the time of the film's production.

While the film met with success on the international film festival circuit, in India it provoked a number of controversies. Partially, these had to do with the film's tenuous status as a representative of "Indian cinema," as the British television station Channel 4 funded it, and most of the film crew (initially, at least) were non–Indian.[77] Because it was not focused solely on an Indian distribution context, the graphic representation of sexual violence and nudity (representations that existed far beyond any cinematic conventions of the Indian film industry) were also contentious. *Bandit Queen* was initially banned outright in India, and when it was finally released uncut, many cinemas offered separate screening sessions for women.[78] In its status as a rape-revenge film, perhaps most significant is the response of Phoolan Devi herself to the supposed biopic. While she had given her permission for the film to be made (it was based on her 1994 book *I, Phoolan Devi: The Autobiography of India's Bandit Queen*), she was so outraged by the final product that she went to some lengths to stop the film from being shown in India. Aside from outright factual inaccuracies, Leela Fernandes suggests that it was the graphic manner in which the rapes were shown that Phoolan Devi felt were "a portrayal that would violate her sense of honor in the context of the hegemonic social norms in India that depicts rape victims as figures of shame and dishonour."[79] While *Bandit Queen* combines a harrowing and powerful display of the violence against Indian lower-caste women with a sympathetic treatment of the emotional trauma that led the character of Phoolan Devi in the film to exact her revenge, that the real Phoolan Devi herself felt that this representation deviated so dramatically from her own experience and political agenda cannot be overlooked. Was the film *Bandit Queen* itself simply another patriarchal construction that Phoolan Devi was forced to rally against? In the context of the many real struggles and hardships she faced, fought and overcame during her remarkable life, there may be evidence to support this claim.

Devashish Makhija's *Ajji* (2017) reimagines the famous fairy tale *Red Riding Hood* in a film where the metaphorical threat of sexual violence in that tale becomes explicit. In this retelling, the young girl's grandmother becomes the rape avenger against the "big bad wolf," here a powerful local man called Dhavle (Abishek Banerjee). The grandmother—Ajji is the Hindi word for "granny"—is played by Sushama Desphpande, and despite the physical ailments that restrict her movement and cause her pain, she brings a refreshing new twist to the figure of the rape avenging woman, not just in Indian cinema but internationally. What is so extraordinary about her carefully planned strategy to avenge the rape of her 10-year-old granddaughter is that she adopts the seduction model to lure her prey. As noted throughout this book, this is hardly unique, and can be seen in famous earlier examples such as *Ms. 45* and *I Spit on Your Grave*. But when seduction is employed as a method of luring a rapist into a trap, there is more often than not an implicit desire to sexually titillate the audience, watching the "evil sexy woman" trope play out before them, just as it did so famously in the film noir figure of the *femme fatale*. Here, however, *Ajji* does not fit that bill; heavily made up in an attempt to disguise her age, Dhavle is not fooled when she approaches him on the street, but eventually gives in due more to her persistence than any particular sexual desire on his part. As she drops to her knees in what he believes is a precursor to fellatio, it in fact facilitates an act of castration as she pulls a pair of scissors from her bag; her culture-transgressing secret lessons with the local butcher on how to cut up an animal providing her with the skills to promptly get the job done. With its shocking twist on *Red Riding Hood* and transgressive rejection of the stereotype of older women as incapable of action and agency, *Ajji* is an important and quietly radical rape-revenge film that speaks profoundly to an international audience.

Japan

It is an understatement to suggest that Akira Kurosawa's Academy Award–winning *Rashomon* (1950) is not only one of the most famous films on the subject of rape, but also one of the most influential Japanese movies ever produced. The film tells the story of the murder of a samurai (Masayuki Mori) and the rape of his wife (Machiko Kyō) from four different points of view; and Colette Balmain has noted that "the manner in which Rashomon deals with rape can be considered typical of Japanese cultural mythology, in which rape has not, until very recently, been considered a crime."[80] The place of rape in Japanese cinema transcends this key cinematic moment, of course. As demonstrated in areas such as Japanese "pink" cinema,[81] sexual violence is deployed in a manner distinct from Western contexts. There is a long history of torture in the Japanese visual arts that predates cinema that differs from dominant European and North American traditions in particular.[82] Katsushika Hokusai's Edo-period ukiyo-e woodcut *The Dream of the Fisherman's Wife* (*Tako to ama*, circa 1820) famously typifies the striking explicitness of earlier depictions of sexual activity: this painting is also often cited as the origins of the so-called "tentacle rape" featured in the infamous hentai *Legend of the Overfiend* (*Chôjin densetsu Urotsukidôji*, Hideki Takayama, 1989). At the same time, there is also a long folk heritage of vengeful, wronged women. Even non–Japanese viewers familiar with J-horror films such as *Ring* (*Ringu*, Hideo Nakata, 1998) will recognize the figure of the *onryo*, a vengeful spirit who returns after death to seek revenge for a wrong committed against them while they were alive. The history of this figure can be traced back to the Kojiki goddess Izanami and medieval *noh* plays.[83]

For Colette Balmain, the depiction of rape in Japanese cinema (particularly in rape-revenge films) "has a direct correlation with the 'real' world," given that "Japanese society is predicated on female obedience and submission."[84] Sharing a focus on Japanese rape-revenge film, James R. Alexander observes that these films not only examine but are often highly critical of the "traditional social norms regarding women's role in public society and the social stigma of rape."[85] This is apparent in Kameto Shindo's 1968 horror film *Kuroneko*, his follow up to the supernatural vengeance tale *Onibaba* (1964). *Kuroneko* has a strongly mythic tone as it delivers its tale of two raped and murder women who return from the grave as feline vampires intent on revenge. An intersection of sexual violence and retribution is also evident in *Ghost of Chibusa Enoki, The Man with a Shotgun, Female Demon Ohyaku* (*Yôen dokufuden hannya no ohyaku*, Yoshihiro Ishikawa, 1968) and in a range of other Japanese rape-revenge films including *Rica the Mixed-Blood Girl* (*Konketsuji Rika*, Ko Nakahira, 1972); *Criminal Woman: Killing Melody* (*Zenka onna: Koroshi-bushi*, Atsushi Mihori, 1973); *Girl Boss Revenge: Sukeban* (*Sukeban*, 1973) and *School of the Holy beast* (*Seijû gakuen*, 1974), both directed by Norifumi Suzuki; *Grotesque Perverted Slaughter: Present Day Bizarre Sex Crime* (*Gendai ryoki sei hanzai*, 1976) and *Please Rape Me Once More* (*Mou Ichido Yaru*, 1979), both directed by Giichi Nishihara; *Entrails of a Beautiful Woman* or *Guts of a Virgin 2* (*Bijo no harawata*, Kazuo "Gaira" Komizu, 1986); *All Night Long* (*Ooru naito rongu*, Katsuya Matsurama, 1992); *High Heeled Punishers* (*Oshioki haihiiru*, Takashi Kodama, 1994); *Serpent's Path*; *Blood Sisters* (*Senketsu no kizuna: Kichiku reipuhan o shinkan saseta shimai*, Daisuke Yamanouchi, 2000); *Weekend* (*Uīkuendo*, Yoshikazu Ishii, 2012); and *Lipstick* (*Rippusutikku*, 2013) and *Camp* (*Kyanpu*, 2014), the latter two directed by Ainosuke Shibata. The excessiveness of the titles here should not suggest that rape-revenge exists only in the terrain of horror and softcore pornography, however. For example, both the Sonny Chiba martial arts vehicle *The Streetfighter* (*Gekitotsu! Satsujin ken*, Shigehiro Ozawa, 1974) and the third installment of the popular *Lone Wolf and Cub* series, *Babycart in Peril* (*Kozure Ôkami: Oya no kokoro ko no kokoro*, Buichi Saito, 1972), revolve around rape-revenge storylines. Additionally, it is worth emphasizing that rape has a strong presence in Japanese cinema well beyond the context of rape-revenge, as typified by a range of texts stemming from *Go, Go, Second Time Virgin* (*Yuke, Yuke, Nidome No Shojo*, Kôji Wakamatsu, 1969), the *Rape! 13th Hour, Hanzo the Razor, Subway Serial Rape* and *Rapeman* series, and anime such as *Legend of the Overfiend* and *Perfect Blue* (Satoshi Kon, 1998). In particular, the exquisite animated fantasy film *Belladonna of Sadness* (*Kanashimi no Belladonna*, Eiichi Yamamoto, 1973) is one of the most creative and original rape-revenge films ever made.

As James R. Alexander states, in pink rape films that do not include an element of revenge, rape itself acts as both a tool of vengeance against, and a method of subduing, women who do not adhere to traditional submissive roles: "Rape is a punishment for display of ambition beyond one's expected role in society and by which the victim is permanently degraded in the eyes of her family and society."[86] In these situations, the idea of the rape survivor herself seeking revenge is therefore illogical, and Alexander looks towards contemporary Japanese rape films like Takashi Ishii's *Freeze Me* (*Furiizu Mii*, 2000) and Takashi Miike's *Audition* (*Ôdishon*, 1999) as demonstrations of what he considers a "maturation" of Japanese cinema. Although convincing and vigorously argued, the absence in Alexander's essay on rape-revenge in Japanese cinema of one of the key figures of Japanese pink cinema, Meiko Kaji, is worthy of note. For non–Japanese audiences, Kaji may be most readily identifiable for her title role in *Lady Snowblood* (*Shurayukihime*, Toshiya Fujita, 1973), which Quentin Tarantino so explicitly paid homage to in structure, theme and style in *Kill Bill Vol. 1*. As Rikke Schubart states, "Meiko Kaji is to Japanese cinema what Pam Grier is to American cinema: a queen of cult cinema and erotic bloodshed."[87] *Lady Snowblood* begins with Yuki Kashima's birth in a prison in 1874, where her mother tells her "you were born for vengeance" before she dies. Yuki's story is told via male voiceover and is split between a series of flashbacks and flashforwards. Set during the Meiji era in a period of corruption and injustice, the film shows Yuki's mother is abducted by a group of three men and a woman, and raped and beaten for three days after her husband has been murdered. Enlisting the assistance of Matsuemon, leader of the beggars, and using the skills learned from Dokai (Ko Nishimura), Yuki strategically tracks down each member of the gang responsible for her mother's rape and kills them. The first of these occurs in a beautiful, highly theatrical night scene with falling snow, and it is in this same environment that Yuki is herself murdered after she kills the last of her intended targets. (Ironically, Yuki is killed by the daughter of one of the men she has previously murdered who has undertaken her own mission of vengeance). As the avenger of her mother's rape, Yuki is very much a protagonist in keeping with rape-revenge traditions.

Meiko Kaji had appeared in an earlier rape-revenge film, *Female Prisoner #701: Scorpion* (*Joshuu 701: Sasori*, Shunya Itō, 1972). Unlike *Lady Snowblood*, here it is not her mother's but her own rape that Kaji's character seeks to avenge. But both films manifest a spectacular fusion of low-brow (exploitation) and high-brow (art-house) elements in a film that attaches an overarching rape-revenge narrative trajectory to what is widely considered one of the best offerings of the "Women in Prison" subgenre, made famous by films such as *The Big Doll House* (Jack Hill, 1971). In *Female Prisoner #701: Scorpion*, Kaji plays Nami Matsushima ("Matsu the Scorpion") who is jailed for attempting to murder police detective Sugimi (Isao Natsugagi). From the bleak, cruel world of Nami's prison cell, a flashback provides the back-story: deeply in love with Sugimi and blind to his corruption, Nami is used as bait by Sugimi to trap a Yakuza gang, who gang-rape her. In prison, Nami suffers at the hands of both sadistic guards and vicious fellow prisoners, and the film follows a series of violent vignettes, including Nami being burned by scalding soup, hung up from the ceiling and beaten, and enduring excruciating and deliberately pointless physical tasks like digging a large dirt hole that other inmates are simultaneously re-filling. At the same time, Nami has to outsmart a plan by Sugimi and other corrupt officials to have her murdered in prison. A riot at the end of the film allows Nami her opportunity to seek her revenge against both the Yakuza who raped her and Sugimi himself. Wearing a large floppy black hat and a long flowing black trench coat, Nami is dressed almost identically to the protagonist in Bo Arne Vibenius' *Thriller: A Cruel Picture*, made in Sweden two years later. She returns to her prison garb for the film's final shot as she walks back to jail.

Filmed from below Kaji's body through a glass floor the rape sequence in *Female Prisoner #701: Scorpion*, suggests Schubart, is shot like this "to enhance the theatrical setting."[88] But it is more than stylistic pizzazz—this unusual formal device places the spectator within the rape itself. This is not the only significant stylistic choice during this flashback, however. In the scene where Nami loses her virginity to Sugimi, a circle of blood (assumedly from her broken hymen) appears as a red circle on a pure white sheet, replicating the Japanese flag. This allusion is made literal at the end of the film when she kills Sugimi. He pulls the knife out of his stomach and throws it up in the air, and a close up shows it passing a Japanese flag. These two shots are crucial. Firstly, it suggests that Sugimi's taking of Nami's virginity with such a malign motive is in itself an act of sexual violence. Even more importantly, however, it links that symbolic rape directly to the state. In the context of the film's broader thematic focus on power and corruption, Nami's search for vengeance is therefore about much more than her own body—it is about the much broader metaphorical "body" of those mistreated by Japanese society as a whole. While this in itself may not single-handedly demonstrate an earlier movement towards James R. Alexander's "maturation" of the Japanese rape-revenge film, Kaji's powerful performances in both the *Female Prisoner*[89] and *Lady Snowblood* films are significant.

Both Nami and Yuki are marked by their almost total silence throughout these films, but in the *manga* upon which the movies are based, this is not the case. Kaji herself felt that the original version of *Female Prisoner #701: Scorpion* in particular was filled with "obscenities."[90] and it was her insistence that the directors of both the *Lady Snowblood* and *Female Scorpion* films decided to make her characters predominantly silent. This silence may be seen as part of what James R. Alexander identifies as the broader social convention for women in Japanese society to be submissive. In the case of *Female Prisoner #701: Scorpion* at least, this silence may therefore be linked to Nami's refusal to physically resist her rapists.[91]

But like Madeleine in *Thriller: A Cruel Picture* and Thana in *Ms. 45*, Nami and Yuki's silence ultimately grants them the status of what Schubart identifies in *Female Prisoner #701: Scorpion* as "a mute image of female mystery [and] dark sensualism."[92] While neither Yuki nor Nami finish the first films of each series as particularly victorious (one dies, and one goes to prison), that they appear (however briefly) to "empower" themselves to some degree through the socially expected norms of the polite, unspeaking woman precisely to assist in their "spooking" of their prey suggests an important comment on the relationship between women, violence and power in Japan at the time.

In terms of contemporary Japanese rape-revenge film, Colette Balmain and James R. Alexander turn to the work of writer and director Takashi Ishii. While Balmain provides a long overdue critical evaluation of Ishii's pivotal involvement in the earlier *Angel Guts* series,[93] Alexander examines *Freeze Me*, a film that received exposure through the international festival circuit at the time and has since been released on DVD with English subtitles. These critics observe a shift in Ishii's work among all of these films away from more traditional Japanese considerations of rape and is in this spirit that this section will conclude with Ishii's rape-revenge thriller *A Night in Nude* (1993), a film made while Ishii was also involved in bringing the last three *Angel Guts* films to the screen. Doubtlessly, the absence of significant critical discussion on this movie has less to do with neglect

136   Rape-Revenge Films

than it does with access to legitimate English-language copies of the film, but its merger of neo-*noir* aesthetics with rape-revenge and supernatural elements (its ending is a direct reference to Herk Harvey's 1962 horror classic *Carnival of Souls*) make it a prime candidate for further critical evaluation in terms of how it "fits" into an understanding of Ishii as a "rape-revenge auteur." That so many of the other films Ishii has written and/or directed feature rape (either with or without an associated act of vengeance)—*Flower and Snake* (*Hana to Hebi*, 2004), *Flower and Snake II* (*Hana to Hebi 2: Pari/Shizuko*, 2005), *Evil Dead Trap* (*Shiryô no wana*, Toshiharu Ikeda, 1988), *Black Angel* (*Kuro no tenshi*, 1997), and *Sweet Whip* (*Amai muchi*, 2013)—also positions him as a key figure warranting further critical attention in regard to the representation of rape and its relationship to Japanese cinema more broadly. As more of these films become available outside of Japan, work in English on this director hopefully will continue to grow.

Korea

In recent years, the subject of rape and rape culture has made headline news in South Korea. In 2017 and 2018, high profile politicians such as Hong Joon-pyo and An Hee-jung were the subject of rape and attempted rape allegations, with a series of sexual assault allegations linked to the globally popular K-pop music genre culminating in the 2019 imprisonment of a number of idols for gang rape and distributing video footage of both consensual and non-consensual sexual acts. The film industry has not been untouched, with the late director Kim Ki-duk accused of rape and assault by three different women in 2018; in 2019 he was fined $6000 for physically assaulting an unnamed woman who worked on his 2013 film *Moebius* (claims that he forced her into sex scenes that were not in the screenplay were dropped by prosecutors due to lack of evidence). Rape and other kinds of extreme violence are a signature of his work, and he was no stranger to revenge narratives either, as seen in movies such as *Bad Guy* (2001) and *Pieta* (2012).

As Darcy Paquet notes, by the middle of the 1990s, the "rape-as-national-trauma metaphor ... had grown wearyingly familiar in Korean cinema,"[94] and rape featured as a key plot point in Korean cinema as early as 1927 in Na Woon-gyu's *Jalitgeola*. Rape permeates Korean film history, with a handful of examples including but certainly not limited to *Between the Knees* (*Muleupgwa muleupsai*, Lee Jang-ho, 1984), *Hope* (*Sowon*, Lee Joon-ik, 2013), numerous films by Hong Sang-soo including *The Day a Pig Fell in the Well* (*Dwaejiga umul-e ppajin nal*, 1996), *Virgin Stripped Bare by Her Bachelors* (*Oh! Soo-jung*, 2000), *Woman is the Future of Man* (*Yeojaneun namjaui miraeda*, 2004) and *Like You Know It All* (*Jal Aljido Mot-hamyeonseo*, 2009), and *Han Gong-ju* (Lee Su-jin, 2013), based on the notorious 2004 Miryang gang rape case. Simultaneously, Korean cinema is internationally renowned for the strength of its revenge cinema, most immediately recognizably in Park Chan-wook's Vengeance trilogy—*Sympathy for Mr. Vengeance* (*Boksuneun Naui Geot*, 2002), *Oldboy* (*Oldeuboi*, 2003) and *Lady Vengeance* (*Chinjeolhan geumjassi*, 2005)—but also a range of films not limited to *A Bittersweet Life* (*Dalkomhan insaeng*, Kim Jee-woon, 2005), *The Yellow Sea* (*Hwanghae*, Na Hong-jin, 2010), *No Mercy* (*Yongseoneun eupda*, Hyeong-Joon Kim, 2010), *Montage* (*Mongtajoo*, Geun-seop Jeong, 2013), *Burning* (*Beoning*, Lee Chang-don, 2018), and culminating most recently in Bong Joon-ho's class-based revenge film *Parasite* (*Gisaengchung*, 2019), famously the first film in a language other than English to win the Oscar for Best Picture. Rape and questions of revenge drove the story of Bong's earlier film *Mother* (*Madeo*, 2009), but Korean rape-revenge films have also been made that manifest along more immediately recognizable lines.

Rape-revenge films are far from new in Korean cinema, Alison Peirse identifying rape and revenge plots—both explicit and implied—across a range of films including *A Devilish Homicide* (*Salinma*, Lee Yong-min, 1965) and *Death Bell* (*Gosa: Piui Junggangosa*, Chang, 2008).[95] In the context of horror, rape-revenge can be found well into the twenty-first century with movies including *Arang* (Ahn Sang-hoon, 2006) and *The Outlaw* (*Mubeopja*, Cheol-han Kim, 2010). Of particular note is Donku Lee's *Fatal* (*Kashi-ggot*, 2012) if only for its original and ethically unconventional twist on the formula; here, a young man who was forced into participating in a gang rape seeks vengeance on those who forced him into it. While Curtis Harrington's *The Killing Kind* (1973) also starts from the perspective of a traumatized young man pressured into taking part in a gang rape, that film follows his continuing turn to violence upon his release from jail. In contrast, *Fatal* focuses explicitly on the redemptive attempt by its protagonist to right the wrongs against not just the rape survivor, but himself. Also atypical for rape-revenge are two films released in 2020 on a broadly ignored subject in cinema internationally— elder sexual abuse. Kim Mi-jo's *Gull* and Lim Sun-Ae's *An Old Lady* (*69 se*) tell the stories of different older women who must find justice on her own terms due to broader cultural biases against women over a certain age, a bias brought to life in two very different ways in each film.

Kim Jee-woon's action rape-revenge film *I Saw the Devil* (*Angmareul boatda*, 2010) employs a more orthodox male agent model in its story about a man whose pregnant fiancée is raped and murdered by a serial perpetrator. An agent at the NSI (Korea's National Intelligence Service), he uses his skills along with information garnered from his fiancée's police investigator father to identify the perpetrator, who continues his rapes and murders as the film progresses. Based largely around a cat-and-mouse structure, while many of the sexual assaults are not shown, it is clear that rape is very much part of the killer's modus operandi, the film's protagonist only able to grieve for his dead fiancée and unborn child once his revenge is complete. A more feminized agent-as-rape-avenger model can be found in Kim Yong-han's *Don't Cry Mommy* (*Don keurai Mami*, 2012) which, while still a crime film, is less action-driven and more focused on melodrama than *I Saw the Devil*. A recently divorced woman attempts to build a new life for herself and her teenage daughter as she starts work on opening a new café and her daughter tentatively makes friends at a new high school. When the latter is flattered by the attention of a handsome classmate, a new female friend is visibly anxious about the crush but says nothing. Believing she is meeting him for a romantic rendezvous, the protagonist's daughter is gang raped, leaving her traumatized. While the police easily locate the perpetrators, the legal system is ill-equipped to exact justice, and it becomes clear that not only is this one of many assaults the boys have committed following a similar pattern, but that they have no intention of stopping. Blackmailing the protagonist's daughter with phone video footage of the first assault, they rape and humiliate her again, driving her to suicide. Paralyzed by grief, her mother tracks down each boy, killing them until she discovers who the ringleader was. In a confrontation with a sympathetic policeman, she stabs the final rapist as she is simultaneously shot dead herself. The film's coda lists on screen rape statistics in Korea at the time (as *The Accused* did 24 years earlier), clearly intent on constructing the film as a social issues drama.

Arguably the most internationally well-known Korean rape-revenge film is Kim Bok-nam's *Bedevilled* (*Kim Bok-nam Salinsageonui Jeonmal*, 2010), where it is the raped and abused woman herself who is the agent of her own revenge. But *Bedevilled* is far from typical, as its central protagonist is a far more morally opaque woman, Hae-won (Ji Sung-won). Cold and socially tone-deaf, the film begins as she witnesses a rape and is indifferent to her role as a witness in the police investigation. Regardless, she is recognized by the assailants and threatened when they see her leave the police station in her car, stealing her business card from the dashboard so they can identify her. Combined with her losing her job after assaulting a colleague at work, she accepts the invitation from her old friend Bok-nam (Seo Young-hee) whose previous (implicitly desperate) invitations she had until now ignored, deciding to visit her on the tiny island of Mudo where they'd spent happy times together as children. Although again largely indifferent and focused on her own relaxation, Bok-nam's life is far from idyllic; raped, humiliated and beaten by her husband and his brother, this behavior is condoned by the matriarchs who dominate the small community. Bok-nam's only source of joy is her daughter, herself the result of rape, and when the child's father begins to show a sexual interest in her, Bok-nam's distress increases further. When the child is accidentally killed when Bok-nam attempts to flee the island and take her daughter with her, Bok-nam snaps, strategically killing everyone on the island. Although Hae-won escapes, Bok-nam knows her old friend witnessed the truth of what happened and refused to tell the police, so she travels to Seoul to complete her revenge. The film's action climax centers around the showdown between the two women, Hae-won surviving when Bok-nam is killed. But Hae-won has learned her lesson and returns confidently to the police station to formally identify the men who she witnessed rape a woman at the beginning of the film. Returning home, she finally opens and reads the many, many letters Bok-nam had sent her over the years, describing her life and asking for help, that Hae-won had left both unread and unanswered.

Bedevilled is both a sad film and a satisfying revenge movie which from a western perspective situates us in an unusual position in terms of our relationship to the film's central character; it is not the tragic Bok-nam who we see the story through, but the far more morally grotesque Hae-won. The middle-class/poor, city/rural divide here is undisguised, Hae-won simply not registering the horrors Bok-nam has faced during her life and even just during Hae-won's time on the island as an adult, choosing to let them go unacknowledged and focusing instead on her own needs and desires. As Michelle Cho argues, the social construct upon which *Bedevilled* is built seeks to aggressively reject Bok-nam's journey as being a particularly unique or individualized one, and rather one that reflects and addresses broader systemic inequalities:

> Although, in invoking the law of retributive justice, revenge narratives point to a generalized social dimension, in many cases, they reduce the collective to the social contract maintained by heroic, self-made men, as fantasized by a liberal ideology of possessive individualism, *Bedevilled*, in contrast, uses the revenge plot to facilitate the cinematic expression of trans-individual culpability. In other words, unlike the typical revenge narrative, which individualizes justice, Jang's film uses the desire for revenge—its affective register of indignation—to indicate the deep structural conditions of violent sociality in South Korea.[96]

For Cho, that *Bedevilled*'s revenge component employs "the affective and visual conventions of the slasher genre," the film is thus capable of disrupting assumptions of "the revenge trope as a depoliticizing, privatizing system of generic representation, and foregrounds the social implications of cinema as an act of witnessing."[97] Again echoing *The Accused*, by its deliberate privileging on the objectively unlikable and unsympathetic Hae-won, *Bedevilled* demands its audience consider their own culpability as spectators who—like Hae-won herself—have the opportunity to simply walk away from the horrors that we witness in these films.

Spain

The most immediately recognizable instances of rape in Spanish cinema to international audiences no doubt appear in the work of two of that country's most famous directors. Scenes that can be understood as attempted rape appear in Luis Buñuel's *Viridiana* (1961) and *Un Chien andalou* (1929); and rape, attempted rape and sexual abuse more generally appear throughout many of Pedro Almodóvar's films including *Pepe, Luci, Bom* (*Pepi, Luci, Bom y otras chicas del montón*, 1980), *Labyrinth of Passions* (*Laberinto de pasiones*, 1982), *Matador* (1986), *Kika* (1993), *Talk to Her* (*Hable con ella*, 2002), *Bad Education* (*La mala educación*, 2004) and *Volver* (2006). Most explicit on the rape-revenge front is Almodóvar's 2011 mad doctor film *The Skin I Live In* (*La piel que habito*), an undisguised homage to Georges Franju's classic French horror film *Eyes Without a Face* (*Les Yeux sans visage*, 1960). The film reunites him with long-term collaborator Antonio Banderas, who plays a plastic surgeon called Robert Ledgard who, for reasons that are initially unclear, has a young woman called Vera (Elena Anaya) held captive in his house that also doubles as his private surgery. Despite her forced captivity, the two also appear to have a consensual sexual relationship. The film's rape-revenge component at first appears relatively straightforward; while Robert is out one day, his housekeeper's son visits and rapes Vera. Without hesitating, Robert kills the man immediately. But via a flashback that makes up the bulk of the film, it is revealed that Vera was in fact a young man called Vincente (Jan Cornet) who possibly raped Robert's daughter Norma (Blanca Suarez) at a party; unable to communicate afterwards due to her trauma, even Vincente himself is unsure what happened as he was on drugs at the time. Norma was already deeply traumatized after witnessing her mother Gal's suicide, and after the (possible) rape she too dies by suicide shortly afterwards. Riddled with grief, Robert abducts Vincente, his revenge taking the shape of a forced gender transition: Vincente becomes Vera, with plastic surgery rendering her the double of Robert's late wife. After years of confinement, Vincente/Vera adapts to their new circumstances, and Vera and Robert become lovers, Robert allowing Vera increasing freedoms such as shopping trips. It is only when Vera sees a newspaper story about Vincente's disappearance that Vera's memory comes back. Shooting both Robert and his housekeeper, Vera returns home tearfully, and although unrecognized tells their family and friends "I'm Vincente" before explaining what had happened to them. *The Skin I Live In* typifies the kind of giddy transgressiveness typical of much of Almodóvar's *oeuvre*, and arguably continues the director's signature queering agenda:

> Almodóvar's films treat questions of sex and gender within the context of a postmodern decentering of traditional notions of social-sexual identity. Indeed, one of the constants of his cinema is the emphasis on sex and gender role reversals, whether masculine or feminine. Emblematic of this concern is the presence and sometimes proliferation of homosexual, transvestite, and/or transsexual characters.[98]

While undeniably challenging when it comes to gender politics more broadly and sexual identity more specifically, *The Skin I Live In* is an important recalibration and deconstruction of the assumed biologically defined binaries that define "male" and "female" that permeates the rape-revenge category—and film history itself—more broadly.

An earlier Banderas rape-revenge film very different to *The Skin I Live In* is Carlos Saura's *Outrage* (*¡Dispara!*, 1993). Saura is also a prolific figure in Spanish cinema and rose to prominence during the 1960s when he built an international reputation stemming from award-winning films such as *The Hunt* (*La caza*, 1966) and *Peppermint Frappé* (1967). While today Saura is most immediately recognized for dance films like *Flamenco* (1995) and *Tango* (1998), *Outrage* was produced shortly after the huge critical and commercial success of his civil war film *¡Ay Carmela!* (1990).

Marco (Banderas) is a journalist writing an article for his newspaper on a visiting circus. Although initially not interested in the assignment, his attitude changes when he sees the glamorous horse-riding sharp-shooter Ana (Francesca Neri). Ana is initially tentative but warms to Marco when she teaches him to shoot, and they begin a romance. The smitten Marco tells Ana he is prepared to join her in her nomadic circus life, and that he'd follow her "to hell." Marco is suddenly sent to Madrid on an overnight assignment, and Ana is gang-raped by three local mechanics that she had met

The Skin I Live In (La Piel Que Habito, Pedro Almodóvar, 2011), Spanish poster art (Everett Collection Inc./Alamy Stock Photo).

earlier while they were repairing one of the circus vehicles. After a brief shower, a numb Ana takes her rifle and her ammunition, looks up the details for the garage where the three men work, and drives there, waiting for them to arrive. She executes them swiftly and coldly, and then, shocked by both the rape and her response, she drives out of the city. Ana tries to call Marco, but he is not at home, so she leaves a teary, incoherent message on his answering machine. She visits a doctor who tells her she is in need of hospitalization because of severe internal bleeding, and the doctor reports the crime to the police, despite Ana's request for her not to. Meanwhile, Marco returns home and, hearing Ana's hysterical message and seeing both the news reports about the murders and the evidence of the attack in her lodgings, pieces together what has happened. With her physical condition deteriorating, Ana takes a family hostage in their deserted country house, and the police, Marco and his editor (who encourages Marco to use his personal connection to the story to his advantage) locate the property. A lengthy siege ensues, and the police finally agree to let Marco into the house. He reminds Ana that he said he would follow her to hell, and she dies in his arms.

Outrage is the product of an experienced director, and while the film's visual flair is inescapable, deciphering the significance of these stylistic choices is a more complex task. Most immediately, the film makes it explicit (both through dialogue and form) that the circus represents a nostalgic view of an old-fashioned world beyond the realities of contemporary living. It is depicted in terms of childhood hopes and dreams, and of tales of true love (not only of Marco and Ana, but of other circus folk). It is a romantic image that Marco succumbs to wholly, not only in terms of his affection and attraction to Ana herself, but also in regard to a clichéd "running away to join the circus" fantasy. While never presenting the circus elements of the story as excessive or over-the-top, Saura fills these scenes with color and life, particularly in the evening scenes with the other circus members, and in the intimate scenes between Ana and Marco. But in the scenes of Ana's captivity, rape and subsequent revenge, the color is dramatically and suddenly desaturated, leaving a *noir*-like palate of black, white and blue. This sudden shift to a dark, shadowy aesthetic allows the visual allusion to extreme violence (including Ana being raped with a wine bottle) without actually showing it. The affect is still shocking and revolting and combined with the highly stylized manner in which Ana's rape and revenge are presented, it is difficult not to share her dazed, trance-like state as she seemingly floats from scene to scene from this point onwards. When Marco returns, the color palate is restored to its original one, suggesting a *Wizard of Oz*–like chasm between the color world of fantasy and romance (coded as masculine/Marco) and the harsh, brutal reality of a realm stripped to a raw black and white (coded as feminine/Ana).

That Ana and Marco are kept physically apart for all but the final few moments after the attack suggests that while the rape transforms her into an avenger, more crucially it transforms her into something more symbolic to Marco, whose story this ultimately is. Formally and narratively, there is a sharp tension in the film between its narrative focus on Ana and its refusal to let this be "her" story. The reference to *film noir* is therefore thematic as well as stylistic, as demonstrated in Christopher Perriam's summation of the film: "Banderas finds himself in a classic, older Hollywood position as the man who should never have tangled with the fascinating, dangerous woman and who finds his life and career perverted."[99] To read rape only as the process by which Ana is rendered dangerous to Marco and his career necessarily diminishes the importance of its effect on her, but it is a reading that the film—particularly in its stylistic attempts to paint her as a *femme fatale*—appears to actively encourage. Despite both her experience and screen time warranting far more of the spectator's sympathy than Marco, *Outrage* ultimately falls on the side of his naïve romantic vision. This is telling of the film's broader difficulties regarding masculine constructions of gender and nostalgia.

There is a diverse range of Spanish rape-revenge films, spanning in budget and intended audience from Paul Grau's *Mad Foxes* (*Los violadores*, 1982) to Jaime Chávarri's *I'm the One You're Looking for* (*Yo soy el que tú buscas*, 1988). An even more complex configuration of rape-revenge in Spanish cinema manifests in writer and director Jorge Sánchez-Cabezudo's debut film, *Night of the Sunflowers* (*La noche de los girasols*, 2006). Opening on a field of its eponymous flowers, a man is seen walking towards a car on the edge of the plantation and driving away. A series of as-yet-unidentified characters are then introduced, as snippets of information through background television and radio reports and conversations build a story: the body of Elena Martos, a 22-year-old local girl who had fought with her father about her curfew before going nightclubbing, was found, raped and murdered, lying among the sunflowers. None of the characters shown appear to pay anything but vague attention to the news, engrossed as they are in their own lives. From this point onwards the film is divided into six separate chapters that introduces these characters more fully, and demonstrates how and where their stories intersect.

The first part, "The Man in the Hotel," follows the banal details of this seemingly ordinary man in a rented room. The as-yet-nameless figure (played by Manuel Morón) is an industrial vacuum cleaner salesman, and he engages in lackluster conversation with what is assumed to be his wife on the telephone as he eats chocolate and watches a news story on his hotel room television about Elena Martos' death. He is shown eating, working and driving in a matter-of-fact, documentary-style tone, emphasizing the apparent dullness of his life. This changes suddenly when he decides to turn off a country road and follow an unidentified woman, who, without any reason, he approaches and rapes in some deserted bushland. Her car rolls away as she attempts to escape from him, and crashes into a tree. When he hears voices approaching, he panics and runs away. Part two is called "The Potholers," and tells the story of geologist Esteban (Carmelo Gómez), who has come to the sparsely populated village of Angosto to investigate a newly discovered cave in the hope that it may provide the village with a much-needed tourist attraction. His colleague Pedro (Mariano Alameda) and girlfriend Gabi (Judith Diakhate) soon join him, and it is immediately apparent that this action is occurring simultaneously alongside the previous story, as Gabi is the woman who we just saw raped. This section follows both Pedro and Esteban's adventures investigating the cave and shows Gabi's version of the rape. Pedro and Esteban find Gabi, hurt and hysterical, in the crashed car. They drive away frantically, and Gabi identifies a man walking along the road in a white shirt as the man who raped her.

The third section, "The Man on the Road," makes it clear that this is not the man who raped Gabi but is instead the elderly Cecilio (Cesáreo Estébanez), who lives in a nearby abandoned village with little contact beyond his squabbling with his mentally challenged neighbor, Amós (Walter Vidarte). In a lengthy sequence, Pedro and Esteban murder Cecilio, but the old man puts up a strong fight as he struggles to survive. Part four introduces Tomás (Vicente Romero), a lazy, dishonest policeman who is married to his commanding officer's daughter. On his way home from seeing his mistress, he comes across Esteban, Pedro and Gabi, who tell him their story and add that Gabi has confirmed that they killed the wrong man. Tomás decides to blackmail them and disposes of the body in the cave Pedro and Esteban had earlier investigated for a large sum of money that he hopes to use to build a new life away from his wife. In part five, Amós confesses to the police that he had seen Cecilio's dead body before it was removed and believes that he must have murdered his antagonistic neighbor. In part six, Tomás' boss and father-in-law, Amadeo (Celso Bugallo), has growing suspicions about Cecilio's disappearance, despite Tomás' insistence that Amós is insane. He follows Tómas to the place where the money is to be exchanged, and tells Esteban, Gabi and Pedro that he does not want to know what they are doing and throws the money in the fire. Knowing that his daughter is pregnant, he silently returns a devastated Tómas home. The final scene of the film shows the man from the hotel returning to his home, and a voice off-screen calls out to him using his name for the first time in the film: "Miguel?" Sadly removing a child's squeaky toy that he has accidentally sat on, the credits roll as he watches a documentary about bees.

Structurally, the influence of both Akira Kurosawa's *Rashomon* and Gaspar Noé's *Irréversible* are evident in *Night of the Sunflowers*, but this is a significant film in its own right. Like *Rashomon*, it presents the same event—the rape of a woman—from both the rapist's and the victim's perspectives. But it is in regard to the rapist himself that this film is most intriguing. Most obviously, he is not punished; there is no moment of catharsis, and there is not even a vague suggestion that moral order can be seen to return. This is a sophisticated rendering of how the lives of strangers can intersect through random acts of violence. The observation by the documentary's voice-over that Miguel watches at the end of the film that "bees don't sting if you don't bother them" appears to comment on Miguel's violent future. But even more importantly, that Tómas' return home to the news that his wife is pregnant parallels so neatly with Miguel's depressed homecoming to TV and children's toys is too specific to be accidental. The linking of these two men this way implies the possibility that Tómas, too, may end up like Miguel. Does the film therefore suggest that men like these become rapists because of unhappy domestic lives, and therefore that it's the wives who are in at least some way to blame? While *Night of the Sunflowers* offers a remarkable insight into the experiences of all of the "players" of its rape-revenge drama, its final chilling impact stems not from bees, but from this ambiguous link between the two misogynists, Miguel and Tómas.

Sweden

It is no understatement to identify Sweden as a significant national cinema in the history of the rape-revenge film, despite it being so broadly assumed to be a North American phenomenon. Between *The Virgin Spring* and *Thriller: A Cruel Picture*, we see the aesthetic, thematic and tonal spectrum of these films most starkly; highbrow Oscar-winning art cinema at one end, and grotty yet enthralling exploitation cinema at the other. But as noted in my previous exploration of Danish rape-revenge film, in terms of Nordic cinema more broadly national boundaries are sometimes slippery. This is perhaps nowhere more apparent than in Jörn Donner's 1978 film *Män kan inte våldtas*, released in English as both *Manrape* and *Men Cannot Be Raped*. Donner was a Swedish-speaking Finnish filmmaker who moved to Sweden in his late 30s where he made his first feature film. While he would move back and forth between Sweden and Finland before turning later in his life to Finnish politics, during his time in Sweden he was appointed head of the Swedish Film Institute. Donner produced Swedish auteur Ingmar Bergman's *Fanny and Alexander*

(1982); which won four Oscars, making Donner the first person from Finland to win an Academy Award.

Adapted from the 1975 novel *Manrape* by Finnish author Märta Tikkanen, the film follows protagonist Eva (Anna Godenius) who is raped by a man she meets at a restaurant when she is out with a friend celebrating her 40th birthday. Distraught by the event, the recently divorced blonde librarian buys a brunette wig and adopts a *femme fatale* persona and discovers his identity, stalking him at work and beyond to learn his patterns. Beginning with her reporting the crime to the police, the film points to broader societal misogyny when she bristles at being interrogated about her marital status and questions over what job her ex-husband performed. The prevalence of sexism becomes further apparent in workplace meetings and, in particular, in the challenges her friend Agneta (Toni Regner) faces with her oppressive, old-fashioned husband and her fears that he will desert her when he discovers she has breast cancer. Almost by accident, Eva learns from a legal perspective that, as the English-language title suggests, "men cannot be raped," and she hatches a plan to hold her rapist captive in his apartment and tells him, "I am going to rape you … just like you raped me" before cutting to an image of him tied to his bed to be discovered by his laughing, mocking friends. While the film does not show her raping him, the twist at the end of the film is that Eva was not at the station to report her own rape but to confess the rape she just committed. Impatiently, the policeman tells her that such a crime is impossible, and the film ends as she throws her wig and gun away, satisfied with her revenge.

While merely replicating the myths about male rape that were dominant at the time of its production, from a contemporary perspective the very title *Men Cannot Be Raped* is deeply offensive, disparaging and even mocking the very real lived experience of male rape victims who even today find speaking up about such experiences immensely difficult precisely because of the endurance of these myths. In Aliraza Javaid's extraordinary book *Male Rape, Masculinities, and Sexualities: Understanding, Policing, and Overcoming Male Sexual Victimisation* (2018) the author bravely situates his research in the context of his own status as a rape survivor, listing this and other myths about male rape such as "male rape is not 'real' rape" and "only women can be raped."[100] For Javaid, "sexual violence is important to me because, not only have I been raped, but I also have been sexually assaulted so many times, so much so that this book could have easily been filled up with many intimate stories of each incident."[101] Speaking of his younger sister who was sexually assaulted by their cousin, his entire academic research project is framed by this personal experience, leading him to state that "Although the physical pains fade away, the memories are in us forever.… It is the memories that are painful, they hurt the most, and they remind us of those painful events of injustice and inequality. They haunt us like living ghosts."[102] While not about rape-revenge cinema per se, Javaid's book—particularly the opening pages cited here—should be essential reading for any filmmaker or storyteller who sees male rape as a witty gender-twist punchline in stories about the rape of women. This is an assumption that is made at the expense of diminishing the real experiences and the real trauma of real rape survivors, be they men or women.

A more contemporary manifestation of Swedish rape-revenge can be readily identified in the blockbuster success of *The Girl with the Dragon Tattoo* (*Män som hatar kvinnor*, Niels Arden Oplev, 2009) and its sequels, *The Girl Who Played with Fire* (*Flickan som lekte med elden*, Daniel Alfredson, 2009) and *The Girl Who Kicked the Hornet's Nest* (*Luftslottet som sprängdes*, Daniel Alfredson, 2009). The international success of late Swedish investigative journalist Stieg Larsson's "Millennium trilogy" novels spawned an equally successful film franchise, the first in the series ranking as the second highest earning independent movie of 2009. By itself, *The Girl with the Dragon Tattoo* appears to be a relatively straightforward crime story that combines a rape-revenge plot concerning its central female protagonist, Lisbeth Salander (Noomi Rapace), with its central investigative enigma revolving around the unsolved disappearance of a young woman in Sweden in 1966 (itself a plot that explicitly incorporates incest and the search for a serial rapist and murderer). The rape-revenge component appears initially to be relatively self-contained: Lisbeth, a young computer hacker with a troubled past, is required to have a lawyer act as her guardian because of earlier psychiatric problems. With only a year remaining of her guardianship, the corrupt and sadistic Nils Bjurman (Peter Andersson) is given the job, and he forces Lisbeth to fellate him to gain access to her own bank account. Bjurman's sexual abuse of Lisbeth becomes even more vicious and graphic when she visits him at his home to request access to her money; there he ties her up and violently rapes her. He does not realize, however, that tech-savvy Lisbeth has videotaped the entire brutal assault. Believing he would only force her to fellate him again, she accidentally gains powerful visual evidence proving that she was raped. Returning to his house once more, Lisbeth sprays Bjurman's eyes with mace, ties him up and anally rapes him with a dildo while beating and kicking him. She then crudely tattoos the phrase "I am a rapist and a sadistic pig" on his stomach, and after playing him the DVD of her rape, she tells him that if he does not authorize her remaining reports and allow her full access to her own money, she will send the DVD to the police and the press.

In the context of the first film alone, this plot line adds greatly to the development of Lisbeth's character development and provides a neat parallel to the main narrative focus concerning her association with investigative journalist Mikael Blomkvist (Michael Nyqvist). At the beginning of the film, Blomkvist is sentenced to three months in jail for libeling powerful Erik Wennerstrom (Stefan Sauk). Blomkvist insists that he was set up, and the security company Lisbeth works for is hired to investigate Blomkvist's credibility. The client is wealthy Henrik Vanger (Sven-Bertil Taube), who hires Blomkvist to investigate the disappearance of his beloved niece Harriet upon receipt of Lisbeth's positive report. While only ostensibly a lesbian in the first of the Swedish film franchise, Lisbeth is fascinated by Blomkvist and assists him with his investigations remotely by hacking into his computer. The two eventually team up, begin a sexual relationship, and determine that a serial rapist and murderer is behind both Harriet's disappearance and the violent deaths of a number of other women, spanning decades. Identifying the neo–Nazi tendencies of the rapist and killer, they discover the perpetrator is Vanger's nephew, Martin (Peter Haber). Lisbeth rescues Blomkvist when Martin captures him, and Blomkvist discovers that Harriet (Martin's sister) did not die but fled to Australia after murdering her father, Gotfried. Harriet explains that both Martin and her father had raped her since she was fourteen, and she fled in fear that Martin's abuse would escalate in the face of their father's death. In the film's coda, Lisbeth supplies the now-jailed Blomkvist with the evidence to properly convict Wennerstrom, and, when released, Blomkvist sees a disguised Lisbeth on the television news enjoying Wennerstrom's money in the Cayman Islands.

The parallels between these two storylines—Lisbeth's rape-revenge plot regarding Bjurman, and the serial rapes and murders by Martin and Gotfreid—are made explicit as Martin explains to Blomkvist that his crimes were committed "mainly for the sex. When I put them down, it's only a logical consequence of the rape." In Swedish, both the book and the film's title *Män som hatar kvinnor* translates to *Men Who Hate Women*, and this sentiment links Lisbeth and Harriet's stories. But even with its more romantically titled English-language moniker, Lisbeth makes this connection explicit when she tells Blomkvist that Martin "was a killer and a rapist and he enjoyed it. He had the same chances as everyone else. You choose who you want to be. He wasn't a victim. He was an evil motherfucker who hated women." Although the next two films do not as explicitly contain the overt rape-revenge scenario of the first movie, this focus on "men who hate women" begins with the micro (private) example in the first film and expands film by film to address the macro (public): first on an individual level between Bjurman and Lisbeth, then by examining gendered power imbalances in the institution of the family (in *The Girl Who Played with Fire*), and finally within the government itself (*The Girl Who Kicked the Hornet's Nest*, where the action plays out in a courtroom). Considered as a whole, these films reflect a world where violence against women is culturally ingrained, permeating every facet of society.

By no means do the Millennium films represent a particularly feminist enquiry into power, although critical treatments of the books upon which they are based may reach different conclusions. As Blomkvist himself states so frequently in the last movie, it is *specifically* about Lisbeth herself, not against any broader institutionalized view of women as a whole. In fact, this individualized, unique status of Lisbeth as a one-off is made nowhere clearer than in her appearance. With her spikes, black leather, patent leather buckle-boots, body piercings and eponymous tattoo, Lisbeth is visually marked as different. With her fishnet and PVC, she is literally fetishized in the film through her fetish wear. Unlike the books, where she has her own "scene," in the films not only is Lisbeth someone whose gender distinguishes her from myriad "men who hate women," but her tomboyish, aggressively alternative style also separates her from the other women in the film. This even includes her girlfriend Miriam (Yasmine Garbi), who, while also styled so as to represent "alternative" identity, is much more feminized and classically "retro" than Lisbeth's androgynous, Deathrock-infused look. Again, in contrast to the novels, Lisbeth's punk/goth aesthetic is crucially not one that unites her to any subcultural community or movement and there is no subcultural value to her striking style beyond it casting her as a lone outsider. In the films Lisabeth is excluded from the community-building processes that Gothic style actively encourages, and her identity does not link her to like-minded subcultural Others, but simply alienates her from a mainstream that marks her as different. This cinematic construction of Lisbeth as Other exoticizes her experience and makes her story diegetically "different" to the experience of "normal" women by default. While other women help her in the film (most notably Blomkvist's colleague Erika, and his sister who acts as Lisbeth's lawyer), they frequently express an inability to understand Lisbeth. The Millennium trilogy films offer a web of rape-revenge scenarios regarding Lisbeth that peel back to expose yet another layer: she punishes Bjurman for raping her, and she avenged her mother's abuse (including sexual abuse) at the hands of her father when she was a child by throwing gasoline on him and setting him alight. Ultimately, though, it is Blomkvist who facilitates the real victory in the third film when he provides evidence proving a government conspiracy against Lisbeth (and exposes the corruption of the sinister rapist psychiatrist Teleborian), one that allowed her near life-long victimization at the hands of institutionalized misogyny. Despite her unrelenting literal and figurative battles against "men who hate women," by the end of *The Girl Who Kicked the Hornet's Nest* it appears that Lisbeth is just as reliant upon men as ever for her freedom and safety.

Amplifying the visibility of transnational flows in rape-revenge, the success of the original Swedish books and films made a Hollywood remake inevitable, and—like Bergman's *The Virgin Spring* so many years before it—David Fincher's adaptation of *The Girl with the Dragon Tattoo* (2011) also went on to become an Oscar winner. Although obviously the cultural context is different and Rooney Mara's Salander is notably more butch than her Swedish equivalent, the two films deviate most notably in their final half hours. While Fincher's adaptation has been widely celebrated, it is in the specific context of this finale and how it pertains to questions of justice and agency that Joaquin Lowe shrewdly articulates a fundamental ideological weakness in the remake:

> In both versions, after rescuing Blomkvist, Salander chases after sadist Martin Vanger on her motorcycle. In both versions, Vanger flees in his car, only to crash off the road. In Oplev's version Salander approaches the car and watches, almost ecstatically, as Vanger pleads for help before the car explodes in flame. In Fincher's version the car explodes before Salander has a chance to make the decision of whether to save him or not. Again, Fincher robs his character of her agency, and by doing so takes from her the moral ambiguity that makes Oplev's version of the character, and the movie as a whole, so interesting.[103]

While true, "interesting" feels too feeble a word when watching these two scenes closely. By removing the American Salander's agency as Lowe indicates, Fincher softens the character, in notable opposition to the "hardening" (masculinization) that her much tougher physical appearance in this film implies compared to that of Rapace in the original Swedish film. This is, therefore, a superficial wardrobe and costuming gesture that disguises a more conservative vision of womanhood that lies at the heart of the Fincher version; Swedish Salander is happy to choose to watch a man burn to death, while her American counterpart can only sit by and passively witness. Again, her power has been removed by a man—this time, the filmmaker himself.

Turkey

Rape has been far from invisible in Turkish cinema, but in the specific context of rape-revenge, there is a notable diversity in how sexual violence is configured in relation to the narratives it propels. As Gönül Dönmez-Colin suggests, the figure of the rapist in Turkish culture is considered an *irz dü£mann* (enemy of honor), but such dishonorable conduct is often deployed in an erotic context to exploit the commercial market to its fullest potential—for example, in such films as *Koçero* (Ümut Utku, 1964) and *Iffet* (Kartal Tibet, 1982). In terms of rape-revenge specifically, Dönmez-Colin claims that "in film after film," rural melodramas in particular often focus on the rape of innocent village girls by wealthy and powerful men, only to have their honor avenged by a courageous village boy.[104]

Rape and revenge is also pivotal to Metin Erksan's *The Well* (*Kuyu*, 1968), described by Dönmez-Colin as "one of the masterpieces of Turkish cinema." Here, a woman is stalked and raped by a man obsessed with making her his wife. She seeks revenge against his endless assaults, but the intensity of her vengeance is so great that she takes her own life at the end of the film. Although celebrated, responses to the film are divided. Erksan himself said at the time that the film was inspired by a verse from the Koran about not mistreating women,[105] and many considered the film to be a sensitive reflection on the plight of Turkish women. For some feminists, however, the film is little more than "the sexual fantasies of a macho man."[106]

The year before *The Well*, another Turkish rape-revenge movie was Tunç Basaran's *The Great Hate* (*Büyük kin*, 1967). Starring popular actor Ayhan Isik as Omar, the film is told in flashback from a house where he is trapped by police and surrounded by dead bodies. Events begin happily enough at his son's wedding, where Omar's younger son and his parents join in the celebrations. That evening, three thugs invade the house where the young couple and the grandparents are staying. They murder the grandfather and the groom, and rape and kill the grandmother and the bride. The criminals do not see the young boy, who witnesses the attack and then rushes the next morning to Omar. Arriving at the scene, Omar is shocked and devastated at the carnage. He declares a "hunt" and tracks down each of the men, sadistically torturing them to their death. The leader of the group is discovered attending a wedding of his own, and his father pulls a gun on Omar and tells him to leave before publicly whipping his son in front of the wedding guests. Omar captures the man and returns him to the house where his family were slain. After killing him, Omar is trapped in the house by police. Returning to the opening moment where his flashback began, Omar is finally lured out by his young son; after the two embrace, Omar surrenders to the police.

The Great Hate is a remarkable film for a number of reasons, the most immediate of which is its striking stylistic construction. Despite (or perhaps because of) its budgetary limitations, Basaran uses high-contrast black-and-white photography to great effect. The film's *mise en scène* is also noteworthy, and some of the movie's most memorable images are the most simple (such as a shot of a small black kitten walking nonchalantly around the corpses of Omar's dead family at the beginning of the film). This is a beautiful movie to look at, but this is not to detract from the brutality and ugliness of its content. Most immediately, unlike the majority (if not all) of U.S. rape-revenge films in particular, *The Great Hate* downplays the rape of Omar's beautiful young daughter-in-law, which happens completely off-screen, and instead opts to focus on the assault of the elderly grandmother (aside from the Australian film *Shame*, this may be one of the rare rape-revenge films that features victims—or potential victims—that are not young, although in recent years this has diminished in films such as Paul Verhoeven's *Elle*, Lim Sun-Ae's *An Old Lady* and Kim Mi-jo's *Gull*, and Helen Mirren's character in Bill Condon's *The Good Liar* which, like the protagonist of Margaret Atwood's 2014 short story "Stone Mattress," avenges a rape from her youth in her later years).[107] The violence in this scene is overwhelming and appalling, and to a contemporary viewer its sadism may come as an extreme shock. Not only is the aged victim tied up and raped, but her clothes are also ripped off and her chest is burned with a cigarette before she is stabbed in the stomach and left to die. But even placing this horrific sequence aside, the scene where Omar tortures and kills one of the rapists in a bathtub bears striking similarities to its parallel scene in Meir Zarchi's *I Spit on Your Grave* that appeared eleven years later. The victim is not castrated as such, but Omar shoots him, and the victim grabs his crotch as he screams in agony. The creative manner with which Omar approaches the torture and destruction of his prey certainly foreshadows the bizarre and flamboyant techniques that would mark the American rape-revenge films of the 1970s in particular.

It would be erroneous to suggest that all Turkish rape-revenge films are as intriguing as *The Great Hate*, and like many other national instances, there is no shortage of examples that wear their exploitative intent on their sleeves. Osman F. Sedan's *The Stigma* (*Damga*, 1984) is typical of this, and despite featuring Turkish superstar Tarik Akan as the male protagonist, there is little about this tale of a man avenging the rape of his fiancée to separate it from American rape-revenge films of the same period. Those familiar with Turkish genre cinema, however, will be aware that the American influence is far more explicit than this. With its notorious disregard for issues of copyright, the Turkish film industry is renowned for its brazen, unauthorized remakes of popular Hollywood films that lift plot and dialogue, and often simply reenact entire scenes or even whole films. To international cult film audiences, the most famous of these would be *The Return of Superman* (*Süpermen dönüyor*, Kunt Tulgar, 1979)—often just referred to as *Turkish Superman*—and *Kelepçe* (Cetin Inanc, 1982), or *Turkish Dirty Harry*. Even *The Well*'s celebrated director, Metin Erksan, participated in this adaptation culture with his 1974 film *Seytan*, a close to scene-by-scene unauthorized remake of *The Exorcist* (William Friedkin, 1973), simply referred to in cult shorthand as *Turkish Exorcist*. Successful American rape-revenge films were not spared from this form of cross-cultural adaptation, as demonstrated in *Kartal Yuvasi* (Natuk Baytan, 1974)—known colloquially as *Turkish Straw Dogs*—and *The Executioner* (*Cellat*, Memduh Ün, 1975) or *Turkish Death Wish*. Sharing a near-identical moustache to Charles Bronson, Orhan (Serdar Gökhan) is this film's Paul Kersey figure, an architect whose wife and sister are attacked by a group of thugs. When the wife is murdered and the sister raped and left in a catatonic state, the previously liberal Orhan turns to a life of vigilantism that closely resembles Kersey's, right down to his use of a coin-filled sock as a weapon. But there is a crucial difference in the way the two films end: while Kersey is finally confronted by the police and moves to Chicago, in *The Executioner*, Ohran—through a series of coincidences—locates the men who raped his sister and murdered his wife and dispatches them accordingly. Kersey does not get the opportunity to do this until Michael Winner's *Death Wish 2* in 1982.

The differences between *Woman of Vengeance* (*Intikam Kadini*, Naki Yurter, 1979)—or as it is informally known, *Turkish I Spit on Your Grave*—and the original are even more pronounced. As both Kaya Özkaracalar and Ian Robert Smith indicate in their insightful analyses of Erksan's *Seytan*, however, it is unwise to dismiss these Turkish remakes as offering no insight into Turkish culture specifically.[108] While *Woman of Vengeance* shares a similar structure to *I Spit on Your Grave*, unlike *The Executioner* it does not replicate specific scenes as much as it implies loosely shared foundations. The film begins as a car containing a group of middle-aged men breaks down, and they enter the house of an elderly man and his daughter for assistance. The daughter—played by Zerrin Dog˘an, who wears a traditional headscarf and a simple dress—brings them food and drink, and the father offers them lodgings until they can get their car repaired. The leader of the group spies on the daughter, and then beats and rapes her. She lies still in a near-catatonic state as the other men also violate her; after the attack, the men panic and beat her father to death. After the men have left, she removes her headscarf and discovers her father's body. She stands on the edge of a cliff and contemplates suicide but changes her mind. Like in the original *I Spit on Your Grave*, she then prays for what she is about to do (this time at her father's grave). After a lengthy makeover montage where she replaces her traditional clothing with seductive, Western-styled attire, she tracks down the men responsible for her rape and her father's death and executes them. Luring the leader of the group to a deserted barn after she seduces him and the two have embarked upon a lengthy sexual encounter, she changes back into her more traditional clothing and kills him with a pitchfork. With her vengeance complete, she leaves sadly but calmly, and is captured by the police.

Both Zerrin Doğan and director Yurter worked together on one of Turkey's earliest adult films, *A Woman Like That* (*Öyle Bir Kadin Ki*, 1979), and their teaming up again on *Woman of Vengeance* perhaps goes some way to explain the thematically inappropriate sex scenes that litter it (most problematic, of course, is the lengthy sex scene near the end of the film between Doğan's rape-avenging protagonist and the man who raped her). While far from symbolically sophisticated, the use of costume offers insight into the tensions between the categories of East and West, and their relationship to female power and sexuality. As Laurence Raw has indicated, one of the central concerns of Turkish cinema is "the struggles—whether social, personal or political—experienced by people caught between two cultures, European and Islamic."[109] Doğan's character makes this tension explicit through her wardrobe. The Western style of dress that she adopts in vengeance mode can be considered overt: wigs, sunglasses, heavy make-up, bikinis, blue jeans and high-heeled shoes. This strikes a dramatic contrast with her traditional outfit at the beginning and ending of the film, and her transformation from rape victim to vampish avenger is coded explicitly through this wardrobe shift from "East" to "West." That she returns to her more traditional outfit to kill the last of the rapists signifies a return to her "true" self. Her calm surrender to the police is therefore an act allied with traditional values, simultaneously acknowledging that her role as vengeful vamp was a deviation from these values and therefore necessarily coded as explicitly "Western."

This global snapshot of rape-revenge film is by no means exhaustive, and some important countries remain unexplored. Italian rape-revenge films in this book thus far have been mentioned only in the context of spaghetti Westerns and horror (particularly the proliferation of *The Last House on the Left*–inspired films), but as films such as Vittorio De Sica's *Two Women* (*La ciociara*, 1960) and Giuseppe Tornatore's *The Unknown Woman* (*La sconosciuta*, 2008) demonstrate, to glean a singular or cohesive treatment of rape from this national context may prove more difficult than this small selection of films otherwise suggests (Dario Argento's 1996 film *The Stendhal Syndrome* will also be discussed in the Afterword). Rape-revenge is not uncommon in Russian cinema, as seen in films such as *The Day of Love* (*Den lyubvi*, Aleksandr Polynnikov, 1991), *The Executioner* (Viktor Sergeev, 1990), Stanislav Govorukhin's *The Rifleman of Voroshilov Regiment* (*Voroshilovskiy strelok*, 1999), and *Twilight Portrait*. Greek rape-revenge films include *The Steam* (*To hamam*, Makis Antonopoulos, 1988) and *Razor* (Philippos Halatsis, 2007), while Yorgos Tsemberopoulos's *The Enemy Within* (2013) and *Miss Violence* are notable entries from the so-called Weird Greek Wave. From Yugoslavia we find films including *Kraljeva zavrsnica* (Zivorad Tomic, 1987) and the earlier *The Girl and the Oak* (*Djevojka i hrast*, Kresimir Golik, 1956), while from the Czech Republic we find films as diverse as Věra Chytilová's *Traps* (*Pasti, pasti, pastičky*, 1998) and Roman Vojkuvka's *Someone Down There Likes Me* (*Nekdo tam dole me má rád*, 2009).

Clearly, rape-revenge films are not a solely North American or European fascination. From the Israeli film *Big Bad Wolves* to *Mya Mya* (Nyo Min Lwin, 2020) from Burma, rape-revenge is an international phenomenon. Brazil's José Mojica Marins (aka Coffin Joe) made a rape-revenge film in 1979 called *Perversion*, which, although strange and violent, pales in comparison to the brutality of *The Girl of Diabolical Sex* (*A Menina Do Diabólico*, Mário Lima, 1987). From Mexico, the extreme horror of *Atrocious* (*Atroz*, Lex Ortega, 2015) stands in striking contrast to the more teen-friendly thrills of rape-revenge slasher *Romina* from the same country. The Nollywood movies *Deadly Emotion* (Afe Olumowe, 2009), *Scorned* (Tokunbo Ahmed and Oluseyi Asurf, 2016), *Alter Ego* (Moses Inwang, 2017) and the opening scene of Kunle Afolayan's *Citation*

(2020) provide examples of rape-revenge from Nigeria's robust film industry, while the Pashto film *Haseena Atom Bomb* (Saeed Ali Kahn, 1990) paves the way for Pakistan's inclusion in this global snapshot of rape-revenge's scope and diversity. Filipino donations to rape-revenge include *Clouds* (Tata Esteban, 1984), *Oh My Ghost!* (Tony Y. Reyes, 2006), and Lino Brocka's *Angela Markado* (1980), and even Cambodia has utilized a supernatural horror rape-revenge framework for the Khmer film *Lady Vampire* (*Nieng Arp*, Kam Chanty, 2004). Rape-revenge films have been made all around the world, and this vast range of movies demonstrates its diversity. And as the next chapter argues, although contrary to popular belief, many have even been directed by women.

CHAPTER FOUR

Women-Directed Rape-Revenge Films

When allegations of powerful Hollywood producer Harvey Weinstein's decades-long reign of sexual harassment and abuse were made public in *The New Yorker* and the *New York Times* in October 2017, it triggered what would be referred to by the shorthand #MeToo, launching activist Tarana Burke's movement established in 2006 into the mainstream. #MeToo has become a catch-all for the collective yet long-repressed horror stories of sexual harassment and sexual violence experienced by women and men well beyond the U.S. context where the Weinstein story broke. In terms of the film industry specifically, Weinstein's atrocities—which resulted in his conviction in early 2020—were an open secret, with everyone from Courtney Love to Seth MacFarlane having gone on the record about it long before the news stories broke. What has since become apparent is that other publications who had tried to break the story previously had been silenced by powerful forces. Previously appearing in *Death Proof*, actor-turned-activist Rose McGowan is one of many women who have effectively rebranded themselves since the Weinstein story broke, finding not just her voice but a welcoming audience now ready to hear the story she had long wanted to tell, going on the record in numerous interviews, in her memoir *Brave* (2018) and a documentary series, *Citizen Rose* that same year. Countless other women in the industry—both high profile and lesser known—also went public with their stories, such as actor Annabella Sciorra who openly testified in court against Weinstein in the case that eventually saw him behind bars.

The revelations of Weinstein's history of violence against women caused a fundamental shift in how both the film industry specifically but public discourse more broadly framed gender discrimination and abuse. The fact that men dominate the film industry demanded reassessment, with attention turning towards what was already an increasing public interest in precisely why women filmmakers had struggled for so long to not just get their films made but taken seriously. In some cases, responses to the Weinstein case took a literal form, as in Kitty Green's *The Assistant* (2019) which, while obviously based on Weinstein though never explicitly stated, explored the behind-the-scenes mechanics that allowed Weinstein to go unpunished for so long. Green's titular young, ambitious office assistant is both humiliated and, despite her best efforts, forced into complicity with her boss's horrendous behavior. The film is a strong reminder of the extent to which Weinstein story shattered the illusion of a functional, level playing ground for women in the film industry.

While it would require impressive rhetorical gymnastics at best and ideological pig-headedness at worst to reduce the diversity of women-directed rape-revenge films to a singular representational template, what is more important is how—rather than male directors telling stories played out on traumatized, violated women's bodies, here it is women directors telling those stories. These films are diverse, but if there is one generally unifying factor, it is that they are made by women working in an industry where by *virtue of their gender alone* they are considered novelties or interlopers. Long before 2017, there were stories about women who struggled to make films that explored rape and revenge: as discussed previously, Lina Wertmüller was thrown off *The Belle Starr Story* (1976) after mere days, and Tamra Davis was removed from *Bad Girls* (1994) and replaced by Jonathan Kaplan.

The history of women-directed rape-revenge films—and rape films more generally—has been largely ignored, denied and buried. As discussed in the Introduction, Ida Lupino's *Outrage* (1950) is a pioneering film regarding the representation of rape trauma, but this film has remained largely obscure until recent years. But as part of the cultural shifts of recent years, visual culture more broadly has been reassessed through the contemporary #MeToo lens, allowing work as far back as Italian Baroque artist Artemisia Gentileschi to be considered explicitly from the perspective of rape-revenge. Genevieve Carlton's article "The 'Savage' Works of Artemisia Gentileschi, The Painter Who Got Revenge on Her Rapist Through Her Art" is typical of such revisions, noting the artist "endured a torturous trial that ended with her abuser walking free before channelling her rage into some of history's most violent paintings,"[1] citing in particular her work *Judith Beheading Holofernes* (1612). While this perhaps is a simplistic reduction of Gentileschi's work framed heavily by contemporary gender politics, it was not the first time her story had been tweaked to suit a contemporary perspective. While ostensibly a biopic, Agnes Merlet's *Artemisia* (1997) controversially framed the relationship as consensual, sparking outrage among some feminist art historians as this interpretation did not reflect the

Rose McGowan at the Paramount Studios Theater in Los Angeles on 31 March 2016 (Kathy Hutchins/Shutterstock.com).

contents of actual documentation from the rape trial itself. Merlet would later turn to rape-revenge terrain in her supernatural horror film *Dorothy Mills* (2008), where a young girl channels the spirit of a dead raped teenager who uses the title character's body as a vengeance-seeking vehicle.

The rich history of women-directed films that address rape is notably diverse not only in tone and content, but production context. Even a preliminary sweep is revealing, challenging assumptions that the interest of women filmmakers in rape is particularly new. Take, for example, *Rape* (Anja Breien, 1971) from Norway, *Love Violated* (Marie-Annick Bellon, using the alias Yannick Bellon, 1978) from France, *A Scream from Silence* (Anne Claire Poirer, 1979) from Canada, *Germany, Pale Mother* (Helma Sanders-Brahm, 1979) from Germany, *Moral* (Marilou Diaz-Abaya, 1982) from the Philippines, *Macu, The Policeman's Woman* (Solveig Hoogesteijin, 1987) from Venezuela, *Flame* (Ingrid Sinclair, 1996) from Zimbabwe, *Eighteen Springs* (1997) by pioneering Hong Kong New Wave filmmaker Ann Hui, *Love Belongs to Everyone* (Hilde Van Mieghem, 2006) from Belgium, *Hemel* (Sacha Polak, 2012) from The Netherlands, *Dry* (Stephanie Linus, 2014) from Nigeria, *Cock-Tale* (Insia Dariwala, 2014) from India, *Princess* (Tali Shalom Ezer, 2014), *Beauty and the Dogs* (Kaouther Ben Hania, 2017), *Flatland* (Jenna Bass, 2019) from South Africa, *Sema* (Macherie Ekwa, 2020) from the Democratic Republic of Congo, and numerous films by French filmmakers Claire Denis and Catherine Breillat. In the United States alone, there is striking diversity, illustrated by a handful of examples including *The Prince of Tides* (Barbra Streisand, 1991), *Strange Days* (Kathryn Bigelow, 1995), *She Cried No* (Kathleen Rowell, 1996), *Jaded* (Caryn Krooth, 1998), *Deep in My Heart* (Anita W. Addison, 1999), *Edge of Madness* (Anne Wheeler, 2002), *Speak* (Jessica Sharzer, 2004), and *I Believe in Unicorns* (Leah Meyerhoff, 2014). There are films based on the filmmakers' own experiences such as actor Lori Petty's directorial debut *The Poker House* (2008) and Jennifer Fox's *The Tale* (2018), and real-life atrocities inspired a number of women to make rape films. At one end of the spectrum we find Irish filmmaker Juanita Wilson's *As If I Am Not There* (2010) and Bosnian director Jasmila Žbanić's *Grbavica* (2006) which are both based on the mass rapes that marked the Bosnian War, while at the other, Katt Shea's *The Fury: Carrie 2* (1999) was inspired by the real life "Spur Posse" case from Lakewood, California, in 1993. This does not even begin to account for the long history of women-directed documentaries about rape including *Rape Culture* (Margaret Lazarus and Renner Wunderluch, 1975), *Calling the Ghosts* (Mandy Jacobson and Karmen Jelinec, 1996), *The Greatest Silence* (Lisa F. Jackson, 2007), *After the Rape* (Catherine Ulmer, 2008), *Within Every Woman* (Tiffany Hsiung, 2012), and *Brave Miss World* (Cecilia Peck, 2013), just as a random selection.

This quick survey briefly illustrates how futile it is to suggest that women filmmakers suddenly became interested in making films overnight with the onset of #MeToo. Such a claim, even an implicit one, necessarily undermines the existence and scope of work made prior to late 2017. Another assumption that likewise accompanies this belief is that women are somehow blessed with the ability to make fundamentally progressive films, an intrinsically sexist claim if ever there was one. When it comes to rape-revenge, the idealism that marks much commentary on post #MeToo women's rape-revenge filmmaking almost by default either actively denies or remains otherwise oblivious to the category's substantial film history.[2] And not all of it fits into an immediately recognizable progressive discourse. Legendary Japanese pink film director Sachi Hamano made the profoundly unpleasant rape-revenge film *Drifted Into Chaos (Kageki honban: Midareru)* in 1989, a reimagining of Tobe Hooper's *The Texas Chain Saw Massacre* (1974) with an unrestrained dollop of rape thrown into the mix. Hong Kong filmmaker and actor Julie Lee did not hesitate in glamorizing rape in her 1995 softcore rape-revenge film *Trilogy of Lust 2*, and groundbreaking American adult filmmaker Ann Perry made two hardcore rape-revenge films, *Teenage Sex Kitten* (1975) and *Sweet Savages* (1979), the latter—as the title suggests—pivoting around representations of First Nations people that from a contemporary perspective prove challenging.

Not all early women-directed instances of rape-revenge fall into such reactionary categories, of course. In 1965, grindhouse icon Doris Wishman featured a rape-avenging protagonist in her iconic roughie, *Bad Girls Go to Hell*. The film stars Gigi Darlene as Meg, who is raped on the stairwell of her apartment block in Chicago by a man when she takes out her trash, cleaning the house while her husband is at work. Sliding a note under her door, he tells her that if she does not come to his apartment, he will tell her husband. She follows his instructions, expecting him to blackmail her, but he tries to rape her again and she fights back, killing him. She flees to New York where she changes her name to Ellen and hopes to blend in with the crowd. Moving from home to home, Ellen meets a parade of violent, sexually aggressive men, until she encounters a lesbian with whom she has a positive, caring relationship. However, when she sees that the Chicago murder has made the front page of the newspaper, Ellen, not wishing to burden her lover with the consequences of her earlier actions, is forced to leave. She finally lands a job as a companion with a kindly old lady, discovering too late that her son is the policeman investigating the case. He confronts her, prompting her to plead "I didn't mean to do it!" referring to the rape-avenging murder of the man in her Chicago apartment building. But it was all a dream; Meg wakes up next to her husband, telling him she had a terrible dream. Before she knows it, however, the cycle begins again: her husband leaves for work, and she finds the same man in the same stairwell with the same intentions. Rape,

Poster for *Bad Girls Go to Hell* (Doris Wishman, 1965) (Everett Collection, Inc./Alamy Stock Photo).

revenge and its associated trauma are for Meg a never-ending cycle and the lines between nightmare and her reality have collapsed entirely.

If not the first woman-directed rape-revenge film, *Bad Girls Go to Hell* is certainly one of the earliest, and more would soon follow. Early in Stephanie Rothman's *The Velvet Vampire* (1971), the title character is attacked by a man who does not realize she is fully capable of killing him on the spot, which she does with satisfying gusto. Beyond the many other films discussed in this chapter, rape and revenge feature either centrally or in notable scenes in many, many other women-directed films include *The Ladies Club* (Janet Greek, 1986), *Blood Games* (Tanya Rosenberg, 1990), *Macon County Jail* (Victoria Muspratt, 1997), *Titus* (Julie Taymor, 1999), *An Eye for an Eye* (Lou Simon, 2015), *Revenge* (Kjersti G. Steinsbø, 2015), and *Amulet* (Romola Garai, 2020). Again, some are based on true stories; two very different films starring Charlize Theron fall into this category, Patty Jenkins' *Monster* (2003) was based on the life of rape-avenging serial killer Aileen Wuornos, and Niki Caro's *North Country* (2005) which was adapted from Clara Bingham and Laura Leedy Gansler's 2002 book *Class Action: The Story of Lois Jenson and the Landmark Case That Changed Sexual Harassment Law*. Not all films directed by women whose action culminates at the intersection of rape and revenge have embraced the label; Jennifer Kent's *The Nightingale* (2018) is perhaps the most high-profile example of this, the filmmaker going on record numerous times in her emphatic rejection of the description, stating in one instance, "I don't think it is a rape-revenge film. I think it actually works in the opposite direction to a film like that."[3] And, to be fair, she has a point; while her protagonist's desire for vengeance is spawned by a vicious sexual assault, this rape occurs almost simultaneously alongside the murder of her husband and her newborn baby; to privilege only the rape as a motivation for revenge therefore necessarily downplays the unambiguous horror of the two murders (the death of the baby in particular is unflinching in its representation).

But while Kent's aversion stems from a perceived inherent misogyny in the category itself, other filmmakers have voiced different reasons for not framing their films through a rape-revenge descriptor. Widely considered a key woman-directed rape-revenge film, Jen and Sylvia Soska's *American Mary* (2012) follows Mary (Katherine Isabelle), a dedicated medical student struggling for cash who turns to underground extreme body modifications to make money in her spare time. When she is drugged and raped at a party held for the most successful male surgeons at the hospital where she is completing her studies, Mary drops out, finds the man responsible and, having abducted him uses him as an unwilling guinea pig for her most over-the-top body modification experiments. Knowing that a video of her rape exists Mary's paranoia grows, but before the police can capture her, the husband of one of her clients finds and kills Mary out of revenge for the consensual surgery she had performed on a woman to make her look like a plastic doll (including the suturing of her vulva and the surgical removal of her nipples). While less hostile to the rape-revenge label than Kent ("it can definitely be described as that," says Sylvia), like Kent and *The Nightingale*, Sylvia see the rape as only one part of the larger picture in terms of what pushes Mary over the edge. "I never intended to make a rape-revenge [film],"[4] she says. "Mary has her world ripped apart three times before she changes into someone darker for good," and the rape is just one of these. For Jen, this complexity was vital to making Mary a character who reflected their broader worldview. "Women can't fit into one box. We're too complex. We can't just be victim girl, then badass. And in being a badass there isn't always strength," she added. "It was important that Mary had a lot going on inside her before." While very different filmmakers, the Soskas' and Kent's shared insistence that to focus only on rape sidelines broader systemic inequalities that women face, such as the economic challenges which in both films are framed through their particular historical settings: late capitalism in *American Mary*, and colonial-era Australia in *The Nightingale*.

Considering the undeniably gruesome misogyny that has traditionally driven many of the more notorious instances of the rape-revenge film historically, it feels appropriate to respect women filmmakers who reject the label. At the same time, however, any film that hinges on the combined plot elements of rape and revenge is going to necessarily find itself tagged with the label, whether the filmmaker likes it or not. But on the other hand, there are hugely important films that demand consideration here that encompass the desire for revenge for male atrocities that include, but are not limited to, rape. Rarely considered a rape-revenge film as such for good reason, the late Sarah Jacobson's *I Was a Teenage Serial Killer* (1992) is both important and instructive here. Starring Kristin Calabrese as Mary, the film begins with her killing a man who gloats about leaving his wife and child, an act which is soon followed by a series of vignettes depicting a broad spectrum of abusive male behaviors towards women. Mary is demeaned, insulted, harassed, and a consensual sex scene becomes non-consensual when her partner removes his condom without telling her mid-coitus. Today, his actions are identified as what is called "stealthing," something widely understood as both an act of reproductive coercion and a form of sexual assault. Mary certainly understands it as such and after she kills him, forces a banana into his mouth as an unsubtle fellatio metaphor to mirror the sexual violence she has just experienced at his hands. Mary witnesses a range of abuses against women, herself and others, and kills in retaliation, before finding true love with a seeming kindred spirit, a man who tells her that he only kills straight men; his violent desires, like hers, are driven by a reaction against heteronormative patriarchy. They embark on a romantic killing spree, but when he brings home a woman for them to rape and murder together, Mary is heartbroken. Beating him to death with a handheld vacuum cleaner, she tells the frightened woman to leave. The film's powerful climax finds her sitting on the steps outside a West African restaurant when a man sits with her and asks her what is wrong. She is unrestrained in her reply, "I've just killed the only man I've ever loved.... I've killed 19 men, one for every year I've ever lived. When I was a kid, my dad abused me—he tried to touch me. It hurts." Failing to read the mood and continuing the misogyny that permeates the film, her companion flirtatiously replies, "Maybe because it's because you're such an attractive, strong woman." This is the last straw for Mary:

> What the fuck? I can't believe this! Every time I kill someone, they say it's my fault. It's not my fault, I didn't do it—I don't have to be ashamed. No one wants to listen to my story, and then I get this anger that I'm not allowed to express because it's not right for a woman to have any rage. You can have your fucking James Dean image and be a hero to society and I have just as much pain—if not more—and no one can look me in the eye and say "I'm sorry."

She continues:

> You're not the enemy. I don't have to kill you. I don't have to kill anyone anymore. My story exists whether anyone is going to listen to me or not. Killing all these men who don't understand is bullshit. You know, I'm going to do something worse; whether you want to ignore me or invalidate my stories, I'm gonna tell 'em anyways, you can't keep me quiet.

Aside from being one of the most raw and exciting underground films of the 1990s, *I Was a Teenage Serial Killer* is worth privileging here for Mary's final speech alone; by directly addressing her desire to have her voice heard—to have her stories acknowledged—Jacobson effectively issued a manifesto for women-directed rape-revenge films, one that explicitly positions extreme violent tendencies as a seemingly rational response to the collective enormity of what women experience under the patriarchal weight of rape culture.

The raw punk sensibility of *I Was a Teenage Serial Killer* continues into the controversial French rape-revenge film, *Baise-Moi* (2000)—whose English translation has ranged the ideological spectrum from "Kiss Me" to "Fuck Me" to "Rape Me"[5]—co-directed by Coralie Trinh Thi and Virginie Despentes and adapted from the cult novel by the latter (itself based upon her diaries). Both Despentes and Trinh Thi had worked previously in the sex industry and the film was cast with porn performers Karen Bach and Raffaëla Anderson in the lead roles. The inclusion of unsimulated sex (including during its graphic rape scene[6]) combined with the film's excessive violence garnered it international notoriety. Right wing and religious groups in France rallied against the film upon its release, leading the government to place its first ban on a film in the country since 1973.[7] The movie also met with censorship scandals around the world; in Australia the police were even called in to shut down screenings.

While the tabloid press rushed to bestow their polarized, pro- or anti–*Baise-moi* sentiment, more reputable film critics also found their opinions split. For Gavin Smith, the film was "a genuinely primitive mongrel movie" that "is either pointlessly degrading Eurosleaze or a profound vision of nihilism and social transgression. Or both."[8] Eric Monder was equally divided, declaring, "The film is both bravely effective and undeniably repellent."[9] Some critics readily identified what Despentes described as her and Trinh Thi's shared "feminist warrior vision."[10] For Colin Nettelback, "the film is driven by an energetic feminist determination both to subvert the existing male dominance of explicit sexual imagery and to shift what society defines as pornography from the margins to the cultural mainstream,"[11] while Phil Powrie suggests, "*Baise-moi* turns the tables on gender and genre, taking neo-*noir* to a feminized hyper-space where the narrative matters less than a new kind of energy: the black whole of hyper-noir."[12] It is this "energy" that both Powrie and Nettelback identify that appears to be the one element of *Baise-moi* that critics agreed upon, captured most simply by Linda Ruth Williams in her observation that "*Baise-moi* itself is actually rather fun, and refreshingly innocent in its cinematic strategies. If it's sensationally confused, it's also energetically driven."[13]

Nadine (Bach) is a sex worker with a nagging housemate whom she kills in a fit of anger, while Manu (Anderson) is gang-raped with a friend by a group of men while they are drinking and talking in a park. Manu's friend struggles and screams during the attack, but Manu herself remains frozen and blank, her lack of shock suggesting that she is more than familiar with this type of violence. (As she explains to her friend, who is confused by her passivity, "If you park in the projects, you empty your car 'cause someone's gonna break in. I leave nothing precious in my cunt for those jerks.") When he finds out about the rape, Manu's brother gets a gun to avenge the assault, but she refuses to give him the information necessary to identify the perpetrators. He interprets her refusal as meaning she enjoyed the rape and calls her a slut. Manu snaps instantly and kills him with a nearby gun. Manu and Nadine meet near a train subway while wandering around aimlessly after their respective murders and become friends. They embark on a self-destructive road trip where they kill random strangers (both men and women, although the killing of men is certainly privileged and tends to be provided with more motivation—usually sexism—than their female victims). During their killing spree, Manu and Nadine engage in a range of less vicious pleasures than their sadistic murders: They dance in their underwear, they drink, they have sex with strangers. but most of all they enjoy each other's company. When Manu is shot at a roadhouse, their adventure ends as suddenly and as inexplicably as it began. A devastated Nadine disposes of Manu's body, and just before she is able to commit suicide herself, the police locate and arrest her. In this final moment, Nadine returns instantly to her submissive role in a violent and misogynistic patriarchal social order, as the policemen scream, "Bitch! Freeze! Where's your friend? Where's the other bitch?"

As Nettleback and Judith Franco have both observed,[14] from the opening moments of the film—with its lengthy close-up of Nadine's unbroken stare in her dominatrix-styled collar—*Baise-moi* seeks to actively defy the normative "male gaze" of Hollywood narrative cinema as identified by Laura Mulvey in 1972. Its combination of road movie elements with feminist fantasy have perhaps unsurprisingly garnered *Baise-moi* comparisons to *Thelma & Louise*, but the French film has a number of crucial differences. As Franco observes, "While *Thelma & Louise* and other American feminine road narratives privilege the psychological emotional process of self-discovery in a predominantly melodramatic mode, *Baise-moi* ... attempt[s] to co-opt the road movie's masculinist ideals."[15] When asked if it is a rape-revenge film, Despentes has answered that while her and Trinh Thi consider it more a female friendship film, "obviously it can be considered as a rape-revenge movie, and why not?"[16] The revenge Nadine and Manu seek, of course, is not specifically in regard to the rape shown at the beginning of the film. As Manu makes clear in the killing of her brother when he suggests she enjoyed the rape because she was not "properly" traumatized, the film's depiction of violence against women is much broader and insidious than this one sexually explicit and harrowing assault. It is in this sense that the film gains its most perversely charming and bleakly comic motifs, as Manu and Nadine continually joke about how they do not fit the "typical" image of the female avenger, acknowledging an awareness of their own heritage as mythological female avengers. "Fuck, we're hopeless," says Manu at one stage. "Where are all our witty lines?" "We've got guns," answers Nadine, "at least that's something." Later they discuss committing suicide so that it can "end as good as it began ... with a good punchline."

The strength of *Baise-moi*, however, is not its knowing subversion of rape-revenge traditions, its punk *vérité* aesthetic, or even the remarkable performances of its two lead performers. Rather, it is about the randomness of both the violent and pleasurable aspects of these women's lives, and that the film allows its female characters to be irrational, confused and unable to easily fit into the pre-decided role of the female action avenger they so openly mock. "I think what is important in our movie is that to me, for the first time, you can see a girl having sex and being a slut and then laughing and then having fun and then being violent and angry and then being stupid," Despentes has said.[17] *Baise-moi* is a unique artifact that consciously lets its female characters respond—to rape, violence and anger, as well as to pleasure, joy, and friendship—in ways that make sense to them *before* they fit into the preconceived assumptions that dominate film history. Like Nadine and Manu, Trinh Thi and Despentes feel they do not owe *anyone* an explanation, and this (combined with the film's explicit depiction of sex and violence) makes for a difficult but unforgettable viewing experience.

Two years before *Baise-Moi*, a very different woman-directed rape-revenge film was released. A key figure of the Czech New Wave, Vera Chytilová's earlier 1966 feminist masterpiece *Daisies* in retrospect shares the same spirit of anarchic glee as both *I Was a Teenage Serial Killer* and *Baise-Moi*, although decidedly more lighthearted and rape-free. But in her rape-revenge comedy *Traps* (1998), Chytilová made one of her most underrated and enduring films in terms of the poignancy and specificity of its themes today. At the time of its release, some critics chose to altogether ignore the ideological powder-keg of the broadly maligned, assumedly exploitative rape-revenge trope as a foundation for Chytilová's film: for David Stratton, Chytilová's presence alone seems to have automatically rendered the film "feminist," though his main complaint was not the controversial gender politics of rape-revenge but simply that *Traps* wasn't funny enough.[18] But the film is impossible to evaluate without a serious consideration of the thematic deployment of sexual violence, and the question it raises—which Chytilová answers with rigor, compassion and deep intelligence—is this: what does rape *mean* in the world of *Traps*? Her answer is, ultimately, disquieting. The film begins with smiling castratrice Lenka (Zuzana Stivínová)—a veterinarian—neutering pigs in grueling, bloody close-up. When her car runs out of fuel on a deserted country road, she crosses paths with misogynistic advertising designer Petr (played by one of the film's co-writers, Tomáš Hanák), and the somewhat feeble yet highly ambitious newly crowned deputy minister for the environment, Dohnal (Miroslav Donutil). Old school friends, Dohnal and Petr reunite at a party for wealthy businessman Bach (Milan Lasica): Petr is hopeful that Bach will like his campaign for a new line of confectionary (a grotesque image, epitomizing rape culture, of a woman having a chocolate forced into her mouth alongside the slogan "Bach's Balls: The Sweetest Suck of All"), while Dohnal quietly negotiates a pay-off to ignore environmentalist protests about a possible new ring-road in Prague where Bach wishes to build a petrol station and hotel. Petr and Dohnal drunkenly leave the party and, as they drive, the former tells the latter of his belief that monogamy leads to impotence. Seeing the vulnerable Lenka by the roadside, Petr challenges Dohnal to prove his masculinity: they drive to a secluded wooded area and viciously sexually assault her. When she pretends to faint afterwards, the two men believe Lenka has amnesia and agree to drive her home, even accepting her offer of a drink. She drugs them and—off-camera—castrates them, placing their testicles neatly in a candy dish on her coffee table.

Much of the film's humor stems from the physical comedy arising out of Petr and Dohnal's newfound literal emasculation. This is not complex satire, but old-school slapstick: they stumble about, hands on their crotches, as schoolgirls laugh at them. A sequence in which Petr fails to hang himself recalls a similar moment in Jerry Lewis's *Cracking Up* (1983), and Lewis' particular brand of physical comedy is a useful reference point for the specific kind of bodily humor Chytilová opts for. In sharp contrast are the scenes with Lenka. Sombre, dark and wholly sympathetic, her experience is presented by Chytilová in direct tonal and emotional opposition to the goofy, humiliated antics of newly gelded Petr and Dohnal. While Stratton sees this as evidence of a general unevenness,[19] this tonal imbalance is precisely *why* the film succeeds in its unification of rape and comedy: to borrow Rebecca Solnit's description of a later Amy Schumer rape sketch, *Traps* too is "not a joke about rape ... but rape culture."[20]

While not totally sold on the success of the film, Peter Hames identifies Chytilová's attempt to link "a story about rape" with "the values of the new political system" in the post–Velvet Revolution Czech Republic, in which "the main focus of the film's humour lies in the men's hope of becoming reattached, but the film is also an allegory about male power."[21] In 2009, Hames suggested this link was "tenuous,"[22] but from a contemporary perspective, the link between political corruption, state power and sexual violence is only too familiar: think, for example, of Harvey Weinstein, or, for that matter, Donald Trump, the former President of the United States who at the time of writing remains unscathed by the twenty allegations of sexual misconduct and sexual assault made against him.[23] This makes *Traps* a particularly difficult film to watch from a contemporary perspective alone: like so many of the real-world scenarios we increasingly see playing out in the news twenty years after Chytilová's film was released, there is, more often than not, no happy ending for women who suffer at the hands of powerful men. *Traps* is a feminist rape-revenge comedy, but it is no fairytale.

Just as *Traps* foreshadows these more contemporary current events, so too does Talia Lugacy's *Descent* (2007), a film difficult to watch beyond the prism of the Black Lives Matter movement. As Claire Henry suggests, this film is an important one as it "confronts the genre's exclusion of women of color and coding of the sympathetic victim as always and necessarily white."[24] As previously noted, while there are other rape-revenge films that do feature Black survivors such as *Chaos*, *A Time to Kill*, *The Perfection*, *Fight for Your Life* and *Rape Squad* in particular, they are undeniably rare. In *Descent*, a low budget independent film made by Rosario Dawson's childhood friend Talia Lugacy, Dawson plays quiet university student Maya, who goes to a party one night as she recovers from an unspecified heartbreak. Here she meets Jared (Chad Faust), an odd but strangely charismatic footballer with whom she agrees to have dinner. After their date, Maya accompanies Jared home where they drink wine and he date-rapes her. What begins as consensual making out escalates suddenly into a vicious assault, complete with him hurling racist remarks at her while the camera stays upon her crying, pleading face. Unlike many rape-revenge films, Maya's fallout from the assault is not narratively clear—there is no single moment of transformation, and she does not "decide" upon revenge as much as a series of coincidences lead her to the point where she feels it is her only possible option. After the rape, she becomes withdrawn and depressed, and falls into a sex and drug-riddled club scene where she befriends the DJ Adrian (Marcus Patrick). Returning to college and acting as a teacher's aide, Jared is enrolled as a student in one of her classes. Seemingly unaware of the impact of the rape on Maya, Jared says he thinks she is "hooked" on him. Without blinking, she tells him she wishes to see him again. That evening they drink wine as Maya flirts with him. She demands that he strip naked, and she ties him to a bed. When Maya tells Jared of her trauma, he realizes that what he was reading as kinky seduction is, in fact, a revenge scenario. She rapes him with a dildo, and Adrian enters the scene and also rapes Jared, calling him a "maggot," a "stupid fuck," and asking, "You like raping smart girls, huh?" During Adrian's rape of Jared, Maya sits on the bed with her back towards them. Hoping the rape of Jared satisfies her desire for revenge and thus will end her trauma, Adrian asks Maya, "Everything's OK now, right?" The weeping Maya responds by looking directly into the camera; she turns her head away as the film ends.

Descent is noteworthy if only for the confronting first rape scene. As mentioned earlier in the case of *Handgun*, date rape is uncommon in rape-revenge films (most opting instead for stranger or home-invasion themed assaults). Here, however, Lugacy confidently demonstrates the terrifying ease with which a scene of consensual romance can "tip" into rape, as the soft music and candlelit mood that sets the romantic tone early in the scene before Maya asks Jared to stop is quickly transformed into something vicious and ironic when his attempted seduction becomes violent, forced and ugly. The strength of the film is this ability to depict the simple process of how rape "happens" in this context; and Dawson's performance as the detached Maya after the rape is to be commended for its quietude. Maya does not withdraw because she is plotting revenge *for* rape, she withdraws because she is traumatized *by* rape. What is significant in this last scene, however, is that final, fourth wall-crumbling glare that Maya gives the camera. This is a telling moment, as her look actively implicates the viewer in the spectacle of both her rape *and* her revenge. That stare confirms that Maya *knows* we are there, and suggests she is aware that the preceding action—not only her rape, but Jared's as well—was a show performed for an audience. It is in this context that the sad, accusing nature of her look addresses the viewer directly, and her tears silently answer Adrian's earlier question: "No, everything is *not* OK now." While stronger in some places than in others, *Descent*'s powerful final shot demands we reflect upon our complicity as viewers in the actions just witnessed. This is, ultimately, all inescapably framed through the factor of race, an element of the film that is embodied by Dawson herself. Noting the actor's diverse heritage (Puerto Rican, Afro-Cuban and American Indian), Jenny Lapekas states that "Rosario Dawson is a powerful force within a film that explores the sensitive connotations that inevitably accompany the issue of rape. Playing the role of a young black woman who consciously makes the decision to respond to her own rape in this particular way is no small task." She continues, "Even audiences who disagree with the moral implications of the final rape scene would admire Dawson's compelling performance in what is a modern tale of rape-revenge."[25] From a production side, however, Dawson herself explicitly stated that having a key role as a co-producer on the film—an important behind-the-scenes job—also helped tether herself emotionally while she played such a grueling role. "I could have disappeared into that character more, you know, and it would have taken me down," she said in an interview in 2012. "It was really depressing.... But I thought it was important

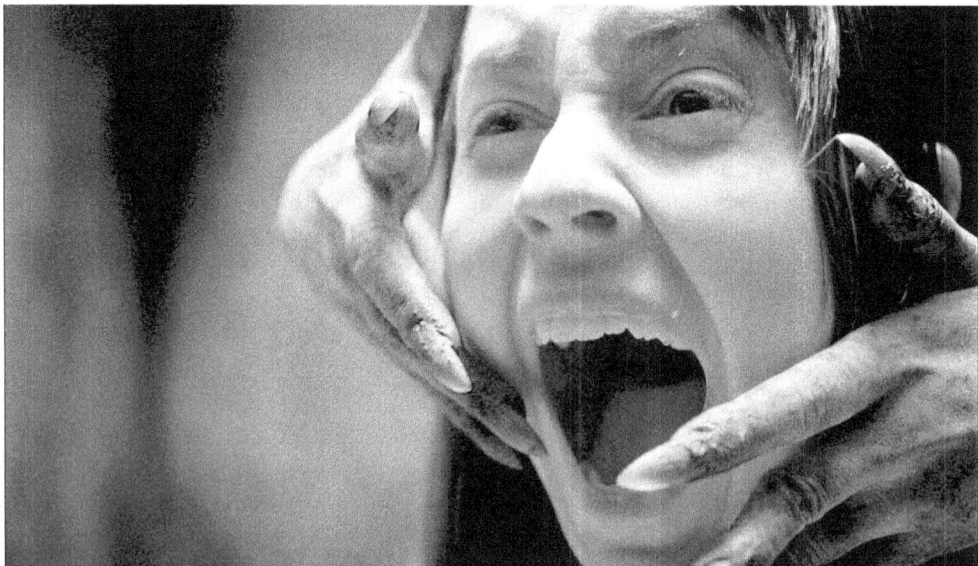

Screen shot of Katerina Katelieva as the title character of Karen Lam's *Evangeline* (2013), director of photography Michael Balfry (courtesy Karen Lam).

Chapter Four. Women-Directed Rape-Revenge Films 163

to show and really talk about revenge, and to put that question into people's minds. People have all these ideas about it, but what it would actually look like is not a triumph. It's actually really degrading and sad."[26]

This blurring with the real world and what happens on the rape-revenge film screen bleed into Karen Lam's 2013 supernatural rape-revenge film *Evangeline* in an entirely different way. As the director outlines, "The Highway of Tears is a northern highway in my province of British Columbia where many young women have gone missing from hitchhiking over decades.... And there was the serial killer Robert Pickton, who was also preying on young female sex workers in Vancouver, and it affected our Aboriginal community extensively."[27] Echoing *I Was a Teenage Serial Killer*, it is not just rape that Evangeline endures, but a series of atrocities—some psychological, but many physical—before she is raped and killed. Lam strategically maps rape as a point on a broader spectrum of gendered violence, and the film is nuanced in regard to the different ways that abuse manifests. Excited about starting college, Evangeline (Katerina Katelieva) takes her first tentative steps into the adult social world and almost immediately falls prey to a violent, sadistic trap laid for her by a handsome, wealthy man she meets at a party. Luring her to an isolated cabin, he abuses her verbally before physically beating her, leaving her for dead. Her journey out of the woods finds her hitchhiking, picked up by a serial killer who rapes and murders her. Rejuvenated by the forest spirits, Evangeline finds a new form with which to seek vengeance and protect other women, but the film's most powerful imagery stems from an abstracted psychological prison we see the young woman trapped in throughout the film, making tangible her emotional subjectivity in a way few other rape-revenge films have.

For Lam, the merger of the real-life horrors in

Evangeline poster (Karen Lam, 2013), designed by Bonni Reid (courtesy Karen Lam).

Canada and the more supernatural elements of Evangeline's story were an organic fit. "The idea of their ghosts and spirits haunting our forests where I assume their bodies have been left, and building up a mythology of these restless spirits is an amalgam of First Nations and Japanese mythology. Our northern communities also housed Japanese families during the internment of World War II, so it seemed to be a natural and organic fit between the two." It was these stories that influenced Lam's 2011 short film *Doll Parts*, the core of which was developed into the feature length project. The inception of *Doll Parts* and its evolution into *Evangeline* are revealing both in terms of Lam's own creative process, but also how women are treated within the industry itself. "*Doll Parts* was a pivotal film for me," Lam continues. "I had just finished my first feature film *Stained* (2010) and after a rather brutal reception, I needed to find out if I even wanted to continue on as a filmmaker":

> A distributor told me that I was incapable of filming sexual violence, based on what he saw in my feature, and if I couldn't "go there" then I had no business being in the industry. I remember that meeting and feeling like I had been kicked in the stomach. The genesis of the short film came when I was in Hong Kong, visiting my grandmother for the last time before she passed. She didn't recognize me at that point in her illness, but spent every night arguing with the demons in her head. I think I felt the veil between our worlds lift at that time, although I don't know if I knew it at the time. I came up with the broken doll image in Hong Kong and the storyline fell into place.

Key to *Evangeline*—released four years before #MeToo—is Lam's conscious decision to make it as a rape-revenge film; unlike Jennifer Kent's *The Nightingale*, in this instance the director embraced the concept, based explicitly on her status as a self-identifying feminist. "I did choose to do a rape-revenge film, and wanted to make sure that there was more to the genre than the conventional," she said. "To me, being a feminist horror filmmaker at my core, it's using the conventional as a springboard. I wanted the film to be a reaction to the genre, to add another voice and perspective to a well-trodden trope." Aside from *Evangeline*'s ability to expand the parameters of what is traditionally assumed a rape-revenge film should be, it is thus also an important film in that it demonstrates a significant diversity in how women filmmakers—and feminist filmmakers, at that—understand the cultural value, meaning and potential of the form.

Women-Directed Rape-Revenge Films After 2017's #MeToo Moment

By 2017, two films in particular made before the Weinstein allegations were published would be, upon their release, inextricably framed by the broader cultural discourse that the *New Yorker* and *New York Post* stories provoked. Both Coralie Fargeat's *Revenge* (2017) and Natalia Leite's *M.F.A.* (2017) are key women-directed rape-revenge films when approached from a #MeToo perspective, the latter released in U.S. cinemas only days after the news stories broke. Brazilian filmmaker Leite is herself a rape survivor and brought her own experience of being sexually assaulted while studying at art school to a film based on a screenplay by Leah McKendrick, who also co-stars in the film as the protagonist's best friend. Set at an American art college, the film follows the story of Noelle, played Francesca Eastwood (daughter of *Sudden Impact*'s Clint Eastwood). Frustrated in her art practice, she excitedly accepts an invitation from a fellow student she has a crush on to attend a party at his house where he date-rapes her. Seemingly oblivious that his actions could even be construed as rape, he cruelly mocks her when the traumatized Noelle confronts him, and she accidentally kills him. With her rage now fully activated, Noelle turns her attention to other women with experiences like hers, transforming into a powerful, *femme fatale*-like vigilante until she is eventually caught by police in the film's final moments. At first, there appears to be something reductive and simplistic about how rape seems to magically turn the once-mediocre student into the college's superstar artist, but when looking closer at the film it is a tidy method of communicating the enormity of her newfound sense of power that stems not from her status as a rape survivor, but her increasing bloodlust. Where *M.F.A.* excels is in how explicitly it communicates that while Noelle takes it upon herself to act on behalf of other rape survivors, those women *do not want her help*, and she in facts retraumatizes them to the point that it ends in one of their suicides. *M.F.A.* is an effective critique of the agent model of rape-revenge, asking the question of its rape-avenging protagonist "you might see yourself as acting on behalf of others, but do those others want or need your help?"

While *M.F.A.* and the Weinstein stories hit almost simultaneously, by the time Coralie Fargeat's *Revenge* went into wide distribution in U.S. cinemas in mid–2018, the anger had kicked in, and the think-pieces were flowing. "*Revenge* is the French, Feminist *Kill Bill*-style Thriller You Need to See" declared Alex Denney at *Dazed*,[28] while Anne Billson at *The Guardian* used the film's release to explore "How the 'Rape-Revenge Movie' Became a Feminist Weapon for the #MeToo Generation."[29] Academic Tim Posada has since labeled *Revenge* "#MeToo's First Horror Film,"[30] with even *Vogue* magazine declaring, "*Revenge* is an Exploitation Movie for the #MeToo Era."[31] While *Vogue* may seem a conspicuous inclusion here, the slick, fashion magazine gloss of Fargeat's film—drenched with seemingly conscious echoes of the French *cinéma du look* tradition—is a shrewd aesthetic deployed to reveal something at the core of not just *Revenge* but arguably the entire rape-revenge category at its most basic level; it's a fantasy. It's a fantasy about getting even, and, more importantly, a fantasy about finding justice when there are no other options available.

The film follows Jennifer, played by Matilda Lutz in one of two rape-revenge films she starred in released originally in 2017 (the other being F. Javier Gutiérrez's supernatural rape-revenge film *Rings*). As Jennifer, Lutz is compelling as the seemingly pliable human sex-doll of her wealthy married lover Richard (Kevin Janssens) who has taken her to an opulent, isolated desert retreat on a hunting trip with his two friends. When one of these friends rapes Jennifer in a scene whose horror subtly shifts from fetishizing her trauma towards the indifferent spectatorship of another of the men who witnesses the assault, Jennifer discovers where Richard's loyalties lie, and it is not with her. Initially believing Jennifer to be dead, when she threatens to tell Richard's wife of their relationship, he refuses to send her home via helicopter, and the men undertake a different kind of hunt when they discover that Jennifer has survived. Reprimanding both Richard and the audience for dismissing the protagonist as an airheaded bimbo, Jennifer rapidly adapts to her circumstances as she fights back. Killing off those who pursue her one by one in a film brimming with gore and more traditional horror thrills, underneath the surface generic pleasures of *Revenge* lies an unspoken but important question: who, in fact, is seeking the revenge of the film's title? Is it Jennifer as we assume, or is her goal in fact just *survival*? Is the revenge in fact Richard's, angered that his control over his disposable young lover is not as secure as he assumed, seeking revenge against a young woman who in his eyes refuses to accept her place?

From Fargeat's *Revenge* to Anvita Dutt's Indian supernatural rape-revenge horror film *Bulbbul* (2020) to Korean filmmaker Lim Sun-Ae's social issues drama *An Old Lady* (2020), women-directed rape-revenge films are neither generically nor regionally specific. The four sections that define Mouly Surya's 2017 Indonesian western rape-revenge film *Marlina the Murderer in Four Acts* structure the journey of its titular protagonist (played by Marsha Timothy). The rape and revenge component predominantly takes place in the first act, where the widow Marlina is visited by a group of men who casually inform her that they are going to steal her livestock and rape her. It is, for them, business as usual, and the raping of Marlina is framed as a property crime, inseparable from the act of stealing her animals. Regardless, Marlina manages to poison all but one of the men with the chicken soup they demanded she cook for them before they manage to execute their planned gang rape. However, one man has slept through the meal in another room and rapes Marlina not knowing his peers are dead: she decapitates him mid-rape with a machete. While the rest of the film largely tracks Marlina's attempt to hand herself in and avoid the wrath of the surviving gang members, the film's focus is ultimately on her hesitant yet growing solidarity with heavily pregnant Novi (Dea Pandendra), a woman suffers at the hands of an abusive husband. After Marlina is raped again by the vengeance-seeking survivors of the gang, it is now Novi who has had enough and beats the man raping Marlina to death just as she is about to give birth. The film ends with the two women and the baby escaping this world of male violence on a motorbike, riding together towards a new life.

As noted in Chapter Three, despite the cultural specificity of *Marlina the Murderer in Four Acts* to Indonesia, Surya was also determined to tell a story with universal appeal. Surya is far from unique in her status as woman filmmaker working across a transnational space. Mexican filmmaker Gigi Saul Guerrero is an impressive example of this, her lived experience as a Mexican immigrant in North America lying at the heart of her feature film debut, *Culture Shock* (2019). The film follows Mexican woman Marisol (Martha Higareda) who, at the beginning of the film, fails in her attempt at an illegal border crossing into the United States and is raped by her boyfriend, who abandons her and leaves her pregnant. With her heart set on the American Dream, the pregnant Marisol is determined to attempt the crossing again, where—after a fraught journey that sees her the target of sexual violence, barely escaping an attempted rape—the intense, chaotic crossing fades away to find her awaking in the pastel-hued ideal of America that she had always imagined. Caring for her and her newborn baby is the smiling blonde embodiment of idealized suburban Americana Betty (Barbara Crampton). Despite having seemingly attaining her dream new life, the intelligent Marisol senses something is not quite right. Following her instinct, Marisol discovers that she and the other Mexican immigrants have been captured by an experimental hospital where they use virtual reality to imprison the demonized Mexicans. In the heat of the escape—led by Marisol—she discovers that the ex-boyfriend who raped her and left her pregnant has also been incarcerated in the medical facility. In the face of his continued hostility and misogyny as he tries to convince her to help him escape, she takes the opportunity to kill him, painfully and slowly, before she and the others make their final break for freedom. In a 2020 interview, Saul Guerrero noted that rape-revenge is almost a subconscious feature in her work, remarking that many people have observed it as a recurring theme across some of her earlier shorts, also. An unapologetic fan of rape-revenge films, she said, "I always thought it was very much a subject matter that caters to women because in the female body that is possibly one of the worst things that could happen to you, that's possibly one of the most horrific things that could happen to you." She continues, speaking to the intersection of rape-revenge in her chosen generic terrain of horror, "To see it in a horror movie—how you can take that ugly thing that we are all afraid of as women—and take that *fucking* revenge.... I mean, *I love it*." The impact of rape-revenge on women viewers like herself is the fundamental recognition of the very ubiquity of rape, and that in reality, revenge or justice are by no means an assumed outcome. "It's truly such a terrifying thing that we walk around the streets thinking 'what if that happened to me?'" she continues. "That subject matter has interested me because I can relate—not that it's happened to me, thank God—to those characters with that fear, and that not everyone *gets* revenge. Sometimes people just get stuck in that trauma. Movies can really bring us that satisfaction."[32]

Marlina the Murderer in Four Acts and *Culture Shock* are powerful examples of how personal trauma is inextricably entwined with the broader social, cultural and political contexts where these women's stories play out. *Black Christmas* (Sophia Takal, 2019) and *Promising Young Woman* (Emerald Fennell, 2020) situate their characters' stories in fictional scenarios that go to great lengths to shatter any opportunity to reduce these women's experiences of gendered violence, sexual abuse and sexual harassment as existing in one-off individualized bubbles. Rather, these narratives present the almost logical outcomes of rape culture itself, defined by Meredith Minister as "a socially accepted pattern that legitimates violence to police socially nonconforming activities, including expressions of sexuality and gender."[33] Rape culture also lies at the heart of a number of recent women-helmed films and television series, including G-Hey Kim's *Don't Click* (2020) at the supernatural horror end of the spectrum, and on television, Michaela Coel's game-changing series *I May Destroy You* (2020). A very loose reimagining of Bob Clark's cult 1974 slasher film of the same name, Takal and co-writer April Wolfe make literal the ambient threat of sexual violence that riddles the original *Black Christmas* in its similarly structured slasher film about a group of young women living in a sorority house who are stalked and killed by a mysterious killer. The central character is Riley (Imogen Poots), who despite her close relationship with her sorority sisters is still deeply traumatized after being raped by the head of one of the college's fraternities. As her friend Kris (Aleyse Shannon) goes on a personal crusade against the brazenly misogynist Professor Gelson (Cary Elwes), it is revealed that he heads a campus-based cult who have invoked the spirit of Calvin Hawthorne, the woman-hating founder of the university. Under Hawthorne's supernatural control, the male members are possessed and murder women students considered to be acting in a manner that is unbecoming of the patriarchy's archaic vision of submissive womanhood. Despite being betrayed by one of their own sorority members, Riley and her sisters fight back in a confrontation that culminates in both Riley physically overpowering the man who raped her so she can destroy the source of Hawthorne's supernatural power, and Kris setting Gelson on fire. *Black Christmas* shrewdly balances the subjectivity of Riley's first-hand experience of rape, with Poots's performance revealing the complexities of rape trauma. But in its depiction of the fallout from sexual violence, *Black Christmas* is aggressively focused on more than the one bad apple; it is unambiguously about the systemic factors in place—validated through the university's own professional hierarchy and very history—all of which have allowed such behavior to flourish.

A shared mission lies at the heart of actor and *Killing Eve* executive producer Emerald Fennell's feature film debut, *Promising Young Woman* (2020). Carey Mulligan stars as

Cassie, whose bright future as a medical student seven years previously has all but vanished; she works in a coffee shop and, on the cusp of thirty, still lives at home with her parents. Once a week, Cassie goes to a bar and pretends to be falling-down drunk, waiting for the inevitable: a self-defining "nice guy" will seemingly do the right thing and try to get her home safely. The opening scene of the film neatly establishes the standard trajectory of these encounters, when the supposedly "nice guy" pressures a visibly confused Cassie to go to his apartment for a drink, where she pretends to pass out. Escalating his unwanted sexual advances—despite her perceived drunkenness, Cassie is still clearly able to refuse consent, repeatedly saying "no"—he aggressively persists in his attempt to have sex with the near-comatose woman. In that moment, when it becomes clear what his intentions are, having willfully ignored her clear refusal of consent, a very sober Cassie leaps to attention, confronting him explicitly about his actions and evident plans, revealing that he is not a "nice guy" after all. Returning home, Cassie has a notebook which reveals this has been a strategy she has undertaken many, many times in the past, a pattern of behavior that is later revealed to be linked to her reasons for leaving medical school; her best friend since childhood Nina was raped by a popular student, Al Monroe (Chris Lowell), leading to Nina's death (an implied suicide) and leaving Cassie devastated. Cassie's trauma is reactivated when—after letting her guard down—she begins a relationship with Ryan (Bo Burnham), another person she went to medical school with who casually mentions that Al has returned to town and is getting married. Infuriated that Monroe and all of those who witnessed Nina's rape not just went unpunished but have blossoming careers and lives, Cassie systematically tracks down everyone involved in betraying Nina, men and women alike. The film culminates when Cassie discovers a video of Nina's rape which shows Ryan was present when it happened; confronting him, he offers the same "nice guy" defense that so many of the men she has targeted in the past have used, leaving her both heartbroken and determined to get her revenge against Al. Pretending to be a stripper at his bachelor party, she handcuffs him to a bed and confronts him, but he murders her. Knowing the likelihood of this, Cassie had sent the video of Nina's rape and a detailed description of her plans to the only man she met during her vengeance-seeking mission who proved himself truly sorry, Al's original lawyer, Jordan (Alfred Molina). Although only a short scene, the brief interaction between Cassie and Jordan remains one of the most astonishing moments in the entire film, and touches on a question very few rape-revenge films have ever seriously addressed: that of the possibility of redemption. Having had what he describes as an "epiphany" that he experienced long before Cassie knocked on his door, Jordan has faced the reality of just how immoral his defense of Al and so many young men like him has been and acknowledges how much damage he has done to women like Nina. Far from insisting he is a "nice guy," Jordan states the opposite, living the anguished life of a man who has done terrible things in the name of his job and has had to face the moral consequences of it. He begs Cassie for forgiveness which, perhaps surprisingly, she unhesitatingly gives, patting his back as he lies weeping with his head on her lap. In one short scene, *Promising Young Woman* shows that there is always a possibility for redemption even for someone who is the very personification of rape culture and the institutions that uphold it: in this case, the lawyer who let rapists go unpunished. Key here in terms of the film's rape-revenge schema is the mature, unambiguous acceptance of guilt and acknowledgment of harm caused by an enabler of sexual violence. That it is Jordan who Cassie trusts at the end of the film—knowing that her confrontation with Al may end in her own death, which it does—speaks volumes to her belief that redemption is possible; it's just that none of the other men she encounters (including Ryan, whom she deeply loved) were ethically capable of accepting that kind of truth about themselves. She gives them all a chance, and Jordan is the only one who passes the test. He has faced the harsh reality that he is anything *but* a "nice guy." In this sense, Fennell's ending is particularly shrewd: having fostered our sense of intimacy with the character of Cassie, her sudden and tragic death at the hands of violent men reprises for the audience Cassie's *own* experience of trauma over the loss of her best friend. The murder that we witness at the film's close thus repositions the audience within the same emotional headspace that motivated Cassie's earlier vengeful actions; we feel the loss of someone we had become close to, we are shocked by the injustice of it all. Thus, Fennell directly implicates the audience not as complicit spectators to a crime but as empathetic onlookers for whom the vicarious experience of sexual violence and death perhaps serves as a passing of the torch. Our anger, confusion and sense of unfairness is a call to action to demand more of a system that lets so many women down.

If *Promising Young Woman* complicates the rape-revenge equation from the perspective of a woman filmmaker, two years earlier Isabella Eklöf's *Holiday* ripped it up, soaked it in lighter fluid and set it on fire. An aggressively and consciously determined rejection of the rape-revenge formula, the paradox to Eklöf's 2018 film is that to clearly describe just how intensely it discards rape-revenge, it becomes difficult to not talk about the very acts of rape and revenge in this film: the Danish filmmaker deliberately sets them up with the precise intent of vehemently shattering them. The film follows Sascha (Victoria Carmen Sonne), a young Scandinavian woman holidaying in Turkey as the guest of her older lover, the crime boss and drug dealer Michael (Lai Yde). Male violence permeates the world Sascha lives in—a slap in the face is business as

Poster for *Promising Young Woman* (Emerald Fennell, 2020) (PictureLux/The Hollywood Archive/Alamy Stock Photo).

usual, as is more extreme violence, we soon discover—which makes her growing friendship with the comparatively passive Thomas (Thijs Römer) come as somewhat of a relief. When Sascha is violently raped by Michael in a sudden and horrific attack that echoes in both its intensity and longevity the rape scene in Gaspar Noé's *Irreversible,* she does not retaliate against him; rather, it is implied this is not the first time this has happened, and such acts of violence against the objectified young woman are simply what she considers the terms of exchange for the opulent lifestyle Michael affords her. When Thomas is outraged that she is so accepting of this abuse, it is *he* who she turns against, murdering not her rapist but the man who dared to criticize her *response* to her rape, leaving Michael and his gang to clean up the crime scene as life for Sascha returns to its unsettling yet superficially pleasant status quo. Aside from being breathtakingly well-made and perfectly cast, *Holiday* at its heart contains a devastating question: what happens when a young woman has been so brainwashed by misogyny that her only way of assessing her own self-worth is as an object herself?

Gender, Authorship and Collaboration

As these films suggest, even when it comes to women-directed rape-revenge film it is not as simple as men being the enemy. We can see this behind the camera, too, across the many collaborations between men and women who have collaborated in these films. Directorial credit for the sole authorship of a movie to be attributed to the director lies at the heart of auteur theory, a position so broadly accepted that it is rarely open to debate. But of its notable opponents, pioneering film critic Pauline Kael remains an important figure.[34] This is certainly relevant to rape-revenge film and the question of authorship, particularly in recent years when the gender of the filmmaker can often radically shift critical reception of a particular film's ideological position on the material in question. As Claire Henry argues in the case of *Descent*, while it is directed by a woman, not only its co-writer but its editor and cinematographer among others were men.[35] This question of collaborations between men and women on rape-revenge is important to consider in regard to the authorship of these films and the assumptions about gender politics that often follow. For example, while Callie Khouri's gender as the screenwriter of Ridley Scott's *Thelma & Louise* is frequently mentioned to beef up that movie's feminist credentials, rarely do we see a male-collaborators on woman-directed rape-revenge films privileged in the same way. Indeed, the entire question of cross-gender collaboration has gone largely undiscussed in this terrain.

We do not need look far for evidence that challenges, or at least destabilizes, widely held views regarding the dominance of the director as sole author of certain rape-revenge films. Zoe Tamerlis, for example, according to both her and *Ms. 45* (1981) director Abel Ferrara's own accounts played an enormous role in making that film the success it was.[36] Although not a revenge film, Ida Lupino co-wrote *Outrage* with two men—Collier Young and Malvin Wald—and Katie Aselton's *Black Rock* (2012) and Melanie Atkinhead's *Revenge Ride* (2020) alone were both based on screenplays written by men. This is not to diminish or undermine the important role of the director, but rather to heighten our sensitivity to the frequently undermined reality of collaboration in film production. In press for the Australian film *Pimped*, director David Barker frequently flagged the centrality of his core collaborators such as editor Marianne Khoo, actor Ella Scott Lynch, and in particular, co-writer Lou Mentor. "We worked together really well and having the outline of the story already developed by David meant that I could explore other areas that he might not have considered like references to menstruation, female identity, and sexuality. Part of the reason David brought me on board was to provide this female perspective in developing the characters and story," said Mentor.[37] This spirit of collaboration with an eye towards centrality of gender politics fed through to the production environment itself. "I was really pleased with the number of women working on *Pimped*," Mentor continued. "I think having so many fantastic women as part of the team did help to create a nurturing atmosphere on set. It always felt like a safe space to be, both creatively and professionally, and I think that was at the forefront of everyone's mind."

From this perspective, Jason Banker's *Felt* (2015) is also worth considering. Like his previous film *Toad Road* (2012), Banker's creative practice is an explicitly collaborative one, working closely in developing his projects with his lead actors, in both cases women artists. *Felt* follows Amy—played by artist Amy Everson—who is struggling to cope with a trauma that occurs prior to the film, her behavior alienating concerned friends who have been trying to help. Marked by her eccentric affection for wearing homemade costumes (an element taken from Everson's own life, part of her practice as a performance artist), the film follows Amy and her women friends through a series of awful encounters with men. Amy's quirkiness escalates to a more extreme level after its is revealed that a man she has been dating has another girlfriend that he has kept hidden. Luring him to the woods, she wears a homemade "man suit," complete with phallus, and encourages him to wear a complimentary "woman suit," before stabbing him repeatedly with a pair of scissors and castrating him. Holding his detached penis in her hand, she attaches it to her own suit, simultaneously appropriating not just his literal penis, but (more symbolically) the entire phallic representational apparatus itself. Becoming man and becoming sexually violent are, in her eyes, the same thing, based on the romantic betrayal we know about and a distant (sexual) trauma that remains deliberately opaque. While Everson is also credited as a co-writer as well as the film's lead actor, in Banker's own words, she was both the originator of the project and a core collaborator: "When I saw Amy and the costumes, I saw her room, it was so rich in visual metaphors and I knew that there would be a great film," he said. "I wanted to make a film with Amy about her, and this is what came out of it ... the voice in the film is a blend of ours."[38]

Men and women filmmakers have co-directed rape-revenge films together, also, from Beverly and Ferd Sebastian's *'Gator Bait* (1974) to *Venus Rising* (Leora Barish and Edgar Michael Bravo, 1995) to *Scavenger* (Luciana Garraza and Eric Fleitas, 2019). Madeleine Sims-Fewer and Dusty Mancinelli's *Violation* (2020) is a significant entry here, made as it was by two filmmakers united by their shared status as sexual assault survivors. Sims-Fewer also plays Miriam who, while attending an emotionally charged country reunion with her partner (with whom her relationship is strained) and her estranged sister and her husband, is raped by her brother-in-law, who was also an old friend. As the film unfolds in a non-chronological manner, her revenge is revealed, resulting in an elaborate and grueling torture sequence and her eventual killing of the man who raped her. The revenge component is shown in part before the rape itself, the story deliberately reorganized in a conscious effort by the filmmakers to represent the disorientation of trauma, based on their own lived experience. For Mancinelli, "we found a structure that maps Miriam's emotional and psychological unravelling, and the structure of the movie is *that*. We knew we were very interested in trying to mimic the kind of post-traumatic stress that she is under, and to create this sense of disorientation that you have as someone who has experienced firsthand a sexual assault."[39] Adds Sims-Fewer, "We wanted to pull the rug out from under people a bit so you get an idea of *why* you think something is happening and then a moment later you get a different perspective." She continues, "We want to create a conflict within people watching it so they start to question things for themselves and wonder about who is right and who is wrong and hopefully discuss with other people and within themselves what the morality surrounding all the issues and ideas is."

Everson and Sims-Fewer's dual roles as central performers and key creative collaborators on *Felt* and *Violation* respectively allow an important reconsideration of the role of Pollyanna McIntosh in the rape-revenge arena. Although known in the mainstream primarily for her work as an actor in *The Walking Dead*, to cult film fans her notoriety is firmly tethered to Lucky McKee's notorious 2011 rape-revenge film *The Woman*. Inspired by a series of novels and characters created by Jack Ketchum, *The Woman* was the sequel to Andrew van den Houten's *Offspring* (2009) which first introduced McIntosh as the eponymous woman of the second film. The last of her feral tribe, she lives in the woods and is captured by Chris (Sean Bridgers), a lawyer in a country town whose pleasant demeanor disguises his violent misogyny. Chained up in the family's barn, he embarks on what he considers a "civilizing" process which is in fact rape and torture, soon joined by his teenage son. Horrified at what is happening, his terrified, long-abused wife Belle (Angela Bettis) enables him, because when she resists, she is beaten. Watching on are their two daughters, the young Darlin' (Shyla Molhusen) and Peggy (Lauren Ashley Carter), the latter who has also suffered from extensive sexual abuse by her father and is hiding a pregnancy that has resulted from incest. As Chris and his son's violence escalates, The Woman fights back, enacting her violent retribution not only on the men of the family, but Belle also. The Woman returns to the wilderness with Darlin', Peggy and a third daughter, nicknamed Socket (Alexa Marcigliano), a girl so badly abused that she took on the dog-like behaviors of the canines with whom she'd been forced to live with outside.

In the third part of the series, McIntosh not only returns as The Woman but also directs the film. *Darlin'* follows the youngest daughter who, now a teenager, has been raised by The Woman and has adapted to a similarly feral lifestyle. While Peggy died in childbirth and Socket ran away, despite Darlin' and The Woman being close, the latter takes Darlin' to a hospital when she is discovered to be pregnant after a consensual sexual encounter with a drifter. The hospital sends Darlin' to a Catholic girls' school where she is taken under the wing of protective nun Sister Jennifer (Nora-Jane Noone), a past student who returned to the school after a difficult period of drug abuse. The reasons for her past self-medication are revealed as the film progresses; the school is under the control of a pedophile Bishop (Bryan Batt), whose long history of abusing those in his care he attempts to justify in a vile speech to Sister Jennifer. As Darlin' learns again to speak, she becomes highly susceptible to the religious teachings of the school, terrified by the fire and brimstone rhetoric. The film climaxes at her First Communion where she attempts suicide—believing her pregnancy means she has the Devil in her—and gives birth on the altar. The Bishop is murdered by the avenging Woman, who then rescues the baby and takes it on Darlin's desperate instructions. For McInstosh, there was a direct line in the politics of *The Woman*—politics she felt was broadly misunderstood in the face of the claims of misogyny it received from some quarters—and her directing *Darlin'*. "I felt that *The Woman* was a feminist movie at heart…. I think that it showed misogyny. That freaked a lot of people out, and so they felt that it was a misogynistic film."[40] When she was invited by producer (and director of the original film in the series) van den Houten to direct *Darlin'*, McIntosh leapt at the opportunity. "That was a really wise choice on his part.... I think he recognized that if we came to it from a female perspective, it would be much harder to make those assumptions."[41] Since she starred and directed *Darlin'*, McIntosh has moved back to more orthodox rape-revenge territory as an actor in Melanie Atkinhead's *Revenge Ride* (2020), spearheading the cast of an all-girl biker gang rape–revenge film that very much carries the spirit of classic grindhouse girl gang films like Jack Hill's *Switchblade Sisters* (1975). As *Revenge Ride* and *Darlin'* both indicate, rape-revenge and rape-revenge aligned women-directed cinema has only continued after 2017's #MeToo moment, with the heightened critical and audience sensitivity to this subject matter and the question of *who* is making these films a clear indicator of the category's broader zeitgeist appeal.

Afterword

Long before this project began, I had a passing interest in rape-revenge films going back to my teenage years that was based on an awareness of more well-known examples like *I Spit on Your Grave* and *Ms. 45* (and, of course, more mainstream instances such as *The Accused* and *Thelma & Louise*). But it was only with Dario Argento's *The Stendhal Syndrome* (*La sindrome di Stendhal*, 1996) that I discovered how much more deserving of critical attention rape-revenge was as a whole. This arises in part from a long love of this particular director's work, including films like *The Bird with the Crystal Plumage* (*L'uccello dalle piumpe di cristallo*, 1970), *Suspiria* (1977) and *Tenebrae* (1982). I was not alone in sensing a decline in the quality of his films around the early 1990s, however, due to what has been viewed as their increasing "Americanization," typified by the broadly maligned *Trauma* (1993).[1] Although *The Stendhal Syndrome* had been originally set in the U.S. and was to star Bridget Fonda, Argento was frustrated by the Hollywood system and returned to Italy to make what he described as a "high-concept European movie."[2] While both fan and critical opinion on the film was divided when it was released, upon further inspection *The Stendhal Syndrome* is a sophisticated and deeply complex text. The more I thought about what Argento was trying to do with this film, the more the rape-revenge category opened up to me as a powerful and important area that had too often fallen prey to critical generalization. It is by no means a perfect film, and its depiction of sexual violence is confronting, violent and harrowing. What makes *The Stendhal Syndrome* so endlessly fascinating, however, is Argento's focus on the relationship between rape and its very representation from within the diegesis of the film itself.

Argento is renowned for his hypertheatrical and excessive horror films, which are often as visceral and visually spectacular as they are seemingly indifferent to complex plotlines and character development. Clover—among many—has quoted his controversial statement "I like women, especially beautiful ones. If they have a good face and a good figure, I would much rather watch them being murdered than an ugly girl or man."[3] But Argento's films potentially offer far less simplistic representations of gender and sexuality that such a statement would suggest, and the blurring of traditional binaries between "male" and "female" is one of the more intriguing elements of his earlier work in particular.[4] While *The Stendhal Syndrome* features graphic scenes of the rape and murder of beautiful women, it also follows, with immense sympathy and compassion, the plight of its central female protagonist, described as his "first three-dimensional heroine ... [who] makes the film work on both an emotional and stylistic level."[5] For Louis Paul, Argento's casting of his own daughter Asia in the grueling role of a rape-survivor pushed beyond sanity by her trauma was "the pinnacle of unsavouriness,"[6] but it can just as easily be argued that it was their close relationship that granted Asia's performance such a remarkable level of intimacy and intensity. From the perspective of #MeToo, Argento's casting is further complicated: as one of Weinstein's original accusers, Argento was a key figure in the movement until allegations against Asia Argento of statutory rape were made by the actor Jimmy Bennett, who played her son in her directorial feature *The Heart Is Deceitful Above All Things* (2004). Argento denied the allegations, but the story has since become synonymous with her association with #MeToo.

The Stendhal Syndrome follows the story of Inspector Anna Manni (Asia Argento), a police investigator for the "anti-rape squad" in Rome. Anna suffers from the Stendhal syndrome, a psychological condition named after the nineteenth-century French author who described the physical and psychological symptoms of being overwhelmed by great art. The movie begins as she visits the Uffizi gallery in Florence, where she is following up on a mysterious phone call offering information on her current investigation. As she walks around the Uffizi, Anna fixates on the representation of rape in great art, including Sandro Botticelli's 1492 painting *Primavera* (1492), where she focuses on the wind-breathing Zephyrus seizing the nymph Chloris. Anna also looks at Caravaggio's *Medusa* (1597), and again focuses upon the representation of mythological rape victim in art. When Anna reaches Pieter Brueghel's 1558 painting *Landscape with the Fall of Icarus* (a painting where mythological tragedy is exposed as insignificant in the face of the toil of everyday life), her condition causes her to faint and she imagines herself drowning until she is revived by a giant fish. She comes to, unaware that she is being assisted by the rapist and killer she is hunting, Alfredo (Thomas Kretschmann). He follows her back to her hotel where, after she has another hallucination (this time triggered by Rembrandt's

Asia and Dario Argento at the 65th Festival de Cannes, 19 May 2012 (Jaguar PS/Shutterstock.com).

1642 painting *The Night Watch* hanging on the wall of her hotel room), he brutally rapes her and cuts her face with a razorblade.

Devastated by the assault, Anna withdraws and becomes increasingly isolated. Her boyfriend, fellow police officer Marco (Marco Leonardi), does not understand her iciness, and when he pushes her for an emotional connection, she threatens him with sexual assault. In an attempt to recover, she begins counseling, cuts her hair short, and spends time with her father and brothers at her family home. There, Anna tries painting as a way of self-treating her sensitivity to the Stendhal syndrome. Over and over again she paints large canvases of the same figure: a face with a large, black, abyss-like mouth. When this does not appear to help, Anna paints her own body; but her creative endeavors are interrupted when Alfredo, the rapist, locates her once again. Knowing about her extreme psychological reaction to art, Alfredo holds Anna captive in a deserted building with large, terrifying graffiti figures drawn on the wall. Here he rapes her repeatedly until she stabs him in the eye with a mattress spring. After disposing of his body in a nearby waterfall, Anna attempts recovery once again. She changes her appearance, donning a long Veronica Lake–style wig that hides the facial scars left by Alfredo, and begins a romantic relationship with Marie (Julien Lambroschini), a young French art student. Despite her efforts to find peace, she becomes increasingly fixated on Alfredo, convinced he is still alive. When Marie is found dead, her worst fears are apparently confirmed. However, when both Marco and her counselor are also killed, it is revealed that it is not Alfredo who is the killer but Anna herself, believing that she is Alfredo. The final image of *The Stendhal Syndrome*, compositionally reminiscent of the film's earlier rape scenes, shows her, hysterically screaming, being surrounded and carried away Pieta-style by her male colleagues.

Argento has constructed a rape-revenge film about a woman literally trapped within the apparatus of artistic representation. In a meta-mirroring of the Stendhal syndrome condition itself, the film contrasts Anna's status as a fictional depiction of a rape survivor with the representational traditions that surround her both diegetically and extradiegetically—not only in regard to the Renaissance and Baroque rape imagery she sees in the Uffizi, but also in terms of the options film history has made available to her as either a tough tomboy or a vampish *femme fatale*. She cannot move, and in the scenes where she literally paints her own body, she explicitly acknowledges—even from within the diegesis of her own rape-revenge story—that her body is simply a forum (a canvas, if you like) for the historical representation of rape, from painting to cinema, to play out on yet again. When Anna collapses at the end of the film, she is crushed by a combination of both diegetic and non-diegetic weight. It is not just a case of her suffering from rape trauma, but—as she was already aware from the earliest scenes in the Uffizi even before the first rape—there is the added knowledge that she cannot escape the historically entrenched patterns of how rape (and rape victims) have been represented. Anna tries all the options this history allows her, and none work. Flailing wildly in the film's heartbreaking final scene, she is literally trying to break out of the frame. She is restrained—not coincidentally—by policemen, figures that represent nothing less than institutionalized patriarchal authority itself, who are compositionally presented in exactly the same way Alfredo was when he assaulted her.

By no means can *The Stendhal Syndrome* be considered a perfect film, and I do not in any way wish to suggest that it is unambiguously the kind of rape-revenge movie to which all should aspire. However, *The Stendhal Syndrome* is both valuable and unique in that it puts the traditions surrounding the representation of rape to the test. In this context, the revenge component—while satisfying at the moment of its execution for both the spectator and Anna herself—is exposed as trivial, redundant and almost irrelevant when compared to Anna's real battle against the representational apparatus against which she fights so fruitlessly. In the face of that history, Anna's struggle is not just against Alfredo, but against a long, unrelenting history that allows the rape survivor only a limited number of choices regarding how she can be artistically configured. These options all fail Anna, and she goes insane. She pays the price for the troubled and often contradictory history of how rape has been represented both in film and in the visual arts more broadly.

Chapter Notes

Preface

1. Ronan Farrow, "From Aggressive Overtures to Sexual Assault: Harvey Weinstein's Accusers Tell their Stories," *The New Yorker*, 10 October 2017, accessed 10 January 2020, https://www.newyorker.com/news/news-desk/from-aggressive-overtures-to-sexual-assault-harvey-weinsteins-accusers-tell-their-stories.

2. Jodi Kantor and Megan Twohey, "Harvey Weinstein Paid Off Sexual Harassment Accusers for Decades," *New York Times*, 5 October 2017, accessed 10 January 2020, https://www.nytimes.com/2017/10/05/us/harvey-weinstein-harassment-allegations.html.

3. Diane Wolfthal, *Images of Rape: The "Heroic" Tradition and Its Alternatives* (Cambridge: Cambridge University Press, 1999), 182.

4. Cate Young, "The Perfection Turns the Rape Revenge Fantasy Into Spectacle," *Jezebel*, 31 May 2019, accessed 10 January 2020, https://themuse.jezebel.com/the-perfection-turns-the-rape-revenge-fantasy-into-spec-1835146913.

5. Aja Romero, "Netflix's *The Perfection* learned all the Wrong Lessons from #MeToo," *Vox*, 28 May 2019, accessed 10 January 2020, https://www.vox.com/2019/5/28/18641735/netflix-the-perfection-review-controversy.

6. Lena Wilson, "*The Perfection* Is A Problematic Body Horror Drama You'll Likely Want To Avoid," *The Playlist*, 22 May 2019, accessed 10 January 2020, https://theplaylist.net/perfection-netflix-review-20190522/.

7. Ashlee Blackwell, "*The Perfection* is Simply Perfection," *Graveyard Shift Sisters*, 23 May 2019, accessed 10 January 2020, https://www.graveyardshiftsisters.com/2019/05/the-perfection-2018-is-simply-perfection.html.

8. Anne Billson, "How the 'rape-revenge movie' became a feminist weapon for the #MeToo generation," *The Guardian*, 11 May 2018, accessed 10 January 2020, https://www.theguardian.com/film/2018/may/11/how-the-rape-revenge-movie-became-a-feminist-weapon-for-the-metoo-generation.

9. Philippa Snow, "Can a Rape-Revenge Film Ever Be Truly Feminist?" *Garage*, 9 August 2018, accessed 10 January 2020, https://garage.vice.com/en_us/article/pawmwk/revenge-review.

10. Peggy Phelan, "Survey: Art and Feminism," in *Art and Feminism*, ed. Helena Reckitt, 14–49 (London: Phaidon, 2012), 18.

11. Claire Henry, *Revisionist Rape-Revenge: Redefining a Film Genre* (Houndsmills: Palgrave Macmillan, 2014), 8.

12. Ibid., 4.

13. Ibid., 5.

14. Ibid., 4.

15. World Population Review, "Rape Statistics by Country 2020" (no date), accessed 10 January 2020, https://worldpopulationreview.com/country-rankings/rape-statistics-by-country.

16. All quotes from Karen Lam in this Preface are taken from email correspondence with the author, 19 November 2020.

17. All quotes from Jim Hemphill in this Preface are taken from email correspondence with the author, 18 November 2020.

18. BJ Colangelo, "'You Just Don't Understand It,' or Why I Love Rape-Revenge," *Icons of Fright*, 6 September 2013, accessed 10 January 2020, http://iconsoffright.com/2013/09/06/you-just-dont-understand-it-or-why-i-love-rape-revenge/.

19. Kate Erbland, "'M.F.A.' Director Natalia Leite Faced Her Sexual Assault By Directing a Rape-Revenge Thriller," *IndieWire*, 13 October 2017, accessed 10 January 2020, https://www.indiewire.com/2017/10/mfa-natalia-leite-sexual-assault-1201887081/.

20. Alexandra Heller-Nicholas, "The Anti Rape-Revenge Film: Madeline Sims-Fewer and Dusty Mancinelli on *Violation*," *Film International*, 27 September 2020, accessed 10 January 2020, filmint.nu/madeleine-sims-fewer-and-dusty-mancinelli-on-violation-tiff-2020/.

Introduction

1. Sarah Projansky, *Watching Rape: Film and Television in Postfeminist Culture* (New York: New York University Press, 2001), 60.

2. Claire Henry, *Revisionist Rape-Revenge: Redefining a Film Genre* (Houndsmills: Palgrave Macmillan, 2014), 3.

3. Philip Green, *Cracks in the Pedestal: Ideology and Gender in Hollywood* (Amherst: Massachusetts University Press, 1998), 190.

4. Diane Wolfthal, *Images of Rape: The "Heroic"*

Tradition and Its Alternatives (Cambridge: Cambridge University Press, 1999), 182.

5. *Ibid.*, 180.

6. Joanna Bourke, *Rape: A History from 1860 to the Present* (London: Virago, 2008), 18.

7. Sabine Sielke, *Reading Rape: The Rhetoric of Sexual Violence in American Literature and Culture, 1790–1990* (Princeton: Princeton University Press, 2002).

8. Diane Wolfthal, 4–5.

9. Susan Brownmiller, *Against Our Will: Men, Women and Rape* (Harmondsworth: Penguin, 1975), 295–299.

10. Trudy Govier, *Forgiveness and Revenge* (New York: Routledge, 2002), 8–9.

11. *Ibid.*, 2.

12. Sarah Projansky, 19.

13. *Ibid.*, 95.

14. Tammy Oler, "The Brave Ones," *Bitch Magazine: Feminist Responses to Pop Culture* (Winter 2009): 30–34, 34.

15. All quotes from Peter Strickland in this chapter are taken from email correspondence with the author, 19 November 2020.

16. All quotes from Sims-Fewer and Mancinelli in this chapter from Alexandra Heller-Nicholas, "The Anti Rape-Revenge Film: Madeline Sims-Fewer and Dusty Mancinelli on *Violation*," *Film International*, 27 September 2020, accessed 10 January 2020, filmint.nu/madeleine-sims-fewer-and-dusty-mancinelli-on-violation-tiff-2020/.

17. Peter Lehman, "'Don't Blame This on a Girl': Female Rape-Revenge Films," in *Screening the Male: Exploring Masculinities in Hollywood Cinema*, eds. Steven Cohan and Ina Rae Hark, 103–117 (London: Routledge, 1993), 114.

18. Tammy Oler, 31.

19. Madelaine Hron, "Naked Terror: Horrific, Aesthetic and Healing Images of Rape," in *Cultural Expressions of Evil and Wickedness: Wrath, Sex, Crime*, ed. Terrie Waddell, 127–145 (Amsterdam: Rodopi, 2003), 127.

20. Susan Brownmiller, 309.

21. Lynn A. Higgins and Brenda R. Silver, "Rereading Rape," in *Rape and Representation*, eds. Lynn A. Higgins and Brenda R. Silver (New York: Columbia University Press, 1991), 3.

22. Tanya Horeck, *Public Rape: Representing Violation in Fiction and Film* (London: Routledge, 2004), 4.

23. Sarah Projansky, 2–3.

24. Sabine Sielke, 2.

25. Sarah Projansky, 61.

26. Mieke Bal, "The Rape of Narrative and the Narrative of Rape: Speech Acts and Body Language in Judges," in *A Mieke Bal Reader* (Chicago: Chicago University Press, 2006), 339.

27. Rhiannon Graybill, "Day of the Woman: Judges 4–5 as Slasher and Rape Revenge Narrative," *The Journal of Religion and Popular Culture* 30:3 (Fall 2018): 193–205.

28. While examples of the transformative power of rape are abundant, one of the most memorable is Blanche DuBois' (Vivian Leigh) descent into madness after she is raped by her brother-in-law Stanley Kowalski (Marlon Brando) in Elia Kazan's 1951 adaptation of Tennessee Williams' play *A Streetcar Named Desire*.

29. Sarah Projansky, 258.

30. Rikke Schubart, *Super Bitches and Action Babes: The Female Hero in Popular Cinema, 1970–2006* (Jefferson, NC: McFarland, 2007), 95.

31. Jacinda Read, *The New Avengers: Feminism, Femininity and the Rape-Revenge Cycle* (Manchester: Manchester University Press, 2000), 71.

32. *Ibid.*, 241.

33. *Ibid.*, 10.

34. *Ibid.*, 12.

35. Laura Mulvey, "Visual Pleasure and Narrative Cinema," in *Movies and Methods, Volume II*, ed. Bill Nichols (Berkeley: California University Press, 1985), 303–14.

36. Carol J. Clover, *Men, Women, and Chain Saws: Gender in the Modern Horror Film* (Princeton: Princeton University Press, 1992), 152.

37. *Ibid.*, 154.

38. Klaus Rieser, "Masculinity and Monstrosity: Characterization and Identification in the Slasher Film," *Men and Masculinity* 3.4 (2001): 370–392, 337.

39. Tony Williams, "Trying to Survive the Darker Side: 1980s Family Horror," in *The Dread of Difference: Gender and the Horror Film*, ed. Barry Keith Grant, 164–180 (Austin: Texas University Press, 1996), 170–2.

40. According to Clover, the "final girl" in the slasher film "is the one who encounters the mutilated bodies of her friends and perceives the full extent of the preceding horror and of her own peril; who is chased, cornered, wounded; whom we see scream, stagger, fall, rise, and scream again. She is abject terror personified" (35).

41. Frank Burke, "Dario Argento's *The Bird with the Crystal Plumage*: Caging Women's Rage," in *Killing Women: The Visual Culture of Gender and Violence*, eds. Annette Burfoot and Susan Lord, 197–217 (Waterloo: Wilfred Laurier University Press, 2006), 202.

42. Andrew Tudor, *Monsters and Mad Scientists: A Cultural History of the Horror Movie* (Oxford: Basil Blackwell, 1989), 3.

43. Jacinda Read, 241.

44. *Ibid.*, 9.

45. *Ibid.*, 10.

46. Yvonne Tasker, "Review: *Reel Knockouts: Violent Women in the Movies* (Austin: Texas University Press, 2001), ed. Martha McCaughey and Neal King; *The New Avengers: Feminism, Femininity, and the Rape-Revenge Cycle*, by Jacinda Read (Manchester: Manchester University Press, 2000)," *Signs: A Journal of Women in Culture and Society* 30.2 (Winter 2005): 1700–1702, 1702.

47. Karen Hollinger, "Review: *The New Avengers: Feminism, Femininity and the Rape-Revenge Cycle*, by Jacinda Read (New York: Manchester UP, 2000)," *Film Quarterly* 55.4 (Summer 2002): 61–63, 62.

48. Jacinda Read, 14.

49. *Ibid.*, 7.

50. Lili Pâquet, "The Corporeal Female Body in Literary Rape-Revenge: Shame, Violence, and Scriptotherapy," *Australian Feminist Studies* 33 (2018): 397.

51. While ironically appropriating the title of Griffith's early film in its telling of the 1931 slave rebellion in Virginia led by Nat Turner, that Parker's film featured numerous rape scenes saw a spike in media attention on a 1999 rape allegation against both Parker himself and the film's co-writer Jean McGianni Celestin. This in itself echoes the uncomfortable parallels between accused serial rapist Roman Polanski and his 1994 rape-revenge film *Death and the Maiden*, and even the shocking 2019 admission by actor Liam Neeson—who starred in Michael Caton-Jones's 1995 historical rape-revenge drama *Rob Roy*—that after a friend's rape by a black man, he felt the desire to kill *any* black man in an act of vengeance. See Catherine Shoard, "Liam Neeson: after a friend was raped, I wanted to kill a black man," *The Guardian*, 4 February 2019, accessed 10 January 2020, https://www.theguardian.com/film/2019/feb/04/liam-neeson-after-a-friend-was-raped-i-wanted-to-kill-a-black-man.

52. James R. Alexander, "The Maturity of a Film Genre in an Era of Relaxing Standards of Obscenity: Takashi Ishii's *Freeze Me* as a Rape-Revenge Film," *Senses of Cinema* 36 (2005), accessed 24 August 2005, http://www.sensesofcinema.com/contents/05/36/freeze_me.html.

53. Jacinda Read, 84.

54. Laura L. Finley, *Domestic Abuse and Sexual Assault in Popular Culture* (Santa Barbara: Prager, 2016), 132.

55. A number of films deliberately complicate the mute rape survivor motif, most dramatically *The Tribe* (Myroslav Slaboshpytskyi, 2014); set in a deaf school (without subtitles, deliberately excluding viewers who do not understand this particular regional sign language dialect), it deliberately subverts the "mute victim" motif—here everyone is mute, rendering it impotent as a signifier of power. Rather, although not a rape-revenge film, that distinction is made through the film's gender politics, vividly displayed in both a shocking rape scene and a distressing illegal abortion sequence. Alternatively, while *Avenged* (Michael S. Ojeda, 2013) features a deaf woman, and while she does not attempt to speak to those who rape and kill her, earlier in the film we see her signing to her mother but also verbalising language also. In *Romina* (Diego Cohen, 2018), we hear her scream but never talk; not explicitly mute, it can be understood that she *can* speak but chooses not to.

56. Pam Cook, *Screening the Past: Memory and Nostalgia in Cinema* (London: Routledge, 2005), 157.

57. Molly Haskell, *From Reverence to Rape: The Treatment of Women in the Movies* (Harmondsworth: Penguin, 1974), 201.

58. Lisa M. Cuklanz, *Rape on Prime Time: Television, Masculinity, and Sexual Violence* (Philadelphia: Pennsylvania University Press, 2000); Lorna Jowett, "Rape, Power, Realism and the Fantastic on Television," in *Feminism, Literature and Rape Narratives: Violence and Violation*, eds. Sorcha Gunne and Zoe Brigley Thompson, 217–231 (New York: Routledge, 2010); and Molly Ann Magestro, *Assault on the Small Screen: Representations of Sexual Violence on Prime-Time Television Dramas* (Lanham: Rowman & Littlefield Publishers, 2015).

Chapter One

1. Neil Fulwood, *One Hundred Violent Films That Changed Cinema* (London: BT Batsford, 2003), 40.

2. Janet Staiger, "The Politics of Film Canons," in *Multiple Voices in Feminist Film Criticism*, eds. Diane Carson, Linda Dittmar and Janice R. Welsch, 191–209 (Minneapolis: Minnesota University Press, 1994).

3. Jonathan Rosenbaum, *Essential Cinema: On the Necessity of Film Canons* (Baltimore: John Hopkins University Press, 2004), xiii.

4. For Sconce, paracinema "includes entries from such seemingly disparate subgenres as 'badfilm,' splatterpunk, 'mondo' films, sword and sandal epics, Elvis flicks, government hygiene films, Japanese monster movies, beach-party musicals, and just about every other historical manifestation of exploitation cinema from juvenile delinquency documentaries to softcore pornography." Paracinema is "a particular reading protocol," less a generic categorization than "a counter-aesthetic turned subcultural sensibility devoted to all matter of cultural detritus." The defining function of paracinematic culture is to assign value to films which have fallen outside the purview of so-called "legitimate film culture." See Jeffrey Sconce, "Trashing the Academy: Taste, Excess, and an Emerging Politics of Cinematic Style," *Screen* 36.4 (1995): 371–91, 372.

5. Matt Hills contends that the binary opposition between trash and legitimate film as described by Sconce ignores the stratification that occurs within paracinema itself, creating a second-class level of less privileged texts that he calls "para-paracinema." See Matt Hills, "Para-Paracinema: The *Friday the 13th* Series as Other to Trash and Legitimate Film Cultures," in *Sleaze Artists: Cinema at the Margins of Taste, Style and Politics*, ed. Jeffrey Sconce, 219–239 (Durham: Duke University Press, 2007).

6. This is a summary of my longer essay "Silence and Fury: Rape and The Virgin Spring," from Issue 28 (2010) of *Screening the Past*. It can be read online at http://www.latrobe.edu.au/screeningthepast/28/rape-and-the-virgin-spring.html. Special thanks to *Screening the Past* for granting permission to use this material in this book.

7. James R. Alexander, http://www.sensesofcinema.com/contents/05/36/freeze_me.html.

8. Bergman was also influenced by Akira Kurosawa's *Rashomon* (1951), see John Kenneth Muir, *Wes Craven: The Art of Horror* (Jefferson, NC: McFarland, 1998), 47.

9. Michael Sicinski, "Review: *The Virgin Spring*," *Cinéaste* 31.3 (Summer 2006): 69.

10. *The Accused* is not the only revenge film in which Foster has starred. In *The Brave One* (2007), radio DJ Erica Bain (Foster) and her fiancé David Kirmani (Naveen Andrews) are violently assaulted, leading to Kirmani's death. While she is not sexually assaulted in the initial attack, there are implications throughout the film that revenge for rape and sexual violence are on her agenda, as she shoots two thugs on a train who grab at her breasts and sexually threaten her, and she later saves a sex worker from a violent assault. Despite the absence of rape from its central narrative core, this movie's most obvious points of reference are *Ms. 45* and Michael Winner's *Death Wish* (1974). sequence where Erica is legally unable to purchase a gun in a store and is assisted by a blackmarket seller who overhears her is almost identical to a similar sequence in Winner's *Dirty Weekend* (1993).

11. The "rape statistic" coda was also used the year before in the rape-revenge film *W.A.R.: Women Against Rape* (Raphael Nussbaum, 1987).

12. Real-life rape survivor Kelly McGillis played Kathryn, which was heavily publicized at the time of the film's release. See: Terry Christensen and Peter J. Haas, *Projecting Politics: Political Messages in American Film* (M.E. Sharpe, 2005), 207.

13. Carol J. Clover, 147.

14. Jacinda Read, 109.

15. Carol J. Clover, 146.

16. *Ibid.*, 149. In response, Jacinda Read suggests "Pollyannaism" can just as easily apply to what Clover admits is the "aftermathless" ending of *I Spit on Your Grave* (26).

17. Carol J. Clover, 138.

18. *Ibid.*, 145.

19. Peter Lehman, 109.

20. Says Rikke Schubart: "He is not sexy, attractive, or strong, ... he is nervous, manipulative, and psychologically unstable" (90). While this is true in retrospect, there is no evidence before the first rape that Gordon is anything but a pleasant young man who is simply star struck by his student's famous sister.

21. Edward Guthmann, "An Assault Victim Turns on Her Attacker: Cinema Rape Parallels Woman's Real-Life Ordeal," *San Francisco Chronicle*, 17 August 1986.

22. *Ibid.*

23. For Joanna Bourke, "Commentators often assume that legal statutes decree that rape involves the forced penetration of a vagina by a penis. But this is not the case. Rape sometimes must involve violence; other times, lack of consent alone suffices. Still other statutes refer to sexual acts committed 'against a woman's will.' In some jurisdictions proof of penile penetration of a vagina might be required, while others insist on evidence of emission of semen. Yet at other times the law accepts non-penile penetration as evidence of rape" (8).

24. Elena Gorfinkel, *Lewd Looks: American Sexploitation Cinema in the 1960s* (Minneapolis: University of Minnesota Press, 2017), 130.

25. In the United Kingdom, the 1984 Video Recordings Bill introduced the requirement of the British Board of Film Censors to base (or deny) classifications for video cassettes available for exhibition in private homes "on the possibility that children might see the video." See Martin Baker, "Introduction," in *The Video Nasties: Freedom and Censorship in the Media*, ed. Martin Baker, 1–6 (London: Pluto, 1984).

26. Roger Ebert, "Review: *I Spit on Your Grave* (Dir. Meir Zarchi)," *Chicago Sun–Times* online, 16 July 1980, accessed 6 March 2006. http://rogerebert.suntimes.com/apps/pbcs.dll/article?AID=/19800716/REVIEWS/7160301/1023.

27. "Interview: Ten Questions with *I Spit on Your Grave* Director Meir Zachari!" *Obsessed with Film*, 2 October 2010, accessed 15 October 2010, http://www.obsessedwithfilm.com/interviews/interview-ten-questions-with-i-spit-on-your-grave-director-meir-zachari.php.

28. See Joe Bob Briggs' commentary track, *I Spit on Your Grave*, Dir. Meir Zarchi, 1978, DVD, Force Entertainment, 2004; Philip Green, *Cracks in the Pedestal*; Marco Starr, "J. Hills Is Alive: A Defence of *I Spit on Your Grave*," in *The Video Nasties: Freedom and Censorship in the Media*, ed. Martin Baker, 48–55 (London: Pluto Press, 1984); Gary Crowdus, "Cult Films, Commentary Tracks and Censorious Critics: An Interview with John Bloom," *Cinéaste* 28.3 (Summer 2003): 32–34.

29. Carol J. Clover, 118.

30. Linda Ruth Williams, "Less Rape, More Revenge: *I Spit on Your Grave*," *Sight & Sound* 12.4 (April 2002): 70.

31. Chris Eggertsen, "Interview: Original *I Spit on Your Grave* Director Meir Zarchi!" *Bloody Disgusting*, 5 October 2010, accessed 15 October 2010, http://www.bloody-disgusting.com/news/21921.

32. Sean Decker, "Exclusive: Director Steven R. Monroe Talks *I Spit on Your Grave*," *Dread Central*, 4 September 2010, accessed 15 October 2010, http://www.dreadcentral.com/interviews/monroe-steven-r-i-spit-your-grave.

33. Anchor Bay Film, *I Spit on Your Grave* (Steven R. Monroe, 2010) Press Kit, 2010.

34. Anton Bitel, "I Spit on Your Grave 2 (2013)," *Projected Figures*, 25 September 2018, accessed 10 January 2020, https://projectedfigures.com/2018/09/25/i-spit-on-your-grave-2-2013/.

35. Anton Bitel, "Mixing It Up: The FrightFest Halloween All-Dayer 2015," *Projected Figures*, 22 July 2016, accessed 10 January 2020, https://projectedfigures.com/2016/07/22/mixing-frightfest-halloween-dayer-2015/.

36. John Martin, *Seduction of the Gullible: The Truth Behind the Video Nasty Scandal* (Liskeard: Stray Cat, 2007), 133.

37. John Kenneth Muir, 46.

38. Michael Brashinsky, "The Spring, Defiled: Ingmar Bergman's *Virgin Spring* and Wes Craven's *Last House on the Left*," in *Play It Again, Sam: Retakes on Remakes*, eds. Andrew Horton and Stuart

Y. McDougal (Berkeley: California University Press, 1998), 162–171, 167.

39. John Kenneth Muir, 47.

40. Michael Brashinsky, 169.

41. Joseph Maddrey, *Nightmares in Red, White and Blue: The Evolution of the American Horror Film* (Jefferson, NC: McFarland, 2004), 163.

42. Jan Bruun, "What the Hell Was He Thinking? Interview with Bo Arne Vibenius," *Cinema Sewer* 15: 13.

43. *Ibid.*

44. *Ibid.*, 14.

45. Kier-La Janisse, "Death Walks in High Heels: The Silent Avenger of Abel Ferrara's Ms. 45," *Women and Hollywood*, 11 December 2013. accessed 10 January 2020, https://womenandhollywood.com/death-walks-in-high-heels-the-silent-avenger-of-abel-ferraras-ms-45-8474c5f409b5/.

46. Alexandra Heller-Nicholas, *Ms. 45* (New York: Columbia University Press, 2017).

47. See Xavier Mendik, "Thana as Thanatos: Sexuality and Death in *Ms. 45: Angel of Vengeance*," in *Necronomicon Book One*, ed. Andy Black, 168–176 (London, 1996).

48. Carol J. Clover, 124–137.

49. Stephen Prince, *Savage Cinema: Sam Peckinpah and the Rise of Ultraviolent Movies* (Austin: Texas University Press, 1998), 126.

50. Peter Hutchings, "'I'm the Girl He Wants to Kill': The 'Women in Peril' Thriller in 1970s British Film and Television," *Visual Culture in Britain* 10:1 (2009): 53–69, 54.

51. Carol J. Clover, 153.

52. Christopher Sharrett, "Review: *Straw Dogs* (Sam Peckinpah, 1971)," *Cinéaste* 28:4 (Fall 2003): 57–59, 57.

53. Stephen Prince, 126.

54. David Andrews, *Soft in the Middle: The Contemporary Softcore Feature and Its Contexts* (Columbia: Ohio State University Press, 2006), 64.

55. According to RAINN (the Rape, Abuse & Incest National Network), only 19.5 percent of rapes are committed by a stranger. "Perpetrators of Sexual Violence: Statistics," RAINN https://www.rainn.org/statistics/perpetrators-sexual-violence.

56. Christopher Sharrett, 58.

57. Linda Ruth Williams, "*Straw Dogs*: Women Can Only Misbehave," *Sight & Sound* 5:2 (February 1995): 26–7, 26.

58. Christopher Sharrett, 57.

59. David Weddle, 23.

60. *Ibid.*, 24.

61. Linda Ruth Williams, "*Straw Dogs*," 27.

62. Xavier Mendik, "Urban Legend: The 1970s Films of Michael Winner," in *Shocking Cinema of the Seventies*, ed. Xavier Mendik, 58–73 (Hereford: Noir, 2002), 66.

63. David Andrews, "Remaking, or Not, the Classics *Straw Dogs* and Biocultural Stability in Rape-Revenge Movies," in *Evolution and Popular Narrative*, eds. Dirk Vanderbeke and Brett Cooke, 43–63 (Leiden: Brill Rodopi, 2019), 56.

64. *Deliverance* is not totally female free: At Griner's garage, Ed sees an elderly woman with a young girl. There are women among the group of elderly patients Ed and Bobby eat with after their arrival in Ainsey, and Ed's pregnant wife is shown briefly in the film's concluding scenes.

65. Carol J. Clover, 160.

66. Rikke Schubart, 87.

67. Carol J. Clover, 118.

68. Rikke Schubart, 85.

69. Michel Ciment, *John Boorman* (London: Faber and Faber, 1986), 117.

70. *Ibid.*

71. *Ibid.*, 121.

72. Rikke Schubart, 28.

73. Carol J. Clover, 132.

74. James F. Beaton, "Dicky Down the River," in *The Modern American Novel and the Movies*, eds. Gerald Peary and Roger Shatzkin, 293–306 (New York: Frederick Ungar, 1978), 293.

75. Sally Robinson, "'Emotional Constipation' and the Power of Dammed Masculinity: *Deliverance* and the Paradoxes of Male Liberation," in *Masculinity: Bodies, Movies, Culture*, ed. Peter Lehman, 133–147 (New York: Routledge, 2001), 140.

76. *Ibid.*, 133.

77. Carol J. Clover, 128.

78. Vincent Canby, "*Death Wish* Hunts Muggers: The Cast Story of Gunman Takes Dim View of City," *New York Times*, 25 July 1974, accessed 27 June, 2010, http://movies.nytimes.com/movie/review?res=9804E3DB1131EF34BC4D51DFB166838F669EDE.

79. Travis Dumsday, "On Cheering Charles Bronson: The Ethics of Vigilantism," *The Southern Journal of Philosophy* 47:1 (Spring 2009): 49–67.

80. Karl French, "Obituary: Charles Bronson: 'Acting Is the Easiest Thing I've Ever Done,'" *Financial Times* (UK, 2 September 2003): 2.

81. Vincent Canby, http://movies.nytimes.com/movie/review?res=9804E3DB1131EF34BC4D51DFB166838F669EDE.

82. Michael Ryan and Douglas Kellner, *Camera Politica: The Politics and Ideology of Contemporary Hollywood Film* (Bloomington: Indiana University Press, 1999), 90.

83. Xavier Mendik, 2002, 64.

84. Michael Winner, "Introducing the Shocking Cinema of the Seventies," in *Shocking Cinema of the Seventies*, ed. Xavier Mendik, 7–10 (Hereford: Noir, 2002), 7.

85. Bill Harding, *The Films of Michael Winner* (London: Frederick Muller, 1978), 106.

86. William Beard, *Persistence of Double Vision: Essays on Clint Eastwood* (Edmonton: Alberta University Press, 2000), 19; Vincent Canby, "Review: *Sudden Impact*," *The New York Times*, 6 December 1983, 153.

87. William Beard, 19.

88. Douglas Thompson, *Clint Eastwood: Sexual Cowboy* (London: Warner Books, 1992), 85.

89. Deborah Allison, "Courting the Critics/Assuring the Audiences: The Modulation of Dirty Harry in a Changing Cultural Climate," *Film International* 5.5 (2007): 17–29, 23.

90. Deborah Allison, 23.
91. Kevin Thomas, "Orgy of Violence in *Sudden Impact*," *Los Angeles Times*, 9 December 1983, 233.
92. Vincent Canby, 153.
93. Gary Arnold, "Eastwood and His Stale Impact," *The Washington Post*, 13 December 1983, 175.
94. Peter Stack, "*Impact*: Torn Flesh, Death, and Big Guns," *San Francisco Chronicle*, 9 December 1983, 246.
95. Deborah Allison, 25.
96. *Ibid.*
97. *Ibid.*, 23.
98. Douglas Thompson, 85; Kevin Thomas, 233.
99. Michel Ciment, 124.
100. Alan Casty, *Development of the Film: An Interpretive History* (New York: Harcourt, Brace, Jovanovich, 1973), 385.
101. Bill Harding, 107.
102. *Ibid.*, 108.

Chapter Two

1. Rebecca Solnit, "If Rape Jokes Are Finally Funny It's Because They're Targeting Rape Culture," *The Guardian*, 10 August 2015, accessed 10 January 2020, https://www.theguardian.com/commentisfree/2015/aug/10/jokes-finally-funny-because-culture-at-the-butt-of-them.
2. *Ibid.*
3. Steve Knopper, "The Oral History of Revenge of the Nerds," *GQ*, 26 July 2019, accessed 10 January 2020, https://www.gq.com/story/revenge-of-the-nerds-oral-history.
4. Elizabeth Wilson, "Bodies in Private and Public," in *Public Bodies/Private States: New Views on Photography, Representation, and Gender*, eds. Jane Brettle and Sally Rice, 6–23 (Manchester: Manchester University Press, 1994), 20.
5. Barbara Creed, *The Monstrous-Feminine: Film, Feminism, Psychoanalysis* (London: Routledge, 1993), 106.
6. *Ibid.*, 7.
7. Kyle Buchanan, "Biting Wit," *Advocate* 1001 (29 January 2008): 57–58.
8. See, for example, Casey Ryan Kelly, "Camp Horror and the Gendered Politics of Screen Violence: Subverting the Monstrous-Feminine in *Teeth* (2007)," *Women's Studies in Communication* 39:1 (2016): 86–106.
9. All quotes from Sam Ashurst in this chapter are taken from email correspondence with the author, 19 November 2020.
10. Katey Rich, "Angelina Jolie Confirms a Key Maleficent Scene Was About Rape," *Vanity Fair*, 12 June 2014, accessed 10 January 2020, https://www.vanityfair.com/hollywood/2014/06/angelina-jolie-maleficent-rape.
11. William Bibbiani, "I Prestidigitate On Your Grave," *Mandatory*, 28 May 2014, accessed 10 January 2020, https://www.mandatory.com/fun/696491-maleficent-review-i-prestidigitate-on-your-grave.
12. Novotny Lawrence, *Blaxploitation Films: Blackness and Genre* (New York: Routledge, 2008).
13. Stephane Dunn, *Baad Bitches and Sassy Supermamas: Black Power Action Films* (Urbana: Illinois University Press, 2008), 126.
14. *Ibid.*
15. Debra Ferreday, "'Only the Bad Gyal could do this': Rihanna, rape-revenge narratives and the cultural politics of white feminism," *Feminist Theory* 18:3 (2017): 268.
16. *Ibid.*
17. Janell Hobson, *Body as Evidence: Mediating Race, Globalizing Gender* (New York: State University of New York Press, 2012), 89.
18. Debra Ferreday, 270.
19. Jocelyn Vena, "Lady Gaga Says 'Bad Romance' Video Is About 'Tough Female Spirit,'" MTV.com, 9 November 2009, accessed 31 October 2010, http://www.mtv.com/news/articles/1625848/20091109/lady_gaga.jhtml.
20. Maria Bevacqua, *Rape on the Public Agenda: Feminism and the Politics of Sexual Assault* (Boston: Northeastern University Press, 2000), 126.
21. While the focus of this book is specifically on rape-revenge film, this by no means undermines its ubiquity on television. In terms of the 1970s and 1980s alone, Lisa M. Cuklanz lists a number of popular series that utilized rape-revenge plots, including *Simon & Simon*, *In the Heat of the Night*, *The Equalizer*, *Barnaby Jones*, *Dallas*, *Starsky and Hutch*, and *Hawaii Five-O*. See Lisa M. Cuklanz, *Rape on Prime Time: Television, Masculinity, and Sexual Violence* (Philadelphia: Pennsylvania University Press, 2000).
22. Sujata Moorti, *Color of Rape: Gender and Race in Television's Public Spheres* (Albany: State University of New York Press, 2002), 188.
23. Peter Lehman, 109.
24. *Ibid.*
25. Jacinda Read, *The New Avengers: Feminism, Femininity and the Rape-Revenge Cycle* (Manchester: Manchester University Press, 2000), 126.
26. Using rape *as* revenge is not specific to *High Plains Drifter*, and again there is some diversity in how this particular trope has been deployed on film. In *The Baby of Mâcon* (Peter Greenaway, 1993), a woman who fakes an immaculate conception and a subsequent virgin birth is gang-raped in a symbolic deflowering. Notably, the play-within-a-play structure allows one of its "internal" audience members to devise this mode of vengeance; thus the film places the responsibility of this abomination squarely upon its "audience."
27. James R. Lewis, "Images of Captive Rape in the Nineteenth Century," *Journal of American and Comparative Cultures* 15:2 (June 1992): 69–77, 75.
28. *Ibid.*, 72.
29. *Ibid.*, 75.
30. Elliott Gruner, "Rape and Captivity," *Jump Cut: A Review of Contemporary Media* 39 (June 1994): 51–56, accessed 3 December 2006, http://www.ejumpcut.org/archive/onlinessays/JC39folder/RapeandCaptivity.html.

31. Barbara Mortimer, *Hollywood's Frontier Captives: Cultural Anxiety and the Captivity Plot in American Film* (New York: Garland, 2000), 29.
32. Linda Colley, "Perceiving Low Literature: The Captivity Narrative," *Essays in Criticism* 53.3 (July 2003): 199–218, 200.
33. Jacinda Read, 223.
34. Philip Green, 192.
35. Jerrold S. Greenberg, Clint E. Bruess and Sarah C. Conklin, *Exploring the Dimensions of Human Sexuality, Fourth Edition* (Sudbury: Jones and Bartlett, 2011), 551.
36. Commentary track for the 2004 Force Entertainment DVD of Zarchi's *I Spit on Your Grave*.
37. Carol J. Clover, 164.
38. Barbara Mortimer, 4–6. There is almost no music in *I Spit on Your Grave*, and there is minimal dialogue also. It is gesture and action, emphasized by the dominant muteness of the text, that most wholly signifies the supposed "virtue" and "villainy" of the film's characters.
39. Ibid., 21.
40. Will Wright, *Sixguns and Society: A Structural Study of the Western* (Berkeley: California University Press, 1975), 59.
41. Ibid., 69.
42. Ibid.
43. Kate Millett, *Sexual Politics* (Champaign: First Illinois Paperback, 2000), 44.
44. Susan Brownmiller, 18.
45. Jacinda Read, 129.
46. Ibid., 125.
47. Ibid., 133.
48. Ibid., 141.
49. Ibid., 134.
50. Ibid., 139.
51. Ibid., 129.
52. Lisa M. Cuklanz, 37.
53. Jacob Knight, "The Savage Stack: HANDGUN (1984)," *Birth. Movies.Death.*, 23 September 2016, accessed 10 January 2020, https://birthmoviesdeath.com/2016/09/23/the-savage-stack-handgun-1984.
54. Christina Lane, *Feminist Hollywood: From Born in Flames to Point Break* (Detroit: Wayne State University Press, 2000), 212.
55. Jordan Crucchiola, "57 Horror Directors on the Scares That Inspired (and Traumatized) Them," *Vulture*, 5 December 2018, accessed 10 January 2020 https://www.vulture.com/2018/12/horror-directors-horror-movies-that-shaped-them.html.
56. Linda Badley, *Film, Horror and the Body Fantastic* (Westport: Greenwood, 1995), 10.
57. Linda Williams, "Film Bodies: Gender, Genre and Excess," *Film Quarterly* 44.4 (Summer 1991): 2–13, 5.
58. Carol J. Clover, 32.
59. Diane Wolfthal, 81.
60. There are parallels between *Demented* and the similarly named *Deranged* (Chuck Vincent, 1987), where a crazy, heavily-pregnant woman murders a masked home invader who beats her viciously (causing her to miscarry) and attempts to rape her.
61. All quotes from Jim Hemphill in this chapter are taken from email correspondence with the author, 18 November 2020.
62. Maximillian Le Cain, "Tarantino and the Vengeful Ghosts of Cinema," *Senses of Cinema* 32 (July–September 2004), accessed 29 September 2009, http://archive.sensesofcinema.com/contents/04/32/tarantino.html.
63. Todd McCarthy, "A Killer Double Bill," *Variety* 406:7 (2–8 April 2007): 25–32.
64. Nick James, "Tarantino Bites Back," *Sight & Sound* (February 2008), accessed 10 January 2010, http://www.bfi.org.uk/sightandsound/feature/49432/.
65. Roger Ebert, "Evil in Film: To What End?" *Chicago Sun–Times*, 19 August 2005, accessed 30 February 2010, http://rogerebert.suntimes.com/apps/pbcs.dll/article?AID=/20050818/COMMENTARY/508190304.
66. Eric Somers, "Down the Block from Bergman: *The Last House on the Left* and Beyond," *Video Watchdog* 151 (September 2009): 14–27.
67. Norman Bryson, "Two Narratives of Rape in the Visual Arts: Lucretia and the Sabine Women," in *Rape: An Historical and Social Enquiry*, eds. Sylvana Tomaselli and Ray Porter, 152–173 (New York: Basil Blackwell, 1986), 153.
68. Paul Fischer, "Rachael Taylor: Shutter Interview," *Femail*, accessed 6 October 2009, http://www.femail.com.au/rachael-taylor-shutter-interview.htm.
69. Jamie Russell, "Review: *Shutter*," *Sight & Sound* 17:7 (July 2007): 71.

Chapter Three

1. E. Ann Kaplan, "Problematizing Cross-Cultural Analysis: The Case of Women in the Recent Chinese Cinema," in *Asian Cinemas: A Reader and Guide*, eds. Dimitris Eleftheriotis and Gary Needham, 156–167 (Honolulu: Hawai'i University Press, 2006), 157.
2. Ibid., 164.
3. Ibid., 166.
4. Patrick Brzeski, "How Indonesia's Oscar Submission, 'Marlina the Murderer,' Became a Revenge Thriller for the #MeToo Era," *The Hollywood Reporter*, 13 November 2018, accessed 10 January 2020, https://www.hollywoodreporter.com/news/how-marlina-murdered-became-a-revenge-thriller-metoo-era-1157608.
5. All quotes from Peter Strickland in this chapter are taken from email correspondence with the author, 19 November 2020.
6. Ofelia de Pablo, Javier Zurita and Giles Tremlett, "Guatemalan war rape survivors: 'We have no voice,'" *The Guardian*, 29 July 2011, accessed 10 January 2020, https://www.theguardian.com/lifeandstyle/2011/jul/28/guatemalan-women-mass-rape-give-evidence.
7. Alice Aslan, *Islamophobia in Australia* (Glebe: Agora Press, 2009), 98.
8. Stuart Cunningham, *Framing Culture: Criticism and Policy in Australia* (North Sydney: Allen &

Unwin, 1992), 149; Rose Lucas "Shame," in *Australian Film 1978–1992: A Survey of Theatrical Features*, ed. Scott Murray (Melbourne: Oxford University Press, 1993), 257.

9. Kathi Maio, *Popcorn and Sexual Politics* (Freedom: The Crossing Press, 1991), 124.

10. Rose Lucas, 257.

11. The U.S. TV movie remake of *Shame* (Dan Lerner, 1995) resituates the Australian original to United States. The basic plot structure, many key scenes and much of the dialogue are retained in the U.S. *Shame*, but the two films deviate crucially in many ways: There is no mobilization of the townswomen after the gang attack Lizzie's home (thus their unity remains at the discursive level only), and there is no attempted rape of the grandmother (rape is therefore implied to be an issue facing attractive young women). Unlike Furness' Asta, Donohoe's Diane is hailed unambiguously as a heroine as she tells another rape victim, "Things are going to change; this is where it starts." Combined with its final textual rape statistic coda, the American *Shame* is a straightforward "social issue" drama, whereas the original Australian version emphasizes the ethical nuance of Asta's position as bourgeois outsider casting her own brand of "feminism" of women of a much different socio-economic status.

12. Olivia Newton-John—from *Xanadu* (Robert Greenwald, 1980) and *Grease* (Randal Kleiser, 1978)—was originally considered for the role of Jessica. See "Olivia Seeks Film Role," *Truth* (Australia), July 7, 1984, 3.

13. Rachel Handler, "Jennifer Kent Doesn't Think The Nightingale is a Rape-Revenge Story," *Vulture*, 1 August 2019, accessed 10 January 2020, https://www.vulture.com/2019/08/the-babadooks-jennifer-kent-on-the-nightingale.html.

14. All quotes from David Barker and Lou Mentor in this chapter are taken from email correspondence with the author, 30 November 2020.

15. Derek Elley, "Review: *Straightheads*," *Daily Variety* 295:19 (27 April 2007): 4, 10.

16. Anna Smith, "Review: *Straightheads*," *Sight & Sound* 17:5 (May 2007): 83–84.

17. Rob Carnavele, "Gillian Anderson: *Straightheads*," *BBC.co.uk*, April 2007, accessed 6 October 2009, http://www.bbc.co.uk/films/2007/04/23/gillian_anderson_straightheads_2007_interview.shtml.

18. A.H. Weiler, "House by Lake Sinks in Blood," *New York Times*, 12 May 1977, 70.

19. Clive Denton, *Cinema Canada*, 3:33 (December 1976-January 1977): 57–58, 57.

20. Canuxploitation.com Review: *Death Weekend*, accessed 6 October 2009, http://www.canuxploitation.com/review/deathweekend.html.

21. Clive Denton, 57.

22. Canuxploitation.com, http://www.canuxploitation.com/review/deathweekend.html.

23. Christina Stojanova, "Denys Arcand," in *Contemporary North American Film Directors: A Wallflower Guide*, eds. Yoram Allon, Del Cullen and Hannah Patterson (London: Wallflower Press, 2002), 19.

24. Pierre Veronneau, "Denys Arcand: A Moralist in Search of His Audience," in *Great Canadian Film Directors*, ed. George Melnyk, 67–77 (Edmonton: Alberta University Press, 2007), 69. *The Cotton Mill* was finally released in its fully uncut version on DVD in 2004.

25. *Ibid.*, 71.

26. Christina Stojanova, 20.

27. Alain Dubeau, "Denys Arcand," in *Guide to the Cinema(s) of Canada*, ed. Peter Rist (Westport: Greenwood Press, 2001), 6–7, 7.

28. Ashitha Nagesh, "Does Denmark Have a 'Pervasive' Rape Problem?," *BBC News*, 11 March 2019, accessed 10 January 2020, https://www.bbc.com/news/world-europe-47470353

29. Gwilym Mumford, "Danish Authorities Investigating Claims of Sexual Abuse at Lars Von Trier's Studio Zentropa," *The Guardian*, 13 November 2017, accessed 10 January 2020, https://www.theguardian.com/film/2017/nov/13/nine-women-allege-sexual-harassment-and-bullying-at-lars-von-triers-production-firm.

30. Imran Siddique, "Why Do We Let "Genius" Directors Get Away With Abusive Behavior?" *BuzzFeed*, 25 October 2017, accessed 10 January 2020, https://www.buzzfeednews.com/article/imransiddiquee/hollywood-abusive-auteur-problem.

31. Lars von Trier is "the P.T. Barnum of modern cinema, a brilliant showman-cum-shaman, part provocateur, all entrepreneur." Damien Wise, "No Dane, No Gain," *The Guardian*, 12 October 2003, accessed 6 October 2009, http://www.guardian.co.uk/film/2003/oct/12/features.magazine.

32. Dendy Films (Australia), *Dogville* Press Kit, 2003.

33. *Ibid.*

34. Jack Stevenson, *Lars von Trier* (London: BFI, 2002), 185.

35. Damien Wise, http://www.guardian.co.uk/film/2003/oct/12/features.magazine.

36. Bryant Frazer, "Review: *Dogville*," *Deep Focus*, 21 March 2004, accessed 6 October 2009, http://www.deep-focus.com/dfweblog/2004/03/dogville.html.

37. Caroline Bainbridge, *The Cinema of Lars von Trier: Authenticity and Artifice* (London: Wallflower, 2007), 151.

38. Obviously there is also a strong legacy of films that make clear connections between women, gender and insanity beyond France, see Kier-La Janisse, *House of Psychotic Women: An Autobiographical Topography of Female Neurosis in Horror and Exploitation Films* (Goldalming: FAB Press, 2012).

39. James Quandt, "Flesh and Blood: Sex and Violence in Recent French Cinema," *Artforum* 42:6 (February 2004): 126–132.

40. Mark Kermode, "Horror Movie," *Sight & Sound* 13:2 (February 2003): 21–22, 22.

41. David Sterritt, "'Time Destroys All Things':

An Interview with Gaspar Noé," *Quarterly Review of Film and Video* 24:4 (2007): 307–316, 312.

42. Elvis Mitchell, "*Irréversible*: Rape, Violence ... It's OK to Look Away," *New York Times* 7 March 2003, E1: 32.

43. Nick James, "Horror Movie," *Sight & Sound* 13:2 (February 2003): 21–22, 21.

44. David Sterritt, 312.

45. Mark Kermode, 22.

46. Anne Billson, "How the 'rape-revenge movie' became a feminist weapon for the #MeToo generation," *The Guardian*, 11 May 2018, accessed 10 January 2020, https://www.theguardian.com/film/2018/may/11/how-the-rape-revenge-movie-became-a-feminist-weapon-for-the-metoo-generation.

47. Aristides Gazetas, *An Introduction to World Cinema* (Jefferson, NC: McFarland, 2008), 275.

48. Hans-Bernhard Moeller and George Lellis, *Volker Schlondorff's Cinema: Adaptation, Politics, and the "Movie-Appropriate"* (Carbondale: Southern Illinois University Press, 2002), 46.

49. *Ibid.*, 43.

50. *Ibid.*, 46.

51. *Ibid.*, 42.

52. This view of Boll is typified in the article "Uwe Boll: Money for Nothing: The Awful Truth Behind the Worst Director in the World," accessed 10 January 2010, http://www.cinemablend.com/features/Uwe-Boll-Money-For-Nothing-209.html.

53. Sally Stockbridge, "Rape and Representation: The Regulation of Hong Kong Films in Hong Kong and Australia," *Asian Studies Review* 17:3 (1994): 43–49, 43.

54. *Ibid.*, 44.

55. Darrell W. Davis and Yeh Yueh-yu, "Warning! Category III: The Other Hong Kong Cinema," *Film Quarterly* 54:4 (Summer 2001): 12–26, 14.

56. Andrew Grossman, "Against Pleasure, Against Identification: Feminism, Cultural Atheism, and the Tragic Subject," *Bright Lights Film Journal* 47 (February 2005), accessed 10 July 2009, http://www.brightlightsfilm.com/47/47rape.php.

57. Darrell W. Davis and Yeh Yueh-yu, 14–18.

58. Linda Ruth Williams, *The Erotic Thriller in Contemporary Cinema* (Bloomington: Indiana University Press, 2005), 386.

59. Andrew Grossman, http://www.brightlightsfilm.com/47/47rape.php.

60. James Mudge, "Review: *Red to Kill*," *Beyond Hollywood*, 17 September 2004, accessed 6 October 2009, http://www.beyondhollywood.com/red-to-kill-1997-movie-review/.

61. Michael Atkinson, "Taboo Ya!" *Village Voice*, 5 November 2002, accessed 6 October 2009, http://www.villagevoice.com/2002-11-05/film/taboo-ya/1.

62. Julian Stringer, "Category 3: Sex and Violence in Postmodern Hong Kong," in *Mythologies of Violence in Postmodern Media*, ed Christopher Sharrett, 361–378, 364.

63. *Ibid.*, 362. Darrell W. Davis and Yeh Yeuh-yu also share this critical approach in their treatment of the Category III film *Intruders* (Tseng Kam-Cheong, 1997), a movie that emphasizes the monstrosity of "ruthless mainlanders" and thus acts in part as "an allegory of the reunion with China" (14).

64. *Ibid.*, 367.

65. Gregory D. Booth, "Traditional Content and Narrative Structure in the Hindi Commercial Cinema," *Asian Folklore Studies* 54:2 (1995): 169–190, 172.

66. *Ibid.*, 180–181.

67. *Ibid.*

68. Urvashi Butalia, "Women in Indian Cinema," *Feminist Review* 317 (August 1984): 108–110, 108.

69. Leela Rao, "Women in Indian Films: A Paradigm of Continuity and Change," *Media, Culture and Society* 11:4 (1989): 443–458, 455. Jyotika Virdi's article "Reverence, Rape—and Then Revenge: Popular Hindi Cinema's 'Woman's Film'" offers a fascinating historical overview of the rape threat and how it was coded in Hindi "women's films." See *Screen* 40:1 (Spring 1991): 17–37.

70. Jyotika Virdi, 28.

71. See Urvashi Butalia, 109.

72. Jyotika Virdi, 29.

73. *Ibid.*, 32.

74. Uryashi Butalia, 109.

75. Jyotika Virdi, 33.

76. *Ibid.*, 30.

77. Udayan Prasad, "Woman on the Edge," *Sight & Sound* 1:2 (February 1995): 14–17, 16.

78. Lalitha Gopalan, *Cinema of Interruptions: Action Genres in Contemporary Indian Cinema* (London: BFI, 2002), 59.

79. Leela Fernandes, "Reading 'India's Bandit Queen': A Trans/national Feminist Perspective on the Discrepencies of Representation," *Signs* 25:1 (Autumn 1999): 123–152, 128.

80. Colette Balmain, *Introduction to Japanese Horror Film* (Edinburgh: Edinburgh University Press, 2008), 95.

81. For James R. Alexander, "The so-called pink films (*pinku eige*) of the 1970s offer(ed) ... a steady diet of violent mayhem, including shootings, beatings, stabbings, torture, mutilation and rape.... Prototypical of these were gangster (*yakuza*) films, films about roving gangs of alienated youth (the staple text of the nihilistic period of the Japanese New Wave), and films that featuring the rape of young girls," http://www.sensesofcinema.com/contents/05/36/freeze_me.html.

82. Pete Tombs, *Mondo Macabro: Weird and Wonderful Cinema from Around the World* (New York: St. Martins Griffin, 1998, 160.

83. Gregory Barrett, *Archetypes in Japanese Film: The Sociopolitical and Religious Significance of the Principal Heroes and Heroines* (Cranbury: Associated University Press, 1989), 98.

84. Colette Balmain, 95.

85. James R. Alexander, http://www.sensesofcinema.com/contents/05/36/freeze_me.html.

86. James R. Alexander, http://www.sensesofcinema.com/contents/05/36/freeze_me.html.

87. Rikke Schubart, 107.

88. *Ibid.*, 111.

89. *Female Prisoner #701: Scorpion* is the first

of four films in this series, the others being *Female Prisoner Scorpion: Jailhouse 41* (*Joshuu Sasori—Dai 41 Zakkyobo*, Shuya Ito, 1972), *Female Prisoner Scorpion: Beast Stable* (*Joshuu Sasori—Kemono Beya*, Shuya Ito, 1973), and *Female Prisoner Scorpion: Grudge Song* (*Josh Sasori—701 Go Urami Bushi*, Yasharu Hasebe, 1973). Meiko Kaji starred in all these films.

90. Chris Desjardins, *Outlaw Masters of the Japanese Cinema* (London: I.B. Tauris, 2005), 68.

91. James R. Alexander, http://www.sensesofcinema.com/contents/05/36/freeze_me.html.

92. Rikke Schubart, 116.

93. There are nine *Angel Guts* films in all. While Takashi Ishii only directed the last three, the whole series is based on a manga series he wrote.

94. Darcy Paquet, *New Korean Cinema: Breaking the Waves* (New York: Columbia University Press, 2009), 42.

95. See Alison Peirse, *Korean Horror Cinema* (Edinburgh: Edinburgh University Press, 2013).

96. Michelle Cho, "Beyond Vengeance: Landscapes of Violence in Jang Chul-Soo's Bedevilled (Kim Pong-Nam Sarinsakon Uichonmal, 2010)," *Acta Koreana*, 17: 1 (2014): 144.

97. Ibid.

98. Víctor Fuentes, "Almodóvar's Postmodern Cinema: A Work in Progress" in *Post-Franco, Postmodern: The Films of Pedro Almodóvar*, eds. Kathleen M. Vernon and Barbara Morris (London: Greenwood Press, 1995), 162.

99. Christopher Perriam, *Stars and Masculinities in Spanish Cinema: From Banderas to Bardem* (New York: Oxford University Press, 2003), 65.

100. Aliraza Javaid, *Male Rape, Masculinities, and Sexualities: Understanding, Policing, and Overcoming Male Sexual Victimisation* (Cham: Palgrave Macmillan, 2018), 1.

101. Ibid., 3.

102. Ibid., 4.

103. Joaquin Lowe, "The Girl with the Dragon Tattoo Side-by-Side," *Fandor*, 16 August 2018, accessed 10 January 2020, https://www.fandor.com/posts/the-girl-with-the-dragon-tattoo-side-by-side.

104. Gönül Dönmez-Colin, *Women, Islam and Cinema* (London: Reaktion Books, 2004), 76.

105. Ibid., 80.

106. Ibid.

107. In popular representations, "the victim is always female, young, and physically desirable" (Julie A. Allison and Lawrence S. Wrightsman, 3).

108. Kaya Özkaracalar, "Between Appropriation and Innovation: Turkish Horror Cinema," in *Fear Without Frontiers: Horror Cinema Across the Globe*, ed. Steven Jay Schneider, 204–217 (Gottalming: FAB Press, 2003); Ian Robert Smith, "*The Exorcist* in Istanbul: Processes of Transcultural Appropriation Within Turkish Popular Cinema," *Portal Journal of Multidisciplinary International Studies* 5:1 (January 2008), accessed 1 July 2010, http://epress.lib.uts.edu.au/ojs/index.php/portal/article/view/489/584.

109. Laurence Raw, "Review: Gönül Dönmez-Colin, *Turkish Cinema: Identity, Distance and Belonging*," *Turkish Cinema Screen* 50.3 (Autumn 2009): 362.

Chapter Four

1. Genevieve Carlton, "The 'Savage' Works Of Artemisia Gentileschi, The Painter Who Got Revenge On Her Rapist Through Her Art," *All That's Interesting*, 6 April 2020, accessed 10 January 2021, https://allthatsinteresting.com/artemisia-gentileschi.

2. There has been some recent tentative work to assess the donation of women directors to rape-revenge but is seen as far more anomalous and contemporary a phenomenon than I consider it here. See, for example, Mary Beth McAndrews, "The History of Rape-Revenge Films and the Importance of Female Directors," *Bloody Disgusting*, 8 October 2019, accessed 10 January 2021, https://bloody-disgusting.com/editorials/3586210/eyes-history-rape-revenge-films-importance-female-directors/, and Kelly MacNamara, "Making Sense of Senselessness: The Bloody History of Rape Revenge Films," *Vice*, 11 April 2015, accessed 10 January 2021, https://www.vice.com/en/article/ezjw3e/making-sense-of-senselessness-the-bloody-history-of-rape-revenge-films.

3. Rachel Handler, "Jennifer Kent Doesn't Think The Nightingale Is a Rape-Revenge Story," *Vulture*, 1 August 2019, accessed 10 January 2021, https://www.vulture.com/2019/08/the-babadooks-jennifer-kent-on-the-nightingale.html.

4. Alexandra Heller-Nicholas, *1000 Women in Horror, 1895–2018* (Orlando: BearManor Media, 2019), 483.

5. Because of the diversity and political impact of these different translations, this chapter will refer to the film by its original French title.

6. Linda Ruth Williams cites an interview where Despentes stated, "I've been raped and one of my actresses has been raped…. It's horrific, so I don't see why I shouldn't treat it this way." See Linda Ruth Williams, "Sick Sisters," *Sight & Sound* (July 2001): 28–29. In a supplementary Q&A feature on the U.K. DVD release of the film, Trinh Thi echoes this sentiment, stating, "We have the right to show how awful can be rape [sic]."

7. The banning of *Baise-Moi* in France caused even greater controversy, so the French government quickly reintroduced an 18+ certificate that meant the film was allowed only to be screened in adult cinemas.

8. Gavin Smith, "Toronto," *Film Comment* 36:6 (November-December 2000): 66.

9. Eric Monder, "*Baise-moi (Rape Me)*," *Film Journal International* 25 (March 2002), accessed 6 October 2009, http://www.filmjournal.com/Article.cfm/PageID/75641304.

10. Potential Films (Australia and New Zealand), *Baise-moi* Press Kit, 2000.

11. Colin Nettelback, "Self-Constructing Women: Beyond the Shock of *Baise-moi* and *A ma soeur!*" *Flinders University Languages Group Online Review* 1:3 (December 2003): 58–68, 61.

12. Phil Powrie, "French Neo-noir to Hyper-noir," in *European Film Noir*, ed. Andrew Spicer, 55–83 (Manchester: Manchester University Press, 2007).

13. Linda Ruth Williams, "Sick Sisters," 28.

14. See: Colin Nettelback, 61; Judith Franco, "Gender, Genre and Female Pleasure in the Contemporary Revenge Narrative: *Baise-moi* and *What It Feels Like for a Girl*," *Quarterly Review of Film and Video* 21 (2004): 1–10, 4.

15. Judith Franco, 2.

16. Virginie Despentes and Coralie Trinh Thi interview, "Q&A Session," *Baise-moi*, UK DVD release, Universal Studios, 2003.

17. Ibid.

18. David Stratton, "Review: *Traps*," *Variety*, 12 October 1998, accessed 10 January 2021, http://www.variety.com/1998/film/reviews/traps-2-1200455558/

19. Ibid.

20. Rebecca Solnit, "If Rape Jokes Are Finally Funny It's Because They're Targeting Rape Culture," *The Guardian*, 10 August 2015, accessed 10 January 2021, https://www.theguardian.com/commentisfree/2015/aug/10/jokes-finally-funny-because-culture-at-the-butt-of-them.

21. Peter Hames, *Czech and Slovak Cinema: Themes and Tradition* (Edinburgh: Edinburgh University Press, 2009), 91.

22. Ibid.

23. Lucia Graves and Sam Morris, "The Trump Allegations," *The Guardian*, 30 November 2017, accessed 10 January 2021, https://www.theguardian.com/us-news/ng-interactive/2017/nov/30/donald-trump-sexual-misconduct-allegations-full-list.

24. Claire Henry, *Revisionist Rape-Revenge: Redefining a Film Genre* (Houndsmills: Palgrave Macmillan, 2014), 80.

25. Jenny Lapekas, "Descent"—'Everything's okay now.' Race, vengeance, and watching the modern rape-revenge narrative," *Jump Cut: A Review of Contemporary Media* 55 (Fall 2013), accessed 10 January 2021, https://www.ejumpcut.org/archive/jc55.2013/LapekasDescent/index.html

26. Kira Cochrane, "The Saturday interview: Rosario Dawson," *The Guardian*, 26 March 2012, accessed 10 January 2021, https://www.theguardian.com/theguardian/2012/mar/17/rosario-dawson-actor-activist-interview.

27. All quotes from Karen Lam in this chapter are taken from email correspondence with the author, 19 November 2020.

28. Alex Denney, "Revenge is the French, feminist Kill Bill-style thriller you need to see," *Dazed*, 11 May 2018, accessed 10 January 2021, https://www.dazeddigital.com/film-tv/article/39999/1/revenge-film-coralie-forgeat-interview.

29. Anne Billson, "How the 'Rape-Revenge Movie' Became a Feminist Weapon for the #MeToo Generation," *The Guardian*, 11 May 2018, accessed 10 January 2021, https://www.theguardian.com/film/2018/may/11/how-the-rape-revenge-movie-became-a-feminist-weapon-for-the-metoo-generation.

30. Tim Posada, "#MeToo's First Horror Film: Male Hysteria and the New Final Girl in 2018's Revenge," in *Performing Hysteria: Images and Imaginations of Hysteria*, ed. Johanna Braun (Leuven University Press, 2020).

31. Taylor Antrim, "Revenge is an Exploitation Movie for the #MeToo Era," *Vogue*, 11 May 2018, accessed 10 January 2021, https://www.vogue.com/article/revenge-coralie-fargeat-review.

32. Emily Taylor Center for Women & Gender Equity, "Feminist Fright Fest: An Interview with Gigi Saul Guerrero," YouTube, 30 October 2020, accessed 10 January 2021, https://www.youtube.com/watch?v=5Tgw8TDG_Ao.

33. Meredith Minister, *Rape Culture on Campus* (Lanham: Lexington Books, 2018), 1.

34. See Pauline Kael, "Raising Kane—I," *The New Yorker*, 20 February 1971, https://www.newyorker.com/magazine/1971/02/20/raising-kane-i; "Raising Kane—II," *The New Yorker*, 27 February 1977, https://www.newyorker.com/magazine/1971/02/27/raising-kane-ii. Both accessed 10 January 2021.

35. Claire Henry, 81.

36. See Alexandra Heller-Nicholas, *Ms. 45* (New York: Columbia University Press, 2017).

37. All quotes from Lou Mentor in this chapter are taken from email correspondence with the author, 30 November 2020.

38. Amy Anna, "Interview: FELT's Amy Everson and Jason Banker," *Cut Print Film*, 26 June 2015, accessed 10 January 2021, cutprintfilm.com/features/interviews/interview-felts-amy-everson-and-jason-banker/.

39. All quotes from Sims-Fewer and Mancinelli in this chapter from Alexandra Heller-Nicholas, "The Anti Rape-Revenge Film: Madeline Sims-Fewer and Dusty Mancinelli on *Violation*," *Film International*, 27 September 2020, accessed 10 January 2020, filmint.nu/madeleine-sims-fewer-and-dusty-mancinelli-on-violation-tiff-2020/.

40. Kristy Puchko, "Pollyanna McIntosh Speaks Out on The Woman's Infamy and Her Directorial Debut Darlin'," *SyFyWire*, 17 May 2019, accessed 10 January 2020, https://www.syfy.com/syfywire/pollyanna-mcintosh-speaks-out-on-the-womans-infamy-and-her-directorial-debut-darlin.

41. Ibid.

Afterword

1. Angela Baldassarre, *The Great Dictators: Interviews with Filmmakers of Italian Descent* (Toronto: Guernica Editions, 1999), 14.

2. Ibid. I do not believe Argento means "high concept" in the way in which it has been applied to mainstream (Hollywood) cinema *à la* Justin Wyatt's *High Concept: Movies and Marketing in Hollywood* (Austin: Texas University Press, 1994). Rather, I understand this as meaning that he aspires to a high art standard.

3. Carol J. Clover, 42.

4. For example, transsexual transgender icon Eva Robins plays one of the key female figures in *Tenebrae*, and Carlo's male lover in *Deep Red* is played by a female actress. The killer in his 1971 film *Four Flies on Grey Velvet* is a woman who was raised as a boy, while in *Cat o' Nine Tails* that same year, the murderer had a mutant chromosomal structure and was thus called the "XXY killer." That being said, this is not to suggest that all representations of LGBT characters in Argento's films should be assumed to be necessarily progressive: The depiction of homosexuality in both *Four Flies on Grey Velvet* and *Tenebrae*, for example, make such a claim challenging.

5. Daniel Schweiger, "*The Stendhal Syndrome* Paints It Red," *Fangoria* 162 (May 1997): 40–41, 40.

6. Louis Paul, *Italian Horror Film Directors* (Jefferson, NC: McFarland, 2005), 57.

Bibliography

Alexander, James R. "The Maturity of a Film Genre in an Era of Relaxing Standards of Obscenity: Takashi Ishii's *Freeze Me* as a Rape-Revenge Film." *Senses of Cinema* 36 (2005) (accessed 24 August 2005), http://www.sensesofcinema.com/contents/05/36/freeze_me.html.

Allison, Deborah. "Courting the Critics/Assuring the Audiences: The Modulation of Dirty Harry in a Changing Cultural Climate." *Film International* 5.5 (2007).

Allison, Julie A., and Lawrence S. Wrightsman. *Rape: The Misunderstood Crime*. Newbury Park: Sage Publications, 1993.

Andrews, David. "Remaking, or Not, the Classics Straw Dogs and Biocultural Stability in Rape-Revenge Movies." In *Evolution and Popular Narrative*, edited by Dirk Vanderbeke and Brett Cooke. 43–63. Leiden: Brill Rodopi, 2019.

———. *Soft in the Middle: The Contemporary Softcore Feature and Its Contexts*. Columbus: Ohio State University Press, 2006.

Arnold, Gary. "Eastwood and His Stale Impact." *The Washington Post*, 13 December 1983, 175.

Aslan, Alice. *Islamophobia in Australia*. Glebe: Agora Press, 2009.

Atkinson, Michael. "Taboo Ya!" *Village Voice*, 5 November 2002 (accessed 6 October 2009), http://www.villagevoice.com/2002-11-05/film/taboo-ya/1.

Atkinson, Mike. "Givers of the Viscera." *Sight & Sound* 17, no. 6 (June 2007).

Badley, Linda. *Film, Horror, and the Body Fantastic*. Westport: Greenwood, 1995.

Bainbridge, Caroline. *The Cinema of Lars von Trier: Authenticity and Artifice*. London: Wallflower Press, 2007.

Baker, Martin. "Introduction." In *The Video Nasties: Freedom and Censorship in the Media*, edited by Martin Baker, 1–6. London: Pluto, 1984.

Bal, Mieke. *A Mieke Bal Reader*. Chicago: Chicago University Press, 2006.

Baldassarre, Angela. *The Great Dictators: Interviews with Filmmakers of Italian Descent*. Toronto: Guernica Editions, 1999.

Balmain, Colette. *Introduction to Japanese Horror Film*. Edinburgh: Edinburgh University Press, 2008.

Barrett, Gregory. *Archetypes in Japanese Film: The Sociopolitical and Religious Significance of the Principal Heroes and Heroines*. Cranbury: Associated University Press, 1989.

Beard, William. *Persistence of Double Vision: Essays on Clint Eastwood*. Edmonton: Alberta University Press, 2000.

Beaton, James F. "Dicky Down the River." In *The Modern American Novel and the Movies*, edited by Gerald Peary and Roger Shatzkin, 293–306. New York: Frederick Ungar, 1978.

Billson, Anne. "How the 'rape-revenge movie' became a feminist weapon for the #MeToo generation." *The Guardian*, 11 May 2018 (accessed 10 January 2020), https://www.theguardian.com/film/2018/may/11/how-the-rape-revenge-movie-became-a-feminist-weapon-for-the-metoo-generation.

Booth, Gregory D. "Traditional Content and Narrative Structure in the Hindi Commercial Cinema." *Asian Folklore Studies* 54, no. 2 (1995): 169–190.

Bourke, Joanna. *Rape: A History from 1860 to the Present*. Virago: London, 2008.

Brashinsky, Michael. "The Spring, Defiled: Ingmar Bergman's *Virgin Spring* and Wes Craven's *Last House on the Left*." In *Play It Again, Sam: Retakes on Remakes*, edited by Andrew Horton and Stuart Y. McDougal. Berkeley: California University Press, 1998.

Brownmiller, Susan. *Against Our Will: Men, Women and Rape*. Harmondsworth: Penguin, 1975.

Bryson, Norman. "Two Narratives of Rape in the Visual Arts: Lucretia and the Sabine Women." In *Rape: An Historical and Social Enquiry*, edited by Sylvana Tomaselli and Ray Porter, 152–173. New York: Basil Blackwell, 1986.

Buchanan, Kyle. "Biting Wit." *Advocate* 1001 (29 January 2008): 57–58.

Burke, Frank. "Dario Argento's *The Bird with the Crystal Plumage*: Caging Women's Rage." In *Killing Women: The Visual Culture of Gender and Violence*, edited by Annette Burfoot and Susan Lord, 197–217. Waterloo: Wilfred Laurier University Press, 2006.

Butalia, Urvashi. "Women in Indian Cinema." *Feminist Review* 317 (August 1984): 108–110.

Canby, Vincent. "*Death Wish* Hunts Muggers: The Cast Story of Gunman Takes Dim View of City." *New York Times*, 25 July 1974 (accessed 27 June 2010), http://movies.nytimes.com/movie/review?res=9804E3DB1131EF34BC4D51DFB166838F669EDE.

———. "Review: *Sudden Impact*." *New York Times*, 6 December 1983, 153.
Canuxploitation.com. "Review: *Death Weekend*." Accessed 6 October 2009, http://www.canuxploitation.com/review/deathweekend.html.
Carnavale, Rob. "Gillian Anderson: *Straightheads*." *BBC.co.uk*, April 2007 (accessed 6 October 2009), http://www.bbc.co.uk/films/2007/04/23/gillian_anderson_straightheads_2007_interview.shtml.
Casty, Alan. *Development of the Film: An Interpretive History*. New York: Harcourt, Brace, Jovanovich, 1973.
Cho, Michelle. "Beyond Vengeance: Landscapes of Violence in Jang Chul-Soo's Bedevilled (Kim Pong-Nam Sarinsakon Uichonmal, 2010)." *Acta Koreana*, 17:1 (2014): 137–162.
Christensen, Terry, and Peter J. Haas. *Projecting Politics: Political Messages in American Film*. M.E. Sharpe, 2005.
Ciment, Michel. *John Boorman*. London: Faber & Faber, 1986.
Clover, Carol J. *Men, Women, and Chain Saws: Gender in the Modern Horror Film*. Princeton: Princeton University Press, 1992.
Colangelo, BJ. "'You Just Don't Understand It,' or Why I Love Rape-Revenge." *Icons of Fright*, 6 September 2013 (accessed 10 January 2020), http://iconsoffright.com/2013/09/06/you-just-dont-understand-it-or-why-i-love-rape-revenge.
Colley, Linda. "Perceiving Low Literature: The Captivity Narrative." *Essays in Criticism* 53, no. 3 (July 2003): 199–218.
Cook, Pam. *Screening the Past: Memory and Nostalgia in Cinema*. London: Routledge, 2005.
Creed, Barbara. *The Monstrous-Feminine: Film, Feminism, Psychoanalysis*. London: Routledge, 1993.
Crowdus, Gary. "Cult Films, Commentary Tracks and Censorious Critics: An Interview with John Bloom." *Cinéaste* 28, no. 3 (Summer 2003): 32–34.
Cuklanz, Lisa M. *Rape on Prime Time: Television, Masculinity, and Sexual Violence*. Philadelphia: Pennsylvania University Press, 2000.
Cunningham, Stuart. *Framing Culture: Criticism and Policy in Australia*. North Sydney: Allen & Unwin, 1992.
Davis, Darrell W., and Yeh Yueh-yu. "Warning! Category III: The Other Hong Kong Cinema." *Film Quarterly* 54, no. 4 (Summer 2001): 12–26.
Decker, Sean. "Exclusive: Director Steven R. Monroe Talks *I Spit on Your Grave*." *Dread Central*, 4 September 2010 (accessed 15 September 2010), http://www.dreadcentral.com/interviews/monroe-steven-r-i-spit-your-grave.
———. "Exclusive: Dread Central Hits Red Carpet Premiere of *I Spit on Your Grave*." *Dread Central*, 30 September 2010 (accessed 15 October 2010), http://www.dreadcentral.com/news/40076/exclusive-dread-central-hits-red-carpet-premiere-i-spit-your-grave.
Denton, Clive. *Cinema Canada* 3, no. 33 (December 1976-January 1977): 57–58.
Desjardins, Chris. *Outlaw Masters of the Japanese Cinema*. London: I.B. Tauris, 2005.
Despentes, Virginie. *Baise-moi: A Novel*. Melbourne: Black, 2003.
Devi, Phoolan, with Marie-Thérèse Cuny and Paul Rambali. *I, Phoolan Devi: The Autobiography of India's Bandit Queen*. London: Warner Books, 1997.
Dickey, James. *Deliverance*. London: Pan Books, 1971.
———. *Deliverance*. Screenplay. Suffolk: Screen Press Publishing, 2003.
Dönmez-Colin, Gönül. *Women, Islam and Cinema*. London: Reaktion Books, 2004.
Dubeau, Alain. "Denys Arcand." In *Guide to the Cinema(s) of Canada*, edited by Peter Rist, 6–7. Westport: Greenwood Press, 2001.
Dumsday, Travis. "On Cheering Charles Bronson: The Ethics of Vigilantism." *The Southern Journal of Philosophy* 47, no. 1 (Spring 2009): 49–67.
Dunn, Stephane. *"Baad Bitches" and Sassy Supermamas: Black Power Action Films*. Urbana: Illinois University Press, 2008.
Ebert, Roger. "Evil in Film: To What End?" *Chicago Sun-Times*, 19 August 2005 (accessed 30 February 2010), http://rogerebert.suntimes.com/apps/pbcs.dll/article?AID=/20050818/COMMENTARY/508190304.
———. "Review: *I Spit on Your Grave* (Dir. Meir Zarchi)." *Chicago Sun-Times*, 16 July 1980 (accessed 6 March 2006), http://rogerebert.suntimes.com/apps/pbcs.dll/article?AID=/19800716/REVIEWS/7160301/1023.
Eggertsen, Chris. "Interview: Original *I Spit on Your Grave* Director Meir Zarchi!" *Bloody Disgusting*, 5 October 2010 (accessed 15 October 2010), http://www.bloody-disgusting.com/news/21921.
Elley, Derek. "Review: *Straightheads*." *Daily Variety* 295, no. 19 (27 April 2007): 4, 10.
Farrow, Ronan. "From Aggressive Overtures to Sexual Assault: Harvey Weinstein's Accusers Tell their Stories." *The New Yorker*, 10 October 2017 (accessed 10 January 2020) https://www.newyorker.com/news/news-desk/from-aggressive-overtures-to-sexual-assault-harvey-weinsteins-accusers-tell-their-stories.
Faulkner, William. *Sanctuary*. Harmondsworth: Penguin, 1958.
Fernandes, Leela. "Reading 'India's Bandit Queen': A Transnational Feminist Perspective on the Discrepancies of Representation." *Signs* 25, no. 1 (Autumn 1999): 123–152.
Ferreday, Debra. "'Only the Bad Gyal could do this': Rihanna, rape-revenge narratives and the cultural politics of white feminism." *Feminist Theory* 18:3 (2017): 263–280.
Finley, Laura L. *Domestic Abuse and Sexual Assault in Popular Culture*. Santa Barbara: Prager, 2016.
Fischer, Paul. "Rachael Taylor: Shutter Interview." *Femail* (accessed 6 October 2009), http://www.femail.com.au/rachael-taylor-shutter-interview.htm.
Franco, Judith. "Gender, Genre and Female Pleasure in the Contemporary Revenge Narrative: *Baise-moi* and *What It Feels Like for a Girl*." *Quarterly Review of Film and Video* 21 (2004): 1–10.

Frazer, Bryant. "Review: *Dogville*." *Deep Focus*, 21 March 2004 (accessed 6 October 2009), http://www.deep-focus.com/dfweblog/2004/03/dogville.html.

French, Karl. "Obituary: Charles Bronson: 'Acting Is the Easiest Thing I've Ever Done.'" *Financial Times* (UK), 2 September 2003.

Fuentes, Víctor. "Almodóvar's Postmodern Cinema: A Work in Progress." In *Post-Franco, Postmodern: The Films of Pedro Almodóvar*, edited by Kathleen M. Vernon and Barbara Morris. 155–170. London: Greenwood Press, London, 1995.

Fulwood, Neil. *One Hundred Violent Films That Changed Cinema*. London: BT Batsford, 2003.

Gazetas, Aristides. *An Introduction to World Cinema*. Jefferson, NC: McFarland, 2008.

Gopalan, Lalitha. *Cinema of Interruptions: Action Genres in Contemporary Indian Cinema*. London: BFI, 2002.

Gorfinkel, Elena. *Lewd Looks: American Sexploitation Cinema in the 1960s*. Minneapolis: University of Minnesota Press, 2017.

Govier, Trudy. *Forgiveness and Revenge*. New York: Routledge, 2002.

Graybill, Rhiannon. "Day of the Woman: Judges 4–5 as Slasher and Rape Revenge Narrative." *The Journal of Religion and Popular Culture* 30:3 (Fall 2018): 193–205.

Green, Philip. *Cracks in the Pedestal: Ideology and Gender in Hollywood*. Amherst: Massachusetts University Press, 1998.

Greenberg, Jerrold S., Clint E. Bruess, and Sarah C. Conklin. *Exploring the Dimensions of Human Sexuality, Fourth Edition*. Sudbury: Jones and Bartlett, 2010.

Grossman, Andrew. "Against Pleasure, Against Identification: Feminism, Cultural Atheism, and the Tragic Subject." *Bright Lights Film Journal* 47 (February 2005) (accessed 10 July 2009), http://www.brightlightsfilm.com/47/47rape.php.

Gruner, Elliott. "Rape and Captivity." *Jump Cut: A Review of Contemporary Media*, 39 (June 1994): 51–56 (accessed 3 December 2006), http://www.ejumpcut.org/archive/onlinessays/JC39folder/RapeandCaptivity.html.

Guthmann, Edward. "An Assault Victim Turns on Her Attacker: Cinema Rape Parallels Woman's Real-Life Ordeal." *San Francisco Chronicle*, 17 August 1986.

Hames, Peter. *Czech and Slovak Cinema: Themes and Tradition*. Edinburgh: Edinburgh University Press, 2009.

Haskell, Molly. *From Reverence to Rape: The Treatment of Women in the Movies*. Harmondsworth: Penguin, 1974.

Heller-Nicholas, Alexandra. *1000 Women in Horror, 1895–2018*. Orlando: BearManor Media, 2020.

_____. "The Anti Rape-Revenge Film: Madeline Sims-Fewer and Dusty Mancinelli on *Violation*." *Film International*, 27 September 2020 (accessed 10 January 2020), filmint.nu/madeleine-sims-fewer-and-dusty-mancinelli-on-violation-tiff-2020/.

_____. *Ms. 45*. New York: Columbia University Press, 2017.

Henry, Claire. *Revisionist Rape-Revenge: Redefining a Film Genre*. Houndsmills: Palgrave Macmillan, 2014.

Higgins, Lynn A., and Brenda R. Silver. "*Rereading Rape*." In *Rape and Representation*, edited by Lynn A. Higgins and Brenda R. Silver, 1–11. New York: Columbia University Press, 1991.

Hills, Matt. "Para-Paracinema: The *Friday the 13th* Series as Other to Trash and Legitimate Film Cultures." In *Sleaze Artists: Cinema at the Margins of Taste, Style and Politics*, edited by Jeffrey Sconce, 219–239. Durham: Duke University Press, 2007.

Hobson, Janell. *Body as Evidence: Mediating Race, Globalizing Gender*. New York: State University of New York Press, 2012.

Hollinger, Karen. "Review: *The New Avengers: Feminism, Femininity and the Rape-Revenge Cycle* by Jacinda Read (New York: Manchester University Press, 2000)." *Film Quarterly* 55, no. 4 (Summer 2002): 61–63.

Horeck, Tanya. *Public Rape: Representing Violation in Fiction and Film*. London: Routledge, 2004.

Hron, Madelaine. "Naked Terror: Horrific, Aesthetic and Healing Images of Rape." In *Cultural Expressions of Evil and Wickedness: Wrath, Sex, Crime*, edited by Terrie Waddell, 127–145. Amsterdam: Rodopi, 2003.

Hutchings, Peter. "'I'm the Girl He Wants to Kill': The 'Women in Peril' Thriller in 1970s British Film and Television." *Visual Culture in Britain* 10, no. 1 (2009): 53–69.

James, Nick. "Horror Movie." *Sight & Sound* 13, no. 2 (February 2003): 21–22.

_____. "Tarantino Bites Back." *Sight & Sound*, February 2008 (accessed 10 January 2010), http://www.bfi.org.uk/sightandsound/feature/49432/.

Janisse, Kier-La. *House of Psychotic Women: An Autobiographical Topography of Female Neurosis in Horror and Exploitation Films*. Goldalming: FAB Press, 2012.

Javaid, Aliraza. *Male Rape, Masculinities, and Sexualities: Understanding, Policing, and Overcoming Male Sexual Victimisation*. Cham: Palgrave Macmillan, 2018.

Jowett, Lorna. "Rape, Power, Realism and the Fantastic on Television." In *Feminism, Literature and Rape Narratives: Violence and Violation*, edited by Sorcha Gunne and Zoe Brigley Thompson. 217–231. New York: Routledge, 2010.

Kaplan, E. Ann. "Problematizing Cross-Cultural Analysis: The Case of Women in the Recent Chinese Cinema." In *Asian Cinemas: A Reader and Guide*, edited by Dimitris Eleftheriotis and Gary Needham, 156–167. Honolulu: Hawaii University Press, 2006.

Kantor, Jodi, and Megan Twohey. "Harvey Weinstein Paid Off Sexual Harassment Accusers for Decades." *New York Times*, 5 October 2017 (accessed 10 January 2020), https://www.nytimes.com/2017/10/05/us/harvey-weinstein-harassment-allegations.html.

Kelly, Casey Ryan. "Camp Horror and the Gendered Politics of Screen Violence: Subverting the

Monstrous-Feminine in *Teeth* (2007)." *Women's Studies in Communication* 39:1 (2016): 86–106.

Kermode, Mark. "Horror Movie." *Sight & Sound* 13, no. 2 (February 2003): 21–22.

Lane, Christina. *Feminist Hollywood: From Born in Flames to Point Break*. Detroit: Wayne State University Press, 2000.

Lapekas, Jenny. "Descent'—'Everything's okay now.' Race, vengeance, and watching the modern rape-revenge narrative." *Jump Cut: A Review of Contemporary Media* 55 (Fall 2013), https://www.ejumpcut.org/archive/jc55.2013/LapekasDescent/index.html.

Lawrence, Novotny. *Blaxploitation Films: Blackness and Genre*. New York: Routledge, 2008.

Le Cain, Maximillian. "Tarantino and the Vengeful Ghosts of Cinema." *Senses of Cinema* 32 (July–September 2004) (accessed 29 September 2009), http://archive.sensesofcinema.com/contents/04/32/tarantino.html.

Lehman, Peter. "'Don't Blame This on a Girl': Female Rape-Revenge Films." In *Screening the Male: Exploring Masculinities in Hollywood Cinema*, edited by Steven Cohan and Ina Rae Hark, 103–117. London: Routledge, 1993.

Lewis, James R. "Images of Captive Rape in the Nineteenth Century." *Journal of American and Comparative Cultures* 15, no. 2 (June 1992): 69–77.

Lowenstein, Adam. *Shocking Representation: Historical Trauma, National Cinema, and the Modern Horror Film*. New York: Columbia University Press, 2005.

Lucas, Rose. "Shame." In *Australian Film 1978–1992: A Survey of Theatrical Features*, edited by Scott Murray. Melbourne: Oxford University Press, 1993.

Maddrey, Joseph. *Nightmares in Red, White and Blue: The Evolution of the American Horror Film*. Jefferson, NC: McFarland, 2004.

Magestro, Molly Ann. *Assault on the Small Screen: Representations of Sexual Violence on Prime-Time Television Dramas*. Lanham: Rowman & Littlefield, 2015.

Maio, Kathie. *Popcorn and Sexual Politics*. Freedom: The Crossing Press, 1991.

Martin, John. *Seduction of the Gullible: The Truth Behind the Video Nasty Scandal*. Liskeard: Stray Cat, 2007.

Matheson, Richard. *I Am Legend*. New York: Fawcett, 1954.

McCarthy, Todd. "A Killer Double Bill." *Variety* 406, no. 7 (2–8 April 2007): 25–32.

Mendik, Xavier. "Thana as Thanatos: Sexuality and Death in *Ms. 45: Angel of Vengeance*." In *Necronomicon Book One*, edited by Andy Black, 168–176. London, 1996.

_____. "Urban Legend: The 1970s Films of Michael Winner." In *Shocking Cinema of the Seventies*, edited by Xavier Mendik, 58–73. Hereford: Noir Publishing, 2002.

Millett, Kate. *Sexual Politics*. Champaign: First Illinois Paperback, 2000.

Minister, Meredith. *Rape Culture on Campus*. Lanham: Lexington Books, 2018.

Mitchell, Elvis. "*Irréversible*: Rape, Violence … It's OK to Look Away." *New York Times*, 7 March 2003, E1: 32.

Monder, Eric. "*Baise-moi (Rape Me)*." *Film Journal International*, 25 March 2002 (accessed 6 October 2009), http://www.filmjournal.com/Article.cfm/PageID/75641304.

Moorti, Sujata. *Color of Rape: Gender and Race in Television's Public Spheres*. Albany: State University of New York Press, 2002.

Mortimer, Barbara. *Hollywood's Frontier Captives: Cultural Anxiety and the Captivity Plot in American Film*. New York: Garland, 2000.

Mudge, James. "Review: *Red to Kill*." *Beyond Hollywood*, 17 September 2004 (accessed 6 October 2009), http://www.beyondhollywood.com/red-to-kill-1997-movie-review/.

Muir, John Kenneth. *Wes Craven: The Art of Horror*. Jefferson, NC: McFarland, 1998.

Mulvey, Laura. "Visual Pleasure and Narrative Cinema." In *Movies and Methods, Volume II*, edited by Bill Nichols, 303–14. Berkeley: California University Press, 1985.

Nettelback, Colin. "Self-Constructing Women: Beyond the Shock of *Baise-moi* and *A ma soeur!*" *Flinders University Languages Group Online Review* 1, no. 3 (December 2003): 58–68.

Oler, Tammy. "The Brave Ones." *Bitch Magazine: Feminist Responses to Pop Culture* (Winter 2009): 30–34.

"Olivia Seeks Film Role." *Truth* (Australia), July 7, 1984.

Özkaracalar, Kaya. "Between Appropriation and Innovation: Turkish Horror Cinema." In *Fear Without Frontiers: Horror Cinema Across the Globe*, edited by Steven Jay Schneider, 204–217. Gottalming: FAB Press, 2003.

Paquet, Darcy. *New Korean Cinema: Breaking the Waves*. New York: Columbia University Press, 2009.

Pâquet, Lili. "The Corporeal Female Body in Literary Rape-Revenge: Shame, Violence, and Scriptotherapy." *Australian Feminist Studies* 33 (2018): 384–399.

Paul, Louis. *Italian Horror Film Directors*. Jefferson, NC: McFarland, 2005.

Peirse, Alison. *Korean Horror Cinema*. Edinburgh: Edinburgh University Press, 2013.

Perriam, Christopher. *Stars and Masculinities in Spanish Cinema: From Banderas to Bardem*. New York: Oxford University Press, 2003.

Phelan, Peggy. "Survey: Art and Feminism." In *Art and Feminism*, edited by Helena Reckitt. 14–49. London: Phaidon, 2012.

Posada, Tim. "#MeToo's First Horror Film: Male Hysteria and the New Final Girl in 2018's Revenge." In *Performing Hysteria: Images and Imaginations of Hysteria*, edited by Johanna Braun. 189–206. Leuven University Press, 2020.

Powrie, Phil. "French Neo-Noir to Hyper-Noir." In *European Film Noir*, edited by Andrew Spicer, 55–83. Manchester: Manchester University Press, 2007.

Prasad, Udayan. "Woman on the Edge." *Sight & Sound* 1, no. 2 (February 1995): 14–17.

Prince, Stephen. *Savage Cinema: Sam Peckinpah and the Rise of Ultraviolent Movies*. Austin: Texas University Press, 1998.
Projansky, Sarah. *Watching Rape: Film and Television in Postfeminist Culture*. New York: New York University Press, 2001.
Quandt, James. "Flesh and Blood: Sex and Violence in Recent French Cinema." *Artforum* 42, no. 6 (February 2004): 126–132.
Rao, Leela. "Women in Indian Films: A Paradigm of Continuity and Change." *Media, Culture and Society* 11, no. 4 (1989): 443–458.
Raw, Laurence. "Review: Gönül Dönmez-Colin, *Turkish Cinema: Identity, Distance and Belonging*; Rekin Teksoy, *Turkish Cinema*." *Screen* 50, no. 3 (Autumn 2009): 362.
Read, Jacinda. *The New Avengers: Feminism, Femininity and the Rape-Revenge Cycle*. Manchester: Manchester University Press, 2000.
Robinson, Sally. "'Emotional Constipation' and the Power of Dammed Masculinity: *Deliverance* and the Paradoxes of Male Liberation." In *Masculinity: Bodies, Movies, Culture*, edited by Peter Lehman, 133–147. New York: Routledge, 2001.
Rosenbaum, Jonathan. *Essential Cinema: On the Necessity of Film Canons*. Baltimore: John Hopkins University Press, 2004.
Russell, Jamie. "Review: *Shutter*." *Sight & Sound* 17, no. 7 (July 2007): 71.
Ryan, Michael, and Douglas Kellner. *Camera Politica: The Politics and Ideology of Contemporary Hollywood Film*. Bloomington: Indiana University Press, 1999.
Schweiger, Daniel. "*The Stendhal Syndrome* Paints It Red." *Fangoria* 162 (May 1997): 40–41.
Sconce, Jeffrey. "Trashing the Academy: Taste, Excess, and an Emerging Politics of Cinematic Style." *Screen* 36, no. 4 (1995): 371–91.
Selbert, Perry. "Plot Synopsis: *Rape Is a Circle*." Allmovie.com (accessed 6 October 2009), http://www.allmovie.com/work/rape-is-a-circle-342395.
Sharrett, Christopher. "Review: *Straw Dogs* (Sam Peckinpah, 1971)." *Cinéaste* 28, no. 4 (Fall 2003): 57–59.
Sicinski, Micheal. "Review: *The Virgin Spring*." *Cinéaste* 31, no. 3 (Summer 2006): 69.
Sielke, Sabine. *Reading Rape: The Rhetoric of Sexual Violence in American Literature and Culture, 1790–1990*. Princeton: Princeton University Press, 2002.
Smith, Anna. "Review: *Straightheads*." *Sight & Sound* 17, no. 5 (May 2007): 83–84.
Smith, Gavin. "Toronto." *Film Comment* 36, no. 6 (November-December 2000): 66.
Smith, Ian Robert. "*The Exorcist* in Istanbul: Processes of Transcultural Appropriation Within Turkish Popular Cinema." *Portal Journal of Multidisciplinary International Studies*, 5, no. 1 (January 2008), accessed 1 July 2010, http://epress.lib.uts.edu.au/ojs/index.php/portal/article/view/489/584.
Solnit, Rebecca. "If Rape Jokes Are Finally Funny It's Because They're Targeting Rape Culture." *The Guardian*, 10 August 2015 (accessed 10 January 2020), https://www.theguardian.com/commentisfree/2015/aug/10/jokes-finally-funny-because-culture-at-the-butt-of-them.
Somers, Eric. "Down the Block from Bergman: *The Last House on the Left* and Beyond." *Video Watchdog* 151 (September 2009): 14–27.
Stack, Peter. "*Impact*: Torn Flesh, Death, and Big Guns." *San Francisco Chronicle*, 9 December 1983, 246.
Staiger, Janet. "The Politics of Film Canons." In *Multiple Voices in Feminist Film Criticism*, edited by Diane Carson, Linda Dittmar and Janice R. Welsch, 191–209. Minneapolis: Minnesota University Press, 1994.
Sterritt, David. "'Time Destroys All Things': An Interview with Gaspar Noé." *Quarterly Review of Film and Video* 24, no. 4 (2007): 307–316.
Stevenson, Jack. *Lars von Trier*. London: BFI, 2002.
Stockbridge, Sally. "Rape and Representation: The Regulation of Hong Kong Films in Hong Kong and Australia." *Asian Studies Review* 17, no. 3 (1994): 43–49.
Stojanova, Cristina. "Denys Arcand." In *Contemporary North American Film Directors: A Wallflower Guide*, edited by Yoram Allon, Del Cullen and Hannah Patterson. London: Wallflower Press, 2002.
Stringer, Julian. "Category 3: Sex and Violence in Postmodern Hong Kong." In *Mythologies of Violence in Postmodern Media*, edited by Christopher Sharrett, 1999, 361–378.
Tasker, Yvonne. "Review: *Reel Knockouts: Violent Women in the Movies* (Austin: Texas University Press, 2001), edited by Martha McCaughey and Neal King; *The New Avengers: Feminism, Femininity, and the Rape-Revenge Cycle*, by Jacinda Read (Manchester: Manchester University Press, 2000)." *Signs: A Journal of Women in Culture and Society* 30, no. 2 (Winter 2005): 1700–1702.
Thomas, Kevin. "Orgy of Violence in *Sudden Impact*." *Los Angeles Times*, 9 December 1983, 233.
Thompson, Douglas. *Clint Eastwood: Sexual Cowboy*. London: Warner Books, 1992.
Tombs, Pete. *Mondo Macabro: Weird and Wonderful Cinema from Around the World*. New York: St. Martins Griffin, 1998.
Tudor, Andrew. *Monsters and Mad Scientists: A Cultural History of the Horror Movie*. Oxford: Basil Blackwell, 1989.
Vena, Jocelyn. "Lady Gaga Says 'Bad Romance' Video Is About 'Tough Female Spirit.'" MTV.com, 9 November 2009 (accessed 31 October 2010), http://www.mtv.com/news/articles/1625848/20091109/lady_gaga.jhtml.
Veronneau, Pierre. "Denys Arcand: A Moralist in Search of His Audience." In *Great Canadian Film Directors*, edited by George Melnyk, 67–77. Edmonton: Alberta University Press, 2007.
Von Kleist, Heinrich. *The Marquise of O—and Other Stories*. New York: Criterion Books, 1960.
Weddle, David. "*Straw Dogs*: They Want to See Brains Flying Out?" *Sight & Sound*, 5, no. 2 (February 1995): 20–25.

Weiler, A.H. "House by Lake Sinks in Blood." *New York Times*, 12 May 1977, 70.
White, Emily. *Fast Girls: Teenage Tribes and the Myth of the Slut*. New York: Scribner's, 2002.
Williams, Linda. "Film Bodies: Gender, Genre and Excess." *Film Quarterly* 44, no. 4 (Summer 1991): 2–13.
Williams, Linda Ruth. *The Erotic Thriller in Contemporary Cinema*. Bloomington: Indiana University Press, 2005.
———. "Less Rape, More Revenge: *I Spit on Your Grave*." *Sight & Sound* 12, no. 4 (April 2002): 70.
———. "Sick Sisters." *Sight & Sound* (July 2001): 28–29.
———. "*Straw Dogs*: Women Can Only Misbehave." *Sight & Sound* 5, no. 2 (February 1995): 26–27.
Williams, Tony. "Trying to Survive the Darker Side: 1980s Family Horror." In *The Dread of Difference: Gender and the Horror Film*, edited by Barry Keith Grant, 164–180. Austin: University of Texas Press, 1996.
Wilson, Elizabeth. "Bodies in Private and Public." In *Public Bodies/Private States: New Views on Photography, Representation, and Gender*, edited by Jane Brettle and Sally Rice, 6–23. Manchester: Manchester University Press, 1994.
Winner, Michael. "Introducing the Shocking Cinema of the Seventies." In *Shocking Cinema of the Seventies*, edited by Xavier Mendik, 7–10. Hereford: Noir, 2002.
Wise, Damien. "No Dane, No Gain." *The Guardian*, 12 October 2003 (accessed 6 October 2009), http://www.guardian.co.uk/film/2003/oct/12/features.magazine.
Wolfthal, Diane. *Images of Rape: The "Heroic" Tradition and Its Alternatives*. Cambridge: Cambridge University Press, 1999.
Wright, Will. *Sixguns and Society: A Structural Study of the Western*. Berkeley: California University Press, 1975.
Wyatt, Justin. *High Concept: Movies and Marketing in Hollywood*. Austin: Texas University Press, 1994.

Index

The Accused (1949) 28
The Accused (1988) 10, 19, 22, 25, 27–9
Act of Aggression (1975) 117
action films 61–2
Adamson, Al see Jessi's Girls (1975)
Ajji (2017) 9, 117, 132
Alfred Hitchcock Presents see "Revenge," television episode (1955)
Almodóvar, Pedro 139; see also The Skin I Live In (2011)
American Mary (2012) 16, 156–7
Anatomy of a Murder (1959) 28
The Animals (1970) 70
Arbuckle, Roscoe "Fatty" 19
Arcand, Denys see Gina (1975)
Argentina 99–102
Argento, Asia see The Stendhal Syndrome (1996)
Argento, Dario see The Stendhal Syndrome (1996)
Aselton, Katie see Black Rock (2012)
Ashurst, Sam see A Little More Flesh (2020)
The Assistant (2019) 152
Australia 102–8
Avenged (2013) 16, 70, 88, 181n

The Baby of Mâcon (1993) 108, 184n
Bad Girls (1994) 76, 153
Bad Girls Go to Hell (1965) 155–6
Bad Reputation (2005) 5, 78–80
Baise Moi (2000) 6, 119, 158–60, 188n
Bandit Queen (1994) 131–2
Barker, David see Pimped (2018)
Bedevilled (2010) 138–9
The Bedroom Window (1987) 60
Being John Malkovich (1999) 55
Belladonna of Sadness (1973) 133
The Belle Starr Story (1976) 75–6, 153
Bergman, Ingmar see The Virgin Spring (1960)
The Birth of a Nation (1915) 119
The Birth of a Nation (2016) 181n
Black Christmas (2019) 167
Black Rock (2012) 106, 170

Blackrock (1997) 102
Blaxploitation 63
BloodRayne (2005) 88, 124n
Boll, Uwe see BloodRayne (2005)
Bollywood see India
Botticelli 12, 176
The Boys (1998) 102–3
Boys Don't Cry (1999) 16
The Bravados (1958) 68, 71–3, 118, 119
The Brave One (2007) 182n
Brazil 150, 164
Britain 35, 38, 56, 98, 102, 108–10, 126, 131
Bronson, Charles see Chato's Land (1972); Death Wish (1974); Death Wish IV: The Crackdown (1987); Rider on the Rain (1969)
Brownmiller, Susan 12, 15, 66, 72
Burke, Tarana 1, 152
Burma 150
Buster and Billie (1974) 77

Canada 110–4
canon formation 25
captivity narratives 68–70
A Case of Rape (1974) 66
castration 35–6, 37, 39, 42, 57–9, 62, 63, 78, 132, 160, 171
Category III films see Hong Kong
A Certain Sacrifice (1979) 65–6
Chaos (2005) 69, 84–5
Chato's Land (1972) 50, 52, 56, 68, 69, 117
Chytilová, Věra see Traps (1998)
Clover, Carol J. 12, 16–7, 28–9, 35, 37, 44–5, 48, 49, 50, 61; see also Final Girl
Colangelo, B.J. 6
comedy 55–60
Cosby, Bill 1, 55
Coward of the County (1981) 15, 65, 66
Craven, Wes see The Last House on the Left (1972)
The Crow (1994) 9–10
Culture Shock (2019) 166–7

Darlin' (2019) 172–3
Davis, Tamra 76, 153
Dawson, Rosario see Death Proof (2007); Descent (2007)

Death and the Maiden (1994) 181n
Death Proof (2007) 80–1, 105, 152
Death Weekend (1976) 111–2
Death Wish (1974) 36, 43, 44, 50–2, 54, 56, 61, 69, 71, 117, 149, 182n
Death Wish (2018) 52
Death Wish IV: The Crackdown (1987) 52, 54, 68
A Degree of Murder (1967) 122–3
Deliverance (1972) 44, 48–50, 54, 66, 183n
Demented (1980) 78, 185n
The Demoniacs (1974) 93–4
Denmark 114–6
Deranged (1987) 185n
Descent (2007) 57, 69, 110, 161–3, 170
Despentes, Virginie see Baise Moi (2000)
Devi, Phoolan 131–2
Dirty Weekend (1992) 18, 21, 52, 56–7, 60, 108, 182n
Dogville (2003) 114–6
Don't Click (2020) 167
Don't Cry Mommy (2012) 137
Drifted Into Chaos (1989) 154–5

Eastwood, Clint see High Plains Drifter (1973); Sudden Impact (1983)
Elle (2016) 60, 121–2, 148
The Entity (1981) 88–9
Evangeline (2013) 5, 88, 162–4
Even Lambs Have Teeth (2015) 63
The Executioner (1975) 149
Extremities (1986) 18, 31–4, 62

Fair Game (1986) 81, 104–5
Fargeat, Coralie see Revenge (2017)
Fatal (2012) 137
Feedback (2019) 98
Felt (2015) 171
Female Prisoner #701: Scorpion (1972) 42, 134–5
Fight for Your Life (1977) 63
"final girl" 17, 81, 87, 180n; see also Clover, Carol J.
France 93–4, 116–22, 158–9, 165, 186n, 188n
Frankenstein 2000 (1991) 90

Index

Freeze Me (2000) 134, 135
Fruet, William *see Death Weekend* (1976)

'Gator Bait (1974) 9, 15, 36, 171
Gentileschi, Artemisia 153
Germany 122–5
Germany, Pale Mother (1979) 122, 154
Get Carter (1971) 108–9
Gina (1975) 112–4
girl gang films 62–3, 173
The Girl with the Dragon Tattoo (2009) 36, 110, 144–7
The Girl with the Dragon Tattoo (2011) 147
Girls Against Boys (2012) 53
The Good Liar (2019) 148
The Great Hate (1967) 148
Greece 150
Growing Up with I Spit on Your Grave (2019) 38

Handgun (1983) 73–5, 161
Hannie Caulder (1971) 68, 73–6
Hemphill, Jim *see Bad Reputation* (2005)
Henry, Claire 4–5, 10, 161, 170
High Plains Drifter (1973) 68, 184n
Holiday (2018) 169–70
Hong Kong 125–8, 154, 164
Horns (2013) 91–2
The Horseman (2008) 105–6
House on Straw Hill (1976) 108
House on the Edge of the Park (1984) 84
Huppert, Isabelle *see The Bedroom Window* (1987); *Elle* (2016)

I May Destroy You (2020) 167
I Saw the Devil (2010) 137
I Spit on Your Grave (1978) 6, 17, 25, 26, 35–8, 41, 44, 45, 48, 70, 76, 78, 82, 84, 101, 103, 125, 132, 148, 149, 182n
I Spit on Your Grave (2010) 36–7, 110
I Spit on Your Grave 2 (2013) 37–8
I Spit on Your Grave III: Vengeance Is Mine (2015) 38
I Spit on Your Grave: Deja Vu (2019) 38
I Was a Teenage Serial Killer (1992)
I'll Never Die Alone (2008) 101, 102
India 128–32
Indonesia *see Marlina the Murderer in Four Acts* (2017)
Iran *see The Salesman* (2016)
Irreversible (2002) 119–21, 170
Ishii, Takashi *see Freeze Me* (2000)
Italy 2, 84, 150, 153, 175–8

Jaded (1998) 53, 154
Janisse, Kier-La 42–3, 186n
Japan 132–6
Jessi's Girls (1975) 76

Johnny Belinda (1948) 20, 21, 22
Jolie, Angelina *see Maleficent* (2014)
Jud Süß (1940) 122
Julia (2014) 62–3

Kael, Pauline 170
Kaji, Meiko *see Female Prisoner #701: Scorpion* (1972); *Lady Snowblood* (1973)
Kaplan, Jonathan 27–9, 76, 153
Katalin Varga (2009) 13–4, 98–9
Keaton, Camille *see Growing Up with I Spit on Your Grave* (2019); *I Spit on Your Grave* (1978); *I Spit on Your Grave: Deja Vu* (2019); *Savage Vengeance* (1983)
Khouri, Callie 33, 170
Kid Vengeance (1977) 68
Kill Bill 1 and *2* (2004/5) 40, 65, 80, 81, 91
The Killing Kind (1973) 137
Korea 136–9, 166
Kusama, Karyn 77

The Ladies Club (1986) 18, 62, 156
Lady Gaga 64
Lady Snowblood (1973) 125, 134, 153
Lam, Karen *see Evangeline* (2013)
Landmine Goes Click (2015) 37
The Last House on the Left (1972) 10, 21, 25, 26, 37, 38–40, 42, 77, 78, 81, 82–7, 103, 106, 111, 112, 121, 150
The Last House on the Left (2009) 85–9
Last House on the Beach (1978) 83, 84
Law Abiding Citizen (2009) 61–2
Leite, Natalia *see M.F.A.* (2017)
Lipstick (1976) 18, 29–31, 33, 37, 43, 88, 130
literary adaptation 18–9, 35, 45, 122, 144–7
A Little More Flesh (2020) 58–60
La Llorona (2019) 99
Loft (1985) 123–4
Lupino, Ida *see Outrage* (1950)

Macon County Jail (1997) 63, 156
Mad Max (1979) 105
Mad Max: Fury Road (2015) 105
Madonna *see A Certain Sacrifice* (1979)
Maleficent (2014) 60
The Man Who Loved Cat Dancing (1973) 70
Manrape (1978) 143–4
Mancinelli, Dusty *see Violation* (2020)
Marlina the Murderer in Four Acts (2017) 15, 73, 98, 166, 167
McGowan, Rose 80, 152–3
McIntosh, Pollyanna 172–3
Men Cannot Be Raped see Manrape (1978)
Mentor, Lou *see Pimped* (2018)

#MeToo 1–3, 6, 56, 121, 152–3, 154, 164, 169, 173, 176
Mexico 150, 166–7
M.F.A. (2017) 1, 6, 164–5
Micheaux, Oscar 19
The "Millenium" Trilogy *see The Girl with the Dragon Tattoo* (2009)
Mortal Thoughts (1991) 60
Mother's Day (1980) 60, 67
Ms. 45 (1981) 20, 21, 25, 26, 29, 35, 36, 37, 42–4, 45, 61, 94, 103, 132, 135, 170, 175, 182n
Mullins, Saxon 1
Mulvey, Laura 17, 29, 57, 159
music videos 63–5
muteness 21, 41, 42, 43, 94, 135, 181n, 185n

Naked Vengeance (1985) 20, 36
Necromancer (1988) 92–3
Neeson, Liam 181n
"New French Extremity" *see* France
Nigeria 151
Night of the Sunflowers (2006) 119, 142–3
Night Train Murders (1975) 82, 83
The Nightingale (2018) 106, 156–7, 164
No One Could Protect Her (1995) 66
Nocturnal Animals (2016) 16, 18
Nollywood *see* Nigeria

The Old Gun (1975) 117
An Old Lady (2020) 137, 148, 166
One Deadly Summer (1983) 118–9
One Way (2007) 110, 124–5
Outrage (1950) 20, 22–3, 24, 153, 170
Outrage (1993) 140–2

Pakistan 151
paracinema 25, 181n
Pepé Le Pew (character) 60
The Perfection (2018) 2, 69, 161
Perry, Ann 70, 155
The Philippines 151
Photographic (2012) 37
Pimped (2018) 106–8, 170–1
"pink" cinema 132–3, 134, 154, 187n; *see also* Japan
Polanski, Roman 181n
pornography 15, 34, 41, 126, 133
Positive I.D. (1986) 21, 25, 61
pre-code Hollywood 19–21
Projansky, Sarah 9, 16
Promising Young Woman (2020) 56, 167–9
The Proposition (2005) 103
The Punisher: Dirty Laundry (2012) 61

Rambo: Last Blood (2019) 61, 73
Rape Squad (1974) 62, 69, 161
Rashomon (1950) 19, 132, 143, 181n
Ravage (2020) 63

Read, Jacinda 12, 16, 17–8, 20, 28, 61, 68, 69, 72–4, 77
Red Sonja (1985) 53
Red Sparrow (2018) 60
Red to Kill (1994) 127–8
"Revenge," television episode (1955) 23
Revenge (1971) 108
Revenge (2017) 1, 164, 165, 166
Revenge for a Rape (1976) 66
Revenge of the Nerds (1984) 56
Revenge Ride (2020) 62, 170, 173
Revengers Tragedy (2002) 18
Rider on the Rain (1969) 117–8
Rihanna 63–4
Rob Roy (1995) 181*n*
Robot Ninja (1989) 61
Rogers, Kenny *see Coward of the County* (1981)
Rollin, Jean *see The Demoniacs* (1974)
Room 205 (2007) 114
"roughies" 35

Safe in Hell (1931) 20–1, 24
The Salesman (2016) 98
Saul Guerrero, Gigi *see Culture Shock* (2019)
Savage Streets (1984) 9, 21, 82
Savage Vengeance (1983) 36
The Scales of Justice (1980) 129–30
Scavenger (2020) 102, 171
science fiction 66–8
The Search (1985) 100–1, 102
The Seasoning House (2012) 21, 108
Seven Brides for Seven Brothers (1954) 64, 75
Shakespeare, William 18
Shame (1988) 10, 103–4, 186*n*
Shame (1995) 186*n*
Shanghai Express (1932) 20
Shutter (2004) 94–6
Shutter (2008) 94–6
Sims-Fewer, Madeleine *see Violation* (2020)

The Skin I Live In (2011) 98, 139–40
SlutWalk 1
Something Wild (1961) 23–4
Soska, Jen and Sylvia *see American Mary* (2012)
Soul Vengeance (1975) 63
Spain 139–43
Steel and Lace (1991) 66–8
The Stendhal Syndrome (1996) 150, 175–8
The Stigma (1984) 48
Stir of Echoes (1999) 89–90
Straightheads (2007) 57, 109–10
Straw Dogs (1971) 18, 25, 44–8, 54, 69, 108, 120
Straw Dogs (2011) 47–8
Strickland, Peter *see Katalin Varga* (2009)
Sudden Impact (1983) 44, 52–4, 61, 67, 68, 69, 71, 164
Sweden 41, 135, 143–7
Sweet Savage (1979) 70; *see also* Perry, Ann

Tarantino, Quentin *see Death Proof* (2007); *Kill Bill 1* and *2* (2004/5)
Taxi Driver (1976) 43, 69
Teeth (2007) 57–8, 60
television movie 15, 66, 186*n*
Thailand 94–6
Thelma & Louise (1991) 20, 33–4, 36, 123, 159, 170, 175
They Call Her One Eye see Thriller: A Cruel Picture (1974)
Thirteen Women (1932) 21
Three Billboards Outside Ebbing, Missouri (2017) 9, 56
Thriller: A Cruel Picture (1974) 21, 25, 26, 40–2, 43, 80, 94, 98, 135, 143
Titus (1999) 18, 156
transnational cinema 98–9, 114, 147

Traps (1998) 150, 160–1
Trauma (2017) 99
The Tribe (2014) 181*n*
Trilogy of Lust 2 (1995) 155
Trinh Thi, Coralie *see Baise Moi* (2000)
Turkey 147–50
Twilight Portrait (2011) 63, 150

vagina dentata 57–8
The Velvet Vampire (1971) 156
"Video Nasties" 35, 38
Violation (2020) 6, 13, 35, 111, 171–2
The Virgin Spring (1960) 9, 19, 26–7, 29, 39, 40, 72, 77, 81, 98, 143, 147
von Trier, Lars *see Dogville* (2003)

W.A.R.: Women Against Rape (1987) 63, 182
Weinstein, Harvey 1, 121, 152, 161, 164, 165, 176
The Well (1968) 147–8
Wellman, William A. *see Safe in Hell* (1931)
Wertmüller, Lina 75, 153
Westerns 50, 54, 55, 61, 68–76, 82, 103, 113, 166
Winner, Michael *see Chato's Land* (1972); *Death Wish* (1974); *Dirty Weekend* (1992)
Wishman, Doris 35; *see also Bad Girls Go to Hell* (1965)
Without Apparent Motive (1971)
Wolfthal, Diane 2, 6, 11–2, 25, 77
The Woman (2011) 172
Woman of Vengeance (1979) 149–50
Woman Thou Art Loosed (2004) 19
Wright, Will 70–1
Wrong Way (1972) 82–3

www.ingramcontent.com/pod-product-compliance
Lightning Source LLC
Chambersburg PA
CBHW080805300426
44114CB00020B/2839